G. W. F. Hegel

System of Ethical Life (1802/3)

and *First Philosophy of Spirit*

(Part III of the System of

Speculative Philosophy 1803/4)

Edited and translated by

H. S. Harris and T. M. Knox

State University of New York Press Albany 1979

The translation of Hegel's text of "The First Philosophy of Spirit" has been made with the consent of the Rheinisch-West-faelische Akademie der Wissenschaften in Duesseldorf from the Collected Writings of G.W.F. Hegel, Volume 6 "Jenauer Systementwerfe I", published by Klaus Duesing and Heinz Kimmerle, 1975. The translation from "System der Sittlichkeit" is based on the work of George Lasson, second edition, 1923, reprinted in 1967, entitled "Philosophische Bibliotek", Volume 144a. Both publications: Felix Meiner Verlag, Hamburg.

Published by
State University of New York Press
Albany, New York 12246

Library of Congress Cataloging in Publication Data

Hegel, Georg Wilhelm Friedrich, 1770–1831.
    System of ethical life (1802/3) and first Philosophy
of spirit (part III of the System of speculative
philosophy 1803/4)

    Translation of System der Sittlichkeit and of
Philosophie des Geistes, Teil 3 of Encyklopädie der
philosophischen Wissenschaften.
    Bibliography: p.
    Includes index.
    1. Ethics. 2. Mind and body. I. Hegel, Georg
Wilhelm Friedrich, 1770–1831. Encyklopädie der philo-
sophischen Wissenschaften. Teil 3. Philosophie des
Geistes. English. 1979. II. Harris, Henry Silton,
1926–   III. Knox, Thomas Malcolm, Sir, 1900–
IV. Title.
B2944.S9513   170   79-14477
ISBN 0-87395-386-X

Contents

General Preface   ix

PART ONE: Hegel's *System of Ethical Life:* An Interpretation
by H. S. Harris   1

   1. The character of the manuscript.   3

   2. The systematic context of the
      System of Ethical Life.   7

   3. Ethical Life on the basis of relation.   20

     A. Feeling   21

     B. Thought   36

   4. The Negative as Freedom.   44

   5. Ethical Life.   54

     A. Virtue   65

     B. Government   70

   6. Religion.   81

   7. Conclusion.   85

   Notes.   87

PART TWO: *The System of Ethical Life*
translated by T. M. Knox and H. S. Harris   97

   Note on the Translation   99

   [Introduction]   99

   1. Absolute Ethical Life on the Basis of Relation   102

     A. [First Level: Feeling as Subsumption
        of Concept under Intuition]   103

     B. Second Level: of Infinity and Ideality
        in Form or in Relation   116

        a) [The Subsumption of the Concept
           under Intuition]   117

Contents

b) The Subsumption of Intuition
under the Concept   119

c) [The Level of the Indifference
of (a) and (b)]   123

2. The Negative or Freedom or Transgression   129

3. Ethical Life   142

First section: The Constitution of the State   145

I. Ethical Life as System, at rest   146

II. Government   156

A. The Absolute Government   157

B. Universal Government   163

a) [The first system of Government:
System of need]   167

b) The second system of Government:
System of justice   173

c) [The] third system of Government:
[System of discipline]   176

C. Free Government   176

Appendix to *System of Ethical Life*   178

PART THREE: Hegel's *First Philosophy of Spirit*
(being Part III of the "System of Speculative Philosophy"
of 1803/4) translated with an Introduction
by H. S. Harris   187

Introduction to the First Philosophy of Spirit
by H. S. Harris   189

[A. The Formal Concept of Consciousness]   206

First Level: [Speech]   218

Second Level: The Tool   228

Third Level: Possession and the Family   231

[B. Transition to Real Existence: The Negative]   235

[C. Real Existence: The People]   242

Contents

Appendix 1: The fragment "ist nur die Form"   251

Appendix 2: The report of Rosenkranz about Hegel's
            Philosophy of Spirit in the early Jena
            period   254

A Note on The Translation   267

Bibliography   270

Index   275

General Preface

This volume contains the two earliest surviving versions of Hegel's social theory. Neither of them is complete, and although it is quite likely that Hegel himself left them both uncompleted, it is certain that some parts of the second manuscript have been lost. The appendixes contain, in each case, the secondary reports (and other surviving fragments) which throw most light upon what is missing from the manuscripts themselves. I have tried to show the relation of all of the translated materials as clearly as I can in my introductions—and I have not scrupled to make these quite lengthy. The reader will find in them the fullest statement of the context and background and the clearest line of interpretation for the manuscripts that I have been able to devise.

Difficult as they undoubtedly are, these highly condensed accounts of Hegel's social theory are both full of interest in themselves and pregnant with portents of his later thought and its influence. If, as I believe, they reciprocally illumine one another, they will together help us to understand better the great works of Hegel's maturity—both the *Phenomenology of Spirit* and the *Philosophy of Right*. We meet here Hegel's first versions of the "life and death struggle" (which leads to the establishment of "lordship and bondage" in the *Phenomenology*) and of the theory of "Civil Society" and its class structure (which is basic to his mature *Philosophy of Right*). We are also presented with statements of basic economy theory which are in some ways prophetic of the Paris Manuscripts of Marx. But these are only the most obvious and striking anticipations of later developments. There are many things less evident to the first glance which may in the end be of even greater importance for the interpretation of Hegel's work and its influence. It has long been recognized that the concept of "spirit" is probably the central notion of Hegel's thought as a whole, but the concept remains extremely difficult to grasp clearly. In these two manuscripts the evolution of this vital focus of Hegel's philosophy can be directly observed as it comes to birth in his own mind.

This volume has been in gestation for a long time. The first version of my interpretation of the *System of Ethical Life* was written in 1971/2 when I was granted a sabbatical leave and a Leave Fellowship. It is my pleasant duty, therefore, to acknowledge gratefully my debt both to York University (who granted the leave) and to the Canada Council (who granted the Fellowship). But there is another kind of debt that is more important. Sir Malcolm Knox had made the first draft of the translation before I ever became interested in the text, and only someone who had compared my first attempt at an interpretation with the essay published here can justly estimate how much it owes to the experience of working over the text with him.

Finally I must record my gratitude to the others who have labored to bring the gestation to a successful *physical* outcome. Several drafts were typed by Mrs. Ida Sabag, and one by my daughter Carol. My wife bore a heavy share of the burdens of proof-reading and making the Analytical Index; and the staff of SUNY Press have been uniformly helpful throughout.

Martinmas 1978   H. S. Harris

Hegel's *System of Ethical Life*

An Interpretation

by H. S. Harris

Hegel's System of
Ethical Life
An Interpretation
by H. S. Harris

1. THE CHARACTER OF THE MANUSCRIPT.

The untitled manuscript among Hegel's Jena papers, to which editors
have given the name *System der Sittlichkeit* (System of Ethical Life)
was written in the winter of 1802 or the spring of 1803. It is the earliest
of Hegel's systematic manuscripts that has survived. The writing of it
followed directly after the composition of the essay on *Natural Law* for
the last number of the short-lived *Critical Journal of Philosophy*, and
it was either contemporaneous with or directly prior to the final drafting of the essay on the *German Constitution*.[1] The manuscript is a fair
copy, and from the way Rosenkranz dealt with it in his *Life of Hegel*
we can safely infer that he had at least one earlier draft before him.
That earlier draft was written for a course of lectures.[2] Our manuscript
does not read at all like a set of lecture notes until we come to the final
pages, where it degenerates into a series of "headings," from which a
connected discussion was still to be written up. Possibly Hegel used
these headings as a basis for oral development, but in view of the reli-
able report that he was "bound to his text" during his first years as a
lecturer we must be doubtful of this. Our manuscript is very dense and
stark throughout; it gives the impression that everything extraneous
has been carefully stripped away. The lecture-manuscript which Rosenkranz had before him, on the other hand, seems to have been somewhat more unbuttoned and flowing.[3]

The best available answer to the question why Hegel should have
written up his own lecture notes in this rather forbidding, and at first
sight not maximally useful, way depends partly on a proper comprehension of his "scientific" or systematic conception of philosophy and
partly on an understanding of his external circumstances as a univer-

sity lecturer. We shall here begin with the external circumstances, but the reader will rapidly perceive that the systematic and the external exigencies are not strictly separate. They interacted to produce the sort of manuscript that we actually have, and the same sort of interaction continued throughout Hegel's academic career first at Jena and later at Heidelberg and Berlin.

On the external side, then, what we principally need to remember is that it was the usual thing for lecturers to appoint a textbook to be studied in connection with their lectures. Hegel himself followed this practice, for example, when he announced a course on mathematics in 1805 and 1806.[4] But in philosophy the only existing texts that he could conceivably make a *constructive* use of were the various writings of Schelling,[5] and it was scarcely to be expected that students would *pay* Hegel to explicate Schelling's texts when they could go and listen to Schelling himself. A lecturer in Hegel's position, who did not have a salaried appointment and was therefore not *allowed* to give "free" lectures even if he had wanted to,[6] had virtually no recourse but to write his own textbook. And since Hegel was never in reality the mere disciple of Schelling that others—including Schelling—frequently took him for, he had the strongest of internal motives to do this in any case. His first course at Jena was on "Logic and Metaphysics." Apparently it did not last long, but broke up quite early. In announcing the course again for the next semester (Summer 1802), Hegel promised the early appearance of a textbook. But the textbook did not materialize. New promises were made and old ones reiterated, but it was only in the last course of lectures that Hegel was to give at Jena (Summer 1806) that his students were finally provided with a printed text from his hand— the sheets of the still unfinished *Phenomenology* as they came from the press.[7]

So what did Hegel (and his students) do in the meanwhile about a textbook for the lectures? A lecturer who did not wish to use someone else's book was obliged, until his own book was ready, to lecture *ex dictatis*. This is what Hegel both promised to do, and did, in his courses on "Natural Law" in 1802 and 1803.[8] Thus his own textbook, when it finally materialized, would take the place of a sequence of dictated propositions or paragraphs. In the normal course of events, therefore, the book itself grew out of such a sequence. The character of Hegel's mature *Encyclopedia*—and at least some part of the peculiar difficulty that it presents for the modern student—is much easier to understand when we realize that the text was not meant to stand entirely alone. It was designed to be read in the context of the oral explanations provided by the lecturer.[9]

The *System of Ethical Life* is best regarded, I think, as a draft for this sort of textbook. It is an attempt to distil the "scientific" essence out of a series of lectures, so that the auditors of future series would have a foundation to start from. It is not meant to be read by itself, but to serve as a skeleton for the lecturer and a guideline for his students. It never actually reached the students' hands, but the fact that there are a few marginal notes, generally of an amplificatory and illustrative kind, strongly suggests that Hegel himself may have used it for "dictation" at least once after it was written.

What course was it written for? In his initial application for permission to lecture at Jena in 1801, Hegel advised the Faculty that he wished to lecture on "theoretical and practical philosophy."[10] For his first semester he lectured only on "Logic and Metaphysics," but subsequently he offered two courses regularly for several terms: "Logic and Metaphysics," and "Natural Law." The initial announcement of this latter topic (for Summer 1802) gave the title more fully as *jus naturae civitatis et gentium*, or in the vernacular *Natur und Völkerrecht*. This, surely, was the lecture course from which our text was written up.

But already in the announcement for this term Hegel was promising a textbook for "Logic and Metaphysics" that would appear in due time, whereas at no time did he promise a textbook specifically for his course on Natural Law. The reason for this silence is not too far to seek. Hegel's "systematic" conception of the subject made it impossible for him to contemplate more than one textbook in philosophy.[11] The one book might be published in parts; but the part dealing with "practical" philosophy could hardly be prepared until the "theoretical" part was completed at least in outline. We can assume that when Hegel gave notice of the impending publication of his "Logic and Metaphysics" he was already hard at work on an outline for that course. In the summer of 1802, however, he was immensely burdened by his labors for the *Critical Journal*. So it is not suprising that he sent nothing to press in his own name. By the fall he felt able to promise that the textbook in "Logic and Metaphysics" would appear within a few weeks (*nundinis instantibus proditurum*). This is fairly good evidence that the manuscript was ready. But it did not come out. Instead Hegel went to work to make a textbook for his course in "practical" philosophy, and what he produced was our present manuscript, which has no heading and no introduction to speak of. The most reasonable hypothesis, I think, is that by the time he began the *System of Ethical Life* Hegel had decided *not* to publish a separate compendium on "Logic and Metaphysics," but to issue an outline of both his "theoretical" and his "practical" philosophy in the same volume. This is confirmed by the next lecture announcement (for Summer 1803), which promises a *philosophiae universae delineatio* (or in the vernacular an *Encyklopädie der Philosophie*) "from a compendium to be published this summer." Our manuscript is a draft for part of this encyclopaedic outline.

The latest manuscript discoveries have revealed that the schema of Hegel's "System of Philosophy" during his earliest years at Jena was based on a fourfold division, rather than the triadic plan (Logic, Nature, Spirit) that formed the skeleton of all of his system-construction from the end of 1803 onwards.[12] The manuscripts have not yet been published, but the division attracted the notice of Rosenkranz as a curiosity. He gives it thus:

1. Logic or the science of the Idea as such;

2. Philosophy of Nature or the realization of the Idea, which in the first place creates its body in Nature;

3. Ethical Nature as the real spirit;

4. Religion as the resumption of the whole into one, the return to the primitive simplicity of the Idea.[13]

The *System der Sittlichkeit*, as we have it, fits very exactly into the third of these four subdivisions. The way that Hegel refers to the *difference* between the level of *Sittlichkeit* and that of *Religion* at several points in our manuscript reflects the fact that he regarded religious experience, not as part of ordinary social life, but as the highest synthesis of theoretical and practical cognition, and hence as the culmination of the whole system. This conception of religious experience was one that he formulated at Frankfurt. He had already injected it into his account of "Schelling's system" in the *Difference* essay.[14]

One might object that on this hypothesis it is strange that Hegel made no mention of his new "compendium" in his announcement of the "Natural Law" course for Summer 1803. Again the probable reason is to be found in the gap that had still to be filled. Hegel's problem now was that he could not send any of his practical philosophy to the printer until his theoretical philosophy was completed by the addition of a systematic philosophy of nature. If he had had any idea of how difficult it was going to be to fill this gap, he would never have promised the early appearance of his compendium at all.[15] But no matter how optimistic he felt in the spring of 1803, he could certainly see that the printing of the practical philosophy would never begin in time to be of any use to his "Natural Law" students that summer.

By the winter he had managed to complete the first draft of his

"Philosophy of Nature" and had come round again to what he now called the "Philosophy of Spirit."[16] At this stage he must have decided to recast everything that he had already done, for there is no further mention of a textbook in his announcements until Summer 1805, when the systematic compendium is again promised, this time for use in the "Natural Law" course as well.[17]

In effect our manuscript fell by the wayside—along with the four-fold division of philosophy to which it belongs—when Hegel's "ency-clopaedic" conception of philosophy assumed its mature form. But there was an important *external* reason for this too. The departure of Schelling from Jena in the spring of 1803 opened up for Hegel a wider field of academic activity. He was now able, indeed morally obliged, to assume responsibility for the entire range of systematic philosophy, as the two of them understood it, whereas philosophy of nature had until then been peculiarly Schelling's province. In view of Hegel's lifelong concern with *organic* ideas of growth and continuity, it is not surpris-ing that a treatise which had been written out of order, so to speak, would not fit properly into its place when everything was finally done, for the first time, in the proper order. We shall have to consider later the unresolved tensions in the manuscript itself, which were virtually bound to lead to significant development in Hegel's views. But it was the form rather than the content that had become unsatisfactory when the essay was first set aside.[18]

2. THE SYSTEMATIC CONTEXT OF THE SYSTEM OF ETHICAL LIFE.

The external data have thus led us to the suggestion that the *System of Ethical Life* represents the third part of a four-part plan in the context of which Hegel had been working since 1801. The fact that it is also the earliest of his "systematic" manuscripts that has survived makes the task of interpreting this wider systematic context into which it fits an extremely difficult one. Here we must rely heavily upon the internal indications offered by the text itself. We have only just enough indirect evidence and secondary reports to provide the barest outline of the way in which Hegel's "system" evolved.

In his essay on the *Difference between Fichte and Schelling* Hegel came forward as the champion of the "philosophy of Identity," which was already associated with the name of his younger friend Schelling.

The original conception of the "Identity Philosophy" was explicitly Spinozist in its inspiration. The two "attributes" of extension and thought were replaced by "philosophy of Nature" and "transcendental philosophy" respectively. The fundamental thesis was, to use Spinoza's expression, that "the order and connection of ideas is the same as the order and connection of things."[19] But the focal problem of the idealism of Kant and Fichte, the problem of reconciling theoretical determinism with practical freedom, was superimposed upon this Spinozist foundation. And the solving of that problem required that a certain supremacy of "practical" philosophy over "theoretical" philosophy, a certain superiority of the "transcendental" philosophy of subjective activity over the "natural" philosophy of objective observation must be admitted. Thus although there was supposed to be a perfect Spinozist parallel between the two philosophical constructions of the one Absolute Identity, there was also, in the single system of "speculation" in which they were both comprehended, a necessary sequential relation between them. Philosophy of nature was *theoretical*, while transcendental philosophy was *practical*. But if the sequential relation was seen to be necessary in the speculative comprehension of the "absolute indifference," it must *also* be present in both of the opposed "constructions of the Absolute." Theoretical (natural) philosophy and practical (transcendental) philosophy must each have both a "theoretical" and a "practical" part. This presented no problem on the side of transcendental philosophy—from which the antithesis of "theoretical" and "practical" was derived in the first place. But it meant that the theory of nature had to be subdivided into a strictly theoretical part (the philosophy of inorganic nature) and a practically theoretical part (the philosophy of organism). These two parts were thought of as anticipatory parallels of the self-constructive (and hence *essentially* practical) activities of "theoretical" and "practical" Reason.[20]

From the fragmentary manuscripts of those first lecture courses we now know that in Hegel's hands the cyclic unity of the "system" became, from the very first, a more complex matter than the summary in the *Difference* essay indicates. Even in that summary it is fairly clear that the theory of the "absolute Indifference Point" or the "resumption of the whole into one" is to be thought of as a separate (third) phase of the system.[21] From the introduction to the first course on "Logic and Metaphysics," we can now see that there was a corresponding "introductory" phase of speculative philosophy: "Logic, or the science of the Idea as such."

This introductory phase was necessarily two-sided. First there was the *critique of finite Reason*, which was the task of critical logic. Then there was the *construction of absolute Reason* (the "Idea as such") which was the task of speculative logic (or "metaphysics"). It was this latter task which eventually became the whole subject matter of Logic in Hegel's mature theory. But he always maintained the negative, critical, conception of the traditional "philosophical logic" (i.e., epistemology) with which he began. Faced by the demand of Reinhold and Bardili that thought should be conceived "objectively," he agreed that the demand was justified, even though its proponents did not understand it.[22] The "reduction of philosophy to logic" which Bardili proclaimed was Hegel's serious object from the first in a sense quite different from that given to it by Bardili.

The necessary complement of his criticism of the essentially "finite," subjective, basis of the whole tradition of empiricist and critical epistemology from Locke to Fichte was a *positive* conception of "Logic and Metaphysics" which completely transcended the bounds of "transcendental philosophy," as described in the systematic outline of the *Difference* essay. Instead of being parallel with the philosophy of Nature, the theory of the Absolute Idea has to be thought as the *beginning* of systematic theory which corresponds (though without any structural *parallel*) to the *end* of speculation in the absolute experience of Religion. Ever since about 1797 Hegel had been thinking of *Religion* as the *experience* of the Absolute. In the *Difference* essay "Art" and "Speculation" are presented as the twin approaches to the "point of indifference" from its opposite sides. Both are there characterized as forms of "divine service." Religion is thus the mode of experience in which the Absolute Identity is comprehended absolutely.[23] In seeking to establish a conception of thought which would be truly *absolute*, because it was completely beyond the antithesis of subject and object, Hegel was opening the way to his mature doctrine that "speculation" or philosophy, not religion, is the absolute mode of experience. But he could not see this yet. What he saw first was that just as "Logic" must be distinguished from the "theoretical part of transcendental philosophy" and given absolute status as "the science of the Idea as such," so "Religion" must be distinguished from the "practical part of transcendental philosophy" (the theory of "ethical life").

We have already noted that our manuscript reflects this distinction between *Sittlichkeit* and *Religion* in several places, where Hegel remarks without further explanation that the situation in religion is "different" from the ethical one that he is analysing. In the notes on the forms of constitution with which the manuscript ends, it is clear that we are approaching the boundary line where this "difference" will need to be discussed. Fortunately Rosenkranz was able to recognize the connection between our manuscript and the lecture manuscript. In spite of his indubitable confusion about the supposed "conclusion" of the *System of Ethical Life*, the connection that he makes appears to be quite secure;[24] and from his account we can see that Hegel's discussion of "Religion proper" was conducted—like the discussion that we still find in the *Phenomenology*—upon a higher plane altogether.

Assuming, then, that our manuscript is designed to fit into the four-part plan of Hegel's first year at Jena, rather than the triadic schema (Logic, Philosophy of Nature, Philosophy of Spirit) which underlies the fragmentary "System of Speculative Philosophy" of 1803/4 and all the subsequent manuscripts that have come down to us, let us now consider the structure of the *System of Ethical Life* itself. The absence of anything resembling an introduction provides further support for the view that it was designed to be part of a larger, continuous whole. It is well known that Hegel disliked philosophical prefaces and introductions generally, but in an independent treatise we should expect to find, at the very least, a page or two on the futility of writing (and reading) prefaces, if he were in fact here making a beginning without one. What we are given instead is more like the opening of a new chapter than the start of an autonomous treatise. Hegel begins baldly: "In order to cognize the Idea of absolute *Sittlichkeit*, the intuition must be posited in complete adequacy to the concept, because the Idea is itself nothing other than the identity of the two."[25] The only "introduction" that he supplies is a two-page elaboration of this thesis in which every new term and every explanatory assertion only makes things more obscure, because none of the familiar words is used in a familiar fashion. The logical and epistemological terms "intuition," "concept," "universal," "particular," "singular," "subsumption," "relation" have all been removed from the "subjective" or "finite" matrix of ordinary discourse and are used in the new "absolute" way. What they mean in this new context has to be discovered and explicated by detailed examination of the way in which this initial programmatic statement is executed in the body of the discussion.

The main body of the discussion, however, bristles with the same sort of difficulty on almost every page. So we must have some idea of the overall structure and method if we are to have any hope of comprehending it in detail. Let us begin then with some general observations about the structure and the method of exposition which can be verified by straightforward observation of an external and formal kind.

We must hope that even an examination of this superficial, noncomprehending, type will enable us to interpret the initial programmatic statement with enough confidence to attempt a detailed study of the main text.

The structural analysis provided by Hegel himself through his headings and subheadings (ignoring for the moment, the further subdivisions, where one might have difficulty deciding what is coordinate and what is subordinate) reveals that the treatise is in three sections. These are:

1. Absolute *Sittlichkeit* on the Basis of Relation

2. The Negative, or Freedom, or Transgression

3. *Sittlichkeit*[26]

Of these three sections, the second is not provided with any subheadings by Hegel. The fact that it has three coordinate titles suggests the possibility of an internal progression, but this is only a hypothesis to be tested. All that is outwardly evident is that this middle section is meant to provide a *necessary* transition of some kind from the first section to the third.

The first and third sections, on the other hand, *are* clearly subdivided by Hegel. In the first section he failed to provide a heading for the first main subdivision, though he marked it clearly enough. In the third he has provided what *may* be a superfluous (purely repetitive) heading at the beginning of the first section. We cannot be sure whether the heading "First Section: The Constitution" is superfluous or not, since the fact that there is no coordinate "Second Section" may simply be a consequence of Hegel's failure to complete the manuscript. But for the functional analysis of what we have it is superfluous precisely because there is nothing we can coordinate with it, so we are justified in ignoring it in this external survey. Setting it aside, we have Part I subdivided into "Finitude: Reality"[27] and "Infinity: Ideality" and Part III into "Ethical Life as a system at rest" and "Ethical Life in motion: Government."

In terms of content the first section of Part I is about the primitive natural needs of a human organism and about the most elementary forms of labor and economic relations; in the second "Infinite" section we find in reverse order the establishment of the necessary institutional context, first the organization of labor and property, then the necessary stages of family life. Part III, on the other hand, is mainly concerned with the character, functions, structure, and interaction of three social classes—the nobility, the bourgeoisie, and the peasantry—within an established political community.

The whole discussion is organized as a sequence of "levels" (*Potenzen*)—though this becomes less insistently obvious in Part III—and the sequence is organized as a pattern of reciprocal "subsumptions" in accordance with the programmatic statement at the beginning. "The subsumption of concept under intuition" is followed by the converse "subsumption of intuition under concept," and then, typically, both "subsumptions" are equalized in their "middle" or "totality."[28]

"Intuition," "concept," and "relation" are terms which come originally from the "subjective" philosophy of Kant. In the Identity Philosophy they gain an "absolute" significance, but with respect to all of them, there is something to be gained from attending to Kant's use. Let us begin with "relation," for which the relevant Kantian context is easy to locate. The categories of "relation" in Kant's table are:

1) Inherence and Subsistence (or Substance and Accident)

2) Causality and Dependence (or *Ursache* and *Wirkung*)[29]

3) Community (or Reciprocity between the agent and the patient).

We shall find that the recollection of *all* the categories and synonyms that Kant mentions under this heading helps us to understand how Hegel employs "relation" as an ethical category. In the *Difference* essay Hegel speaks of the substance-accident relation as "the true relation of speculation."[30] The speculative focus of the *System of Ethical Life* is the *Volk* as a self-conscious, self-moving, *substance*. Hence it is the substance-relation that dominates Part III. But this "ethical substance" is materially constituted by mortal living organisms which are only transient moments in the more comprehensive substantial whole of Nature. Their mortal lives and motions are cycles of action and reaction which can only be stabilized as a perfect reciprocal balance of cause and effect. "Natural" ethics, the "ethics of relation" in Part I, is thus inevitably an analysis of "causality and dependence."

So much for the Kantian context of Hegel's concept of "relation." It must be admitted that there is very little in the "transcendental aesthetic" or the "transcendental analytic" that has an equally obvious relevance to Hegel's use of "intuition" and "concept." Certainly there is an analogy of some sort between the Hegelian "totality" of intuition and concept and the Kantian doctrine of a necessary "synthesis" between them. But the preponderant role played by the strange principle of "subsumption" in arriving at the "totality" plainly forbids us to look to the first Critique for any real help here.

It is not the first Critique that provides the clue in this instance but the third. In the "Critique of Teleological Judgement" we find the following:

It is, in fact, a distinctive characteristic of our understanding, that in its cognition—as, for instance, of the cause of a product— it moves from the *analytic universal* to the particular, or, in other words, from conceptions to given empirical intuitions. In this process, therefore, it determines nothing in respect of the multiplicity of the particular. On the contrary, understanding must wait for the subsumption of the empirical intuition—supposing that the object is a natural product—under the conception, to furnish this determination for the faculty of judgement. But now we are also able to form a notion of an understanding which, not being discursive like ours, but intuitive, moves from the *synthetic universal*, or intuition of a whole as a whole, to the particular—that is to say, from the whole to the parts. To render possible a definite form of the whole a *contingency* in the synthesis of the parts is not implied by such an understanding or its representation of the whole. But that is what our understanding requires. It must advance from the parts as the universally conceived principles to different possible forms to be subsumed thereunder as consequences. Its structure is such that we can only regard a real whole in nature as the effect of the concurrent dynamical forces of the parts. How then may we avoid having to represent the possibility of the whole as dependent upon the parts in a manner conformable to our discursive understanding? May we follow what the standard of the intuitive or archetypal understanding prescribes, and represent the possibility of the parts as both in their form and synthesis dependent upon the whole? The very peculiarity of our understanding in question prevents this being done in such a way that the whole contains the source of the possibility of the nexus of the parts. This would be self-contradictory in knowledge of the discursive type. But the *representation* of a whole may contain the source of the possibility of the form of that whole and of the nexus of the parts which that form involves. This is our only road. But, now, the whole would in that case be an effect or product the *representation* of which is looked on as the *cause* of its possibility. But the product of a cause whose determining ground is merely the representation of its effect is termed an end. Hence it follows that it is simply a consequence flowing from the particular character of our understanding that we should figure to our minds products of nature as possible according to a different type of causality from that of the physical laws of matter, that is, as only possible according to ends and final causes. In the same way we explain the fact that this principle does not touch the question of how such things themselves, even considered as phenomena, are possible on this mode of production, but only concerns the estimate of them possible to our understanding. On this view we see at the same time why it is that in natural science we are far from being satisfied with an explanation of natural products by means of a causality according to ends. For in such an explanation all we ask for is an estimate of physical generation adapted to our critical faculty, or reflective judgement, instead of one adapted to the things themselves on behalf of the determinant judgement. Here it is also quite unnecessary to prove that an *intellectus archetypus* like this is possible. It is sufficient to show that we are led to this Idea of an *intellectus archetypus* by contrasting with it our discursive understanding that has need of images (*intellectus ectypus*) and noting the contingent character of a faculty of this form, and that this Idea involves nothing self-contradictory.[31]

The basic claim of the Identity philosophy is that our understanding both of ourselves and of the world is ultimately intuitive and that we must use the concept of an *organism* (or "natural end") constitutively, and not just regulatively (as Kant allows), if we are to have any knowledge at all. Thus we must "follow what the standard of the intuitive or archetypal understanding prescribes, and represent the possibility of the parts as both in their form and synthesis dependent upon the whole." Thus "intuition" in the present work refers to "*synthetic universal*, or intuition of a whole as a whole," and "concept" refers to the "motion" of the understanding "from the whole to the parts." How far Hegel's attempt to meet Kant's challenge is successful is the ultimate question, both about this present piece of systematic exposition and about his later philosophy as a whole. But at least this passage from Section 77 of the *Critique of Judgement*—with all the surrounding context from Section 76 to Section 84—shows us both what Hegel was attempting to do, and why the first formulation of his endeavor was in terms of "intuition" and "concept."

Just as "intuition," "concept," and "relation" remind us of Kant, so *Potenz* directs us to Schelling. From the very moment when he began to break out of his initial allegiance to Fichte,[32] Schelling employed the term *Potenz* as one of his basic conceptual tools. In one of his early polemics about the Identity Philosophy, a dialogue between "the author" and "a friend" "On the Absolute Identity-system," Schelling implies that the first to use the term (at least in print) was his friend Eschenmayer in a work called *Propositions from Nature-Metaphysics*, published in 1797.

Unfortunately for us it is a very flexible conception easily adaptable to different contexts and scarcely definable apart from some definite context.[33] Its origin was the mathematical theory of "powers," and in combination with the signs *plus* and *minus* and the elementary logical formulas for identity and difference "A=A" and "A=B," it provided Schelling with an algebraic notation for his theory. Thus in the *Exposition of My System* (1801), which remained the fixed foundation stone of the Identity Philosophy, we find the following: "The formula $A^2 = (A=B)$ thought as a relative totality, signifies the Absolute Identity, not in so far as it exists, but in so far as it is ground or cause of its existence through the organism, and so also it signifies the organism itself (as product). The formula $A^3 = (A^2 - A = B)$ signifies the Absolute Identity existing under the form A^2 and A=B."[34] The A^3 formula expresses a higher *Potenz* than the A^2 formula, which is, in turn, a higher formula than A=B, which is the elementary basis of all *Potenzen*. These three levels are to be found in finite consciousness and in all finite realities, for they express the structure of the Absolute itself. Hence they express also both the way the Absolute is in things and the way that things are in it. "The unique reality in everything, in the singular thing and in the whole alike, is for me the A^3, that in which the universal and the particular, the infinite and the finite are absolutely one, or in a word the eternal."[35]

According to the *Exposition of My System*, "The Absolute Identity only exists under the form of all *Potenzen*."[36] The theory of *Potenzen* enables Schelling to articulate the relation between the different aspects of finite reality and activity and the Absolute Identity. If pressed about the fact that he offered a series of variant accounts of the *Potenzen*, he would probably have responded that a certain relativity in the account of experience on its finite side was inevitable. His best non-

technical explanation of the meaning of *Potenz* was in the lecture
course on the *Philosophy of Art* (Winter 1802/3):

> There is only One philosophy and One science of philosophy;
> what are called distinct philosophical sciences are just expositions
> of the One and undivided whole of philosophy in distinct
> *Potenzen* or under distinct ideal determinations. . . . this expres-
> sion . . . is connected with the general doctrine of philosophy
> about the essential and inward identity of all things and of every-
> thing which we distinguish at all. There is truly and in itself
> only One essential being, One absolute real, and this being an
> absolute is indivisible, so that it cannot pass over into distinct
> beings through division or separation; since the one being is
> indivisible, diversity of things is only possible at all, in so far as
> it is posited as the undivided whole under distinct determinations.
> These determinations I call *Potenzen*. They change nothing
> whatsoever in the essential being, which remains always and
> necessarily the same, which is why they are called *ideal* deter-
> minations. For example, what we cognize in history or in art is
> essentially the same as what also exists in nature: in each of them
> the whole absoluteness is innate, but this absoluteness stands at
> distinct levels [*Potenzen*] in nature, history, and art. If one could
> take the *Potenz* away, so as to see the *pure essence* naked, so to
> speak, One being would truly be in all of them.
>
> But *philosophy* in its complete appearance emerges only in
> the totality of all *Potenzen*. For it ought to be a true image [*Bild*]
> of the Universe—and this equals *the Absolute set forth in the
> totality of all ideal determinations*. God and the Universe are one,
> or they are only different aspects of One and the same being.
> God is the universe regarded from the side of identity; he is *All*
> since he is the only real being, and hence there is nothing outside
> of him, while the *Universe* is God grasped from the side of to-
> tality. But in the absolute Idea which is the principle of philoso-
> phy, both identity and totality emerge only in the totality of
> all *Potenzen*. In the Absolute as such, and therefore also in the
> principle of philosophy, there is *no Potenz* precisely because it
> comprehends *all Potenzen*, and conversely just in virtue of the
> fact that there is no *Potenz* in it, all *Potenzen* are contained in it.
> I call this principle the *absolute point of identity* of philosophy
> precisely for this reason, that it is not equal to any particular
> *Potenz*, and yet it comprehends all of them.

Now this indifference point, just because it is the point of
indifference, and it is strictly unique, indiscernible, and indivis-
ible, necessarily exists again in every *particular* unity (another
name for a *Potenz*); and this is not possible unless in each of
these *particular* unities all unities, hence all *Potenzen*, return once
again. Thus there is in philosophy overall nothing but the Absolute, or we meet with nothing in philosophy but the Absolute—
always just strictly the One, and just this unique One in
particular forms.[37]

The proper formula for this indifferent unity of all *Potenzen* would
be "A=A." Hegel's *System of Ethical Life*, which seeks to exhibit the
existence of the Absolute as the *ethical organism*, would be summed
up by Schelling in an A^3 formula. But since, to the best of my knowledge, no one has ever found the algebra of the Absolute enlightening,
that topic is scarcely worth pursuing.

The dynamic connotations of the term are more interesting.[38] Schelling used it to formulate his philosophy of nature as a series of energy
levels, and it is clear that Hegel is using it in the same way for social
philosophy. For us, therefore, the most interesting aspect of *Potenz*
theory in Schelling is his architectonic use of the concept as a way of
articulating the Spinozist parallel between nature and thought, the real
and the ideal, the object and the subject. In the *Exposition* Schelling
says, "Every definite *Potenz* signifies a definite quantitative difference
of subjectivity and objectivity . . . relative to the whole or the Absolute
Totality."[39] Thus there are two "series" of *Potenzen*, the real series
(where the object is positive) and the ideal one (where the subject is
positive). In his *Further Expositions from the System of Philosophy* of
1802 Schelling adds that the fundamental triad in both series consists
of a first *Potenz* of "reflection" (the "reception of the infinite into the
finite") and a second *Potenz* of "subsumption" (the "reception of the
finite into the infinite"). These two phases achieve their "totality" (the
A^3 formula) in the *Potenz* of "Reason."

This basic triadic pattern is preserved in many variant versions in
Schelling's subsequent essays.[40] But it is only in this first account that
the concept of "subsumption" plays an important role. This was also
the latest version that Schelling had published at the time when Hegel
was working on the *Sytem of Ethical Life*. For this reason the coincidence of terminology deserves a fairly close examination. The total
scheme which can be extracted from Schelling's account is a follows:[41]

	REAL WORLD (Nature—the realm of finitude)	IDEAL WORLD (God—the realm of Infinity)
First Potenz (Reflection—reception of the infinite in the finite)	World-structure (in the whole) Body, material forms (in singulars) Spatialization	Knowledge, Science, Concepts Temporal sequence
Second Potenz (subsumption—reception of the finite into the infinite)	Light (universal principle) Dynamically determined bodies (in series of three Potenzen: Magnetism—one-dimensional Electricity—two-dimensional Chemical process—three-dimensional) Divine light and Gravity Universal Mechanism and Necessity	Action God Freedom
Third Potenz (Reason—absolute equality of finite and infinite)	Organism—identity of form and matter Objective Reason (Truth)	Work of Art Imagination (Beauty)

Absolute
Indifference
Point

In view of the importance of "subsumption" in the organization and procedure of the *System of Ethical Life* it may well be significant that Schelling regards the whole sphere of human action as the *Potenz* of "subsumption." We cannot be sure how much of Hegel's theory and method was directly inspired or suggested by Schelling because there is no extended discussion of this second *Potenz* of the "ideal series" in Schelling's published work during this period. There are some reasons for thinking, however, that Hegel developed his own procedure, working within the context of the general scheme given above, but adapting it to a purpose of his own, which was subtly different from Schelling's monochromatic concern with seeing all things in God and God in all things. Schelling's "subsumption" is the "reception of the finite into the infinite." It is a process of intellectual subordination of the many to the One; and we can follow it *either* in the realm of thought *or* in that of extension. But on both sides it is a one-way process. Hegel's "subsumption," on the other hand, is *essentially* a reciprocal procedure going first one way, then the other, and continually weaving back and forth from the real side to the ideal side. This interaction of the "real" and the "ideal" is perfectly concordant with Schelling's conception of the second *Potenz*. For this is the *Potenz* of *motion* in space *and* time; in Schelling's real series it is the *Potenz* where the inward essence (an "ideal" principle) utters or realizes itself. So, by parity of reasoning (whether Schelling's or Hegel's), we should expect that in the "ideal" series it is where the outer reality "inwardizes" and so "idealizes" itself. The important thing for us is not to decide whether it was really Schelling who originally thought of this, but to see that the use of "subsumption" in this *reciprocal* way is more closely analogous to what Schelling calls "reception" or "formation" (*Einbildung*) than to what *he* calls "subsumption" proper; and secondly we need to recognize that because of the equilibrium established by this reciprocity the finite *Potenz* gains in Hegel a firmer standing, a greater measure of independent subsistence, than it ever seems to enjoy in Schelling's discussions.

In place of Schelling's antithesis of "Nature" and "God," we find in Hegel's treatise the antithesis of "nature" and "spirit," or "nature" and "ethical life." "Nature" embraces man as a living organism contextually embedded in the organic life of the earth. It is important to remember that Schelling and Hegel regarded the world, and in particular our Earth, as an animate organism. The essential contrast between *Natur* and *Sittlichkeit* is a contrast between two levels of *life*. We begin in the side of natural life, and we move up and over toward the side of ethical life. Thus in all the stages of "ethical life as relation"— which means the life of the rational organism in the context of natural necessity, there is a lower "natural" pole from which we begin, and an opposite "rational" or artificial pole, through which we move to the higher, truly ethical "middle," which is their "totality." But when we arrive at the higher level of independent ethical life, this whole pattern is reversed. For *Sittlichkeit* is itself only a "side"; it is the higher "ideal" side of the Absolute, but it needs to be integrated with its lower analog in nature. So here it is the higher ethical pole, the pole of "totality," from which we begin; and we move through an opposite pole of reflective separation or difference to the *natural* middle which is the *point of identity* between them. Thus at the level of "nature" we go from desire, through labor, to the tool; whereas at the level of *Sittlichkeit* proper we go (several times, at different levels) from the nobility, through the bourgeoisie, to the peasantry. This alternation of pattern reflects Schelling's basic doctrine about the *Potenzen*. Schelling liked to express the "quantitative difference" between a *Potenz* and the Absolute in terms of a "constructed line":

$$\text{(Ideal Pole) } \overset{+}{A} = B \qquad\qquad \underset{A = A}{\text{(O)}} \qquad\qquad A = \overset{+}{B} \text{ (Real Pole)}$$

In the *System of Ethical Life* Hegel proceeds from right to left in the first part and from left to right in the third. His second section, "Freedom," is where the absolute midpoint emerges. It comes forth in its negative aspect (the zero-point) as the annihilation of everything finite (i.e., everything expressible by the formula A=B). Thus "O" is a better designation for it on Hegel's "constructed line" than the "A=A" that Schelling prefers. But Hegel's procedure shows us what Schelling's axiom "The constructed line is the form of the being of the Absolute Identity, both in single instances and in the whole"[42] meant to him.

3. ETHICAL LIFE ON THE BASIS OF RELATION.

We are now as well prepared as we can easily manage for the study of the text in detail. According to Hegel, ethical awareness begins as the self-awareness (the "intuition") of a single individual in the controlling environment of nature as a whole. Before he/she[43] can emerge as a free agent, he/she must come to terms with the necessities of nature (both inward and outward). The whole *concept* of man as a free rational agent is first presented to each of us in the shape of the natural world in which we exist. This is the stage on which we are to perform as free agents, and in order even to know what it *means* to be a rational agent, we must first discover what is *necessary* to our own maintenance as active natural organisms, and we must be able to secure it; secondly we must know what is *possible* for us as natural organisms and what the natural consequences of different possible patterns of behavior are. We find all this out either by trying, and suffering the consequences ourselves, or by seeing others try and suffer them. Nature rewards or disciplines our efforts, and in this way we come to know what we naturally are and what we need. This is the "subsumption" of our own singular existence or self-awareness under the "concept" which is objectified or realized in the organic totality of nature as a whole. At first I wrote "instantiated or realized," but I had to cross out "instantiated" because it carries the misleading implications that the concept might be exemplified otherwise or elsewhere and that it is definable in abstraction from its actual existence in and as the order of things. The Identity Philosophy follows Spinoza in denying both of these positions. All of our ordinary "finite" concepts, whether they are mere "possibilities," or are actually exemplified in one or many real "instances," arise from the matrix of our cognitive and practical relations to the one system of "nature" which is the objective and necessary existence of Reason itself.

Even the capacity to survive to biological maturity as parts of the order of nature is something that we only possess as members of a natural community, the family. Hence this community is the "totality" of ethical life on the basis of relation.[44] But the mastery over nature that is requisite to our existence as free rational agents we can only achieve through membership in a wider community, the *Volk*. Thus the "subsumption" of our singular "intuition" under the concept of rational humanity requires for its proper fulfillment the contrary subsumption of the concept of humanity under the ethical intuition of the *Volk*. The process of reciprocal subsumption at this highest *ethical* level is what Hegel calls, for the nonce, "the concept's absolute movement."[45] It is something that happens in real life, as well as in speculative thought. To understand what the "intuition" of the *Volk* is, and what the "subsumption" of the concept of human nature under it can be, is the hardest *major* problem of interpretation in the *System of Ethical Life*. But that is not yet our concern. For the moment that ideal of ethical life can either be said to be buried deep within us or to be floating above and beyond us. There is a sense of *striving* which belongs to this feeling of something deep within that must be brought out, or something far above or beyond that must be reached. This sense of imperfect union with one's own real essence, of not being what one actually can be, is the way in which "relation" appears to the "dependent" consciousness throughout the treatise.

a) *Feeling*

Basically then, at this first stage, "intuition" refers to the particular side, the self-conscious single individual with his wants, his capacities, and his satisfactions; while "concept" refers to the system of Nature as the universal array of possibilities and necessities. But as soon as the striving sets things in motion it is, more obviously than anything else, the functional designations "universal" and "particular" which move. For they are logically tied to the process of "subsumption." What subsumes is always, at that moment, the universal; and what is subsumed is the particular. In the second paragraph of his introductory note Hegel tells us that "what is truly the universal is intuition, while what is truly particular is the absolute concept." This situation, which is the exact reverse of the initial conditions that he sets up in the very next paragraph, is our *goal*. But the very first step is a subsumption of concept under intuition. The intuition has "stepped over" to the side of the particular—that is to say, we are speaking of a singular individual— but it here subordinates the content of nature (as concept) to itself as the inward essence. In the contrary subsumption of intuition under concept, on the other hand, the essence, the real universal or the identity to be achieved "floats above" the order of nature (as concept) and the particular individual (as intuition). This "floating essence" is not identical with the concept, just as the "inward essence" is not properly identical with the intuition—although there the connection is closer. Properly speaking, however, the essence is in both cases the *relation* between concept and particular. Since it is a *relation*, a *relative* unity, it is not absolutely identical with the absolute unity. But it can only qualify as a *unity* of inner and outer—of intuition and concept—at all, to the extent that the inward essence does come out and coincide with or get realized to some degree in external nature. This coincidence is a "satisfaction" (of the subsuming moment), a "totality" of intuition and concept, of the real and the ideal sides. Thus something comes into existence which has a significance beyond the urge of the moment that was its immediate occasion. But all the same the satisfaction is not final; it leads on to a new drive, but one which is logically of a higher type. This will continue to be the case until the inward essence ("absolute life" or "absolute intuition") finally coincides perfectly with the outward essence (the system of nature as a whole or the "absolute concept").

All the pages that I have so far devoted to the explication of these few introductory paragraphs are probably worth less to the puzzled reader than a few concrete examples. But one cannot give *general* examples. Every concrete case necessarily belongs to a definite level or *Potenz*, and should therefore be given in its place. The first stage of "Natural ethics" is what Hegel calls "feeling." This is the simplest, most primitive form of intuition.[46] It has to be opened out somehow until it embraces the whole natural environment of the organism's life in a subordinating or subsumptive way. Hegel tells us as well as he can what the subsumption of the concept under "feeling" means when he calls this the *practical Potenz*. We subsume nature under our own feeling by acting upon it. Thus work or labor will be the crucial moment of this stage. But work is the *negation* of feeling as the spontaneous awareness of our own living energy. Thus within the overall subsumption of concept under intuition labor is the moment of opposition, the moment when intuition is subsumed under concept.

A good example with which to begin this very first stage—we shall see why later—is a baby. The concept of feeling has three moments:

a) desire or need (subsumption of concept under intuition)

b) satisfaction (subsumption of intuition under concept)

c) the totality of need and satisfaction: the tool

A healthy baby, awake but not hungry, active only at the theoretical level of simple awareness, e.g., learning to focus its eyes and fascinated by the play of light and color, is the simplest model of what Hegel calls "the complete undifferentiatedness of ethical life . . . or nature proper." As he gets hungry or thirsty or wet or cold, the cycle of practical life begins. But the baby exemplifies as strictly as possible the subsumption of concept under intuition, for when he is in need, it is someone else who must labor to satisfy his needs. The baby sets before us the cycle of need and satisfaction, but the only *work* that he contributes to keep the cycle going is to signal his need by crying. If we regard this signal as essential, if we feed or change the baby "on demand," then he is a paradigm of "natural ethics as intuition." On the other hand, if we ignore his "normal" cries and feed him, etc., "on schedule" (as we typically do with our domesticated stock), then the baby—like the beasts —continues to belong only to the realm of nature so far as his own practical initiatives are concerned; he is not yet an *agent* at all.

The basic *contrast* in feeling is between need and satisfaction. This contrast is what makes feeling *practical*. Before it becomes practical, feeling is unconscious. But a practical need, a *felt* need, is still not yet a *desire*. Desire, as Hegel analyzes it, is the starting point of labor, its ideal pole. For desire involves an imaginative awareness of what is needed. At the very beginning, a baby presumably does not have desires in this sense; it has only needs. We can say with certainty that it has "desires" in Hegel's sense, when its crying is checked or stilled at the sight of what it needs—or when the crying is redoubled. But it never *labors* in the full sense, for labor is properly concerned with the real production of what is ideally envisaged as desirable. Even in the case of adult hunger and thirst, the primitive models that Hegel himself employs at this level, the labor may be nothing more than hunting for and finding the desired object somewhere in the natural order and then reaching out and taking it. This dependence of the organism on nature for the satisfaction of its needs is what Hegel calls "the subsumption of feeling under the concept, or the more real concept of practical feeling unfolded in its three dimensions." His apparent inconsistency in dealing with this here—since we are supposed still to be at the level where concept is subsumed under intuition—arises from a change of perspective which he finds useful at this point. He is here looking at the problem from the *more general* level of "natural ethics" as a whole (which is precisely the subsumption of intuition under concept, or the discovery by a finite organism of its place in nature). He indicates his move to the more general point of view by speaking of "the more *real* concept of practical feeling." The theory of feeling as *subsuming* the concept is the *formal* (i.e., phenomenal) concept of it. In "the *real* concept of feeling" it is precisely this *formal concept* (the needy *subject*) who, in spite of the particularity of his feeling can be recognized as "the universal, the subsuming power."

This "more real concept" contains very little that was not already in the "formal concept." But it gives Hegel the opportunity to describe the "unconscious" state of enjoyment (satiated desire) which is the beginning and the end of practical feeling. This constitutes only a *background* for the formal concept, which is an analysis of how feeling appears to the intuiting subject.[47] In the "real" concept the content of the formal concept is described as it appears for a scientific observer. The need which absorbs the subject's whole consciousness "formally" is "really" only a minute detail in the total economy of life. But as Hegel says, this is not our present concern. The absolutely particular need, with which we are concerned, particularizes the environment for the organism. Thus there is nothing in the order of nature which is in itself food or drink. Nothing would appear as "food" or "drink" in a scientific account such as Schelling's "dynamic series" of finite things (to take the obvious philosophical instance); nothing appears in the "dynamic series" as a mere particular of any kind. Everything there is "universal," being both "identical" (with itself in the Absolute), and "quantitative" (i.e., *different* from the Absolute as a *Potenz* of it). But for a hungry and thirsty organism what appears is *this* loaf of bread, *this* glass of milk, etc. In the "theoretical" course of nature the loaf would mold and eventually disappear as "this" thing altogether, the milk would sour, and so on. It is the practical need of the subject that identifies these things here and now as food and drink; and they only *are* food and drink when they are consumed, i.e., when they pass away into the organic process of the subject, rather than into some lower cycle of nature. When that happens, the subject settles back into his self-enjoyment, and action ceases. As a result of action, however, the agent has learned something. He has discovered that his comfortable self-absorption is dependent on the system of nature. He has a consciousness of the "objectivity of the object."

This consciousness of objectivity is what must now be developed. From the process *in* which need is satisfied, we must turn to the means *by* which it is satisfied. The *essence* is not now "within" the subject; it "floats over" him as the relation of subject and object. In this *relation* the living energy which he *intuites* as feeling is subordinated to the real order of nature in order to change that order. We have arrived finally at the analysis of labor proper.

A satiated baby may, very probably, go to sleep. This is "the indifference and emptiness of the individual or his bare possibility of being ethical or rational." But, as we have suggested, even a baby learns to cry for food, etc., in a fairly deliberate way, stopping (or increasing its efforts) when it perceives that its cries are about to be answered. For adults who are actually, not just potentially, rational, conceptual comprehension of the full cycle of feeling makes its objectification possible. Because we understand that hunger and thirst will keep on recurring, we can begin to prepare for them before they occur. Thus we begin laboring to produce something that we can have in our *possession* against the time when need returns; and when we give our whole attention to the problem of labor we finally begin to produce possessions designed to make labor easier or more effective. These possessions produced by labor for the sake of labor are *tools*. The tool is thus the *totality* of labor and possession. Notice that labor has here become quite independent of a felt need or desire, and possession has similarly become independent of enjoyment. Primitively, possession and enjoyment are *negatively* dependent on one another—as the proverb says, you *cannot* eat your cake and have it too. But you *can* use your tool and have it too, for that is essential to the concept of a tool.

Hegel's analysis of labor is a logically structured survey of the types of labor that are possible in relation to different levels of the scale of nature and of the different ways in which nature can come into our possession for purposes of enjoyment or tool-use. We are still acting on nature to satisfy our needs (in this general perspective the concept is being subsumed under intuition), but in so far as our attention is focussed on *possession* and *use*, our activity is not directed to our own enjoyment but towards objective ends. A possession can be given to or taken by someone else; a tool can be used by anyone who has learned how. Thus in the narrower, more immediate, perspective "intuition" is subsumed under "concept" in a sense that is quite easy to grasp.

Labor occurs when we change what is there in space for our intuition into something else that we envisage in our minds. Thus the subject is the subsuming agent, indifferently aware both of the thing that exists and the thing that he wants. The object is "subsumed." But the subsumption is quite different from the baby's subsumption of his bottle or the hungry man's subsumption of his dinner. There it was the inner intuition, here it is the inner concept that dominates. Everything is now objectified and the process of transformation (the laboring activity of the subject) becomes continuous and does not terminate in enjoyment as soon as some envisaged transformation is achieved. Adam digs, and the ground is turned; now he can sow; after that he can water, hoe, etc. Enjoyment is deferred.

In order for this lengthy deferment to be possible, Adam must take possession of his field; he must also have last year's crop in store to live on while he works; and finally he must have his spade. These are three forms of possession which were not present in the primitive cycle of needing, finding, and consuming. In the Garden of Eden Adam had momentarily to *take possession* of whatever he needed for consumption, but he did not *have* possession of the Garden or its fruits.

It should be noted that we are not yet thinking of any kind of legal "possession," but of the attitudes one must have in an agricultural relation to nature. Obviously the need to have secure possession of the necessities of life *leads* to the establishment of a legal system of property relations, but that comes later. For the moment Hegel is only concerned to clarify his own version of the labor theory of property. "Possession" is the synthesis of two moments, the conceptual moment of *taking possession* and the real moment of *labor*. The first moment is the moment of rest, for Adam *thinks* of the field as *his* even before he turns the first sod, and he must continue to think of it so through all the transformations produced by his labor; and of course he thinks of the crop as his when he finally *possesses* it properly in his barn.

But in this possession of the product, the gathered crop, we have something different from the possession of the field. The activity of labor by which the ideal concept of possession was realized has now stopped, but the "difference" that it has made in the world is visibly piled in the barn. The object now "subsumes" the activity of labor; or in other words the objective, external, intuition subsumes the concept (whereas at the level of need it is the subjective, internal, intuition that subsumes the concept). This object, the gathered crop, *belongs* to Adam as a singular individual, it is his *private* possession, a singular characteristic of his. So when labor is "subsumed" in the object produced, the singularity of the subject gets its "rational place" as "implicit concept." Labor is the *active* concept, the *Begriff für sich*; the product is the resting concept, the *Begriff an sich*; but both of them have this conceptual status as aspects of the practical subject.

So far we have considered labor only as a mechanical activity, as the expenditure of physical energy, without regard to the different ways in which the energy is expended. I mentioned Adam's digging, sowing, hoeing, etc., but the reader was supposed to attend to the continuing flow of activity, not to the variation. There is a steady stream of activity, and the laboring subject is the efficient cause of all of it. The field which Adam digs, etc., exists always in some particular state, it is "one with the particular," but it abides indifferently through all the states that Adam imposes on it; these states are "purely external forms," not its "being as a subject." Adam's field does not have "being as a subject," though the Earth of which it is part was conceived by Hegel as a living organism and hence as having something analogous to the "being of a subject."

The differences, to which we now turn, arise from the product, but the product is not the *efficient* cause of them. Hence Hegel says that "causality is absent."

For what is true of the ploughing of the field is not true of the growing of the crop. The seed that Adam sows is not "indifferently one" with any condition. It has a life cycle that belongs to it. Since Adam wants the best crop he can get, "the object is in the relation as real." His agricultural labor is not just a mechanical activity; it is concordant with the life cycle of his crop. Labor as "real and living" (not just mechanically causal) is thus differentiated according to the patterns of the life cycles which it subserves. Adam's digging, etc., in so far as it is all concerned with moving the soil around, *creating the conditions* for the desired plant life and destroying or inhibiting other life, is regarded by Hegel as purely mechanical. The life cycle of the plant itself is determined by the earth and its elementary processes. Moreover such effective practices as grafting, slip-setting, and so forth, are evidence, in

Hegel's view, that plants are not true individual organisms. Thus on both sides, with respect to the labor and with respect to the living thing labored on, the intuition is subsumed under the concept.

Animals, on the other hand, are individuated living things; they offer us the simplest paradigm of the concept subsumed under intuition. The individual animal is not conscious of itself as a "living thing," so there is no reciprocal subsumption of intuition under concept except in the mind of its human keeper and breeder. Hence the different possibilities of animal life can only be realized in spatial dispersion. But the human labor of "domestication" can transform the animal in ways which are quite impossible in the cultivation of plants. Plants can enter only into the primitive cycle of need and consumption, but animals can be trained as fellow laborers. Plants provide us with the food that maintains what Hegel calls our "inorganic" nature. He uses "organic" and "inorganic" in the contextually relative way that Aristotle uses "form" and "matter." In the present context "inorganic nature" means our animal nature as distinct from our rational nature, or our natural as distinct from our ethical or conscious life.

Hegel remarks further that with respect to "enjoyment" (positive as opposed to negative intuition) the "subsumptive" relations are the converse of those involved in labor. Now labor is basically subsumption of intuition (subjective image of what may be, and objective impression of what is) under concept (the thought-guided activity that transforms desired image into real impression and real impression into remembered image). In the labor to produce a plant crop it is the concept of the plant, the development of its living form to perfect fruition, that guides and controls the working activity. But in growing flowers for enjoyment it is the sensation of the viewer that is the grower's end. This is a "subsumption of the concept under intuition" because "the enjoyment of the single sense is the dispersal of the same"—i.e., perhaps the expression of our feeling for our theoretical awareness?

The "enjoyment" of our relation with animals cannot be fully considered at this stage because it "would not be a subsumption of the concept under intuition." Hegel is probably thinking here of "domestication" in the full and etymologically literal sense, the treatment of animals as friends or pets. This is an active relationship and we must presumably regard it as a primitively ethical one, which falls beyond the horizon of the moment, since it is an anticipatory form of the process of *Bildung*. At this stage we can only consider the enjoyment of the sense of freedom and increased power that comes from harnessing animals to do our work with us.

The highest object of labor is the human being himself. Plants can be quantitatively maximized as a harvest to maintain the animal existence of both man and his livestock. Animals can be trained individually to assist man in his labor. But the human individual is laboriously trained to make his own nature into the tool of reason which is his concept. Here the labor of molding the life process is a direct assistance of the life process itself, to enable it to reach its own goal. The teacher begins in the position of the worker who imposes his own "concept" on the pupil. But this is the very concept of which the pupil is himself the intuition, so the process of his formation is a process of his own self-formation and we can no longer say what is subsuming what. Each side "makes its particularity immediately into universality." As we shall see, this is the characteristic of rational communication in language. Rational communication is not a matter of causal interaction because the parties are self-conscious subjects or self-determining agents.

This relationship between two rational agents at the culmination of a self-suspending process of labor has its own natural course of evolution. The intuition and concept that are united in it are not, after all, those of plant and animal: they are the intuition and concept of man. So here Hegel's analysis touches for the first time on the family as the natural means by which man is made. The process of human reproduction begins with something that is outwardly analogous with the instinctive coupling of animals and moves to a terminus that is inwardly analogous with the simple multiplication within conceptual identity of plants. Between these limits lies all the physical and mental effort that sustains the human family.

For six or seven years before he wrote this treatise Hegel had been pondering about the feeling of union that arises from sexual coupling. As a natural phenomenon he now regards it as the objective realization of the moments of the absolute concept. The male is the universal, the female the particular. In the coupling of an animal pair the unity of the species exists as a feeling, but there is no mutual recognition at the conceptual level. The recognition of equality at the conceptual level, the recognition that each partner, regardless of the sex difference is a rational human individual, is the distinctively human relation that is achieved between man and wife. Properly human love is not, therefore, as Hegel had held in 1797/8, an incomprehensible miracle.[48] It is only natural desire that is incomprehensible, because it is *below* the level of reflective consciousness altogether.

The subject-object relation, where the subject is dominant as intelligence (not as a singular agent satisfying his desires) is realized in the relation between parents and children. But here the determinacy of the opposites is superficial because temporary. In the course of nature, and through the work of nature, the child grows up. Through "practice"—the human activity of parents and children alike—both parties finally become aware of their own humanity in each other.

It is only at this stage that the real cultural formation of man begins. *Bildung*, as Hegel understands it is the reciprocal communication of rational agents. Helping one another in the general enterprise of knowing ourselves and our place in nature is the highest *work* of mankind. It is through this cultural exchange that men become really independent individuals. The bonds of feeling, need, desire, and of loving emotion become mere outward forms. What matters for each man as an individual is to discover the truth for himself.

We have now reached the "totality" of this first *Potenz* of practical feeling. The two moments through which we have passed were *relative* identities, which is to say that the identity between the subjective side and the objective side exists in them as a necessary causal relation between the two terms and reveals itself as a see-saw motion in which first one side and then the other dominates. The "totality" will show the see-saw at its moment of perfect equilibrium. Thus the first stage (concept under intuition) showed us the alternation of need and satisfaction (as the way in which the objective process of nature appears in subjective experience) but did not show us the fulcrum on which the alternation depends. All that we could see there was the top edge of the fulcrum, the bare necessity of action to satisfy need when the stimulus of need is felt. That fulcrum, when we examined it on its own account in the second stage (intuition under concept), was found to be a complex process of subjective activity in and upon the organic reality of nature. Out of the simple alternation of need and satisfaction (the cycle of the human *body*, or of the human organism as a stimulus-response system) there emerged the great arc of the forms of human labor, involving the whole odyssey of the human spirit in miniature, from Adam's bondage to the soil at one end to the perfect equality in freedom of a society of cultural "enlighteners" on the other. Thus, in studying the fulcrum of the first see-saw we discovered a far greater see-saw. We shall see how the one real see-saw comes to rest as the two views of it coincide.

This coincidence and resultant equilibrium comes about through the examination of the fulcrum of the second see-saw. In his analysis of the process of need Hegel did say a little about the "middle" between need and satisfaction, which is the objective moment of labor. But in his analysis of labor and its products he has not said a word about the "totality" of labor and possession beyond naming it as "the tool." In the first *Potenz* all that was really analyzed was the state of need. Having seen that the satisfaction of need requires labor, we went on to analyse that. It is only now that we have shown how human labor reaches its climax in man's *self*-creative activity, that the third moment of "enjoyment" can come to have a positive content. Thus far the term "satisfaction," meaning just the removal or abolition of need, was more appropriate. Labor was the process by which need is abolished. But we have now seen labor finally *abolish itself* by becoming enjoyable. Thus enjoyment has become a conscious subjective condition, whereas to begin with it was merely an unconscious objective state of organic equilibrium. We shall now watch man's subjective self-enjoyment of his rational nature reach back over the whole range of the laborious activities by which he satisfies his needs, until everything that he does can be recognized as the self-enjoyment of Reason. At the same time we shall see how the process of *Bildung*, the process where enjoyment finally reveals itself as something that has positive content for the subject, is the most absolute of all human needs, the absolute precondition of our capacity to satisfy even the primitive organic drives of hunger and thirst. Thus need and enjoyment will be shown to be "identical," and instead of a relative identity we shall have before us a true *Potenz* of the Absolute.

In the first two stages, "the Absolute Identity is something subjective outside them." The hungry man *knows* why he must eat now, and why he will be hungry again in a few hours. That is the way life is. Similarly when Adam goes out into his field in spring, he knows that he must work now if he is going to live through next winter. The Absolute Identity is "life," which involves hunger and necessitates labor, but it is not identical with being hungry, still less with digging. Hegel would be willing to say that "life" *is* identical with what a baby *feels*, but the baby does not really *know* that he is hungry, and he cannot dig. He is only the formal possibility of rationality. As he grows up, the child does come to know what he feels, but at first he has no concept of his own desires at all. He is a bundle of needs. I remarked earlier that we should eventually see why the baby was a good example of Hegel's first stage. It is because the new born child *is* the substratum, the unconscious unity of the whole cycle of need and satisfaction. He is the reality of feeling as bare intuition. We adults say, "Here is *the baby*," but *he* does not yet know what we are saying; and when his mother protests a few years later against the imposition of some task on her little boy because "he is not old enough to work yet," her common sense is again at odds with the speculative truth; for in fact the child began to work at being human when he learned to talk.

Hegel presents the baby as the "identity" of the sex-distinction which was the first moment of the totality of work. As far as the connection is concerned explanation is superfluous here, for it is obvious enough that the baby is the *product* of sexual congress. What was not at first clear was why sexual congress should be regarded as an aspect of labor at all; and what is still anything but obvious is why the baby should be regarded as the first moment of the concept of a "work tool." The key to both problems is the recognition that the real topic of the philosophy of Identity is the self-formation of Reason. The child is the "instrument" of Reason and his begetting as a natural organism is the first step in the self-making of man. The proper task of "practical" philosophy is to put all human practical activities into their proper perspective as part of that self-making. All animals reproduce themselves as part of the self-maintaining cycle of nature. But nature is only the raw material from which Reason fashions the "instruments" of its own existence. So when the rational animal reproduces himself "in the course of nature," this reproduction has for him an instrumental function; it is not the achievement of a final goal as it is for the organisms that are simply part of nature.

The child is what makes the bond of sexual desire "comprehensible." In him the *feeling* of the parents becomes an external *intuition* for them. Of course there is a formal *concept* ("baby") that expresses that intuition. But that formal concept is only "the indifference and emptiness of the individual, or his bare possibility of being ethical or rational" (420). The *actual* concept that the parents have of their child is the concept both of what they believe he is and of what they hope he will become, the concept that guides all of their conduct towards him. For themselves they might live from day to day; but for him they must make a home and secure their livelihood. He is a possession that makes other possessions necessary.

Thus the transition from this *natural* stage in the making of man is to its direct opposite—to all the *artificial* making that man does in order to create a stable home for himself. The child, presumptively, has all the normal potential of a human being—"in this identity . . . no circumstance is missing"—and until he/she reaches physical maturity, there will be no sexual "one-sidedness." But what are the "circumstances" that are none of them missing? In an obvious sense *everything* is missing, the baby is, as yet, *nothing* human at all—except a *real* potentiality. That real potentiality cashes out as a full complement of human *needs*. This is where "no circumstance is missing." Everything he needs has to be supplied for him.

Actually this is not quite correct. Nature has provided for the baby's food to begin with; and the production of food always remains essentially a natural process. It is scarcely correct to regard the endless cycle of Adam's mechanical labor in his field as a kind of tool-making, because he is always at the mercy of the changing seasons. But in all his labor man is using nature as an instrument for his purposes, though this is a fact that only becomes *explicit* in his *home*. There all the needs of life have to be spelled out in an *actual concept* of human existence, realized in *things*. The range of this concept extends from the baby's cradle to the family Bible—but we have a long way to go before we can put the Bible in its correct perspective.

Adam's *spade* is the elementary paradigm of the *tool*, for his digging shows us this moment of the alienation of the concept in *things* at its simplest. The spade is a piece of dead matter that has been formed by Adam himself for the mechanical purpose of digging to which he directs his own energies. It forms a mediating term between Adam's intelligently directed activity and the mechanism of the natural order. But in order to use it Adam, with all his rational powers, must become a mere quantum of energy. The digging in which Adam uses his spade is a mere negation of both object and subject, without any *realization* of rationality at all. On the subjective side it produces nothing but weariness and a blunting of all his human capacities; and on the objective side it produces the satisfaction of the natural needs of himself as a singular individual and of certain other singular individuals. But when he was making the spade itself Adam was realizing his rational capacities, he existed as a universal subject. Once Adam has made it, others can use it when he is tired; and anyone who grasps what it is for can make another one like it. Thus the making of tools sets the boundary between nature and culture. Labor here becomes rational self-expression (craftsmanship) instead of being a mechanical expense of energy (toiling).

But all tool-making and tool-using has its mechanical aspect, because it involves the realization of a concept in the natural order. As the child grows up, he begins to realize his own concept. Thus he makes himself the "tool of reason." The extreme at which the living agent is reduced to a stream of energy that moves the dead things in which his real nature is expressed, is now brought together with the opposite extreme of pure reason *enjoying* itself. The spirit must guide the hand in the craftsman's self-expression, whereas both spirit and muscle alike were merely spent in the laborer's struggle with nature; and at the higher limit spirit must express itself spiritually. This is what it does in *speech*. As a momentary sound speech is, on its material side, a vanishing quantity. The barest minimum of living energy is consumed in producing it, and it makes a minimal impact on the objective world of natural processes. And "because of the immediacy of the nature of this being, its subjectivity is immediately objectivity" (429): the word spoken is nothing but an immediate coming-to-be-and-passing-away unless we catch its *meaning*; and the meaning is a *concept* which is the form of objectivity on its ideal side. This objectivity is at the same time absolute subjectivity, for it is the actual existence of the subject. In the formal concept of speech, the concept of words as a set of "possible meanings," the very concept that has its real existence in a dictionary, "objectivity" itself is a *word* with a fixed meaning such that "objectivity" and "subjectivity" can never coincide absolutely. But in the *actual* concept of speech, i.e., in actual speech, this coincidence is just what is necessarily brought to pass.[49]

The "totality of speech" is the final development of the concept of *Bildung* at this level. It begins with "gesture, mien, and their totality the glance of the eye." This is an "unconscious" language of the kind that we have to interpret in dealing with the needs of babies. In so far as it is not deliberate—I believe the intended contrast between "gesture" and "mien" is that the latter is not deliberate—there is no "concept" here. It is the direct expression of feeling in and for intuition. Crying ought to belong here just as much as laughing does, but Hegel does not say so because he wants to treat the types of vocal sound as the totality of the totality.

It is clear that Hegel intends to include all forms of *writing* under the next heading, *corporeal sign*, which embraces all the ways in which we use the external world to make signs to each other. A child conveys a great deal by his "mien," but as a rule he does not intend to do so. But we cannot make *external signs* without knowing exactly, and in the most objective way possible, what "message" we want to send. All the meanings conveyed in an external sign system have been established by *conscious* convention; and of course no such sign is capable of interpreting itself. It is not a sign *for* itself and does not mean anything *to* itself, yet it has its own being *in* itself. When we come finally to *audible speech*, none of these assertions holds good. We might plausibly object at this point that writing is a much higher cultural achievement than speaking. Hegel does not mean to deny this, for he comments on the high level of rationality involved in writing. But writing is a dead communication, not a living one. For this reason, as Plato was the first to point out, written communication is not a self-correcting process, and one cannot be fully "dialectical" in writing. Hegel, like Plato himself, certainly struggled against this limitation. But it *would* be easier to understand him if we could talk to him. As it is, we have to "tack on" the meaning that he sought to express in his "objective speech" as best we can.[50]

What is new in the discussion of speech as the totality of gesture and sign, as compared with Hegel's introductory discussion of it, is the concept of "recognition." Spoken language is addressed to someone else, who is thereby recognized as a rational agent who can receive and interpret it. Written language is "dumb" recognition because it is only for someone who can *read* it—i.e., make it speak by lending it his own voice—that it exists as language. The objective existence of *speech* is "according to the mode of the concept," i.e., it is that of a living and self-conscious intelligence which has its being in the "inner" world, or on the "ideal" side. Hegel did not know how much effective animal communication there is through cries and other behavior at the level of what he calls "mien"; but he would have had no trouble in accommodating all of it within his analysis. Indeed it would fit in better than the romantic fancies about the death cries of lower animals with which he did have to deal. In any case he does have a very sharp awareness of how different the song of a poet is from the song of a bird. He says that the lyrical capacity for direct linguistic expression of one's own inward feeling is the "highest flower of the first *Potenz*." This first *Potenz* is the *Potenz* of feeling, the level of absolutely singular existence. Except for the "song" of the lyric poet, the universals of culture exist at this level only in the objective form of tools. In the poet's speech singular consciousness is finally exhibited as a proper monadic reflection of the Absolute Identity.

In conclusion Hegel adds a short note about "the negative of this *Potenz*." First, there is the negative of intuition. Necessity (*Not*) is the point where need (*Bedürfnis*) overwhelms all other consciousness. An example of the negative extreme which Hegel gave in his own earlier writings was the hunger that drove David to eat the shewbread.[51] Natural death is the negative of all feeling, being the negative moment present in life itself. As we shall see presently, the havoc of natural forces and even of man himself, so far as he appears simply as a force of nature, are the negatives of rational activity, and achievement, the negative of the concept, rather than of intuition. But all of these active forces form the lower levels of the negative as such, and Hegel will deal with them more fully later on.

b) *Thought*

The second stage of natural ethics is an abstract conceptual one. In the first stage we were concerned with the articulation of feeling as the living process of the singular individual. But in the "conceptually" dominated submoments of that analysis we saw how the wider context of nature made certain structures necessary. Now we shall look at those structures from the point of view of the thinking consciousness that language makes possible. Thus the second stage as a whole will be a subsumption of intuition under concept; and it will be largely concerned with the conceptualization of the laboring process and of "possession," which, as we have already seen, is the conceptual framework without which the organization of labor as a way of life would not be possible. The singular organism that needs, works, and enjoys life from cradle to grave now appears as an abstract concept, the *person*.

Whereas the first stage was *finite* and *real*, this stage is *infinite* and *ideal*. The first stage was that of feeling, this one is the stage of thought. But both stages are "formal," for both are concerned with the conditions that must be satisfied if the singular human organism is to reach maturity. The first stage was concerned with the relation between the sentient organism and nature; this one is more concerned with social relations outside the family. (The family is a natural structure and belongs to the first stage.) But in both stages we are dealing with man as a *possibility*. First we dealt with his "real" nature as an abstract possibility. This stage culminated in the concept of actual speech, because that is the "point of union" between the real and the ideal sides. Now we shall deal with the "ideal" side as an abstract possibility likewise.

Because we are now dealing with abstract *thoughts*, not feelings, we lose contact with living men altogether. In the conceptually dominated substages of our previous discussion we found ourselves dealing with dead *things*, but they were the singular things that constituted the life environment of a single individual and his family. They were *Adam's* things, even when we arrived at his tools and his speech. But his tools and his speech have universal import, and the speech is a point of transition because it *demands* a response of the same sort. Hence it posits (or logically presupposes) the *recognition* of the "other" who is addressed as Adam's *conceptual* equal. Now we shall deal with the *con-*

cepts that are implicit in that recognition of others as equals and with the new relationships which become possible in a community of independent equals. Adam becomes "Mr. X," and his wife and children temporarily disappear from the scene altogether. When they return in the moment of "totality," they will be accompanied by a new character, the bond-servant, who is not entitled to the prefix "Mr."

The "intuition" under which the concept is subsumed in the first stage of this conceptually dominated *Potenz* is the "negative" intuition of labor. This appeared previously in the opposite role of intuition subsumed under concept when it was differentiated objectively in terms of the aspect of nature that the labor was directed upon. But then it was just the one man Adam, who partitioned his energies between digging, planting, stockkeeping, and raising his children. And even at the higher level of tool-making and tool-using we had before us only one man, who devoted all of his intelligence and energy to one special craft. The subsuming intuition now is the one task of life-maintenance that is partitioned between indifferent intelligences. This unique and absolute task of life-maintenance, in its unity of subjective and objective sides, is what "intuition" always refers to in some way throughout the whole range of its uses in the first part. But whereas earlier the focus point was the singular feeling of subjective need, the emphasis is now on the objective task. Through the parcelling out of the different aspects of the work of living, and even the stages of a single craft, to different agents, all agents approach more closely to the "mechanical" ideal of simply providing the energy to keep a causal cycle going. Life is divided up into single working activities or equal tasks. Carried to its limit, the process makes everyone the minder of a special tool which provides its own energy and needs only to be turned on and off at the right moments. Thus we move from the *tool*, which presupposes the skill of the specific craftsman who made it and/or uses it—the smith who made the shield of Achilles or the bard who exalts him to the level of the gods—to the *machine*, which presupposes an impersonal intelligence that does not *do* any more than turn switches and press buttons.[52]

This impersonal labor produces a surplus commodity; in order to have any bearing on the needs of the producer the surplus commodity has to be exchangeable. Hence the formal alienation of possession from one agent to another has to be possible. Instead of being a man who possesses things that are useful to him, the agent must be a *person* who *owns property*.

With these legal abstractions we arrive at the point where the recoil of the concept can begin. The "ideal" tie of possession will now become a "real" one in virtue of its public recognition and legal status. The "infinity" of this *Potenz* is subjectively the concept of legal personality and objectively the concept of "acknowledged property." As an *identity* transcending the subject/object antithesis it is simply *legal right*. The bare concept of a surplus product is the concept of the present *Potenz* "at rest"; it is implicitly alienated, its destiny is clearly indicated, when it is marked as "surplus." The process of exchange is the concept "in motion." Exchange presupposes that each of the two parties involved needs what the other possesses, and each recognizes the other's "right" as owner. As rightful owners they are like the oppositely charged bodies involved in a discharge of static electricity, whereas work, as the connecting of desire to enjoyment, is analogous to the attraction between the poles of a bar magnet.[53] Each side *can* be separated from its own energy (as embodied in the product of labor). The "magnetic" relation between me and my labor can be severed, whereas if we try to sever the poles of a magnet we only get two magnets. Thus "true ideality" begins here, for practical intelligence (the energy of man as such) can be severed from need and labor altogether. Someone else can work to supply my needs while I devote my mind to other pursuits. But this must come about "rightfully," or else the equilibrium of nature will be disturbed, and a see-saw of quite a new kind *between* families will be set up.

Therefore the exchange must be an exchange of things which are *in themselves* equal, even though each side finds what the other has more desirable. The equality of the two sides of the "concept in motion" is the *price*. The price is the empirically found *value*. The value of something is what the owner *ideally* possesses when the thing he owns is not useful to him *per se*. He *realizes* this ideal value in actual utility by getting something that he actually does need and can use through the exchange. We should note that although Hegel speaks of the "price" already at this stage, he has not yet introduced "money" as a *real middle*. This he will do only in the "totality" of this *Potenz*. At the moment we have the ideal value of the thing possessed, on the one side, exchanged directly for the real utility of the thing desired, on the other. This is the moment of simple opposition, and as long as the exchange is a simple barter-relation, there is no need for a "real middle." But when the exchange is complicated and is completed over a time interval, some guarantee of fulfilment at the stipulated time becomes necessary. Thus we arrive at *contract*, the "totality" of abstract right and exchange, where the legal right itself becomes what is evidently real and effective. The exchange may not actually take place until after the harvest, or service at harvest time may be promised in return for goods delivered now, and so forth. But the contract is already signed, sealed, and delivered. It is a "rational middle" which does away with all the differences of time and place. On the ideal side the exchange is already completed.

Hegel treats "contract" as the *formal* emergence of the *spirit*. Men often *trust* one another to perform promises without invoking legal sanctions. This is an important element in social relations, and Hegel certainly does not underestimate it, as we shall see in due course. But this relation of "trust" belongs to the *inwardness* of the spirit. In a legal contract the spirit exists "formally," i.e., abstractly, in the shape of something absolutely outward and nonspiritual. The *formal* existence of the "spirit" is the "letter."

The "totality" of these two stages of property and exchange is two-sided. On the external side the "totality" of property and exchange is *money*, which is the medium of exchange in the form of property, the resting concept of exchange itself, and *trade*, which is the actual process of exchange, or the concept in motion.

So far there is no great difficulty. Money is a concept that is always necessarily singularized, but one can see how it is the "realization" of a universal, for it circulates from hand to hand indifferently in commerce, keeping always the same significance and depending always for its currency on the generally recognized convention about its value. It is, indeed, precisely the realized form of the abstract concept of *value*.

But according to Hegel this is just "the relative identity or the relation." The implication here is that in order to be an absolute identity the external process of money circulating in the course of trade has to be brought into equilibrium as a stable pattern of human existence. The object (money and trade) must be equalized with the subject. The object is a concept that is necessarily singularized in intuition when it is real. The subject, correspondingly, is an intuited singular that is necessarily universalized as a concept when it is realized. This is the individual as *person*. The individual exists as a person only for another person who recognizes him and whom he recognizes. The process of this recognition has the usual three stages.

First, there is the subsumption of concept under intuition: as perceived by others, the individual as person is the owner of all his possessions and of rights generally. He is a living being who has rights and owns things. This is his formal character, and it is no concern of anyone else what capacities for living this person has, or what external equipment he actually owns. He has the generalized right to be recognized as a person as long as he is alive. What then is this "life" that entitles him to recognition? Hegel says that "like recognition and empirical intuition in general" it is "a formal ideality" (441). In its actuality an individual's life is his freedom: "the supreme indifference of the singular," i.e., the capacity of being indifferently A or not A. This is not one of his "personal" possessions, for he cannot alienate it—at least he cannot hand it over to another in the way that he can give up his possessions generally. But his life is "also something formal," since it is the "empty unity of the singular characteristics." Here, as before, the best model of an "empty unity" is a baby. The baby is already a person with the generalized right to recognition even though he is not yet a rational free agent. For at the very least, at the absolute limit of abstraction, he is a living being and his life is human life. To be a "person" is to be acknowledged as a living human being in this absolutely abstract sense. Thus the concept of "personality" is the formal concept of rationality; and Reason is, of course, "the Absolute Concept itself."

When we recognize another being as human, even if he is only a baby, we are already thinking of him as the realization of the Absolute Concept, or as a free rational agent. But this recognition involves also necessarily a consciousness of its own freedom, for it is a recognition freely given, and it can equally well be withheld or denied. It is not a simple fact that this human being is free when he might not have been free, as it is a simple fact that his skin is black when it might have been white or white when it might have been black. Every intelligible concept involves some possible alternative or contrast; but the actual concept of intelligence, the concept of freedom, is "the indifference of all specific characteristics" including "recognition," which is freedom itself as a specific characteristic.

Thus when the concept of personality subsumes intuition, or when our baby grows up and goes out into the world as an actual concept, a free intelligence, he finds other living individuals there from whom he *demands* recognition. They make the same demand. But it is a simple matter of economic fact that some are rich and others are poor, and for this reason some can employ others as servants and some are forced by their circumstances to become servants. One is "caught" (*begriffen*) in a "difference" and another is not. (We should remember that the primitive "difference" is that between need and satisfaction.) Some persons have more "living might" (*Macht des Lebens*) than others, and so they can satisfy their needs. The less fortunate must give service in return for the satisfaction of their wants out of the surplus of the more prosperous.

The mention of *Macht* and the use of the terms *Herrschaft* and *Knechtschaft* must give rise to the suspicion that Hegel is here discussing the master-slave relation. But he calls "this relation of bondage" a relation "of person to person" when he goes on to the next stage where the difference is equalized. He has not clearly identified the *Knecht* as a *person* before this, though he is very explicit that the *Herr* is a person. Still, the bond that he is discussing is not one of physical dominance of lord over slave, for he explicitly says that what constitutes it is *Not*. Now *Not* stands for the point where the ordinary need (*Bedürfnis*) of life becomes *compelling*; the fear of death may enter into it, but it is not yet a fear of death through the violence of the mastering personality. Hegel insists that the relation is natural and that it is directly involved in the very concept of a plurality of men living together.

It is plain I think, that Hegel means this formal *Potenz* to embrace all the forms of servitude, from the slavery of a vanquished foe to the servile dominance of Jeeves or the admirable Crichton. The only thing that he explicitly contrasts it with is the "obedience" involved in a relation of individuals "in connection with what is most ethical." In that ethical relation obedience is also necessarily involved, but there the "power or might" is an absolute universal, whereas here we are concerned with the authority of another's particular need (which the servant labors to satisfy). In the ethical relation "individuality is only something external and the form," whereas in servitude "it is the essence of the relation . . . since bondage is obedience to the single and the particular." Thus when an army officer gives a military order we have ethical obedience, for the safety and prosperity of the *Volk* is *das Sittlichste*; but when the same man gives instructions to his batman we have *Knechtschaft*.

Primitive servitude—slavery or serfdom—is certainly embraced within this *Potenz*. It is the natural pole to which ethical obedience is opposed. The very fact that Hegel develops the formal concept of recognition into its own negation as his way of making the transition is a warning of this; and he speaks of the *Knecht* at first as "the one who is not free" and who must therefore intuit his inner freedom as its opposite, i.e., the external freedom of the *Herr*. But the full development of our present *Potenz* is the relation of paid service, where the formal equality of personality or legal right is recognized on both sides and objectified in the money paid. In the primitive condition of servitude the opposite moments of "being a person" and "being a possession" are realized on the side of subjectivity. But since the relation is natural, and is immediately established where men are living together, it must still exist when the moments of "recognizing" and "being recognized" are not dissociated but are in their proper reciprocal equilibrium. This is also where the objective concept of value (money) is in perfect equilibrium with the subjective concept of personal right.

But even in the society of free persons, there still remains the relation, the "difference" between "master" and "servant." Only within the family is this difference finally equalized. In the family the difference and the dependency remains—indeed it is accentuated, for there is no one else so incapable of independent survival as a baby—but it is not what is important. Of course the formal identity of the baby as a living being with the free rational agent that he will become, or the real identity of the child with the parents themselves as Hegel likes to put it (because the actual *Bildung* of the new individual is their work), does not show on the surface. But that just reflects the abstractness of this *Potenz*. On the one hand the baby is recognized as human and possesses human *rights*; on the other hand he is loved by his parents as the expression and meaning of their union. The family, which has thus far been treated strictly as a set of natural ties, is now given its properly ethical dimension as a system of "recognition."[54]

As the totality of natural feeling with ethical right the family is *first* the institution by which natural needs are kept at bay. Adam's incessant struggle to take possession of his field, his actual possession of his house and its furniture, is all for the sake of his family; and when he demands and gets recognition from his neighbors as landowner and householder, this too is for the sake of his family. He does not assert his claims against the members of his family or they against him. His sons do not make contracts to work for him in the field or his wife and daughters in the house. He is the recognized holder of the family property, but his "holding" is just that: the property is a patrimony to be handed on to the next generation. Thus in the order of natural ethics he has no right to bequeath the family property to an alien heir. But within the family he is the authority. In the public world he is the householder, having equal legal rights with other householders; in the private world of the household, as a plurality of men living together, it is the "difference of living might" that makes itself evident, so that the master's word is law. But the obedience involved here is ethical obedience. The family members are not father's servants; he gives orders, and they obey, in the interest of the family as a whole.

Secondly, the natural difference of the sexes passes into an ethical identity in the family. "These twain are one flesh" permanently and by general recognition, not just in the momentary intuition of "the beast with two backs." If either of the parties now follows the promptings of sex in a new direction, they will be guilty of adultery, which is a violation of fundamental natural right. It is proper to speak of *natural* right here, for husband and wife form an "empirical universal," they are together a particular instance of the natural species *homo sapiens*.[55]

A marriage is made by a man and a woman in order to have a family. In that sense it is a naturally determined relationship, not an accident of personal choice. But the couple do *choose* one another, and from this side their union has the outward appearance of a contract. In its inward meaning, however, marriage transcends the limits of contractual relations altogether. It is impossible to "own" one's own life as a whole, yet the parties to a marriage give themselves up to their union completely. Of course as a matter of legal form it is quite possible for a family member to be treated as property; wives, like slaves, can be bought and sold. But this involves a contract between the owners, not between master and slave or husband and wife. So *this* contract does not, and cannot, constitute an ethical relation between them. The marriage contract, like the authority of the householder, is only an outward form. If the husband and wife begin arguing about the due exercise of their "conjugal rights," they will make their marriage an ethical monstrosity. For a marriage is a *union*, and it must not be treated as a *relation*.

Finally, the family is an absolute unity of form and actuality. The marriage comes to its fruition in the child. The parents must care for all of his needs, so that the marriage as the moment of difference is "subsumed" under the first moment of external need. This is a natural necessity, and as such we dealt with it in the first *Potenz*, but now we have returned to it as the crowning ethical duty imposed by nature. In subordinating their own fully developed rationality to the natural needs of the living thing which is as yet human only in outward appearance, the parents come to terms with their own mortality as natural organisms. Death as the negative aspect of life is the mode in which the concept as the universal inward essence manifests itself against the inescapable particularity of external nature. Reason itself is preserved, and the foundation of Reason's own independent level of existence—the realm of *Sittlichkeit* proper—is laid through this surrender of the parents' own lives, not to one another as rational adults (as in their marriage), but to this life whose complete fruition they may perhaps not live to see. By this reversal of values in which the strong serves the need of the weak, and the actual labors on behalf of the merely formal, the absolute identity of form and essence, intuition and concept, of the inward and the outward, is known and shown to be what matters, even though the identity must "remain inward" as a feeling, or "float above" family relations as a thought. It is because the whole function of the family is the raising of the children that "the family is the supreme totality of which nature is capable" (445).

4. THE NEGATIVE AS FREEDOM.

At the end of the *Potenz* of feeling, Hegel mentioned "the negative" for the first time. We have now seen how the *natural* negations of feeling—*Not* and *Tod*, necessity and death—function to make natural relations into ethical ones for rational beings. It is through *Not* that men are naturally brought into institutional relations of service and obedience with each other; and it is through the conscious recognition of the inevitability of need and death that men are led to transform the natural bonds of desire and instinct into ethical institutions. Thus death, as the negative of natural life, is the link between the natural and the ethical level of the rational individual's existence.

But now that the family has emerged as the totality of natural *relation* and rational *identity*, or as the stable equilibrium of nature and ethical life, the further development of ethical life into full independence is only possible through the negation of what the family itself represents. Thus need and death must come forward as ethical negatives, as selfishness and murder, so that ethical life can be established in its own right as the power by which they are controlled.

Hegel said at the beginning that "nature itself is nothing but the subsumption of intuition under the concept" (416). Now he says that this whole stage of "Nature" that we have gone through is "the Absolute subsumed under the concept." It appears, therefore, that the life of mankind in the "state of nature" is the existence of the Concept as Nature—and what is subsumed under it is man as a rational agent. The totality of life itself (*Sittlichkeit* or *ethical* life) has not come forth to be individuated or "subsumed under intuition." We have advanced from the single organism or person to the particular family or household, but "singularity" remains the principle. The family is created by single agents, and we shall now watch it being destroyed by single agents. The right will come forward as something fully real only in the ethical resolution of this self-destructive dialectic.

Hegel's first concern is to explain the difference between the negative activity of ethical life itself and the destructive act of the murderer. So far we have viewed ethical life as a positive process, setting up a stable equilibrium between need and satisfaction, male and female, parent and child, value and utility, strong and weak, actual and formal. But ethical life is not only positive, reintegrative; it is negative and disciplinary. It is not just *felt* needs that have to be superseded; there are also natural impulses that have to be formally abrogated. Contracts must be kept, marriage must not be violated, lessons must be learned, skills practiced, the rights of others respected, and so on. Here the natural impulse itself, when it conflicts with one of these obligations, becomes negative; and instead of being satisfied it must be negated. This negation is a matter not of *realizing* a goal, but of *changing* the goal to be realized. In dealing with these forbidden desires and impulses, things which he has renounced, the individual acts freely. So far his goals have been given by nature, and reason has been the slave of the passions. But now "the form as negative is the essence. The real will be posited as something ideal; it is determined by pure freedom" (447).

At this point Hegel draws an analogy between the practical and the theoretical levels of the "ideal series." The negative activity of freedom is like the negative activity of thought in relation to sensation. The sensation is necessarily a real particular, while the thought of what was sensed is an ideal universal. But the thought still refers to the sensation in its particularity. "Red" as a sensation is an objective intuition; as a thought it is a subjective one. It has been raised to infinity, for it is now contemplated as possible at any time and in any place, but "its finitude remains definitely persistent." In objective intuition it was *discriminated* against the spatial background of other colors, now it is thought of as one *color* among the others. But at both levels we need the determinate intuition of "red."

Absolute ethical life involves the same sort of idealization of what is naturally given. The negative act of the murderer does what ethical life does, but it does something else as well. Ethical life obliges the individual to come out of his natural context, to forget all his natural impulses (as the murderer removes his victim from this context and as the color is abstracted from its physical background). But, whereas the murderer does away with the objective existence of his victim altogether, so that he becomes just a corpse which returns into the cycle of natural change at a lower level, ethical life leaves the subject's essence as a living being alone (just as thinking about it does not change the color of anything). Ethical life nullifies the individual's subjectivity only as an *ideal* determinacy (not as a real determinacy too, which is what happens in a murder).

The ethical agent is *free*, and ethical life makes him conscious of his freedom in all of the pressures of his natural existence. The murderer, too, is asserting this freedom (though he may be doing so under extreme pressures). But the freedom of ethical life is not a "fixed negative" opposed to the "positive" (which is life itself in its natural determinacy). The "fixed negative" is what we have when the freedom that ethical life reveals is turned (by the murderer) against life itself. Hegel does not explain very clearly how and why freedom gets fixed in its negative moment. He merely says that this is "a determinacy posited by the same moment of negation according to the preceding level of necessity" (448). This "preceding level of necessity" (*Notwendigkeit*) must be the level of natural feeling, and its negative moment is *need* (*Bedürfnis*), which rises to the extreme of *Not*. I cannot see any sign of a "trial-of-strength" doctrine in Hegel's account of "lordship and bondage" in the following "infinite *Potenz*" or *Potenz* of freedom, but it is fairly obvious that violence, rather than recognition, must come about when both of the opposed parties, or even just one of them, is subject to *Not*. If we look forward to the way that Hegel develops the present *Potenz*, this interpretation of what he means appears to be confirmed.[56]

The general pattern of that first "practical" *Potenz* was a cycle from need to satisfaction and back again. But violence, when it reaches the pitch of murder, or even when it simply deprives the loser of the means of subsistence, produces death, which means that "the practical sphere falls under the control of the inorganic and objective levels." In this willingness to destroy life altogether what shows itself as essential is freedom itself. But because it goes to the pitch of destruction, there is bound to be a reaction. Life is only *injured* by violence, not elevated to a higher level as it is by the negative aspect of ethical action. But also it is *only* injured, not destroyed. The "person" who is killed or deprived of his right by violence had only a "formal" existence in any case. He was really a member of some family in which life continues. If he had died in the normal course of nature, the family would simply have buried him and given him the honors due to a member with his status (whatever it may be). This is no longer a matter of ethics but of religion.[57] But if he dies by violence, the family must also take steps to reassert and reestablish his ethical right in this world. There must be an equal and opposite reaction for what was done to him. No matter how he dies, his body is restored to the earth in a ceremony that expresses recognition of the great cycle of the life of nature to which all mortal life belongs. But when he dies by violence, it is not just his body, but the whole sphere of practical action, that falls back under the law of causal reciprocity. This is what the "fixation" of the negative really means: the *lex talionis*, "an eye for an eye, and a tooth for a tooth." The natural justice of vengeance is itself the fixing of the negative, for it is in the vendetta-cycle of injury and revenge that "the negative" is made into the essence. In the positive cycle of need and satisfaction life itself is the essence, and the free personality of the agent is only something "external and superficial." Since each family regards what is done to it as *injury* and what it does as *vengeance*, it is quite correct to say that "the one is the opposite subsumption of the other." If the original injury was an act of *Not*, then free rational consciousness, the concept, does here "constitute itself into intuition" as "negative vitality" having its own absolute right. For *vengeance* belongs to the Lord, and no man can take the law into his own hands. When we grasp the essential endlessness of the vendetta process, we are forced to admit this. Wherever the agent of vengeance is human, the hand of the Lord does not clearly *appear*; but the making of the law into a singular "intuition" is very much apparent.

There is an internal dialectic in the mind of the agent which arises in the same way. The killer knows that the spilling of blood is injury to life. This is the pang of *conscience*; but it is only an ideal or inward vengeance, it does not *appear* outwardly at all. Hegel's analysis of how this inward torment "presses on to a totality" seems to me to have been suggested by *Macbeth* more than by any ancient tragedy.[58] But the source is not important. What *is* important is the doctrine of the life-and-death struggle that begins to emerge here. Conscience makes the guilty one *look for* the avenger. Yet in the presence of the avenger conscience is overcome and drowned by the spur of *Not*. When life itself is threatened *in* oneself, the absolute right of self-preservation comes to the fore. In a life-and-death struggle the parties are equal in the sense that both are defending life itself. This wipes out all their other differences, including the difference of good and bad conscience, because conscience is only a "determinacy" of life. At the same time every "guilty" victory through the death of the opponent in such a struggle increases the inner torment of guilt. Hegel does not appeal to this internal dialectic of conscience in his account of the actual development of criminal justice, but the implication that the guilty man always knows that he is guilty, and must in some sense assent to and approve of his own punishment so far as it "matches" his crime, is important to the understanding of Hegel's doctrine as a whole.

The first moment of this process of "negative vitality" is life itself as a natural force which resists the civilizing power of Reason. In the first moment of practical life we saw how intuition subsumes the concept, how Reason emerges as a slave of the passions. But now we have a very different subsumption of everything that Reason has produced under a single blind passion for simple destruction. This is the opposite of the whole subsumption of nature under "intuition and life." But it is *not* itself a "subsumption of intuition under the concept." Logically it *has* to be a "subsumption of concept under intuition" and the description of the following moment as "this havoc subsumed under the concept" confirms this. The present moment of *natural annihilation* (or "havoc") is logically a moment of intuition, but Hegel is in a difficulty with it (as he was with "feeling") because it is the moment of "pure" or *unconscious* intuition. The agency in this *Potenz* is not a force of nature like fire or flood, but a human horde. What we have here is the *Volk* as a felt community of blood, united in a free activity that is blind or antirational. It is free precisely by being purposeless, or having no purpose beyond sheer destruction. In the total economy of nature and spirit it has a purpose or function, but like the plants and animals it is a natural force that fulfils its function without any awareness of it. This function is to wipe the slate for a new beginning, as when the barbarian invasions overwhelmed the Roman Empire. But those northern barbarians were in "the determinacy of the understanding": they had at least a minimal culture of their own, and they wanted to take over the *imperium* themselves (and did so). The permanent presence of pure barbarism in the natural order is rather the Mongolian hordes. Hegel always thought of the East as the region where human nature existed in a state of natural equilibrium, so it is not surprising that he should take this view of the eastern barbarians. They are simply "brooms of God" who sweep away a decaying culture without replacing it. The horde is an absolutely united *Volk*, but one that is "formless," i.e., without consciousness of itself because it has no "constitution." Thus it really is a natural force, like fire or flood, and cannot be conquered (at least not in a pitched battle, for that is where havoc becomes universal). But it breaks down by itself because it only has an active form by contrast, it is natural devastation as opposed to the active force of Reason and culture. In its triumph it becomes "pure formlessness" properly, and through the abolition of the contrast it goes from the formlessness of "pure unity" to that of pure multiplicity, like a bubble bursting into tiny droplets of water. This happens because the spirit of *Verwüstung* infects even the forces that are seeking to contain and overcome it. Thus we have what Hegel calls *Wut*: "the absolute and unmediated urge, the absolute concept in its complete indeterminacy, the restlessness of the infinity of the absolute concept." This happens because *Wut* intensifies its opposite, *das Reine*, into the opposite of itself, i.e., it turns the self-conscious reason of the civilized defenders into *Wut*. Now the bubble can only burst and all the droplets of which it is composed must fall to the ground in death. *Wut* is the unchaining of absolute freedom in its pure negative form. It shows itself to be "the real being of absolute subjectivity," because in seeking to annihilate all objective form, it leaves nothing but objectivity. By going thus from the battle-madness of the barbarian to the berserk fury that comes over a defender of hearth and altar, Hegel has shown that this first *natural Potenz* is indeed the formal concept of the whole stage.

By definition, havoc can only destroy. It is "negative intuition" in this primitive sense, that it simply replaces one perceptible intuition, one state of the world, by another. Conceptual changes such as "transfer of possession" do not concern it. It is at the opposite pole from *theft*, because it is vital to the thief that what he steals should keep its character and not be destroyed or spoiled. Theft makes apparent the universality that belongs to something as a *tool*; it also makes the purely ideal character of "possession" apparent. Thus theft is the subsumption of havoc under the concept, in as much as it is only something conceptual that is destroyed. Havoc destroys men and things indifferently; theft destroys neither; it merely destroys the relation between them. Only someone who properly understands and recognizes rights can *steal*. The barbarian who makes havoc cannot steal, any more than an animal can; indeed the barbarian has to be regarded and dealt with like an animal on the rampage. But the thief recognizes the very rights that he denies, for he expects the recognition of his own supposed right to possess, enjoy, or alienate what he has stolen.

The natural avenger of theft is the person injured. If he does not care about the injury to his right as such, he may be content with the simple restoration of the thing stolen or with an equivalent payment for its value. But we have not yet reached the level of social development where a settlement of this sort is really conceivable. Before a human community can securely achieve that stage, it must pass through the phase where it is a point of *honor* to defend one's right and where an injury cannot be overlooked without dishonor. We are dealing now with the biblical "strong man who keepeth his goods"; and if he cannot keep them then he is shown to be no strong man. How is such a one to deal with a thief if he catches him? He must subjugate him, compel him to submit to discipline. But as long as his strength is respected and his right admitted, he cannot go so far as to enslave the thief either in terms of justice, since the thief has not threatened his life, or in terms of prudence, since the thief has shown himself untrustworthy. The *lex talionis* must be observed; but I believe Hegel is being deliberately cautious when he refrains from giving any examples. The Bible may speak of "an eye for an eye," but the equivalence of crime and punishment is generally symbolic rather than direct—as when the thief loses his hand. There is no simple natural scale for the application of the natural principle of justice.

The "totality" of the two moments of "havoc" (against civilized existence) and "deprivation" (of personal right) is "battle." For in a fair fight both aspects (subjective and objective) are equalized for both parties. The issue (which may be either death, the fate of havoc, or bondage, the fate of one who seeks to deprive another of his right) is uncertain as between the parties (whereas it is quite definitely the thief and the barbarian who are to be subjected to it in the contributory moments). But how can there be an adequate occasion for such a battle between equals? The very fact that they are equally conscious of their own personal integrity makes anything at all which touches that integrity in any way a possible ground for battle. Any injury, however slight, can be a matter of "honor." Thus honor can be injured through the denial of a mere possession, as the wrath of Achilles over the fact that Briseis was taken from him graphically illustrates. Ordinary theft is not an affair of honor because a thief usually has no honor to defend; generally speaking he will admit his fault and accept the penalty, rather than make a life-and-death struggle of it. Once the struggle has been accepted, however, all lesser questions of right and injury fall away. The threat to life confers right, and the willingness to put life at risk constitutes the justice of one's cause. The issue must be bondage or death for the vanquished party, though if their strength proves equal, both may die (as in the conflict between Eteocles and Polynices).

There is a noticeable ambiguity in this "totality" on the question of whether "battle" is really a conflict of two singular individuals, or whether we have now arrived at a relation which essentially and necessarily involves groups. The "formal" concept of "havoc" from which we began would seem to call for some sort of communal response, and we should therefore expect to find this communal aspect reflected in the "totality" of the whole stage. This expectation certainly appears to be confirmed in some places. Thus the distinction that Hegel draws between murder and political assassination as an act of war makes no sense outside of a communal context; and when his discussion concludes finally with *War* we have just the sort of integration of the formal concept that we might have expected.

Hegel seems, none the less, to be of two minds about the question; and the only interpretation of his argument that can be made fully consistent with all that has gone before and with what immediately follows is one in which the main emphasis is placed on single combat, and where no community larger than the family or clan is invoked. The remark about assassination must be treated as an incidental aside that refers either to a more developed social situation altogether or, more probably, to the faction-fights of "families" like the Montagues and the Capulets;[59] and both the initial discussion of "havoc" and the closing discussion of "war" must be carefully reexamined to discover exactly what perspective Hegel means us to view them in.

This general line of interpretation is made absolutely mandatory by the fact that Hegel explicitly says at the beginning of the next section (on *Sittlichkeit* proper) that "in the foregoing levels there is the totality of particularity in both of its aspects, particularity as such and universality as abstract unity. The former is the family. . . . But in none of the foregoing levels does absolute nature exist in a spiritual shape; and for this reason it is also not present as ethical life; not even the family far less the subordinate levels, *least of all the negative*, is ethical" (460; my italics). In the development of *Sittlichkeit* we shall come upon "war" again in a quite unambiguous perspective, and its supremely ethical character will be emphasized along with its negativity. This is a clear indication that we ought to look very carefully at this preliminary discussion of it in a context which is so explicitly declared to be not properly ethical.

Hegel himself recognized the ambiguity of his discussion of the "totality" of this *Potenz* of "the negative." For in his marginal note—which, no matter when it was written, must surely have been subsequent to the drafting of the text[60]—he summarized the stages of his argument thus: "3 *Potenzen*: (a) Murder, (b) Revenge, (c) *Zweikampf*; the middle is *Kampf*, the swaying. *Zweikampf*, personal injury on the singular point." It is clear that he wanted to focus attention therefore on "single combat" (*Zweikampf*); and although he needed the more general concept of "battle" (*Kampf*), which occupies the limelight in his actual text, he was especially concerned with the definition of the species *Zweikampf* in relation to this genus. "War" (*Krieg*) does not appear in this summary at all, even though his discussion actually culminates with it.

The first moment of the totality, then, is *murder*. Murder is any intentional homicide that does not occur in a fair fight. It is the extreme case of *oppression*, which is the violent subjugation of someone who lacks the strength or a fair opportunity to defend himself. But Hegel is not concerned here with any and every murder. He is not concerned, on one side, with assassination as a political act, where the murder of some notable individual is intended as a declaration of war; nor is he concerned, on the other hand, with murder committed for economic motives, e.g., in pursuance of a robbery. For in this latter case there is "nothing personal," that is to say, the victim has not previously given offense to the murderer in some way which he chooses to take "personally." The giving of personal offense or "injury to personality" is an essential component in the whole concept of crime that Hegel has developed up to this point. Even robbery is here dealt with as a personal offense. The barbarian hordes could not give personal offense because they knew nothing of personality. But now in the "raw" moment of the totality their natural "havoc" is synthesized with the moment of "recognition" against which the "havoc" of theft is directed. The offended self simply wipes out the offending one, without any recognition of his right as a person and without any shadow of natural justice or parity between the offense given and the penalty exacted.

This is precisely the "injury to life" which gives rise to "avenging justice." So the second moment of the totality is the vendetta, which can be recognized abstractly by the understanding as an equilibrium of causal reciprocity, where negation is made real and permanent by being endlessly repeated. Here the family emerges as the offended personality and vindicates its own violated right. But there is no overt "honor" in the process, although "honor" was the original ground of the whole feud. The "negative is fixed," for death is appointed as the penalty for the offender on the other side; and it is what the concept requires, for it is in perfect parity with the offense. We have already analyzed this stage (and its subjective correlate in the guilty conscience) sufficiently above.

It is easy to see now why the developed totality of this relation is single combat over the point of "honor" which would otherwise set off the ruinous cycle of the vendetta. The middle term is death itself, so far as that absolutely conceptual reality can be presented in living intuition. For the fair fight is an equal risk and an equal consciousness of death. Thus the indifference of justice appears and the judgment of God, not of a biased human judge, is made evident in the result of the combat.

Trial by combat is thus a perfect method of avoiding or eliminating the sort of murder that was set forth as the "raw" totality, for it gives everyone whose "honor" is touched in some particular a method of redress which does not create offense against life itself. But it is also a method of resolution for a family feud or vendetta. That is why Hegel insists that the combatants participate here as *family* members. If personal combat were not here being regarded as the "totality" of murder and vendetta, "family matters" would simply be one special area in the completely indefinite range of possible "points of honor." But just as Hegel was not concerned about any and every murder, so he is not concerned about any and every personal combat or duel. He is only concerned with murder for "personal" reasons and with combat as the champion of one's clan. The "fixed negative" of the feud must be rationalized, made indifferent, brought back within the *living* equilibrium of the ethical. The family can afford to lose a member, but it cannot stand to go on doing so continually.

In this combat there is a "judgment of God," but it is not a judgment of guilt or innocence. A family may deny the guilt imputed to it; each side may impute guilt to the other, while claiming innocence themselves; the defending champion may with evident truth, unchallenged by anyone, deny that the offense given was any of his doing; or he may be guilty without question and accept the challenge in open acknowledgement of that fact. None of this matters in the least, since the battle is fought for honor's sake, and "honor," as Hegel says bluntly, "is the urge to subsume" (i.e., to gain the mastery). This brings us back to that subsuming "mania" of the barbarians; and it is precisely here that Hegel makes his final transition to the general concept of *war*. In *war* it does not matter which side is "in the right" and which is "in the wrong"; this difference is "external and formal," like the difference between the *Wut* of the barbarian and its opposite *das Reine*. The "berserker," the man who can forget himself completely, along with all the distinctions and justifications with which his consciousness is filled, he it is, who, like the natural force of "havoc," cannot be conquered.

Finally, then, what war are we talking about? It is a war in which defeat means slavery for the survivors. Therefore it is not a war at the level of *Sittlichkeit* proper, for in the ethical community, as we shall see, there are no slaves or at least they have no proper place.[61] This is war regarded as an affair of the clan and fought for family and dynastic reasons, for the sake of honor and for the vindication of personal right. The Trojan war is a case in point, having been occasioned by the abduction of Helen and almost lost through the injury to Achilles' vanity. But the key instance is the culmination of the Theban saga in the struggle between Eteocles and Polynices. By the "judgment of God" both brothers fell in that battle. This was philosophically appropriate, for their right was equal and their conflict was not properly ethical. Their problem was only "who is to dominate?" The singular individual is still the only *reality* in this sort of war. The universals of "right" and "justice" are only abstractions that "float above" any stable equilibrium of family and personal relations. The family relationship may, indeed, be more fictional than real, but it is still the supposed "tie of blood" that counts, not yet the tie of citizenship.

This war may end in a *peace* which is the recognition of equality in strength, rather than in victory for one side and subjugation for the other. But this peace is not the foundation of a new relation; it is rather the reestablishment of an old one. The "equality" here is simply a mutual recognition of difference. Each side recognizes the other as *foreign* but as too strong to be subsumed or absorbed. This recognition of difference is, I suppose, the only permanent or rational relationship that can exist between civilization and barbarism, if barbarism is regarded as a necessary part of the total balance of nature. But in practical, ethical terms, this simple recognition of difference is just the acceptance of failure. It is the opposite pole from the achievement of Theseus in persuading a group of warring clans *not* to regard each other as foreign, but to accept one another as fellow-citizens. The highest moment we have yet reached is the moment when the clans are locked in combat and the battle hangs in the balance, with each side still hoping to win and no decision in sight: "In the antitheses, the rationality of this totality is the equality of indifference [i.e., equality of strength, equal hope of victory, and equal peril of defeat]; the middle term between them [i.e., the battle] is their unity in their complete confusion and uncertainty" (460).

5. ETHICAL LIFE.

The third section of Hegel's manuscript is simply called *Sittlichkeit*.

This is "absolute ethical life"; the first level was *natural* ethical life or the ethics of natural relations. Natural ethics is the ethics of family life, including the essential economic relations with other families; absolute ethics is the ethics of *political* existence. Within these two "levels" the sublevels are organized so that there is natural continuity and rational transition from each stage to the next. But there is no similar continuity or rational transition from the family to the *polis*. Between them we find only "the negative," which is connected with both certainly but not at all in the way in which it, "the negative," is internally connected. Hegel does make the connections explicit in both directions, but these connections are in surprising places. "The negative" as a whole is connected as negative with "absolute ethical life," not with the family; and this connection is made at the *beginning* of Hegel's discussion of "the negative." His introductory pages on the negative are concerned precisely with the contrast between the *fixed* negative, or the negative as such, and the negative as an integrated aspect of absolute ethical life itself. This is where "absolute ethical life" makes its first appearance in his discussion. The "formal" *Potenz* of the negative, the one that contains the "empty" essence which is both its inward nature and the outward form which will "float above" it throughout its development in the world of conscious experience, or of appearance, is the "havoc" of nomadic barbarian hordes to which only fully developed political societies organized for war can hope to offer effective opposition. Small agricultural communities with a complement of skilled craftsmen and a marketplace, the only social complexes suggested by the "relations" analyzed under "natural ethics," have no military organization at all. On the other hand, the whole objective development of this formal *Potenz* of "havoc" is conceived in terms which run directly parallel with a plausible account of the development of criminal justice and military organization in agricultural *villages* of this type. The justice is "personal" throughout; and although the family takes it up on behalf of the injured personality when he is wiped out altogether, it is only with the return of the person as champion of the family cause in single combat that a stable equilibrium is achieved. The champions thus produced can now be led to war by tribal chieftains, and so by extrapolation we can see how a military class capable of defending civilization against barbarism could be generated. But *this* connection is *not* made at the end of the discussion. Instead we are presented with a war between neighboring tribal communities, similar in strength (and hence in rational organization presumably); and this war ends either in subjugation or in stalemate. Again either of these issues *could* have provided Hegel with a transition to properly political existence, thus making "the negative" into a *positive* connection between the family and the city. At other times and in other places he used both routes. The hero of his earliest independent reflections on society was Theseus, who did not subjugate the warring tribes of Attica, but reconciled them and made them into one *polis;*[62] and the contrast between this "natural" friendliness and the unnatural exclusiveness of the children of Abraham was a favorite topic in Hegel's early essays.[63] In the *First Philosophy of Spirit* the "struggle for recognition" provides the transition from the state of Nature to political existence (Theseus fashion); and in the *Phenomenology* Hegel treats the master-slave relation and cultural subjection as the cradle of political existence. Here he offers us neither, but rather ignores the whole problem. In the "ethics of relation" he develops "civil society," the society of burghers, as the rational context of the family; under "the negative" he develops patriarchal or tribal society as its natural context. But he does not directly connect either of them with political society proper.

The family, whether in the context of marketplace equality or of tribal aristocracy, is one *Potenz* of the Absolute Idea, and political society is another one, the next higher one. They are connected by having the same "negative" in crime and warfare. This is their indifference point as "identity," the center point on the line of speculative development that Hegel is "constructing" for us. At one end (in family-relations as a "system of need") Nature, or the objective moment, predominates; at the other end (in the "absolute estate" of the priests and elders who have passed out of the bonds of family life altogether) Spirit, or the subjective moment, predominates. The "indifference point" is the consciousness of the "Absolute Concept" as the unity of the opposites: life (the natural pole) and freedom (the ethical pole). This indifference point comes before us in its bare "identity" in the "middle term" of *battle*—and that is why Hegel explicitly denominates the *Wut* in which "havoc" becomes indistinguishable from its civilized opposite as "the absolute concept" (451).

In Hegel's exposition we first approach this "indifference point" from the side of Nature; but we do *not* depart from it again on the side of Spirit. This is because the "constructed line" is *also* a process of development, an ascent. Spirit is in perfect balance with Nature; there is a parallel that creates a perfect equilibrium in the scale—for which the "absolute concept" is the fulcrum. But Spirit is also *higher* than Nature; and this is shown by exhibiting Spirit itself as the "totality" of the "indifference point" between them. We know, for instance, that we shall meet *War* again at the level of *Sittlichkeit* and that Hegel will then treat it as *absolutely* ethical rather than "least of all" ethical—i.e., he will treat it as the negative of nature and private happiness, rather than of Spirit and freedom. But we shall also meet all the other moments of the negative, along with all the positive moments of "ethics as relation." The discussion upon which we are now embarking will reach back and assimilate into itself every aspect of family existence, together with its perishing in crime and war, until finally we do have the civilized pattern of social life before us for which barbarian invasion represents a kind of natural death. This "construction of identity into totality" is the same "indifference point" which we approached from below as a point on a line, or as bare "unity" in the earlier discussion, but we shall come to it now from above, as a "totality" or as the fixed end of that line which moves as a radius to generate a circle.[64]

The change in the direction of approach can be apprehended and confirmed immediately. I have already pointed out that whereas every sub-*Potenz* in the ethics of "relation" moves upwards towards a higher "middle" or spiritual point of equilibrium, the sub-*Potenzen* of *Sittlichkeit* move downwards towards a "middle" at the level of *nature*. The dialectic of "the negative," we may notice, goes *both* ways. For the resolution of the "formal" *Potenz* of "havoc" appears to be a return to the unconscious self-assertion of pure freedom against pure life, while the material development through robbery, murder, and vendetta to single combat is plainly an ascent from human arbitrariness to "the judgment of God."

But if the starting point for the development of *Sittlichkeit* is not the battle-consciousness that we reached at the culmination of "the negative," what is it? "Ethical life must be the absolute identity of intelligence, with complete annihilation of particularity and relative identity . . . an incomplete self-objectification and intuition of the individual in the alien individual, hence the supersession of natural determinacy and shaping, complete indifference of self-enjoyment" (460–61). Where have we encountered something like this already? We met with the self-intuition of one single consciousness in another in the love-relation between the sexes. But Hegel does not mean *that*, for he specifically denies that it is properly ethical. It is a "relative identity"—i.e., it belongs to the ethics of relation—because, like all other family relations, it is "afflicted with a difference." The man is the universal, the woman is the particular.[65] We might add that when the child is born we have a *complete* self-objectification of both parents, whereas what we are presently looking for is an *incomplete* one. But also the begetting of a child is not an intelligent objectification at all—as Hegel remarks: "it is more rational to make a tool than to make a child" (431).

What then is the objectification of intelligence itself? *Language.* It is only in expressing their own absolute individuality to one another in language that our singular human organisms have thus far risen to anything that deserves the name "complete indifference of self-enjoyment." *Bildung*, as the mutual education of free rational agents (not as the teacher-pupil relation, which is "afflicted with a difference"), is what we are looking for. But in language the "objectification" is transient. Where is it more permanently realized? In property exchange and contract. Here we have "intuition of self in the other"—though not "self-enjoyment"—in the basic phenomenon of "mutual recognition."

Recognition—subjective in *Bildung*, objective in commerce—is the element of political existence. Just as "the negative" connects with the family through theft and murder, so ethics proper connects with it through the bonds which theft and murder negate. Recognition is "the absolute concept" on its positive side, the concept as life rather than as death, or as intelligence rather than nature. The soldiers who followed the Homeric heroes to battle, and the citizens who are represented by the (male) chorus of a Greek tragedy recognize one another, but they also recognize their natural subordination to their heroic leaders or to the members of the royal *family* whose tragedy they witness. Yet in so far as the soldiers face death, and the chorus expresses opinions in their own right, as men or as citizens, even their obedience is ethical and not servile.[66] The development of civic recognition from slavery, through obedience, to civil equality does not concern Hegel here, as it does in the *Phenomenology*.[67] But by presenting the dialectic of "right" in a bourgeois-civic context, and the dialectic of "wrong" in a familial-tribal one, he has given us all the clues we need to close the circle between the family and the city.

The citizen on business in the marketplace is not yet "truly infinite," for it is not then true that "all his specific determinacy is annulled." But this is true of him when he acts as a "witness" (whether to a contract or to a tragedy). Here he acts in his citizen capacity. In order to understand the hard saying that the "intuition of the Idea of ethical life is the *Volk*" (462) we must attend carefully to the working of Hegel's doctrine of free recognition. When a citizen recognizes another as his fellow-citizen, what is it that he "intuites"? Not simply another adult male human who lives in his market-community area. He recognizes someone who is committed to maintain in any and every way that he can the law and custom of that community. In certain boundary situations he is committed to do this even at the cost of his own life, and if he fails to meet his commitment when such a situation arises, he may be found guilty and banished or even put to death through the normal processes of one of the institutions he is committed to maintain. In his capacity as citizen he is not just "Mr. X" who has certain family responsibilities, certain known assets and liabilities, and certain proved capacities and failings; he is the incarnation of that law and custom. They have made him the free agent that he is, and as a free agent he makes them what they are. Neither could exist without the other, even though "the Laws" existed long before this citizen was begotten in the order of organic nature, and they will remain after his body has returned to the cycle of inorganic nature. What makes a man a citizen is this commitment, and it is identically the same commitment for every citizen. Thus in *intellectual* intuition, in the direct perception of what exists *as and for* intelligence because it *generates itself* as and for intelligence, every citizen is quite simply the law and customs of his city incarnated. When we look at him as a family father coming to the market with his own basket of produce and his own list of things needed, this universal aspect remains "inward," and the law "floats above" him as a formal matter of external record; but when we look at him as a citizen, as the product and the producer of *Bildung*, it is just this inward essence that we intuit. Of course we cannot just see *him* concretely in this way, for this "intuition" is a "*self*-objectification" so far as its intuitive character is concerned; we perceive *ourselves* thus in every other individual. And this self-objectification is only partial, not complete as it was when the parents perceived their own flesh and blood—i.e., the reality of the family which is their own *substance*—in the child; for each citizen has his private life and his private concerns (in that family). But it is a very different matter from the self-positing of Fichte's Absolute Ego, which is what Hegel is referring to when he speaks of "an artificial independent consciousness, and an intellectual intuition in which empirical intuition is superseded" (461). The "objectivity" that exists in the practical intuition of Fichte's Ego is the *Sollen* of absolute moral duty. It is a *Sollen* precisely because all ordinary consciousness and all empirical intuition has to be superseded. This is quite different from Hegel's intellectual intuition of partial self-objectification, because here it is precisely the necessity of the universally shared structures of our ordinary experience that is intuited. The "object" here is not the Categorical Imperative, but the constitution of Athens as known to an Athenian in the history of the City's deeds and

fortunes and expressing for him what he means when he says "I am
an Athenian;" or the British or the American constitution incarnated
in the same way. Each citizen is aware that he is a private person quite
distinct from all the others. But this subjective personal existence is
just the apparent aspect of his real objective essence. The clearest example that Hegel gives anywhere is to be found in *Faith and Knowledge*, in his comment on the story of Sperchias and Bulis. These two
Spartans, being ambassadors at the Persian court, spoke to the satrap
Hydarnes in one way and to the Great King, Xerxes, in quite another:

> They showed their contempt for the satrap plainly, when they
> spoke to him of *his* and *their experience* and *inclination*. They
> confronted his subjectivity with their being in the form of a sub-
> jectivity. To the majesty of the monarch, on the contrary, they
> showed their respect in that they made themselves *wholly explicit*
> before him: they named what was most objective, and just as
> holy for him as it was for them, namely country, people,
> and laws.[68]

This then is the intuition of the *Volk* as a *practical reality*. At the
higher, purely spiritual level, this unity of the City is intuited not as
"country, people, and laws," not as human life at all, but as the City's
God: Athena *is* Athens. So far I have spoken of the intuition of the
Volk as if it were strictly a matter of "equal recognition." But Hegel
explicitly denies that the "intuition of oneself as oneself in every other
individual" is a matter of "equality of citizenship." "Recognition," we
should remember, is implicit in all *speech*. Anyone who shares in the
life of the City as a full *speaking* partner, using its language to express
his own deepest feelings and recognizing those inner depths in the holy
things and sacred traditions of his City, can intuite the *Volk* equally in
himself and all others who reverence the same things and traditions.
Thus a child can perceive what he hopes to become, and boys and girls,
as well as womenfolk, can have their essential part to play in the City's
pattern of worship. Even native-born slaves can intuite the *Volk*. Here
the Identity Philosophy simply provides a theoretical framework for
the "Greek ideal" of Hegel's earlier years:

> the Athenian citizen whose poverty deprived him of the chance
> to vote in the public assembly, or who even had to sell himself as
> a slave, still knew as well as Pericles and Alcibiades who Aga-
> memnon and Oedipus were when Sophocles or Euripides brought

them on the stage as noble types of beautiful and sublime man-
hood or when Phidias and Apelles exhibited them as pure models
of physical beauty.[69]

Thus, civic equality is not a necessary characteristic of the intuition
of the *Volk*, for the *Volk* is an "absolute" or a "living" *indifference*.
As such it is equally all the differences that we have seen to be necessary in the "ethics of relation." It is the moment of *realized* equilibrium
for all of them, the stable fulcrum upon which they all sway, and the
motionless totality of cycles which their swaying establishes. So it is
both the substance, the absolute *one* intuited indifferently in all, and
the accidents, the absolute *many* or the "display of all differences" intuited differently in each member when he is seen as contributing
something distinctive that is necessary to the life of the whole. When
I view these contributions as essential to my own personal existence,
I see them as a set of "relations" in which I stand or of dependencies
and needs to which I am subject. In ordinary experience this is typically how I do perceive the society of which I am a member. The one
"body" of which we are all "members" is not usually apparent to us,
except when we find ourselves opposed to it. One essential function of
religion is to make us aware of it, not as an external system of relations, or a crushing external power, but as our own inward essence.

At the level of action this intuition of the *Volk* is the State-Consti-
tution or the Idea of ethical life. The "Idea" is the identity of intuition
and concept.[70] Intuition and concept are now no longer the opposed
terms of a relation which have to be brought into equivalence through
the stabilizing of the relation itself. They are aspects of an already
stable Idea which has to be made to reveal itself in its living motion as
the substance that appears in a relation. Thus the Idea of *Sittlichkeit*
reaches back and incorporates the necessary "relations" of natural
ethics. This embracing of practical life within its Idea is the process of
"government."

At this point in Hegel's account we encounter the structural ambiguity alluded to earlier.[71] For he now proceeds to give us a *division* of the
"totality" of *Sittlichkeit*, in which there are only two "moments"—the
"Idea at rest" and the "Idea in motion." These two moments are, as we
shall see, opposed to one another as *inner* and *outer*, just as the first
two moments of each *Potenz* of natural or relative ethics were. But the
opposition is now merely a formal one. The *same content* is now going
to be looked at from inside and outside. What is now before us is "the

Idea of absolute ethical life," which was the announced goal and terminus of our inquiry. A *higher* reconciliation of the opposed "moments" in a new "totality" is no longer necessary. The two moments of "inner" and "outer" are self-reconciled inwardly and outwardly as the discussion of them will demonstrate. The same whole is evolving from stage to stage.

The difficulty that arises here is partly an ambiguity of terminology—which is easily removed—and partly one of structure—which Hegel never completely overcame, but which led almost at once to his abandoning the four-part plan of the system of philosophy that he had projected in 1801.

Terminological ambiguity arises because Hegel first gives the "resting" and "moving" moments *different* names ("Constitution" and "Government"), and then in his actual headings he makes it clear that the name first given to the "resting" concept is in fact the name of the Idea as such. "Constitution" becomes his *main* heading with "Resting Concept" and "Government" as its inward and outward sides. The natural name for the "resting concept" is not "Constitution" at all, but "Virtue," since what Hegel offers us under this subheading is his theory of the political virtues. Hegel's whole approach is plainly inspired by Plato, who set forth his theory of what "justice and injustice are *in the soul*" in a work entitled *Constitution* (i.e., the *Republic*).

The deeper structural difficulty arises from the fact that the heading *Constitution*, which has the "resting" and "moving" concept (or "virtue" and "government"—i.e., political activity) as its moments, is itself called the "First Section" (*scilicet* of the exposition of the Idea of *Sittlichkeit*). The initial analysis of the moments of the Idea—which created a false impression concerning the relation of the terms "Constitution" and "Government"—is again shown to be misleading. For that analysis of the moments of the "totality of the Idea" only covers the contents of the "First Section." It gives no hint that any "second section" will be needed, and it might plausibly be taken to imply the contrary.

Again it is plainly Hegel's own heading that must be considered decisive. "Constitution" is the first name of the Idea, the name of the *intuition*, the existing reality, of which *Sittlichkeit* is itself the *concept*. If we ask what the *substance* is, which *is* the "absolute Identity" of this intuition and concept, the answer is the *Volk*. We already know that the primitive *particular* intuition that is to be developed into the universality of the Idea is the intuition of the *Volk*. In order to discover what more there is to the exposition of the Idea than can be contained under the heading "Constitution," we have only to ask what else there is in the life of the *Volk* apart from its political existence.

In Hegelian terms the answer is now obvious. What *unites* the classes, the sexes, and the age-groups, which are divided and set in motion by the Constitution, is their artistic and religious experience. The *Volk* intuits itself as a *Volk* in the tutelary deity of the *polis*. Thus the complete exposition of the "Idea of the absolute ethical order" requires as its culminating phase a discussion of the religious experience of the community.

This put Hegel into a difficulty. He could not simply treat religion as an aspect of *Sittlichkeit*, because in his view the evolution of religious experience belonged to the human race as a whole—not to the ethical life of *any* one *Volk* or even to the race itself at a particular moment. For this reason he wished to keep his discussion of Art, Religion, and Philosophy separate from his account of Nature as the "body" and human history as the "real spirit" which the Idea generates for itself. In the fourfold division of the Identity Philosophy the eternal Alpha and Omega (Logic and the self-conscious Absolute Identity) are carefully segregated from the spatiotemporally determinate realm of the finite. One might very well want to fill in the "eternal" background of temporal *Sittlichkeit* in a course of lectures. But in a systematic presentation everything must be dealt with at its proper level.

This difficulty is not (or need not be taken to be) the reason for Hegel's failure to complete his manuscript. He could have made the transition to the higher *Potenz* of "Religion"—with Art and Speculation as its intuitive and conceptual *moments*—when he came to it, just as the fourfold structure required. It is evident from the manuscript itself that he was not trying to write an independent treatise on *Sittlichkeit*. Nevertheless the heading "First Section" does reveal a tension between what his systematic standpoint required and what he himself wanted to achieve as a historic agent. Philosophy itself, according to Hegel's own historical diagnosis, answers a "need." The "need of philosophy" is something that arises in a particular culture, at a particular stage of its development. Specifically it answers the *need* of a culture that has lost the integrity of *Sittlichkeit*; and its historical function is to restore that integrity or at least to show the way to its restoration when the time is ripe. The question is: how should philosophy itself regard its own genesis? What view should the philosopher take of the historic occasion that brings him to birth? The answer given by the Identity Philosophy itself is plain—and Hegel repeats it faithfully in the *Difference* essay and elsewhere.[72] Philosophy is participation in an eternal vision. It is always one and the same, and if one achieves it, the occasion or path by which one does so becomes irrelevant, indifferent. Speculation is the end in and for itself.

Hegel repeats this faithfully, and he never abandons it. But by defining philosophy from the start in terms of a cultural "need," he tempered the opposition between the eternal and the finite and so remained faithful to the practical "ideal of his youth." His philosopher, like Plato's is a "just" man who cannot simply turn his back upon the Cave once he has got out of it. He must honestly meet the "need" of his time.

The *System of Ethical Life* is *both* part of the system of philosophy as such *and* an attempt to meet the need of the time.[73] As part of the system it cannot properly deal with Religion; as a response to the need of the time it must do so. This was Hegel's dilemma.

The "need of the time" could not be made paramount without destroying speculative philosophy altogether. Philosophy is not simply the theory of *Sittlichkeit*, because religious experience is not simply a reflex of the ideological structure of the time. To deal with Religion merely as a moment of *Sittlichkeit* would have reduced it to this and would have reduced philosophy itself to the "sociology of knowledge" (and of values). Hegel was unalterably opposed to this, though the possibility of adapting his concepts and method to this end accounts for a great part of his following at the present time.

All the same, having come to philosophy himself only when driven to it by his diagnosis of the "need of the time," he could not accept the dichotomy between philosophy and that need, between the temporal and the eternal, imposed by the Identity Philosophy. So what went by the board was the fourfold structure itself. The continuity of the temporal and the eternal was established by transforming the theory of the "Absolute Identity" into the final phase of the Philosophy of Spirit itself. Art, Religion, and Philosophy kept their *absolute* status, but the theory of Absolute Spirit became part of the general theory of Spirit. In this way the twin functions of Religion, as the actual foundation of the State in this and every other time and as the eternal self-revelation of the Absolute Identity, could be reconciled without injustice to either. The change may seem to be a relatively slight one, but it is not. Hegel always insisted from 1801 onwards that philosophy and religion were different modes of awareness of the same ultimate reality. Thus the change in the structure of his philosophical system through which the temporal and the eternal functions of Religion are reconciled is a change in the conception of philosophy itself. It involves the upgrading of the *practical, social* function of philosophy (as the critical consciousness of the State, so to speak), which the Philosophy of Identity might very well lead us to despise.

a) *Virtue*

The introductory paragraph of "Ethical Life as System, at rest" sums up the general doctrine of the *Volk* as intuition and contrasts it with the doctrine of Kant and Fichte, in which there is a reflective separation of the particular self and his circumstances from the universal law of duty. But there is a mysterious sentence in this very telegraphic set of statements which seems to refer to the religious level of experience and to belong to a Judaeo-Christian religious context for which nothing earlier has prepared us: "The grief would not endure, for it would not be intuited in its objectivity and would not be detached." All the other conditional statements with which this one is surrounded are aimed at the "reflective philosophy of subjectivity" criticized in *Faith and Knowledge*.[74] So we must assume that this one refers to that philosophy too and that the situation is somehow better if "the grief" does endure and is intuited in its objectivity or in detachment from the subject. We do indeed find "the infinite grief" identified as a "moment of the supreme Idea" on the last page of *Faith and Knowledge*:

> Formerly [says Hegel,] the infinite grief only existed historically in *Bildung* and as the feeling upon which the religion of recent times rests, the feeling that "God himself is dead" . . . . By marking this feeling as a moment of the supreme Idea, the pure concept must give philosophical existence to what used to be either the moral precept that we must sacrifice our empirical essence, or the concept of formal abstraction . . . . Thereby it must reestablish for philosophy the Idea of absolute freedom and along with it the absolute Passion, the speculative Good Friday in place of the historic Good Friday.[75]

The "speculative Good Friday" *endures* always, whereas the historic Good Friday happened only once.

That "the absolute Passion" must go with "absolute freedom" in the intuition of "ethical life" is a surprise. This is a higher level of "the negative" than any we have encountered previously. This "objectification" of religious grief so that it "endures" is part of Hegel's projected reform of Christianity, not of his essentially Hellenic political philosophy. We shall come to it in due course, although we cannot hope to make much of it because of the loss of the manuscript.[76]

When it is "subsumed under the concept," this absolute intuition (both positive or ethical, and negative or religious) becomes the system of the virtues. The "concept" of ethical life is the whole range of possible human excellence. The "absolute One" of infinite joy and infinite grief differentiates into the "absolute many" of moral obligations. The accidental, capricious character of "reflective" duty which Hegel complained of in Kant and Fichte, the need for "insight," is avoided here; or perhaps we should rather say it is presented in its proper objective form, since every agent is conscious of himself as a limb of the social Briareus. His "station" determines his duties for him, but not as if the "station" itself was a structure of requirements *imposed* on him.

The two aspects of virtue, absolute unity and absolute multiplicity,[77] are differentiated by the great social contrast of war and peace. "Absolute ethical life"—the unity of virtue—is courage. It is not a state of feeling, or an attitude, but a way of life: "absolute life in the fatherland and for the *Volk*." Hegel characterizes it in heroic terms, emphasizing the positive moment of joy and freedom. He explicitly says that "all difference *and all grief* is *aufgehoben* in it. It is the divine . . . unveiled." We should notice that this comes only a page after his insistence that "the absolute grief" must *endure*. In both contexts he is talking about the "intuition" of absolute ethical life. But the earlier passage is about the intuition of it "in its objectivity," i.e., from a contemplative or religious viewpoint. Here we are concerned with it as an activity of the subject. Absolute ethical life is the identity of infinite joy and infinite grief, but where it exists as perfect courage, all "singularity" is sacrificed joyfully. It is not the soldier who grieves for mortality as a moment in the divine life.

We should also notice that although Hegel's language about death in battle is full of Greek overtones, he thinks of modern warfare (typified by the use of firearms) as being more truly ethical, just as the religion of "the absolute grief" is higher than Greek religion. A modern soldier must face not just a living enemy whom he can hope to kill in single combat, but the abstract force of death against which all are helpless. He will die "if the bullet has his name on it," to use an expression which is, I think, post-Hegelian.

It is precisely as self-sacrifice, self-surrender, that courage is "absolute" virtue, the "indifference" of all virtues, the inward essence that makes all the different virtues virtuous. But it is only in the soldier's courage in battle that virtue comes forward in its *absolute* indifference. All ordinary, differentiated, virtue is *Bildung*, self-sacrifice for the sake of self-formation, putting off the old man in order to put on the new one. Thus the danger of battle is the absolute test of one's intuition of the *Volk* in oneself; and there is, after all, a direct transition from "the Negative" (as freedom) to *Sittlichkeit*.

Now a virtue that can only completely and finally reveal itself in death is only formal. The man who dies "nobly"[78] for his country reveals his ethical status, his freedom, his absolute identity with the *Volk*. But there is no life left in which the freedom can realize itself. The soldier gives up his life in order that the life of the *Volk* may go on.

The life that does go on is the ordinary peacetime existence of virtue as *Bildung*. But all the virtues of this ordinary life are ambivalent. We cannot tell whether the "justice" of the bourgeois is merely rational selfishness, the honesty that is the best policy, until we see whether at the appropriate moment of social crisis it turns into its opposite, into prodigality and willful destruction of property. The "dishonest" man of ordinary life is an "outer" hypocrite (one who deceives others about his real motives). But the "honest" man is, very often, an "inner" hypocrite (one who deceives himself, because he does not have the intuition of the *Volk*, he only thinks that he has it, and therefore he does not exemplify it objectively any more than the dishonest man does).

So we have two opposite "formalities." A purely *inward* virtue, which proves itself by dying, and an *outward* virtue, which shows itself in all its concrete fullness, but cannot prove its own inwardness. War and peace are the "see-saw" that unites these two extremes. The life of peace justifies the sacrifice of life in the indifferent virtue of war, and the test of war validates the differentiated virtue of peacetime. In peace the rule of right is "to each his own." Hegel's brief discussion clearly shows the influence of Aristotle's discussion of justice and equity in Book V of the *Nicomachean Ethics*. But neither Plato nor Aristotle has much to do with his conception of "trust" as the natural foundation of all virtue. Trust is the peasant virtue, resembling bourgeois "honesty" in being subordinated to the needs of life and noble "courage" in its absolute commitment, but unlike either of them in that it is only vaguely felt, not rationally intuited. This is the "solid" virtue of the Athenian peasant in the story, who wanted to vote for the ostracism of Aristides because he did not like hearing him continually referred to as "the just," but was so little familiar with the Assembly and its leaders that he asked Aristides himself to write the verdict on his potsherd.[79]

Thus we have three forms of virtue and three social classes in which they are to be exemplified. In a tribal society all the forms will be mingled, and this society will therefore have no "wisdom," no intellectual awareness of what virtue is. Plato's definition of "justice" as "minding one's own business and not meddling" is thus the basic form of social "wisdom" in Hegel's analysis;[80] without it ethical life could not develop into self-conscious freedom at all. But because ethical life *is* free, and is not simply the interdependence and relatedness of natural ethics, each class with its own distinctive virtue must exhibit in some way the *total* structure of the political whole that has all the virtues. The single individual can only express the aspects of ethical life *momentarily*; but in the different classes each level of virtuous activity is presented as an objectively real way of life in a stable ethical and natural context. Thus a "class" is not just a collection of individuals with certain common characteristics. It is a complex of institutions or of objectified patterns of thought and action. "Slaves," for example, are *not* a class, because they have no structural relations to one another as slaves or to the wider society as a structured group. They belong to the family and are related to the wider society only through their "master."

Hegel's account of the classes must therefore include an account of how they meet the needs and perform the functions which are *not* their specific social function. The military nobility has to have property and be maintained by the work of the others, for by its very nature it cannot manufacture things or labor for itself. Its only proper "work" is the waging of war (and training for it); apart from this it must be at leisure, "for its immediate activity in the people is not work, but something organic in itself and absolute" (472).

This "absolute, organic, activity in the *Volk*" is not too easy to grasp. We might expect that it includes the "governing" functions that the military nobility has. "Government" is properly an "organic" function, as we shall see; but it can hardly be the "immediate" activity which is "not work," for Hegel subsequently amends his earlier remark about the "work" of the class to include "government." "Immediate activity in the people" refers rather to the way in which the nobility exemplifies the "real ethical shape" for the other classes. This is the spiritual significance that it has for them. If we were to confine our attention to the material benefit that it produces for the rest of society, the "national security" that the nobility sustains by its "work," in exchange for which it receives its own natural maintenance, then we would be treating the classes as if they were terms in a natural "relation." It is only in the nobility that the rest of society can intuit completely what "life in the Volk" is. And without this intuition, honesty and trust would decay into hypocrisy and natural hostility. There is thus, finally, a *connection*, at least, between the "absolute organic activity" of the nobility and the task of "government" which Hegel belatedly adds to fighting and military training as their "work"; for this absolute activity is the root of the political authority that belongs to the nobility. As we shall soon see, this authority is of particular importance in the relations of the nobility with the peasantry, who have to share the work of bravery with it.

Because of its "absolute activity in the *Volk*" the nobility is the class that has wisdom as well as courage. The bourgeoisie are "without wisdom" for one reason and the peasants for another. The peasants do not have it because their virtue is still natural, rather than ethical; it is not differentiated into its aspects, and so they do not have intellectual awareness of it. The bourgeoisie, on the other hand, have no wisdom because their virtue is *too* intellectual. The burgher is aware of himself as a free citizen with his own rights, but "citizenship" is for him an abstraction. What matters is his own private life, his personal affairs. He is "independent," but he is not wise enough to grasp what independence really means. In his world Reason takes the shape of the "invisible hand"; it is an external, impersonal force which dominates the market in which the achievements and contributions of the bourgeoisie are all weighed and measured. The noble is wise because the "sense of honor" which was the guarantee of *all* right in natural ethics is still the foundation of noble existence, though it is now no longer "personal" but "national" honor. But in the bourgeois way of life honor is replaced by the impersonal might of civil justice. Everything (including the bond of service) becomes a matter of legal contract. Family survival and prosperity are the aspect of natural ethics that remains as the essential subjective concern of this class. The bourgeoisie is incapable either of "a virtue" or of "bravery." "A virtue" here means some *specific* form of self-sacrifice, whereas "bravery" is the absolute or indifferent form. Thus it is only by partial negation of its principle (family prosperity) that this class achieves any proven virtue at all. But even then the sacrifice is either quite impersonal (as in the taxes which the burghers pay for the upkeep of the military, which are regulated by the principle of abstract justice), or else the sacrifice is accidental in character (as in private charity). The peasantry *is* capable of real virtue because in its way of life virtue is still a natural totality. The peasants do not abstract things out of their natural context in order to make artificial things; they rather collaborate in, and with, natural processes. Their existence is still patriarchal, and they still look to their noble lords to lead them in the war in which their virtue is demonstrated.

b) *Government*

Having thus completed his survey of the forms of virtue, Hegel now begins on the forms of government. "Government" is the "motion" of the Constitution. We have already distinguished between the "organic" and the "'inorganic" aspects of the social whole, the nobility being organic and the bourgeoisie inorganic—the peasantry being both or neither depending on how one wants to interpret the question. The "absolute movement" of the concept, the subsumption of "absolute intuition" under the concept, is precisely the "organizing" of the inorganic. But each class is itself an "organic" whole. So this "absolute movement" is something that also happens *within* each class, and it is what organizes each of them into a true class. Thus there has to be an organic/inorganic distinction within the "absolute" (or "organic") class and within the "relative" (or "inorganic") class. The organic moment is the internal government of the class itself, and this self-government of each class is the real "separation of powers" in the political organism. Hegel says that "this system . . . is the true Constitution." This is not quite the conventional view—which would tend rather to see the operation of the central government as the real expression of the Constitution—but it is certainly closer to it than his Platonic identification of the Constitution with the "resting concept" (i.e., with "virtue in the soul").

Government is the essential function of "wisdom." So the "absolute government," the governing function as it is distinctly articulated within the "absolute class," is the analog, in Hegel's account, of the Rulers, in Plato's *Republic*, as distinct from the Auxiliaries. But Hegel's Guardians are "guardians of the law," like the governing class in Plato's *Laws*; and this "absolute government" is not recruited exclusively from the military nobility.[81] One can enter its ranks through the avenue of the priesthood, and the one absolute prerequisite for that is a certain seniority in age. Like warriors, the old live in the presence of death, and they can achieve the practical indifference which is both the highest form of *political* consciousness and the practical side of religious contemplation.

Of course it is only in the naive ethics of natural relations that the "elders" are *ipso facto* wise. But aging is an instrumental aspect of wisdom, and aging consciousness is the proper tool of wisdom. One who lives nobly does become naturally wise as he grows old; and one who sets himself consciously to pursue wisdom by becoming a priest must still wait upon old age for the proper maturing of his wisdom.

Everyone who does participate in this absolute government is *ipso facto* a member of the absolute or noble class. Hegel clearly holds that in the absence of the class structure which is established by nature, and by the ethical interdependence of warring and peaceful existence, *any* absolute government would be a tyranny. Fichte's Ephorate would be as bad as any Roman despotism.[82] The proper business of "absolute government" is to keep the "estates of the realm" in a healthy equilibrium. This cannot be conceived either as a negative, regulatory activity in which dangerous initiatives are vetoed, or as a positive oversight of everything that happens to, or is done by, anybody.[83] Just how it should operate, Hegel does not say; and what he says about how it is established needs pondering over if we are to understand it rightly: "it is God's appearance . . . the direct priesthood of the All highest . . . everything human and all other sanction ceases here" (483).

This is essentially the position that Hegel always maintained, that "religion is the foundation of the State."[84] Anything that is fundamentally religious in character must have for consciousness the quality of being *given*, being beyond all argument and beyond the need of confirmation. In view of all the conscious and deliberate constitution-making which had gone on since 1775, and more particularly since 1789, both in political meetings and in professors' studies, it was important to emphasize that an act of deliberate choice cannot make something holy; choice is bound to have rather the opposite effect, by making explicit the fact that what has been decided does not *have* to be the way it is, that the decision could have been different, and is always open to revision. For the *Volk* its own existence is not a decision; it is rather the given context within which all decisions of the *Volk* are made.

"Absolute government" is the activity by which this absolute foundation maintains and defends itself. All that Hegel says about its activity is that "it is legislative, establishing order where a relation is developed which intended to organize itself independently, or where some hitherto insignificant feature . . . begins to get strong." The "relations" here are relations between the classes or estates. The German Empire was a mass of "estates" which had developed various degrees of independence. Some had advanced to the recognized status of sovereign nations which made war on one another and on the *Reich* itself. In this situation Hegel could say, "Germany is a State no longer,"[85] because the *Reich* no longer had an "absolute government." The empire was "holy" in name, but in fact it was no more than a legal fiction according to Hegel's analysis, since a legal fiction was all that solemn pronouncements of the Imperial Courts or votes of the Diet could preserve.

We should notice that the fact that popular election cannot make something sacred does not mean that the principle of popular election cannot *be* what is sacred. For the Athenians their "democracy," meaning popular assembly and direct popular vote, was sacred; it was part of the wisdom of Athena herself. And we can see both from Hegel's essay on the German Constitution and from the surviving fragments of, and reports about, his pamphlet on the Wurtemberg Estates Assembly of 1797 that he did not believe that any constitution should continue to be held sacred which did not incorporate the principle of popular election for legislative functions.[86]

"Absolute government is the resting substance of the universal movement, but universal government is the movement's cause" (484). We have seen that the "resting substance" is the abiding structure of institutions and values which the political community holds sacred. We are now moving on to examine how that structure functions, and what makes it go. The traditional analysis of the structure involves the distinction of three branches of government, the legislative, the executive, and the judiciary. Hegel does not find this division very satisfactory, since government is always finally a matter of executive action, of causing things to happen. What is at first sight more surprising is that he does not find the division of government business into "internal" and "external" affairs satisfactory either. We might have expected him to make much of this distinction, since the cyclic opposition of war and peace is so important in his theory. The distinction of internal and external affairs is, in fact, more important in his theory than the distinction of legislative, executive, and judiciary, but it is not *fundamental*. Instead, the division that Hegel offers us has the internal/external antithesis built into it as its basic subdivision. His division is between:

a) economic policy and commerce

b) judicial and military policy

c) education and colonization.

The last two aspects are regarded by Hegel as logically connected. But we cannot say how he would have worked the connection out in detail, since the manuscript declines into a mere list of topical headings by the time we reach section c.

The business of "universal government" is to relate the abiding Constitution of the *Volk* to the actual historical situation. With respect to its foundation in nature this situation is a constant. Men always need food, clothes, shelter, etc. But the vicissitudes both of nature and of human intercourse affect even this level of human existence in society, so that it necessarily becomes an object of governmental concern. The surprising thing is that Hegel places it first. The analogy of his procedure thus far at the level of *Sittlichkeit* leads us to expect that this would be the natural "totality" to which his argument would descend. Instead we find an ascending scale, culminating in the self-reproduction of the City by colonization. Colonization is a totality like that provided by the rearing and education of the child at the level of natural ethics. Since a new colony needs first of all a Constitution, its establishment would bring the wisdom of the "absolute government" into play. Thus the "motion" of the concept apparently involved a renewal of the upward spiral movement that was characteristic of Hegel's earlier discussion. We cannot be sure about this because Hegel has left us too little to go on, but I take this reversal to be a reflection of the fact that in the "true constitution" our inquiry has reached its goal.

Apart from this natural substratum the business of "universal government" is the "subsumption of particular under universal." This logical function explains its title. But to identify the referents here is not easy. At the level of natural relations, "the *Potenz* of inwardly concealed identity and outwardly revealed difference," the universal government was the law of universal mortality, the reign of death. But now we have the people governing itself. "Universal," "particular," "concept," "intuition" become very difficult to apply and to interpret because all distinctions are largely formal, i.e., they are only distinctions of reason.

On the internal side the governing process has traditionally been analyzed into three branches, legislative, executive, and judicial. Hegel identifies these branches with the moments of the concept; the legislative being the resting universal and the other two arms being its ideal and its real motion against the particular. But since government is a real process, all governmental action is really executive action. This is not difficult to follow, but just how it fits into Hegel's discussion of the external and internal relations of the people is not so easy to see. Apparently Hegel simply wants us to set it aside because it is not the real problem. The real problem is to "know the executive as government."

The "executive as government" is concerned on the one hand with external relations. This is the subsumption of intuition under concept, for one or both of the parties concerned must submit to higher control. War, as we have already seen, produces only a momentary recognition, and the conclusion of peace need not lead to any permanent relation at all. Only conquest or colonization produce stable results: conquest extends the range of internal relations, while the planting of a colony produces a new kind of relation altogether: "the reconstruction of identity."

Internal relations are the "subsumption of concept under intuition"; because now it is the particular character which the people has gained in its history that is paramount. But the whole distinction of "internal" and "external," "intuition" and "concept," is a formal one. The "movement" of the people always has both an internal and an external side. Its phases are the three given earlier, but the second moment (of justice and war) is one where the "particular remains what it is," so the universal is "merely formal," i.e., it exists when the opposed particulars, whether they be warring nations (in "foreign affairs") or litigating estates (in "home affairs"), "recognize" one another. In the "totality" of education and culture on the internal side, or of conquest and colonization in external relations, the particular is completely absorbed into the universal.

Hegel's remarks about economic policy show the influence of his early "mercantilist" studies. We cannot be certain that he has even read Smith's *Wealth of Nations* yet, though it is quite probable.[87] We have already seen that the division of labor and the establishment of a market are necessary elements in the natural ethics of family relations. The problem now is how markets are to be regulated and how the needs of the noble class, which does not produce marketable goods, are to be provided for.

The market is itself a "power" than can overwhelm the greatest efforts of individuals. Price levels fluctuate according to the total state of supply and demand, and these fluctuations cannot be foreseen by the normal employment of human intellectual capacity. The mechanical operation of the law of supply and demand can therefore threaten the very existence of ethical life if it is not controlled by human agency. Through the exercise of social control "blind fate" comes under "government" (489). The government can tell when an economic crisis threatens by watching the fluctuation of prices. A crisis exists whenever what we would call the "standard of living" of a sizeable fraction of the population is seriously threatened; and the "standard of living" is a function both of the prevailing natural conditions and of general social expectations. "Stability" rather than "growth" is the goal that Hegel sets up for public policy. Economic crisis destroys "trust," which is the natural "solidity" out of which the higher social virtues of "honesty," "courage," and "wisdom" develop. Hegel is willing, like Adam Smith, to rely on the mechanical self-regulation of the market as long as the fluctuations of prices and incomes are not too great, but a serious economic crisis has revolutionary political implications. Need itself cannot be controlled and regulated, for the advance of civilization breeds ever more sophisticated desires. For this reason, too, trade and commerce are essentially world-wide, and economic policy must be made in the context of the world market. The natural difference of strength among men translates in ethical life into a difference in economic resources. The ethical class structure is therefore subjected to the destructive tension between rich and poor, the haves and the have-nots. Hegel calls this economic dialectic "the unmitigated extreme of barbarism"; the reduction of everything to a price, and subordination of every aspect of life to the quest for a profit is, in his eyes, "the bestiality of contempt for all higher things." The urge toward private material prosperity breaks the ethical bonds of society. Just as economic poverty destroys the "trust" of the peasants, so economic prosperity turns the "honesty" of the bourgeois into hypocrisy. Economic policy must therefore be directed towards moderating these extremes. The only method that Hegel suggests is "by making big gains more difficult." We shall see in a moment how the taxation system is adapted for this purpose.

Hegel speaks rather glibly of "sacrificing one part of the burgher class to mechanical and factory work and abandoning it to barbarism" (492). But he was actually much more disturbed by the emergence of an urban proletariat than his words here indicate. This problem of the impoverishment of life through the natural tendency of intelligence to make labor even more "mechanical" was one that had troubled him in his earliest studies of economic life;[88] and the persistence of his concern is evident in the economic analyses contained in the first Philosophy of Spirit. These analyses anticipate Marx in a quite startling way.[89] In the present context the whole emphasis of the Identity theory would naturally lead Hegel to minimize this sort of disturbing development, which did not fit into his theory of the natural classes of society. He was, perhaps, less quick to recognize that the Greek ideal could not simply be extrapolated mechanically for the economic sphere than he was to admit this at the opposite pole, in religion. But the industrial revolution had hardly touched Germany as yet.

Hegel relies partly upon the spontaneous activity of the bourgeois class to secure economic stability. The rich should be obliged by the customs and mores of their own class to support public initiatives of a cultural kind, just as the Athenians imposed special "liturgies" on their richest citizens. In this way private charity, which was the only avenue for subjective virtue in this class, could come to have more than an accidental significance.

We come, finally, to the economic life of the governing class itself. The governing class now includes the "formally universal" class, i.e., public servants of all kinds, drawn from all classes, and possessing only the normal virtues of the class from which they come. The expenses of this class can be met partly through rents received as owners of landed estates; but a system of taxation is also necessary, so the principle of fair taxation must be laid down.

Hegel holds that the only objectively fair system of taxation is a levy on the cost of raw materials for all productive purposes. The peasant will make his contribution in the form of rents, we should notice. This is the closest possible analogy to a levy on his raw materials. A good farmer will get better crops out of a farm than a bad one, and a good craftsman will likewise get better goods out of a given quantity of raw materials. Thus "skilfulness is taxed" but "not according to its receipts, which are something particular and the individual's own." Presumably traders and retailers would pay a levy on what they buy for resale. This system provides the government with its means of "restricting gain," for by raising the levy it can force prices up and drive consumption down in any sector of the economy.

So much for the "system of need." Here "need" was the fulcrum through which the universal "value" and the particular "needs and possessions" of the classes and their members were related in the see-saw of supply and demand. The opposition of universal and particular was only formal, because it is precisely the possessions that have value, and the value is determined by the general need for them.

The second system of "universal government" is the "system of justice." This system includes "war" as a punitive instrument in external relations. But Hegel's discussion is now becoming increasingly condensed, and in the course of this section it ceases altogether, declining into a simple list of the topics that have to be discussed.

The "system of justice" is virtue in its moment of externality. An external concept, justice, here subsumes the property and lives of the citizens (and by implication the property and independence of the City and its foes are similarly subsumed in war, which is the divine judgment). Everything in this moment depends on "recognition" for its reality, for what is "intuited" here is not things and people, but property rights and persons (including "national rights" and "sovereign nations" in the international court of war). The real essence of economic relations is "need" which is *felt*. The real essence of judicial relations is "right" which is *thought of*.

Hence the system of justice is also the moment of abstract equality. Everyone is equal before the law. Class members litigate against one another and against members of another class. They can also litigate against the class itself as an organized whole or against one of its organs. All come into court as legal persons, with rights established by the constitution. If all rights could be systematized in a code, the different classes could each be left to run their own affairs; or, to be more precise, the nobility and the burghers would each run their own affairs, and the peasantry would come to the local manor courts established for them by the nobles. For what matters is the decision of the singular case and the best judges for this would be those who best understand the circumstances. But this Fichtean ideal is impossible to achieve. The government of the people should be self-government; hence the judicial process in civil cases should be a composition of dispute according to equity, which "satisfies the parties and is reached with their consent." What Hegel means by "consent" and "satisfaction" here is apparently just the fact that the parties both want what is right, and although the judgment may go against them, they accept it without compulsion. It is only some *Bestimmtheit* that is at issue, though it may be a performance (e.g., of a contract), or a piece of work, or some personal matter, not just physical property. (It seems that what Hegel calls "war" must, by parity of reasoning, include the peaceful diplomacy through which nations settle many disputes without resort to arms.)

Criminal justice, on the other hand, must not just establish right; it must punish the attempt to establish a private right of one's own. When we look at crime in this way, it is easy to understand how "war" can be assimilated to justice. In a civil suit "damages" are awarded; in criminal justice punishment is imposed. The "essence" of the first is the establishment of what is right; the "essence" of the second is to establish that a crime has been committed, and by whom. War brings the opposed peoples into court, as in a civil suit; ordeal by battle finds one of them guilty like a criminal; and the peace settlement awards "damages" as in civil suit once more. Hegel's notes contain just enough to enable us to descry the pattern of the "totality" that he was intending to construct.

The third system of government is the completed equilibrium where the universal moment does not just momentarily "subsume" the particular, but absorbs it. And the "universal" here is not an abstract ratio of pure quantities, as it was in the operation of supply and demand that determines value. Now it is realized subjectively as well as objectively; it satisfies a need that is felt.

In his introductory survey Hegel gave "education, culture, conquest, and colonization" as the moments of this "system" (488). The notes for his detailed discussion omit "conquest." But since he made no notes for the "external" part of the discussion at all, I do not believe this is significant. "Colonization" only gets into the discussion as the culmination of the City's self-reproduction. We must assume that in the fully developed argument, colonization would have taken its place as the final synthesis of both internal and external policy.

The "internal" process, which we can follow, passes through "education," by which the array of individual talents are developed and in which particular discoveries are made, to *Bildung*, the realm where science is established as a communal activity and achievement. We caught sight of this realm at the extreme limit of the development of natural ethics (just as we also caught sight of the world market at that point, and of the concept of legal right). But here *Bildung* emerges as the universal force (*Zucht*) that *disciplines* us, making us self-conscious members of the *Volk*, enabling us to intuit the *Volk* in ourselves and others, and causing us to "live in the *Volk*." This process of "training" is the work of the school and of the police, but the primary agent is the people itself: "the great discipline consists of the universal *Sitten*, the order of society, *Bildung* for war and the testing of the reliability of the single individual in war" (498). This stage of "subsumption of intuition under concept" has two sides: *Erziehung*, which is formation from within, the maturing of inward nature; and *Zucht*, which is formation from outside, the action of the universal that "floats above."

The totality of "education" and "training and discipline" is "child-rearing" regarded in its social aspect. Here Hegel proposed to deal with population control, the training of the next generation of citizens, and finally with colonization as the chief means of controlling population by disposing of the surplus. Conquest would come in here as the means by which colonization is made possible when the right of the *Volk* is challenged.

The next paragraph begins abruptly: "Possible forms of a free government. I Democracy. II Aristocracy. III Monarchy" (498); and the last page of the text is devoted to this topic. Lasson has rightly divined that this is the final section of the discussion of "Government" and that the "totality" of "absolute government" and "universal government" is "free government." I believe that if this section had been fully written up, it would also have been the totality of "Resting concept" and "Government," and so the conclusion of "Section I: The Constitution." The classification of constitutions forms a natural and appropriate conclusion for this section.

The classification itself derives from Aristotle, and the distinction between "free" and "unfree" constitutions is likewise his. For when the ruler governs in the interest of all, rather than in his own interest (which is Aristotle's distinction between a "true" and a "corrupt" constitution), then in Hegel's terminology the "essence" of ruler and ruled "is the same." This is what "free" government, or "self-government," means in his usage. But in Aristotle's view a corrupt monarchy is the worst of constitutions, whereas Hegel regards a corrupt aristocracy as the worst. Here we have "the form of the absolute constitution, and not its essence." This implies that the "absolute constitution" that we have so far been describing is a "free aristocracy." But since both the hereditary character of the nobility and their possession of entailed landed estates are specifically condemned as departures from the ideal, this conclusion puts us in a difficulty.

The first part of the way out of this difficulty is provided by Hegel when he makes clear that his "absolute constitution," like Aristotle's "best" one, is a "mixed" one. Political activity should *not* be restricted to the noble class. The democratic principle of equality destroys the natural class distinctions, but the absolute constitution "is democracy too, within the classes." Thus Hegel's remark about a hereditary, landed aristocracy being the worst constitution does not imply that the best constitution is a Platonic aristocracy without private property or personal heirs. What Hegel condemns is any constitution in which participation in politics and the holding of public office is a matter of hereditary right and depends on the inheritance of an entailed estate.[90] The nobility of his own "first class" must have their inherited estates; the relations of the nobility and the peasantry could not be what Hegel means them to be on any other basis. But his "priests and elders" are recruited on Platonic principles, and the "formally universal" class would consist mainly of burghers. This much is clear from the manuscript as we have it. The proposals that Hegel makes for the reconstitution of the *Reich* at the end of his "German Constitution" essay further suggest that his distinction of "absolute" and "universal" government would have been articulated into a bicameral legislature, or a senate and an elected assembly, if he had ever completed his *System of Ethical Life*.[91]

Hegel's final notes are about the relation between the constitution and the religion of the *Volk*. Here the emphasis on genetic development is once more evident; it becomes clear also that a "free" constitution really *does* mean popular self-government. A monarchy will only be a "free" constitution when the king governs *with* the people and allows them more and more to govern themselves. And as their political freedom develops, the religious experience of the people will involve increasing resistance to and rejection of the "monarchic" religion.[92]

The comment that there is "little imagination or religion" in an aristocracy "on account of its patriarchal character" needs to be glossed by inserting a qualifying adjective: "little <public> imagination or religion." What "patriarchal" religion is like we can infer fairly reliably from the description of "vendetta justice" earlier. Each tribe has its own cult and its own rites. The political achievement of Theseus was consummated by his religious achievement. He managed to gather the tribal gods into a pantheon which was the object of public worship by all the tribes. This religious achievement broke through the bulwarks of aristocratic privilege and set Athens on the path towards democracy.

It is the Athenian democracy in its great days that exemplifies the democratic "religion of nature." But it was unstable; and when it passed away, the Epicureans demythologized nature. The religion of nature develops from the primitive level which Hegel believes we find in Homer "where Jupiter and Juno are air, and Neptune is water" to the point where the religion is purely ethical, and the artistic representation of it is completely human. Then the "infinite grief" of the separation of God from man can begin. The Epicurean secularization of nature was thus the prelude to the "death of God" in man himself, which was portrayed for intuition and as feeling in the Crucifixion.

6. RELIGION.

According to Rosenkranz, Hegel had material in his lecture manuscript which he could have used to develop his discussion of constitutions along evolutionary lines.[93] He certainly had plenty of material there with which he could have filled out these brief memoranda on Religion. But I have already shown why Hegel could not deal with Religion properly at the level of *Sittlichkeit*. His notes on the parallel between constitutional and religious evolution give some hint of what "section II" of the discussion of *Sittlichkeit* could have contained. Hegel had been meditating on the problem of the relation of state and church for years. This was the proper place for him to state whatever formal conclusions he had arrived at.[94] But only a formal discussion would have been possible. According to the fourfold plan within which Hegel was operating, the content of religious experience—the history of God's self-revelation—belongs to a higher *Potenz* of the Absolute Identity altogether. It belongs in fact to the final phase of speculation: "the resumption of the whole [i.e., of the philosophy of nature and of the ethical spirit] into one, the return to the primitive simplicity of the [Logical] Idea."[95]

It is certain, however, that Hegel laid out this "history of God" in the lectures from which our manuscript was written up. And since his concept of ethical life cannot be properly understood in abstraction from it, we must do our best to recover it from the accounts that we possess. Rosenkranz tells us that Hegel "claimed that in religion the reality of the objective world itself, and subjectivity and particularity along with it, are posited as *aufgehoben*."[96] His introductory discussion included an analysis of the Protestant "religion of subjectivity," which reached its apogee in Schleiermacher's *Addresses*. He attacked Schleiermacher's refusal to "let spirit appear in spiritual shape."[97] Against Schleiermacher's theory of the pastor as a subjective virtuoso he set his own doctrine of true religious democracy, "the spirit is not ashamed of any of its individuals." Any true Athenian, being capable of the intuition of the *Volk*, is capable of intuiting Athena. But when he does so, "the ideal shape of the spirit is real, while its real side is ideal." The inward essence is expressed in the outward form of the goddess, and all the outward reality of life in *agora* and Assembly is collapsed into his inner thoughts. The ancient Athenian was not an idolator. Athena is the very spirit that lives and moves in Athenians when they are conscious of themselves as Athenians. In the speculative knowledge of the philosopher the absolute spirit receives its objective (i.e., conceptual) shape, but this is only one pole of religion. The other is the intuitive contemplation made possible by the religious artist. And still this difference between "subjective" and "objective" or "intuition" and "concept" is "purely formal," as we have by now learned to say.[98]

Pure speculative knowledge is indeed the absolute apex of religious experience. It is when philosophy and religion are completely reconciled that religion reaches its own perfection. Being the actual process of "resuming the whole into one," religion itself goes through a natural cycle of development. Thus a religious tradition expresses the people's consciousness of the Idea in its indissoluble unity with their own history and life. This unity has two aspects: the speculative, or universal, side and the historical, or particular, one. And the relation between universal and particular, the way that the absolute Idea is "bounded" in religion, is not quite the same as the way in which the Idea is "bounded" in art. We cannot be certain what the difference is here, but in his essay on the *Difference between Fichte's and Schelling's Systems* Hegel makes Art the intuition of the "indifference point" from the side of natural philosophy and Speculation the intuition of it from the side of transcendental philosophy. Only a very slight shift in his use of "theoretical" and "practical" would be involved if we suppose that he now regards Art as the theoretical moment and Religion as the practical moment in the absolute knowledge of the speculative Idea. He emphasizes here that religion is the *practical* complement of both art and "science" (i.e., philosophy). In his mature philosophy the triad of the Absolute Idea (Art, Religion, Philosophy) forms a definite sequence with Philosophy at the top. The most consistent interpretation of his various statements about the "absolute Identity" of the Identity Philosophy seems to be that he did not wish to make *any* sequence or grant any preeminence among them.

In any case Religion is certainly the highest activity of practical life. And the basic activity of all religion as cult is *sacrifice*.[99] By offering sacrifice we show that our inward devotion is not hypocritical. We are *reconciled* with the Infinite through this deliberate adoption of an ironical attitude toward our own finite life and affairs.

Hegel called *reconciliation* "the basic Idea of religion." We have already seen how in the *Potenz* of "the negative," he referred to the contrast between causal reciprocity, as exhibited in penal justice ("an eye for an eye"), and the "reconciliation" in religion.[100] As far as can be seen, the explanations which he gave here were consistent with the doctrine of "reconciliation with fate" as he had developed it in his

Frankfurt essays.[101] Reconciliation restores at the spiritual level the original harmony of life that existed before injury established the pattern of hostile interaction. It changes nothing at the level of fact. The transgressor must accept whatever consequences are naturally or ethically "fated." But the discovery of ethical freedom is necessarily the discovery of the possibility of making a fresh start and so of being reconciled with fate.

After this general introduction Hegel gave his systematic exposition of the *Potenz* of Religion in the usual triadic pattern. Religion evolves through three moments:

a) the simple identity of intuition and concept, or the natural reconciliation of spirit (the universal) with its real being in individuality. (Greek religion is the paradigm here).

b) the moment of *difference* between the universal spirit and its real being; the condition where they come into "relation" with one another and a relative identity is established. (Here the paradigm is harder to identify. The whole Judaeo-Christian tradition can easily be subsumed here.)

c) the moment of absolute reconstruction. (This is in the future, but the whole development of Christianity will be "resumed" in it along with Greek religion.)

Haym tells us that this division as given by Rosenkranz, together with his exposition of it, was taken almost verbatim from Hegel's manuscript.[102] The first stage is easy enough to follow. This is the "nature-religion" of the Greeks, for which the whole system of nature is living and holy. The different aspects of this living spirit are "the Gods." Thus in Homeric religion, as Hegel conceived it, the four elements themselves are the Gods. But the principle of reconciliation requires that the divine spirit should be intuited in human form. Thus classical Greek religion, nature-religion in its mature form, becomes "the religion of art" which Hegel presents to us in the *Phenomenology*. We may notice that Hegel distinguishes the three moments of "artistic beauty," "truth of the Ideas," and "actuality" (this last being plainly the "religious" moment) and insists on their "indivisibility."

The next stage is the moment of "absolute difference" or "infinite grief." The remark about Epicurean philosophy at the end of the *System of Ethical Life* itself shows us where this stage begins. When Alexander triumphed, the "natural reconciliation" of man and God, or of politics and religion, was ruptured. Nature became in the Epicurean philosophy a merely mechanical concourse of physical atoms, and in the triumph of the Roman Empire and of Roman law the ethical world became a concourse of spiritual atoms. This is what Hegel refers to as the "boredom of the world," which is something very different from "infinite grief." The Romans took over the "pantheon" of natural religion, but the Gods were no longer spiritual "intuitions" of free peoples; they were no longer really alive. The "boredom of the world" reached its climax in the deification of the emperor. In the Roman pantheon "the ideal constituted itself in the form of universality"—but externally; and in the emperor "the real principle sets itself up firmly as singularity." The actual *religious* consciousness of this situation was first expressed as "infinite grief" by the Jews. Here we have a *Volk* whose God has fled from nature and is Lord over it. This God will allow no pantheon, and there can be no graven images. In his presence men have only the consciousness of sin and of their own nullity.

Orthodox Christianity in all of its historical forms is the reconstruction of a sequence of "relative identities" out of this "infinite grief." The living man Jesus was himself the absolute identity in a simple intuition. But as the dead Saviour he became the mediating term through which Christians were *related* to God; and in being thus "redeemed," they were saved *out of* nature, which remained lost. Thus the Christian "contempt for the world" was bound at first to extend to the world of ethical life as well as that of nature. But when Christianity became the religion of the empire, this was no longer the case; as a result the Judaic principle of "infinite grief" was threatened. Hence the focal ceremony of the cult became a reminder of the religious significance of the Crucifixion. The Christian Eucharist celebrates the sacrifice of God himself who died on earth, and at the same time it establishes the identity of the worshipper with God. The whole human world was consecrated afresh in universal Catholicism. The pope crowned the emperor, and every nation had its own apostles and saints.

The new religion developed its conscious or speculative side in the doctrine of the Trinity, thus rising from the level of nature—for which the ideal expression is Art—to that of spirit. Catholicism developed the natural aspect, and Protestantism the spiritual one. But where the Catholic emphasis overcame the principle of "contempt for nature," the Protestant emphasis accentuated it. They need now to be reconciled. This is the problem that confronts the world in Hegel's own time.

It seems that Hegel was convinced that the advent of the truly *absolute* religious consciousness was imminent. The speculative "totality" of religion, being thus reached, will "resume" the infinite grief into the infinite joy of a genuine reconciliation with nature. All the moments of the above development will be taken up as moments, but they will be mere moments in the religion of *absolute* identity or spiritual freedom.[103] This will be a philosophical religion, but it will demonstrate its speculative character by overcoming the excessive subjectivity of the Christian flight from the world and restoring nature and art to a position of honor. The "infinite grief" of universal mortality and transience will be accepted as an eternal moment in the new synthesis. The grief must "endure," for without it the speculative side of religion cannot develop. But it will no longer be dominant, as it still is in Protestant "yearning." The direct quotation with which Rosenkranz ends his account[104] should be compared with the concluding sentence of *Faith and Knowledge*:

> The pure concept . . . must reestablish for philosophy the Idea
> of absolute freedom, and along with it the absolute Passion, the
> speculative Good Friday in place of the old historical one. Good
> Friday must be reestablished in the whole truth and harshness
> of its Godforsakenness. Since the serenely happy, but less well
> grounded, and more individual style of the dogmatic philosophies
> and of the natural religions must vanish, the highest totality can
> and must achieve its resurrection from this harsh consciousness of
> loss in all its earnestness and out of its deepest ground, encom-
> passing everything, and at the same time possessing the most
> serenely happy freedom of shape that it can.[105]

7. CONCLUSION.

The examination of Hegel's views about the next higher *Potenz*, Religion—the highest *Potenz* of all in fact—has helped us to understand the *System of Ethical Life* better. For it enables us to put the influence of Hegel's "Greek ideal" into proper perspective. The ideal model of *Sittlichkeit* is quite evidently the *polis*. But several tensions are visible in Hegel's discussion. First there is a tension between the speculative and the historical influence of Greek culture itself—a tension between the philosophical model provided by Plato's *Republic* and the historical experience of Athens as Hegel found it in Thucydides and in various lesser writers. In this respect I think we can say that the empirical influence predominates. There is another deeper tension between ancient

and modern influences, where the Hellenic models seem to predomi-
nate, but the truth is more complex. Here the knowledge of Hegel's
religious views and hopes, fragmentary and unsatisfactory as it is because of the state of the evidence, helps us to see that Hegel's concern
was really quite contemporary. His projected reform of religion goes
hand in hand with a projected reconstruction in politics: indeed neither
is possible without the other. Hegel believes that his own society is
now in a position to "reconstruct" the Greek ideal, but on the scale of
a modern nation and on quite a new level of self-conscious awareness.
The reconstruction, when it comes about—and 1789 was a portent of
its imminent arrival—will be a higher thing altogether than the original
creation of the *polis*.

This is where we discover the most important tension of all. For the
projected reintegration of "ethical life" has not yet even begun. Speculation can recollect and integrate all the elements that are spread out in
time behind us. But the logic of the absolute Identity theory requires
that the philosopher should comprehend what actually is, not create a
bridge between a lost world in the past and a dream world of the future. Fichte, and the other philosophers of subjective reflection, thought
it was quite all right for philosophers to build Utopias. The burden of
Hegel's criticism in the *Difference between Fichte's and Schelling's
System* and again in *Faith and Knowledge* was that this was one of
their worst mistakes. Yet by seeking to anticipate history, as he does
in the *System of Ethical Life*, he comes perilously close to doing the
same thing himself. The utopian element in his construction is not
great, but it is there. This fact was dramatized for Hegel himself by
his strictly contemporaneous discovery that "Germany is a state no
longer."

We must be careful not to exaggerate the difference between Hegel's
enterprise in the *System of Ethical Life* and that of his mature *Philosophy of Right*. Philosophical comprehension always continued to be in
Hegel's view an activity of critical *reconstruction*, not just a matter of
descriptive analysis. And the Greek ideal always retained in his mind
much of the authority that it has here as a criterion for use in political
criticism. The general outlines of his mature political theory can be
clearly descried already in the *System of Ethical Life*. But the ideal of
a living organic society portrayed in this early essay is one which Hegel
consciously set up against the "machine-State" of Fichte and of Prussia; and while the Holy Roman Empire was certainly a corpse, Frederi-
cian Prussia was very much alive. The practical ideal of "reconciliation
with fate" was one that Hegel never abandoned. This basic principle of

the Identity Philosophy remained always with him as the speculative axiom that what is actual is rational. By this standard he was bound to adjudge the *System of Ethical Life* to be a philosophical mistake in so far as it was merely the expression of a *hope*. But hope is an essential element in all practical existence; for this reason it will not, and cannot, ever be entirely banished from a political philosophy that seeks to be "systematic" in Hegel's sense. It is always present in Hegel's political thought, and it is always severely disciplined by a conscious effort to comprehend historical actuality. But in the *System of Ethical Life* and the essay on the *German Constitution* hope is allowed to dominate, whereas in the *Philosophy of Right* it is subordinated. Since Hegel's own time, prophecy has occupied a prominent place in political philosophy, especially in the work of the thinkers who owe most to him. The mature Hegel condemned all efforts at philosophical prophecy, but he did not do so without knowing whereof he spoke. The chief benefit that we can derive from the study of his earlier social thought, and especially from the *System of Ethical Life*, is the opportunity to make our own assessment of the wavering assessment of the "principle of hope" that Hegel himself made.

NOTES

1. See H. Kimmerle, "Zur Chronologie von Hegels Jenaer Schriften," in *Hegel-Studien* IV, 153–54. Kimmerle would like to make the *System der Sittlichkeit* later than the final version of the *German Constitution* essay, in spite of the objective evidence of the handwriting, about which he is the expert witness. But since the *German Constitution* essay had its origin in a project on which Hegel had embarked before he came to Jena; and since it was clearly destined for a more general audience, I do not think we should place any weight on his arguments concerning the relative complexity and maturity of Hegel's social theory in the two essays. The general literate public to whom the *Constitution* essay was addressed would have been quite unable to fol-

low the argument of the *System of Ethical Life*.

2. Rosenkranz believed that our manuscript was part of the "system" of which Hegel spoke in his letter to Schelling on 2 November 1800. Hence he was forced to regard the lecture version(s) as later. It is quite possible that he did *also* have a later draft before him, since the lecture lists show that Hegel *announced* a course on "Natural Law" in Summer 1803, Winter 1803/4, and Summer 1805; and some things that Rosenkranz says suggest that he was dealing with *more than one* lecture draft. But since the *connection* of the main lecture manuscript with our *System of Ethical Life* was evident both to Rosenkranz and to Haym, it is virtually certain that the fair copy that we have was written up from an *earlier* version used in lectures. In that case the primary lecture-

draft was for Hegel's first announced course on the topic (Summer 1802). See Rosenkranz, pp. 132–33, translated in the Appendix, pp. 178–79.

3. The part of Rosenkranz's discussion that derives from the first lecture-manuscript is translated on pp. 179–86.

4. He announced the course twice, but he probably gave it only once (see *Hegel-Studien* IV, 78).

5. It was possible, of course, to lecture critically about someone else's work. Hegel did once specifically propose to do this, when he announced a course on Fichte's theory of natural law. That course had to be cancelled (for reasons given in the following note). But much of what Hegel had in mind to say probably went into the essay on *Natural Law* in the *Critical Journal*. When we consider that Hegel's initial conception of "Logic" (as opposed to "Metaphysics") was "critical," we may fairly surmise that *Faith and Knowledge* also contains much material from his earliest lecture courses. One did not, in this period, have to tell students in advance that they must read the *Critiques* or Fichte's latest publications.

6. Hegel always *needed* whatever student fees he could earn—though it is recorded that he sometimes remitted or excused payments when the student himself was short of money. But in order to get students he had to become known (another *external* reason for publishing a textbook). To this end it was in Hegel's interest to give free lectures on topics of general interest if he could afford to do so. In his first year at Jena he lived almost entirely on his small inheritance from his father (plus whatever savings he had accumulated from his years as a private tutor with "all found"). He did not even apply for permission to teach until he had lived in Jena more than six months (and had published

his essay on the *Difference between Fichte and Schelling*). Then in his first teaching semester he participated with Schelling in a "disputatorium" given *gratis* for beginners in philosophy; and for his second he announced the course on Fichte's theory of Natural Law *gratis*. But at this point the faculty intervened. Someone pointed out that according to their rules only the regular professors were allowed to give *gratis* courses.

7. Rosenkranz, *Hegels Leben*, p. 214. His authority for this was Gabler, who took the course. (Compare *Hegel-Studien* IV. 71.)

8. In his last "Natural Law" announcement (for Summer 1805) he promised to lecture from the coming textbook of his own "system of philosophy."

9. The editorial policies of the committee that edited Hegel's works after his death must be understood in this same context. We may—indeed we must—regret their often cavalier treatment of the surviving manuscripts. But we have to recognize that they were only doing their best to make a properly autonomous treatise out of a slightly peculiar pedagogical device.

10. The application (in Latin) can be found in *Hegel-Studien* IV, 28.

11. He did, of course, in his maturity, produce a textbook for his regular course on the philosophy of law. But the special problems which this created for his editors (who had to leave the corresponding part of the *Encyclopedia* without its lecture-commentary) illustrates the point I am trying to make. The project for the *Encyclopedia* was born from Hegel's continuing effort to provide the one necessary textbook for his Jena lectures.

12. The first system to be organized on the triadic model of Hegel's maturity was the "system of speculative

philosophy" of 1803/4. The surviving fragments of the manuscript for this course are printed in *N.K.A.* VI. (The fragments of the third part—Hegel's first "Philosophy of Spirit"—are translated in the present volume.)

13. Rosenkranz, *Life of Hegel*, p. 179. The newly discovered manuscripts—which are plainly texts selected by Rosenkranz for citation in his biography—will be published in *N.K.A.* V.

14. For the earliest form of Hegel's theory, see the "Fragment of a System" translated in Hegel, *Early Theological Writings* (ed. Knox and Kroner), pp. 309–19 (and my discussion in *Toward the Sunlight*, pp. 379–99). For his reformulation of Schelling's theory of the Absolute Identity in terms of this conception, see *Difference*, pp. 171–72. When I wrote my discussions of this passage (*Difference*, pp. 20, 51–52, 58–60), I did not know that the fourfold structure mentioned by Rosenkranz belonged to a manuscript of 1801. But the latest discoveries appear to me to be fully concordant with my hypothetical reconstruction of the system that Hegel ascribes to Schelling in the *Difference* essay.

15. All of his efforts during the summer were bent upon the problems of the philosophy of nature—see Kimmerle's chronology of the manuscripts, *Hegel-Studien* IV, 142–43.

16. As the reader will see, the first "Philosophy of Spirit" preserves much of the content and sequence of the *System of Ethical Life*, but the method of exposition and progression is quite new. (See further my Introduction to the "First Philosophy of Spirit".)

17. The publisher was always willing to send the printed sheets to his own bookshop as soon as they came from the press (or even to send them away to another place as Goebhardt sent the sheets of the *Phenomenology* from Bamberg). One could subscribe for a

work of this sort almost as if it were a journal, because binding was always a quite distinct matter, at the purchaser's discretion. The first edition of Fichte's *Science of Knowledge*, and several of his other works were published in this way. Thus if Hegel thought that he could get at least the first sheets out in time, he could announce his textbook for the course in which those sheets would be used.

18. I assume that this was some time in the summer of 1803 (as far as publication was concerned). But Hegel may have used the manuscript for lectures after that. He announced his "Natural Law" course for Summer 1803 and again for Winter 1803/4. The marginal notes in the manuscript suggest that he probably based his course upon our manuscript at least once, and perhaps twice. The evidence is by no means conclusive. We know from the manuscripts of Winter 1803/4 that Hegel had abandoned his quadripartite theory in favor of a triadic one by then. This would explain why he stopped working on his fair copy, but it would not necessarily make the manuscript unusable for his lectures on Natural Law. On the other hand we must never forget that the announcement of a course is not conclusive proof that it was in fact given; if it were not for our manuscript, and the inferences we can reliably draw from the reports of Rosenkranz and Haym, we could not decisively prove that Hegel gave any particular course on Natural Law (despite five announcements), since there are no surviving enrollment lists (such as we have for some of Hegel's other courses) or known references to a "Natural Law" course in the letters, testimonials, or memoirs of former students who took it.

19. Spinoza, *Ethics*, Part II, Prop. 7; compare *Difference*, etc., p. 166.

20. This sketch is based on the almost equally sketchy outline provided by Hegel in *Difference*, etc., pp. 167–69.

21. Compare my reconstruction in *Difference*, pp. 51–52, 58–60 (which was proposed without any knowledge of the lecture manuscripts).

22. Compare *Difference*, pp. 97, 176–92.

23. Compare *ibid.*, pp. 170–72.

24. The relevant passages from the report of Rosenkranz are given in full on pp. 178–86.

25. Compare pp. 99–100 of System of Ethical Life below.

26. See the Contents (where everything not given by Hegel himself has been placed in square brackets).

27. Lasson supplies the heading "First level of Nature, subsumption of concept under intuition," but this has nothing except the safety of absolute triviality to recommend it. If we want to follow Hegel's own indications in the text, we should probably call the section "First Level: Feeling or the practical." Hegel does not give us *antithetic* headings: Finite/Infinite, Real/Ideal; but these antitheses are the only "gap-fillers" that come spontaneously to mind in a cursory external inspection. I hope to show that they are, at least, not misleading.

28. The antithesis of "intuition" and "concept" was also used by Schelling in his formulations of the Absolute Identity. One minor pointer to his usage that will be familiar to many readers is his bewildered comment when he began to read the *Phenomenology*: "I confess that up to now I do not comprehend the sense in which you oppose the *concept* to the intuition. But you cannot mean anything else by the former except what you and I have called "Idea," whose nature is just this, to have one side from which it is concept and another from

which it is intuition" (Letter 107, 2 Nov. 1807, in Hegel, *Briefe*, ed. Hoffmeister, I, 194). It must be left to the attentive reader to decide whether the *System of Ethical Life* is not already closer to the *Phenomenology* in this respect than it is to Schelling's understanding of a shared terminology.

29. These are, of course, the German terms that are quite normally used for "cause" and "effect." But translation would obscure the difference between this pair and the more scholastic *Kausalität und Dependenz*.

30. *Difference*, p. 116; Compare also p. 161.

31. *Critique of Judgement*, Section 77, (*Akad.* V, 407–08); Meredith, *Teleological Judgement*, pp. 63–64.

32. The earliest occurrence I have found is in *On The World-Soul* (1798): "But the Absolute is not just a willing of itself, but a willing in an infinite way, hence in all forms, grades, and *Potenzen* of reality" (*Werke* II, 362). But I cannot be certain that this is not a revision introduced in the second edition of 1806—just as the occurrence in the *Ideas for a Philosophy of Nature* (1797) belongs to the "Addition" of 1803—see *Werke* II, 66. In that case Schelling's first use of the term is presumably the one which he cited himself (when he awarded the priority to Eschenmayer) from his "Introduction to Nature-Philosophy" (June 1799) —see Hegel, *N.K.A.* IV, 161–62.

33. One must agree with Tilliette (*Schelling*, vol. I) who reiterates, every time he returns to the topic of *Potenzen* in Schelling, that "the study of the *Potenzen* is indubitably not the best guideline for cataloguing the evolution of Schelling" (331); "it is the use that clarifies the term, not the other way round" (377); "the theory of the powers, through the whole length of the philosophy of Identity, never ac-

quires precise contours" (422).

34. Schelling, *Werke* IV, 205.

35. "Ueber das Absolute Identitäts-System," in Hegel, *N.K.A.* IV, 162n.

36. Schelling, *Werke* IV, 135 (Section 43).

37. Schelling, *Werke* V, 365–67.

38. The Leibnizian inspiration of the Identity theory was clearly evident to its earliest critics. Compare, for example, Schelling's indignant footnote in the dialogue for the *Critical Journal* (Hegel, *Werke* IV, 160n). I believe, though I cannot definitely prove, that the earliest form of the *Potenz* theory was mainly inspired by the equivalence which Leibniz established between "power" and "existence." In any case the theory is fundamentally different from the Aristotelian doctrine of "potentiality." A *Potenz* is an actuality rather than an Aristotelian potentiality. In Aristotelian terms it is best identified as a self-actualizing form.

39. *Werke* IV, 134. The note that Schelling added here, which was supposed to elucidate the concept of *Potenz*, actually elucidates the formula A=A.

40. A conspectus of his efforts to arrange the "real series" and the "ideal series" is provided by Tilliette, (*Schelling* I, 417–21). Note how often the "ideal series" is absent.

41. Schelling, *Werke* IV, 412–23; I have also used the summaries of the "real series" in the second edition of the *Ideen* (1803)—*Werke* II 68–69 and 174–77—which clarifies a few vaguenesses. For instance the *organism* is the objective or real aspect of Reason, the object of the "absolute act of cognition." Thus the "real series" connects at its terminus with the beginning of the "ideal series" (and I take the connection of Truth and Beauty to be the joining of the two ends of the ideal series). In the second edition of

the *Ideen,* however, Schelling no longer speaks of "subsumption" but of "subordination under the real unity."

42. For the "constructed line" in Schelling, see, for instance, the *Exposition of My System* (1801), Section 46 (*Werke* IV, 137). I have added the zero for the reason indicated in the text. Schelling's "axiom" will be found in Section 47 (*Werke* IV, 139).

43. Hegel thinks in terms of "he"; and his conception of human *nature* gives him grounds for regarding "man" rather than woman as the ethical agent in the fullest sense. So I shall generally write "he." But the connection between sex and rationality appears to me to be empirically rather than rationally grounded in Hegel's theory; and since we presently regard his empirical grounds as socially misdetermined, rather than as naturally determined, they have little relevance for us. Compare note 65 below.

44. The fact that "community" is Kant's preferred synonym for "reciprocity" as the "totality" of "relation" should always be kept in mind.

45. In its completely general form (not just as restricted to the concept of *Sittlichkeit*) "the concept's absolute movement" combines the procedure of Kant's hypothetical intuitive understanding with that of the analytical understanding to produce this circular motion. But it is also a "real" process, not just an "ideal" one.

46. The insertion of "feeling" into the basically Kantian conceptual scheme of the Identity theory derives from Fichte. "Feeling" is "deduced" as the basic category of practical experience in Part III of the *Science of Knowledge.* But the discussion there is very difficult and abstruse.

47. When Hegel speaks of a "formal" concept, he means the sort of

theoretical understanding of something that can be formulated in a definition. A formal concept is the concept of something as "possible," and the contrast is with an *actual* concept, or with the concept of something actual. The contrast formal/actual may overlap with the contrast ideal/real; but it does so only at the limits of the range of the terms "ideal" and "real." An "ideal" can be a very potent actuality; and in the context of Hegel's practical philosophy "ideal" factors are typically "actual" concepts. (The tripled alpha in the text should be just 'a'. Lasson misunderstood Hegel's own indecision about his divisions here.) The correspondence of the three moments in the "formal" and the "real" concepts are shown by the doubling of the Greek letters: α) becomes $\alpha\alpha$), β) becomes $\beta\beta$) and γ) becomes $\gamma\gamma$).

48. See the fragment on "Love," in Hegel, *Early Theological Writings*, (ed. Knox and Kroner), pp. 302–08; also the other fragments cited in my *Toward the Sunlight*, pp. 316–17n.

49. It seems to me that the text is faulty here (429–30) and that Hegel may have meant to write: "die Realität des Objects ist auf andre Weise subjektiv als es [*das Objekt*] objektiv ist." But I do not feel confident about this or any other simple correction that occurs to me. I feel slightly *more* confident that I have grasped the principal difference between "the formal concept of speech" and Hegel's exposition of actual speech.

50. The whole discussion of *corporeal signs* and *speech* should be compared with the theory of *imagination* and *memory* (the corresponding moments on the *inward* side of consciousness) in the first "Philosophy of Spirit," pp. 219–22 below.

51. See "The Spirit of Christianity," in Hegel, *Early Theological Writings*,

(ed. Knox and Kroner), p. 208. (This example can only be used properly within the full context of *Sittlichkeit*, which has not yet been developed. But I think it shows clearly what *Not* means—compare my *Toward the Sunlight*, pp. 283n, 300.

52. The status of the craftsman (and even of the farmer as soon as there are craftsmen) may seem to be somewhat ambiguous. For all craftsmen produce a surplus and meet some part of their needs through exchange. But tool-making is a special skill, and Hegel ascribes that to the "finite" *Potenz*. Probably he regarded personal commissions executed by and for specific individuals (like the forging of Achilles' shield) as belonging, together with barter and reciprocal exchange of services, to the "finite" level. But the *Potenzen* are only "ideal determinations" of a fluid reality. We must not expect to be able to cleave the things of nature with a hatchet. The attempt to do that is just what typifies the present *Potenz*.

53. Hegel's analogy here was a bow towards the ideal of a perfect parallel between Schelling's "real" and "ideal" series. For as the reader will see from the table on p. 18 above, the "dynamic series" of bodies was regarded as the natural parallel of the levels of human action. In order to understand the analogy we have to remember that for Schelling and Hegel the paradigm case of an electrical phenomenon was what we call "static electricity"—the attraction of a positively charged object of one type for a negatively charged object of another. Thus the inseparable poles of a bar magnet were "dissociated" in electricity.

54. "The child is the parents themselves" Hegel wrote in the first draft of the fragment on "Love" in 1797. In his revision he cancelled this romantic excess, but he let stand the

claim that "in the child their union has become unseparated" (see Hegel, *Early Theological Writings*, ed. Knox and Kroner, p. 308). The translation of the bonds of blood into a system of recognized obligations is the clearest illustration of "ethics as nature or in relation." The identity is the inward feeling of love (a natural bond) or else it "floats above" the child and his family as his "natural rights" (and they are all ethical by virtue of their relation to this "identity" of "human nature").

55. Hegel adds parenthetically: "In Religion wird es ein anderes." This may refer to the dictum of Jesus about there being no marriages in Heaven. But Hegel does not elaborate so we cannot tell just what he means. Perhaps it is somehow the case that particulars can be united without being an *empirical* universal at this level.

56. Hegel's theory of natural barbarism is an added complication. But, at least he supplies the necessary connecting links for that in his brief paragraph on "the negative" of the first *Potenz* as a whole (432). That is the clue which I have followed here.

57. Hegel simply contrasts the ethical *Wiederherstellung* of life with that which occurs in religion, saying that "the restoration through religion does not affect actuality." Since we do not have his account of religion, we cannot be quite certain what the *Wiederherstellung* through religion is, but I think that my implicit appeal to Hegel's treatment of the *Antigone* in the *Phenomenology* is not a very risky conjecture.

58. For the influence of *Macbeth* in Hegel's earlier reflections, see "The Spirit of Christianity" in Hegel, *Early Theological Writings*, (ed. Knox, Kroner), pp. 205, 229.

59. Hegel had studied the history of Italy and would not need to depend on Shakespearean examples. So I do not mean to suggest that he has any Shakespearean model in mind here.

60. Kimmerle makes no remark about the marginalia in the manuscript —which are too slight to provide a sufficient body of text for dating by the handwriting. But Hegel typically used his broad margins for *subsequent* revisions and notes; also this manuscript has the general appearance of a fair copy, so one would not expect him to use the margin for preliminary planning—and if he did so one would expect him to cross his notes out afterwards.

61. Clearly there *can* be slaves in a political community, but they are not an "estate" (*Stand*) within it ([471] see below p. 152). Also there can be serfs or helots. They do form a necessary estate, but it is one that has been forced out of its proper shape (see p. 156).

62. See especially the "Tübingen fragment" (in my *Toward the Sunlight*, p. 488); the "Positivity" essay (in Hegel, *Early Theological Writings*, ed. Knox, Kroner, p. 146); and the "German Constitution" essay (in Hegel, *Political Writings*, ed. Knox, Pelczynski, pp. 219, 241).

63. See, for instance, Hegel, *Early Theological Writings*, ed. Knox, Kroner, pp. 185–88.

64. For the "indifference point" as "identity" and as "totality," compare Hegel, *Difference*, pp. 169–70. The *System of Ethical Life* is a particular illustration—the best and the most detailed that we are likely to find—of the difficult doctrine that is there put forward.

65. Compare p. 29 above. It is not very clear what Hegel takes the *natural* basis of this distinction to be. But presumably, like the immediate positing of the lordship/bondage relation, it is a matter of natural strength and

aggressiveness; certainly the "spiritual" aspect of it is a supposedly *innate* rational authority of man over woman (and specifically of husband over wife).

66. For the distinction of ethical from servile obedience, see p. 41 above.

67. It *did* concern him in the lecture draft upon which our manuscript is based. But our manuscript declines into mere headings, just at the point where the lecture draft apparently provided Hegel's first sketch for the discussion of "noble service" in the *Phenomenology*. Compare p. 179 below and Miller's translation of the *Phenomenology*, sections 493–520.

68. *Faith and Knowledge*, p. 145. (The story comes, via Jacobi's *Letters on Spinoza*, from Herodotus VII, 134–36).

69. "Is Judaea, then, the Teutons' Fatherland?" (1796), in Hegel, *Early Theological Writings*, pp. 147–48. The attempt to collapse the culture of fifth-century Athens into a single example has here produced a rather odd image. But the intent is clear (Apelles is historically out of place, but he is the stock representative of Greek painting).

70. Compare the remark of Schelling quoted in note 28 above.

71. See p. 11 above.

72. See especially *Difference*, pp. 89–94, 114; compare the Introduction for the *Critical Journal*, N.K.A. IV, 117–28.

73. This is evident enough when we study the closing section of *Faith and Knowledge* (pp. 189–91) and *Natural Law* (pp. 129–33). The latter passage, in particular, makes plain the relevance of the *System of Ethical Life* to the "need of the time."

74. For the absence of necessity in practical life, the possibility of other duties, and the accidental character of

ethical insight, see especially *Faith and Knowledge*, pp. 183–87.

75. *Ibid.*, pp. 190–91. The Protestant-ism in which "the grief does not endure" achieves its highest level of development in the *Addresses on Religion* of Schleiermacher (*ibid.*, pp. 150–52).

76. See pp. 81–85.

77. An "absolute" multiplicity is one which is "complete and self-sufficient," to use Aristotelian terminology. Thus virtue as an "absolute multiplicity" includes all the virtues that are necessary to the full articulation and completely adequate expression of human nature. Virtue as "absolute unity," on the other hand, is the living soul of all the articulated virtues, the spirit of self-sacrifice and self-abandonment apart from which they would not be virtuous.

78. When Hegel speaks of ethical life as "beauty" or "beautiful," we must remember that the normal Greek word for "beauty" and "the beautiful" is also the word for "nobility" and "the noble."

79. See Plutarch, *Aristides* (Everyman I, 497). I do not wish to imply that the story was certainly in Hegel's mind, but I think it illustrates what he has to say about the mistrustfulness of trust.

80. *Republic* IV, 433. But Hegel's peasantry, unlike Plato's, remains in the natural condition of "solid" virtue. For this reason it has no "wisdom" and becomes politically dependent on the nobility.

81. The historic analogue at Athens was the Areopagus. Hegel's reflections about this were much influenced by his study of the *Oresteia* of Aeschylus (see his essay on *Natural Law*, Knox and Acton, pp. 104–05).

82. I think it is legitimate to regard the remark about "the nothing" which

hovers over the indifferentiated "clump" (482) as an anticipation of Hegel's discussion of "Absolute Freedom and Terror" in the *Phenomenology* (Miller's translation, sections 582–95).

83. This was the extreme which Hegel thought Fichte's theory would approach in practice (compare *Difference*, pp. 146–47).

84. *Lectures on the Philosophy of World History*, trans. J. Sibree, pp. 49–52; or Nisbet, pp. 101–111.

85. "The German Constitution" in Hegel's *Political Writings*, Knox and Pelczynski, pp. 143, 150–51; compare my *Toward the Sunlight*, pp. 438, 450–52, 456–57).

86. See Hegel, *Political Writings*, ed. Knox and Pelczynski, pp. 73, 234–35, 239–41, 243–45; and my *Toward the Sunlight*, pp. 474–75.

87. It was translated by Garve and published in German between 1796 and 1799. Hegel first refers to it explicitly in his first "Philosophy of Spirit" of 1804. The edition from which he quotes there was apparently the Basel edition of 1791 (in English). He owned this edition, but we do not know when he acquired it; obviously, however, he would be more likely to purchase it *while* he was in Switzerland, and *before* the German translation was available.

88. See Rosenkranz, *Hegels Leben*, pp. 86; and my *Toward the Sunlight*, p. 435.

89. See pp. 246–49; and compare further Avineri, *Hegel's Theory of the Modern State*, pp. 104–05, 107–09. (Avineri rightly emphasizes how different Hegel's attitude to the problem was from that which Marx adopted later. But by the time of Marx it was a matter of the "real motion" of the concept.)

90. The example with which Hegel was himself most familiar, having lived in it for more than three years, was the aristocratic republic of the Canton of Bern.

91. See Hegel, *Political Writings*, ed. Knox and Pelczynski, pp. 239–41. On the other hand, the absence of any legislative structures in the "Constitution" section of the second "Philosophy of Spirit" (1805/06) might be taken as an indication that Hegel believed, at this time, that no such articulation could be philosophically justified—but see further note 93.

92. The final remark here, "and then by reconciliation with the world and itself it passes through the lack of imagination in irreligion and in understanding," seems to look forward to Hegel's lengthy critique of the *ancien régime* and the Enlightenment in the *Phenomenology*.

93. "He worked out the concept of the distinction of constitutions further, and identified the free estate in Monarchy as the Nobility which stands over against Majesty, in a tacit *battle* that has the *form of obedience*" (Rosenkranz, *Hegels Leben*, p. 133). This "battle in the form of obedience" is put before us at length in the *Phenomenology*. For the "form of obedience," see also p. 41. If the analysis of this "class struggle" was carried through to the point of social revolution (as in the *Phenomenology*), then it could have culminated in the justification of a formally established "assembly of Estates."

94. For a summing up of what we know about Hegel's earlier reflections on the problem of church and state, see my *Toward the Sunlight*, pp. 409–16.

95. Rosenkranz, *Hegels Leben*, p. 179; cf. p. 6 above.

96. Rosenkranz, *Hegels Leben*, p. 133. The whole report is printed in an

appendix on pp. 178–86.

97. The general line of his criticism can be gathered from *Faith and Knowledge*, which he wrote in the summer of 1802; see the translation by Cerf and Harris, pp. 150–52.

98. I am here depending on the indications supplied in *Difference*, pp. 171–72, for the interpretation of what Rosenkranz says about the relation between "religion" and *das Wissen*. I cannot be far wrong if Religion is indeed "the return to the primitive simplicity of the Idea."

99. For the origins of this contention in Hegel's religious thought, see the "Tübingen fragment" (in my *Toward the Sunlight*, pp. 503–04).

100. See pp. 46–47.

101. For a detailed exposition of the doctrine as he held it in 1797/98, see "The Spirit of Christianity" (ed. Knox and Kroner, pp. 224–53; see also my

Toward the Sunlight, pp. 346–55).

102. *Hegel und seine Zeit*, p. 509, note 13. He supplies one sentence that was omitted by Rosenkranz (see p. 185), and he indicates that there are other omissions, but he apparently felt that they were not of any great importance.

103. Hegel's attention is mainly concentrated on the Protestant moment of "infinite grief." But we should not overlook his attempt to develop the doctrine of the Trinity *aesthetically*. The three Persons, with the Mother of God, form a sort of "universal" living pantheon. Also he treats the "communion of saints" in a *patriotic* way. So we can see in a general way how the *political* "totality" would be integrated.

104. See Appendix, p. 185–86.

105. *Faith and Knowledge*, p. 191.

G. W. F. Hegel
System of Ethical Life
(1802/3)
Translated by T. M. Knox
and H. S. Harris

Hegel
System of Ethical Life

A NOTE ON THE TRANSLATION

Of all Hegel's posthumously published manuscripts, the *System der Sittlichkeit* is perhaps the most enigmatic. Even German scholars who have studied all of the posthumous publications closely do not seem to dissent from this verdict. For example Haering, who made the most comprehensive study of Hegel's early writings, says: "It is true that the difficulties of understanding it are quite extraordinary" (*Hegel, sein Wollen und sein Werk*, ii, 338). For this reason we have not always found it entirely possible to render into clear and intelligible English what is scarcely intelligible in German. It has, nevertheless, seemed to us that the effort was worth making because this essay is the earliest of Hegel's systematic manuscripts that survives intact, and it represents his mature social thought in embryonic form. Its importance, long recognized by German scholars, has now been made clear to Anglo-Saxon students by Shlomo Avineri (*Hegel's Theory of the Modern State*, Cambridge, 1972).

The translation is based on the edition of Georg Lasson (originally published by F. Meiner Verlag in 1913). We have used the second edition, of 1923, and have indicated the pagination of this edition in square brackets in the margin of our text. The original draft for the translation was made by T. M. Knox and it is in essence his work. But we have both gone over it thoroughly, and we now share responsibility for whatever errors and imperfections may still be found in it.

T. M. Knox

September 1977

H. S. Harris

[*Introduction*]   [415]

Knowledge of the Idea of the absolute ethical order[1] depends entirely on the establishment of perfect adequacy between intuition and con-

1. *Sittlichkeit*—here not a moral philosophy but an ethical order or ethical social and political life.

cept,[2] because the Idea itself is nothing other than the identity of the two. But if this identity is to be actually known, it must be thought as a made adequacy. But because they are then held apart from one another in an equation [as its two sides], they are afflicted with a difference. One side has the form of universality, the other the opposed form of particularity. Therefore, in order that the equation be completely established, what [was] first [put] in the form of particularity [must] be put in the form of universality, while what [was] given the form of universality must now be given the form of particularity.[3]

But what is truly the universal is intuition, while what is truly particular is the absolute concept. Thus each must be posited over against the other, now under the form of particularity, again under the form of universality; now intuition must be subsumed under the concept and again the concept under intuition. Although this last relation is

2. The terminology derives ultimately from Kant. What is at issue is the "synthesis" of the particular and the universal aspects of experience. Ordinary "finite" consciousness never gets beyond a "relation" between the two, in which either the "particular" or the "universal" pole is dominant: either "concept" is subsumed under "intuition," or vice versa. But in Hegel's view, ultimate truth in metaphysics is the identity of universal and particular, or subject and object, in and as the Absolute; while the Idea (i.e., ideal or true form) of political or ethical life is an identity of ruler and ruled, or of individual welfare and the welfare of the whole. This is adumbrated here, but made clear and explicit in the *Philosophy of Right* (or Law).

In his Introduction Georg Lasson says: "For Hegel ethical life is actuality proper, the totality of life which brings all the moments of life together under itself, and thus what he elsewhere calls subject-objectivity. This actuality grasped according to the moment of objectivity, and so as objective subject-objectivity is a nature, a givenness. On the other hand, grasped according to the moment of subjectivity, and so as subject-objectivity, it is the individuality of self-consciousness which grips actuality in itself. The first, the side of givenness, Hegel calls "intuition," the second, the side of individuality, he calls "concept." The totality of ethical actuality is built up by the reciprocal subsumption of one side under the other." Lasson's own opinion is that "this dualism of intuition and concept is more like a shackle than an aid to the development of his thought." We have rendered Hegel's terminology literally here, but it is possible that his meaning could be made clearer if his terminology were completely abandoned and a paraphrase substituted for translation. However the literal rendering becomes less unintelligible if the following interpretations of Hegel's phraseology are kept in mind. "Intuition" is equivalent to "a perceptible particular" as "concept" is to "an abstract universal." Intuitions separated from concepts are both, in Hegel's view, abstractions, although for a philosophy based on the understanding (as distinct from reason) they are constituent parts of our experience, related together but not synthesized or united in a concrete whole. For Hegel the truth is that

the absolute one, for the reason given, the first one is just as absolutely necessary for their perfect equality to be known, since the latter
relation is one and only one relation and therefore the absolute equivalence of intuition and knowledge is not posited in it. Now the Idea of
the absolute ethical order is the resumption of absolute reality into
itself as into a unity, so that this resumption and this unity are an
absolute totality. The intuition of this totality is an absolute people,
while its concept is the absolute oneness of the individuals.

In the first place, intuition must be subsumed under the concept.   [416]
Thereby the absolute ethical order appears as nature, because nature
itself is but the subsumption of intuition under the concept, with the
result therefore that intuition, the unity, remains the inner, while the
multiplicity of the concept and the concept's absolute movement rises
to the surface. In this subsumption, in that case, the intuition of the

---

they *are* so synthesized and they do form a concrete whole, even if that whole is
"ideal," and even if in "reality" they are "realized" separately. For example, in
the real world we can distinguish between an individual citizen and the whole
people to which he belongs, or between a criminal and the arm of the law. But
the truth lying behind this distinction between "intuition" and "concept" is their
ideal and real unity. In the ideal ethical order government and governed are one.
And although this is "ideal," it is also the "truth" of what really exists. Hegel
was later to put the point more clearly and explicitly by his distinction between
"real" and "actual": a bad government may be "real," but it is not "actual," just
as a man may be "real" but not "actual" because he is not in conformity with
what it is to be a man. This reminds us of Platonic "forms," but Hegel regards
these as "merely" ideal; in his view the ideal is not so impotent as not to exist
really also. The ideal is not transcendent and far off, but the inner truth and
essence of reality. The "Idea" is what is absolutely true; it is the synthesis of
intuition and concept, universal and particular, real and ideal, form and matter,
in short of all the opposites which, for a preceding philosophy, were merely "related" and never unified.

Such a philosophy of "relation" may begin with, or emphasize, one opposite
and "subsume" the other under it. But *which* to begin with is arbitrary. To begin
with one to the exclusion of the other produces results contradicting the original
presupposition. Consequently Hegel starts by examining what ethical life is like
if it is regarded as based on *relations* and not on absolute unity or synthesis.
This examination must be twofold: first, we presuppose that concept is subsumed
under intuition, i.e., that the particular is *related* to the universal by *dominating*
it, or by being taken as the basis of the whole, from which, no doubt, abstract
universals can be derived. Secondly, we perform the reverse procedure, i.e., we
presuppose universals as dominant and particulars as merely illustrative of them
—the particular "intuition" is "subsumed" under the "concept."

The result of the examination is unsatisfactory. Both ways of looking at the
social and political sphere are possible; one may supplement the other; one may

ethical order [its particular aspect] which is a people becomes a mani-fold reality or a single individuality, a single man; and as a result the absolute resumption of nature into itself becomes something hovering over this single individual, or something formal, because the formal is precisely the unity which is not in itself either absolute concept or absolute movement.[4] At the same time, precisely because this unity hovers over the single individual, he does not emerge from it or ab-stract himself from it; it is in him but is concealed in him; and it ap-pears in this contradiction, namely, that this inner light does not abso-lutely coincide or unite with the universal light hovering over him as something according to which he is driven on, as impulse or striving. Or in this way the identity of the particular (i.e., the side onto which the intuition has now stepped) with the universal is determined as an imperfect unification or as a *relation* between the two.

[417] 1. ABSOLUTE ETHICAL LIFE ON THE BASIS OF RELATION

Here too, as before, there must be subdivision. This absolute ethical life on the basis of relation, or *natural* ethical life must be so treated that (a) concept is subsumed under intuition and (b) intuition is subsumed under concept. In (a) the unity is the universal, the inner, while in (b) it enters over against [the inner] and is once more in a *relation* with the concept or with the particular.[5] In both cases ethical life is a drive [or impulse]. This means a drive which (α) is not absolutely one with the absolute unity, (β) affects the single individual, (γ) is satis-

---

be a lower stage superseded by the other as a higher one; but both imply that universal and particular are only related to one another, and it is as if social life were split into its extremes and so killed. "There is missing, alas!" as Goethe said, "the spiritual bond." By being split in this way the bond of connection has been snapped, and instead of a living whole we are left with dead abstractions. The true absolute ethical order is a living *whole*, within which there are differ-ences indeed, but they are differences united, like the parts of a living body, by a common life.

3. I.e., there can be no identity, as distinct from mere equality, of universal and particular unless the universal is particularized and the particular universalized.

4. Haering (*Hegel*, ii, 348) describes this passage as a "stone of stumbling," and this is not surprising.

5. Each subsumption has two opposite subsumptive processes as its "moments." So whether the unity is an inward thought or an outward reality, it will appear on both sides of the equation as concept in relation to particular or particular in relation to concept at the appropriate stage of the logical development.

fied in this single individual—this singular satisfaction is itself a totality, but (∂) it goes at the same time beyond the single individual,
though this transcendence is here in general something negative and
indeterminate.

The satisfaction itself is nothing but the union of concept and intuition. Thus it is a totality, living but formal, precisely because this level,
at which it is, is itself a determinate one, and thus absolute life hovers
over it just as much as it remains something inner. But absolute life
remains something inner because it is not the absolute concept, and so,
as inner life, is not present at the same time under the form of the
opposite, i.e., of the outer. And for this very reason it is not absolute
intuition because it is not present to the subject in the relation as such,
and so its identity likewise cannot be the absolute one.

A. [First Level:[6] Feeling as Subsumption of Concept under Intuition]

The first level is natural ethical life as *intuition*[7]—the complete undifferentiatedness of ethical life, or the subsumption of concept under
intuition, or nature proper.

But the ethical is inherently by its own essence a resumption of   [418]
difference into itself, reconstruction; identity rises out of difference
and is essentially negative; its being this presupposes the existence of
what it cancels. Thus this ethical nature is also an unveiling, an emergence of the universal in face of the particular, but in such a way that
this emergence is itself wholly something particular—the identical,
absolute quantity remains entirely hidden. This intuition, wholly immersed in the singular, is *feeling*, and we will call this the level of
practice.

The essence of this level is that feeling (not what is called "ethical
feeling") is something entirely singular and particular, but, as such,
is separated, a difference not to be superseded by anything but its ne-

6. *Potenz*. The word means "power" and is drawn from the vocabulary of
mathematics, where x is raised to the second, third, or nth power. Schelling describes his Absolute as a series of *Potenzen*. Hegel uses the same metaphor at
this time, but he later discarded it on the ground that it was purely quantitative,
not qualitative as well. "Level" rather than "power" seems to convey Hegel's
meaning here less ambiguously.

7. I.e., the dominance of the individual or the particular. Subject differs from
object and is driven to overcome this difference. The drive or instinct is natural,
and thus "natural" ethical or social life is identical with that life as relation. Subject and object are related, not unified. Difference is not overcome.

gation, the negation of the separation into subject and object; and this supersession is itself a perfect singularity and an identity without difference.

The feeling of separation is *need*; feeling as separation superseded is *enjoyment*.

The distinctive character [of feeling] as a level [in ethical life as relation] is that feeling lies in the particular and concerns the singular and that it is absolute feeling; but this feeling which proceeds to supersede the separation of subject and object must display itself as a totality and therefore be the totality of the levels [of ethical life as relation].

This feeling (a) subsuming the concept, and (b) subsumed under the concept [is now to be considered].

(a) If feeling is presented as subsuming the concept, the formal concept of feeling is presented. This is properly its concept which is adduced above, namely, that [there is present]

(α) the supersession of what is wholly and absolutely identical and unconscious—separation, and this separation as feeling or *need*,

(β) difference in contrast to this separation; but this difference is negative, namely, a nullification of separation—(*margin*: desire, ideal determination of the object); and so a nullification of the subjective and the objective and of the empirical objective intuition according to which the object of need is outside; or this nullification is effort and *labor*;

[419]

(γ) the nullification of the object, or the identity of the first two factors—conscious feeling, i.e., unity arising out of difference, i.e., *enjoyment*.

The subsumption of feeling under the concept or, more objectively, the concept of practical feeling unfolded in all its dimensions, necessarily presents feeling (a) in its dimensions according to the nature of the form or the concept, (b) but in such a way that a whole, feeling, remains throughout, while the form is something wholly external for the feeling.

(a) Practical feeling, or enjoyment, an identity void of intuition, of difference, and, therefore, of reason, proceeds thus to the absolute nullification of the object. Consequently, it is a complete indifference of the subject for ethical life, without making conspicuous a middle term uniting the opposites in itself; so there is no resumption of intuition into itself and there is no self-knowledge in the subject.

($\alpha\alpha$) Need here is an absolute singleness, a feeling restricting itself to the subject and belonging entirely to nature. This is not the place for comprehending the manifold and systematic character of this feeling [of need]. Eating and drinking [are the paradigms].[8]

(ββ) By this difference an inner and an outer are directly established and the outer is plainly determined (e.g., as edible or drinkable) according to the specific character of the feeling. Thereby this external thing ceases to be something universal, identical, quantitative, and becomes a single particular. The subject, despite his singularity in this feeling and in the relation posited in the separation [of subject from object] remains in himself undifferentiated; he is the universal, the subsuming power. The specific character which the object of enjoyment acquires at this level is entirely ideal or subjective—the object is directly its own opposite.[9] The specific character does not enter the objectivity of intuition in such a way that something might arise for the subject which he may recognize as the identity of subject and object. —Or this identity is transferred into the individual subject alone, [420] with the result that, being determined purely ideally [or subjectively], the object is simply annihilated.

(γγ) This enjoyment in which the object is determined purely ideally, and entirely annihilated, is purely sensuous enjoyment; i.e., the satiation which is the restoration of the indifference and emptiness of the individual or of his bare possibility of being ethical or rational. The enjoyment is purely negative because it pertains to the individual's absolute singularity and therefore involves the annihilation of the object and the universal. But it remains essentially practical and is distinguished from absolute self-feeling by reason of the fact that it proceeds from difference and to that extent involves a consciousness of the objectivity of the object.[10]

(b) This feeling in the form of difference or of the subsumption of intuition under the concept must itself be likewise comprehended as

8. Need is subjective, satisfied by the destruction of the object, e.g., in eating. Feeling is practical when, as need, it proceeds actively to satisfy itself. At this stage the union of subject and object involves the physical assimilation, and so the destruction, of the object.

9. I.e., it is for the subject that it is edible, so that its character as edible is subjective, not inherent in the object itself.

10. Need implies a difference between itself and what is needed. Enjoyment presupposes this difference. It is not a feeling of self alone, with no consciousness of the object. Thus a difference and a relation between subject and object persists, despite the annihilation of *this* edible object.

a totality: ($\alpha\alpha$) as negative practical intuition (labor), ($\beta\beta$) difference (product) and possession, ($\gamma\gamma$) tool.[11]

($\alpha\alpha$) (*margin*: This is intuition subsumed under the concept; labor is itself the subsuming of the object; the subject is indifference, the subsumer; where the subject is the subsumer, the concept is dominant.) Practical feeling subsumed under the concept displays the dispersed moments of the totality as realities. These moments are:

(α) The nullification of the object or of the intuition, but, *qua* moment, in such a way that this annihilation is replaced by another intuition or object; or pure identity, the activity of nullifying, is fixed; in this activity there is abstraction from enjoyment, i.e., it is not achieved, for here every abstraction is a reality, something that *is*. The object is not nullified as object altogether but rather in such a way that another object is put in its place,[12] for in this nullification, *qua* abstraction, there is no object or there is no enjoyment. But this nullification is [421] labor whereby the [object] determined by desire is superseded in so far as it is real on its own account, an object not determined by desire, and determination by desire *qua* intuition is posited objectively. In labor the difference between desire and enjoyment is posited; the enjoyment is obstructed and deferred; it becomes ideal or a relation, and on this relation, as a result of labor, there is posited as now immediately emerging

(i)[13]   the bearing of the subject on the object, or the ideal determining of the object by desire: this is *taking possession* [of the object];

(ii)   next, the real annihilation of the object's form, for objectivity or difference remains—the *activity* of labor itself;

(iii)   finally, the *possession* of the product, or the possibility of annihilating the product as something [explicitly real], through a connection of the first kind [i.e., consumption in eating] with respect to its matter, as well as through this second one [i.e., working on it], which consists in annihilating its form and in its being given a [new] form by the subject—i.e., the possibility of a transition to enjoyment

11. ($\gamma\gamma$) disappears altogether at this stage, and ($\beta\beta$) partially.
12. I.e., the object as worked upon by the subject.
13. Roman numerals are substituted here and below for the Hebrew characters which Hegel used.

which, however, remains wholly ideal [or purely sub-
jective].

Possession is not present at all at the first stage of practical feeling,
and likewise taking possession is there purely as a moment; or rather
neither of them is a real moment; they are not fixed or kept distinct
from one another. (There can be no question at all here of the legal
basis or aspect of possession.)

Taking possession is the ideal [moment] in this subsumption [of
the product under the subject], or the moment of rest; labor [the second moment] is the reality or movement, the entry of the subsuming
subject into the reality of the object; the third moment, the synthesis,
is the possession, preservation, and saving of the object. In this third
moment there is present that ideal character according to the first moment, but it is present in the object as real according to the second
moment.

(β) The product has already been defined formally in (α) as the
identity of the ideal character, but of it as objectively real and separate; but the essential thing was the identity, activity as such, and so
as something inner and so as not emerging; it must emerge on the
object, and this second stage ββ considers the relation of the inhibited
feeling to the object inhibited by its nullification [i.e., by the labor ex- [422]
pended to change it], or the difference present even in labor, namely,
the difference between the reality and proper nature of the object and
the way it is to be, and is, ideally determined by labor. In (αα) it was
the object that was subsumed, here it is the subject. Or, in (αα), the
ideal relation in labor was considered, here the real one. Here labor is
properly *subsumed under intuition*, for the object is in itself the universal, so, where the object is subsuming, the singularity of the subject has its proper rational place; the subject is concept in itself, difference, and it subsumes [or is dominant].

In (αα) labor is wholly mechanical, since individuality, abstraction,
pure causality is present in the form of indifference; it is dominant
and is therefore something external to the object. For therewith causality is posited in truth, since this subject is something single, absolutely existing on its own account, and therefore absolute separation
and difference. Whereas, when the object and the universal are subsuming, causality is absent, since the object in itself is the indifference
of the particular and one with the particular for which, it follows,
particularity is a purely external form, not the inner essence, not subjective being.

Because the object is subsuming labor under itself, it is in the relation as real (as previously it was nullified, posited as the pure abstraction of an object), for, as subsuming, it is an identity of universal and particular, of the latter in abstraction against the subject. In this way labor too is real and living, and its vitality is to be known as a totality, but each moment [of the totality is to be known] as itself a living individual labor, as a particular object.

For the subsuming [or dominating] living object and living labor there is (a) intuition subsumed under the concept, then (b) the concept under intuition, and (c) the identity of the two.

(ααα) The living object [the individual] subsumed under the concept [the universal] is the *plant* bound up with the element or the pure quantity of the earth and producing itself towards the element of air in the production, infinitely varied (by the concept), of its own entire individuality and totality. Every part of the plant is itself an individual, a complete plant; it maintains itself against its inorganic nature only because it produces itself wholly at every point of contact, or, withering on the stem, is devoted to producing (to the absolute concept, to being the opposite of itself). Because in this way the plant is in the power of the element [the earth], the labor [of horticulture] too is principally directed against the element and is mechanical, but it is left to the element to compel the plant to produce. Labor can have little or nothing of the specific life of the plant and is therefore alive in the sense that it alters just the external form of the element alone and does not destroy it chemically; and this form is an inorganic nature which itself is only *related* to something living and lets it alone.

[423]

(βββ) The concept of the living thing subsumed under intuition is the animal. For since this subsumption itself is one-sided, not intuition subsumed under the concept in the like way over again, life here is an empirically real, infinitely dispersed life, displaying itself in the most manifold forms. For the form or the absolute concept is not itself unity or universality again. Thus here there is an individuality without intelligence, not, as in the case of the plant, where each unit of the individual is itself a mass of such units; on the contrary, here there is indifference in more extended difference and distinction.

Labor on the animal is thus less directed to its inorganic nature than to its organic nature itself, because the object is not an external element but the indifference of individuality itself. The subsumption is determined as a taming of the animal's particular character for the sort of use appropriate to its nature—now more negatively, as compulsion, now more positively as trust on the part of the animal; and now too, just as plants are determined by the elements, so the animals which are destined to be annihilated in being eaten, simply have their natural breeding [and rearing] determined.

If the use of plants is very simple and if labor for them is to be ex- [424] hibited as a need of the subject, or as how this labor is present in a subjective form, then [the need they supply is that of] nourishment, is nonorganic, or only slightly organic and individualized, and so not a nourishment of a higher difference of the individual, whether human or animal—a weak irritability, impotent outgoing, a nullification which is itself a weak one owing to the weak individuality of the plant—and for our delight they provide sensuous enjoyments (smelling and see- ing) which are finer than [those of] nullification, since the plant is not nullified. Or this is the level of the enjoyment of plants just as the level for animals is their domestication. The enjoyment [involved] is sensuous because the senses are the animal level in man, an individ- uality of feeling which as sense is an individual, not [a member] like an arm, etc., but a complete organism. As enjoyment, the eating of plants is the subsumption of the concept under intuition as feeling; whereas labor for plants is the subsumption of intuition under the concept. Thus, from the point of view of labor, the cultivation of plants, taming them, is the subsumption of concept under intuition; the converse is the case from the point of view of enjoyment, for the enjoyment of the single sense is the dispersal of enjoyment. (*margin*: N.B., as regards subsumption, enjoyment and labor are converse).

Subjectively regarded, the domestication of animals is a more many- sided need, but in so far as they are means [to enjoyment], they can- not be considered here yet, for this would not be a subsumption of the concept under intuition, not the aspect of living labor. This labor is an association of animals for movement and strength, and the delight of this propagation is above all the aspect that is relevant here.

(γγγ) The absolute identity of these two levels is that the concept of the first is one with the identity of the second or is the absolute concept, *intelligence*. Labor, subsumed under this intuition, is a one- sided subsumption, since in this very process the subsumption itself is superseded. The labor [which produces intelligence] is a totality, and with this totality the separate subsumptions of the first and second levels are now posited together. Man is a power-level, universality, for his other, but so is his other for him; and so he makes his reality, his own peculiar being, his effectiveness in reality into an adoption into indifference, and he is now the universal in contrast to the first level. And *formative education* (*Bildung*) is this absolute exchanging in the [425] absolute concept wherein every subject, and universal too, makes its particularity immediately into universality, and in the see-saw posits itself as universal at the very moment when it posits itself as one level and is thus confronted by its "being a level," and by the unmediated universality in that being, so that it itself becomes a particular. The ideal determination of the other is objective, but in such a way that this objectivity is immediately posited as subjective and becomes a cause; for if something is to be a power [or level] for another, it must not be pure universality and indifference in a *relation* to it; it must be posited for itself [as what the other is to become] or a universal truly and absolutely—and the intelligence is this in the highest degree. In precisely one and the same respect it is a universal and a particular, both of these absolutely at once and without any mediation, whereas the plant and the animal are universal in ways distinct [from their particularity].

The concept of this relation is the identity of both the two first levels, but as a totality it falls itself under the form of the three levels.

(i) As feeling or as pure identity: for feeling, the object is characterized as something desired. But here the living thing is not to be determined by being worked upon: it should be an absolutely living thing, and its reality, its explicit [being]-for-self, is simply so determined as what is desired, i.e., this relation of desire is by nature made perfectly objective, one side of it in the form of indifference, the other in that of particularity. This supreme organic polarity in the most complete individuality of each pole is the supreme unity which nature can produce. For it cannot get past this point: that difference is not real but absolutely ideal. The *sexes* are plainly in a relation to one another, one the universal, the other the particular; they are not absolutely equal. Thus their union is not that of the absolute concept but, because it is perfect, that of undifferentiated feeling. The nullification of their own form is mutual but not absolutely alike; each intuits him/herself in the other, though as a stranger, and this is *love*. The inconceivability of this being of oneself in another belongs therefore to nature, and not to ethical life, for the latter, with respect to the different [426] [poles], is the absolute equality of both—and, with respect to their union, it is absolute union on the strength of its ideality. But the ideality of nature remains in inequality and therefore in desire in which one side is determined as something subjective and the other as something objective.

(ii) Precisely this living relation, in which intuition is subsumed under the concept, is ideal as a determinacy of the opposites, but in such a way that, owing to the dominance of the concept, difference remains, though without desire. Or the determinacy of the opposites is a superficial one, not natural or real, and practice does proceed to the supersession of this opposite determinacy, yet not in feeling but in such a way that it becomes intuition of itself in a stranger, and thus ends with a perfect opposing individuality, whereby the union of nature is rather superseded. This is the relation of *parents and children*: the absolute union of both is directly sundered into a relation. The child is man subjective but in such a way that this particular is ideal, and the form [of humanity] is only an outward [appearance]. The parents are the universal, and the work of nature proceeds to the cancelling of this relation, just as the work of the parents does, for they continually cancel the external negativity of the child and, just by so doing, establish a greater inner negativity and therefore a higher individuality.

(iii) But the totality of labor is perfect individuality and therefore equality of the opposites, wherein relation is posited and superseded; appearing in time it enters every instant and turns over into the opposite moment, according to what has been said above; this is the universal reciprocal action and *formative education* of mankind. Here too the absolute equality of this reciprocity exists in the inner life and, throughout the level we are at, the relation persists solely in the single individual—a recognition which is mutual or supreme individuality and external difference. In these levels there is a process from the first to the third separately, or [i] the unification of feeling is superseded, but for this very reason [ii] [the same is true of] desire and its corresponding need, and [iii] [at the third level] each is an essential being, alike and independent. The fact that the relation of these beings is one of love and feeling too is an external form, not affecting the essence of the relation which is the universality in which they stand.

(c) The first two levels are relative identities. Absolute identity is [427] something subjective, outside them. But since this level is itself a totality, rationality must enter as such and be real; it lies concealed in the idea of the formal levels. This rational element is what enters as mediator; it shares the nature of both subject and object or is the reconciliation of the two.

This mediating term consequently exists under the form of the three levels.

(αα) Concept subsumed under intuition. This therefore belongs entirely to nature, because the difference involved in intelligent being is

not present in the intelligent being as the subsumption of intuition
under the concept. It is absolute indifference, not like the indifference
of nature which occurs in the formal levels and cannot liberate itself
from difference. At the same time this middle term is not the formal
identity which came before us hitherto as feeling, but a real absolute
identity, a real absolute feeling, the absolute middle term, explicit in
this entire aspect of reality, existing as an individual. Such a middle
term is the *child*, the highest individual natural feeling, a feeling of a
totality of the living sexes such that they are entirely in the child, so
that he [is] absolutely real and [is] individual and real in his own eyes.
The feeling is made real so that it is the absolute identity of the natural beings, so that in this identity there is no one-sidedness, and no
circumstance is missing. Their unity is therefore real immediately, and
because they [the parents] are real and separate within the context of
nature itself and cannot supersede their individuality, the reality of
their unity is thus an essential being and an individual with a reality
of its own. In this perfectly individualized and realized feeling, the parents contemplate their unity as a reality; they are this feeling itself
and it is their visible identity and mediation, born from themselves.
—This is the real rationality of nature wherein the difference of the
sexes is completely extinguished, and both are absolutely one—a living substance.

($\beta\beta$) Intuition subsumed under the concept is the mediating term
in difference or this is alone the form in which the real mediating term
is, while the substance is dead matter; the mediating term as such is
[428] wholly external, according to the difference of the concept, while the
inner is pure and empty quantity. This middle term is the *tool*. Because in the tool the form or the concept is dominant, it is torn away
from the nature to which the middle term of sexual love belongs, and
lies in the ideality, as belonging to the concept, or is the absolute reality present in accordance with the essence of the concept. In the concept, identity is unfilled and empty; annihilating itself, it exhibits only
the extremes. Here annihilation is obstructed; emptiness is real and,
moreover, the extremes are fixed. In one aspect the tool is subjective,
in the power of the subject who is working; by him it is entirely determined, manufactured, and fashioned; from the other point of view
it is objectively directed on the object worked. By means of this middle term [between subject and object] the subject cancels the immediacy of annihilation; for labor, as annihilation of intuition [the particular object], is at the same time annihilation of the subject, positing in
him a negation of the merely quantitative; hand and spirit are blunted

by it, i.e., they themselves assume the nature of negativity and form-lessness, just as, on the other side (since the negative, difference, is double), labor is something downright single and subjective. In the tool the subject makes a middle term between himself and the object, and this middle term is the real rationality of labor; for the fact that work as such, and the object worked upon, are themselves means, is only a formal mediation, since that for which they exist is outside them, and so the bearing of the subject on the object is a complete separation, remaining entirely in the subject within the thinking of in-telligence. In the tool the subject severs objectivity and its own blunt-ing from itself, it sacrifices an other to annihilation and casts the sub-jective side of that on to the other. At the same time its labor ceases to be directed on something singular. In the tool the subjectivity of labor is raised to something universal. Anyone can make a similar tool and work with it. To this extent the tool is the persistent norm of labor.

On account of this rationality of the tool it stands as the middle term, higher than labor, higher than the object (fashioned for enjoy-ment, which is what is in question here), and higher than enjoyment or the end aimed at. This is why all peoples living on the natural level have honored the tool, and we find respect for the tool, and conscious-   [429] ness of this, expressed in the finest way by Homer.

(γγ) The tool is under the domination of the concept and therefore belongs to differentiated or mechanical labor; the child is the middle term as absolutely pure and simple intuition. But the totality of both [intuition and concept] must possess just this [intuitive] simplicity, yet also the ideality of the concept; or in the child the ideality of the extremes of the tool must enter its substantial essence, while for this very reason in the tool an ideality must enter [into] its dead inner be-ing, and the reality of the extremes must vanish; there must be a mid-dle term which is perfectly ideal. The absolute concept, or intelligence, is alone absolute ideality; the middle term must be intelligent, but not individual or subjective; only an infinitely vanishing and self-mani-festing appearance of that; a light and ethereal body which passes away as it is formed; not a subjective intelligence or an accident of it, but rationality itself, real but in such a way that this reality is itself ideal and infinite, in its existence immediately its own opposite, i.e., non-existence; and so an ethereal body which displays the extremes and therefore, while real according to the concept, also has its ideality, since the essence of this body is immediately to pass away, and its ap-pearance is this immediate conjunction of appearance and passing-away. Thus such a middle term is intelligent; it is subjective or in intelligent individuals, but objectively universal in its corporeality, and because of the immediacy of the nature of this being, its subjectivity is immediately objectivity. This ideal and rational middle term is *speech*, the tool of reason, the child of intelligent beings. The substance of speech is like the child—i.e., what is most indeterminate purest, most negative, most sexless, and, on account of its absolute malleability and transparency, capable of assuming every form. Its reality is completely absorbed into its ideality, and it is also individual; it has form or a reality; it is a subject aware of itself; it must therefore be distinguished from the formal concept of speech, for which [i.e., speech] objectivity itself is a [form of] speech; but this objectivity is only an abstraction, since the reality of the object is sub-[430]   jective in a way different from the way the subject is subjective. Objectivity is not itself absolute subjectivity.

The totality of speech in the form of the levels:

(i) of nature, or inner identity. This is the unconscious attitude of a body which passes away as quickly as it comes, but which is something single, having only the form of objectivity, not bearing itself in or on itself, but appearing in a reality and substance foreign to itself. *Gesture*, mien, and their totality in the glance of the eye—this is not fixed objectivity or objective in the abstract; but it is fleeting, an accident, a shifting ideal play. But this ideality is only a play in another who is its subject and substance. The play expresses itself as feeling and pertains to feeling, or it exists in the form of pure identity, of a feeling, articulated indeed, but changing, yet the play is entire in every moment, without the ideality of its objective character or its own corporeality to which nature cannot attain.

(ii) When the intuition of speech is subsumed under the concept, it has a body of its own, for its ideal nature is posited in the concept, and the body is the bearer, or what is fixed. This body is an external material thing, but one which as such is completely nullified in its substantial inwardness and self-awareness; it is ideal and without meaning. But because the concept is dominant, this body is something dead, not something that endlessly annihilates itself inwardly, but something which, being here at the stage of difference, is annihilated only externally for the dominant [concept]. Thus its doubled being is likewise an externality; it expresses nothing but the reference to the subject and the object, between which it is the ideal middle term; but this linkage is made clear by a subjective thinking outside the object. On its own account it expresses this linkage negatively, by its being annihilated as subject, or, having an explicit meaning of its own, it expresses the linkage by its inner meaninglessness, so that it is a middle term, in so far as it is a thing, something explicitly determinate, and yet not explicit to itself, not a thing, but immediately the opposite of itself—self-aware but flatly not self-aware, but being for another; and so the absolute concept is here really objective. A *corporeal sign*: this is the ideality of the tool, just as demeanor is the ideality of the child; [431] and just as to make a tool is more rational than to make a child, so a corporeal sign is more rational than a gesture.

Since the sign corresponds to the absolute concept, it does not express any shape adopted by the absolute concept that has been assumed into indifference. But because it expresses only the concept, it is bound up with what is formal and universal. Just as mien and gesture are a subjective language, so the corporeal sign is an objective one. Just as subjective speech is not torn loose from the subject and is not free, so this objective speech remains something objective and does not carry knowledge—its subjective element—in itself directly. Hence knowledge is also tacked on to the object; it is not a determinate character of the object but is only accosted by it and remains accidental to it. Precisely because the linkage is accidental, knowledge expresses in the object, but free from it, a reference to something subjective which, however, is set forth in a quite indefinite way and must first have thought added to it. Knowledge therefore expresses also the connection between the possession of an object and a subject [who possesses it].

(iii) The *spoken word* unites the objectivity of the corporeal sign with the subjectivity of gesture, the articulation of the latter with the self-awareness of the former. It is the middle term of intelligences; it is logos, their rational bond. Abstract objectivity, which is a dumb recognition, gains in it [an] independent body of its own, which exists for itself but according to the mode of the concept, and which, namely, immediately destroys itself. With the spoken word the inner directly emerges in its specific character, and in it the individual, intelligence, the absolute concept displays itself as purely single and fixed, or its specific character is the body of absolute singularity whereby all indefiniteness is articulated and established, and precisely on the strength of this body it is at once absolute recognition. The ring of metal, the murmur of water, the roaring of the wind does not proceed from within, changing from absolute subjectivity into its opposite, but arises by an impulse from without. An animal's voice comes from its inmost point, or from its conceptual being, but, like the whole animal, it be-

[432] longs to feeling. Most animals scream at the danger of death, but this
is purely and simply an outlet of subjectivity, something formal, of
which the supreme articulation in the song of the birds is not the
product of intelligence, of a preceding transformation of nature into
subjectivity. The absolute solitude in which nature dwells inwardly at
the level of intelligence is missing in the animal which has not withdrawn this solitude into itself. The animal does not produce its voice
out of the totality contained in this solitude; its voice is empty, formal,
void of totality. But the corporeality of speech displays totality resumed into individuality, the absolute entry into the absolute [mo-
nadic] point of the individual whose ideality is inwardly dispersed into
a system. —This is the supreme blossom of the first level, but treated
here not in its content but only in form as the abstraction of the supreme rationality and shape of singularity; but as this pure speech it
does not rise above singularity.

The negative side of this level is distress, natural death, the power
and havoc of nature, as well as of men reciprocally, or a relation,
though a natural one, to organic nature.

B. *Second Level: of Infinity and Ideality in Form or in Relation*

This is the subsumption of intuition under the concept, or the emergence of the ideal and the determining of the particular or the singular
by the ideal. There is causality here, but only as purely ideal, for this
level is itself a formal one;[14] the ideal is only the abstraction of the
ideal. There is not yet any question of the ideal's being constituted as
such for itself [or realized] and becoming a totality. Just as the single
individual was dominant at the first lev   so the universal is dominant
here. At the first level the universal was hidden, something inner, and
speech itself was considered there only as something singular, i.e., in
its abstraction.

In this subsumption singularity immediately ceases. It becomes
something universal which plainly has a bearing on something else.
Beyond this formal concept, however, the living natural relation becomes nevertheless a fixed relation which it was not previously; also
[433] universality must hover over this natural relation and overcome this
fixed relation. Love, the child, culture, the tool, speech are objective
and universal, and also are bearings and relations, but relations that

14. I.e., one in which the universal is still abstract and present only as ideal.

are natural, not overcome, casual, unregulated, not themselves taken up into universality. The universal has not emerged in and [out of] them themselves, nor is it opposed to them.

When this subsuming universality is looked at from the point of view of particularity, there is nothing in this level that is void of a bearing on other intelligences,[15] with the result that equality is posited among them, or it is universality which thus appears in them.

a) [*The Subsumption of the Concept under Intuition*]
This is the relation of the universal opposed to the particular as it appears in the particular, or the subsumption of the universal [the concept] under intuition. The universal, dominant itself in the singular or the particular, bears solely on this single being; or the single being is first, not the ideal hovering over it, nor a multiplicity of particulars subsumed under the ideal. The latter consists in the purely practical, real, mechanical relation of work and possession.

(i) The particular, into which the universal is transferred, therefore becomes ideal and the ideality is a partition of it. The entire object in its determinate character is not annihilated altogether, but this labor, applied to the object as an entirety, is partitioned in itself and becomes a single laboring;[16] and this single laboring becomes for this very reason more mechanical, because variety is excluded from it and so it becomes itself something more universal, more foreign to [the living] whole.[17] This sort of laboring, thus divided, presupposes at the same time that the remaining needs are provided for in another way, for this way too has to be labored on, i.e., by the labor of other men. But this deadening [characteristic] of mechanical labor directly implies the possibility of cutting onself off from it altogether;[18] for the labor here is wholly quantitative without variety, and since its subsumption in intelligence is self-cancelling, something absolutely external, a thing, can then be used owing to its self-sameness both in respect of its labor [434] and its movement. It is only a question of finding for it an equally dead principle of movement, a self-differentiating power of nature like

15. "Intelligences" means "individuals in whom a universal element has emerged."
16. I.e., the labor is divided up between many individuals.
17. This refers to the "division of labor." The machine takes the place of the individual craftsman, and what originally was the product of one individual is now so divided up that many individuals are involved. This is a remove from a living whole to a more mechanical one.
18. The labor is given to a machine instead of to an individual craftsman.

the movement of water, wind, steam, etc., and the tool passes over into the *machine*, since the restlessness of the subject, the concept, is itself posited outside the subject [in the energy source].

(ii) Just as the subject and his labor are determinate here, so the product of the labor is too. It is parcelled out and hence it is pure quantity so far as the subject is concerned. Since his quantity [of the common product] is not in a relation with the totality of [his] needs, but goes beyond them, it is quantity in general and abstractly. Thus this possession has lost its meaning for the practical feeling of the subject and is no longer a need of his, but a *surplus*;[19] its bearing on use is therefore a universal one and, this universality being conceived in its reality, the bearing is on the use of others. Because, from the point of view of the subject, the need is explicitly an abstraction of need in general, the bearing [of the surplus] on use is a general possibility of use, not just of the specific use that it expresses, since the latter is divorced from the subject.

(iii) The subject is [not] simply determined as a possessor, but is taken up into the form of universality; he is a single individual with a bearing on others and universally negative as a possessor recognized as such by others. For recognition is singular being, it is negation, in such a way that it remains fixed as such (though ideally) in others, in short the abstraction of ideality, not ideality in the others. In this respect possession is *property*; but the abstraction of universality in property is *legal right*. (It is laughable to regard everything under the form of this abstraction as legal right; right is something entirely formal, (α) infinite in its variety, and without totality, and (β) without any content in itself.) The individual is not a property owner, a rightful possessor, absolutely in and of himself. His personality or the abstraction of his unity and singularity is purely an abstraction and an *ens rationis*. Moreover it is not in individuality that law and property reside, since individuality is absolute identity or itself an abstraction; on the contrary, they reside solely in the relative identity of possession, in so far as this relative identity has the form of universality. A right to property is a right to right; property right is the aspect, the abstraction in property, according to which property is a right remaining for its other, the particular, as possession.

[435]

The *negative* of this level is the bearing of freedom as against the universal, or the negative in so far as it constitutes itself positively and

---

19. At the earlier level enjoyment followed on the satisfaction of a need. Machinery makes possible the accumulation of capital, a surplus going beyond the satisfaction of a particular individual's need.

sets itself up in difference against the universal, so that it bears on it and is not the lack and concealment of difference. In the latter undeveloped respect the preceding levels would be its negative.

The mechanical negative, i.e., what conflicts with and does not fit a particularity determined by the subject, does not belong to this context. It does not apply at all to this determinacy in so far as this is practical; on the contrary, mechanical negation is a matter belonging entirely to nature. —The negative comes into consideration here only in so far as it conflicts with the universal as such, and in so far as it, as a single individuality, gives universality the lie and abstracts from it; not when singularity really annihilates the form of the universal—for in that case the negative posits the universal as truly ideal and itself as one with it—but, on the contrary, when the negative cannot annihilate the universal or unite itself with it but is differentiated from it.[20] —The negative thus consists in the nonrecognition of property, in its cancellation. But property itself is here posited as not necessary, not tied to the use and enjoyment of the subject. The matter [owned], so far as posited here as something universal, is itself therefore posited as something negative. The subject's tie with it is itself determined as merely a possible one. Thus negation can affect merely this form, or not the matter itself but only the matter as universal [quantity]. A surplus, i.e., what already has no explicit bearing on need, is cancelled. As a surplus its destiny is to pass out of [the producer's] possession. Whether this supersession, this negation, is or is not compatible with this destiny must emerge from the following level.

b) *The Subsumption of Intuition under the Concept*   [436]
A relation is established between the subject and his surplus labor; the bearing of this labor for him is ideal, i.e., it has no real bearing on [his own] enjoyment. But at the same time this bearing has emerged as something universal or infinite, or as a pure abstraction—possession in law as property. But what is possessed here has by its nature a real bearing on the subject [on his enjoyment] only when it is annihilated [consumed], and the previously ideal tie of possession by the

20. Hegel excludes two sorts of negation from consideration here: (a) the mechanical negative, e.g., when an "act of God" or some natural process like fire destroys property; (b) either the moral negation involved in theft, or the speculative negative, when individuality annihilates the abstract form of the universal and embodies it, e.g., when property is destroyed by fire-fighters to prevent the fire from spreading. This leaves alienation of ownership as the sort of negation in question here.

subject is now to become a real one. The infinite, i.e., legal right, as the positive element in this whole level, is something fixed and is to persist; the ideal tie of possession is to persist too and yet it is to be made real. This whole level is in general the level of difference, and the present dimension [of this level] is likewise difference, and so the difference of difference—previously difference at rest, here in movement. Difference is implied [in] the concept, i.e., the relation of a subject to something characterized as merely possible. Owing to the new difference, the relation of the subject to his labor is superseded, but because infinity, i.e., legal right as such, must remain, there appears instead of that ideal connection with the surplus [possession] its conceptual opposite, the real connection with use and need. The separation is starker, but for that very reason the urge for unification [is stronger too], just as the magnet holds its poles apart, without any urge of their own to unity, but, when the magnet is severed, their identity being cancelled, [we have] electricity, a starker separation, real antithesis, and an urge for unification.[21] What is cancelled here is oneness with the object through one's own labor, or the individual special characteristic of it [as "mine"] (magnetism [in the proposed analogy]). What is substituted is real difference, cancellation of the identity of subject and object; and therefore a real annihilation of the opposite or a difference which has a bearing on need. —In this whole level, both (a) and (b), thoroughgoing ideality first begins, as well as the true levels of practical intelligence; with surplus labor this intelligence ceases even in need and labor to belong to need and labor. The relation to an object which this intelligence acquires for need and use, and which is posited here, namely, the fact that intelligence has not worked up the object for its own use since it has not consumed its own labor on it, is the beginning of legal, and formally ethical, enjoyment and possession.

[437]

What is absolute and ineradicable in this level is the absolute concept, the infinite itself, legal right at rest in (a), or subsisting in its opposition and therefore inwardly concealed and hidden; and, in (b), legal right in motion, one accident being cancelled by another, passing through nothingness, so that legal right emerges and stands over against [the accidents] as causality.

21. Hegel is here employing the "dynamic series" in Schelling's philosophy of Nature for purposes of analogy. Since this was the direct parallel in the real series to human action in the ideal series (see the table in the Introductory Essay on p. 00), this is not surprising. The reader should compare also the lectures on the *Philosophy of Nature* (324, Addition) where Hegel remarks that Schelling called electricity "a fractured magnetism."

This pure infinity of legal right, its inseparability, reflected in the thing, i.e., in the particular itself, is the thing's equality with other things, and the abstraction of this equality of one thing with another, concrete unity and legal right, is *value*; or rather value is itself equality as abstraction, the ideal measure [of things]—but the actually found and empirical measure is the *price*.

In the supersession of the individual tie [of possession], there remains (α) legal right, (β) the same appearing in something specific in the form of equality, or value; (γ) but the individually tied object loses its tie and (∂) there enters in its stead something really determinate linked to [the individual's] desire.

[α] The inner essence of this real exchange is, as has been shown, the concept that remains the same [throughout], but is real in intelligences, more precisely in needy intelligences, beings who are concerned with both a surplus and an unsatisfied need at the same time. Each of them enters upon the transformation of the individual thing with which he is linked ideally and objectively [as its legal owner] into something that is subjectively linked with his need. This is *exchange*, the realization of the ideal relation. Property enters reality through the plurality of persons involved in exchange and mutually recognizing one another.[22] Value enters in the reality of things and applies to each of them as surplus; the concept enters as self-moving, annihilating itself in its opposite, taking on the opposite character in place of the one it possessed before, and indeed so determined that what was formerly ideal now enters as real, because the first level is that of intuition, the present one that of the concept; the former is ideal, the latter naturally prior, [but] the ideal in practice comes before enjoyment.

[β] Externally exchange is twofold, or rather a repetition of itself, for the universal object, the surplus, and then the particular element in need is materially an object, but its two forms are necessarily a repetition of it. But the concept or essence [of exchange] is the transformation itself, and since the absolute character of the transformation is the identity of the opposite, this raises the question of how this pure identity, infinity, is to be displayed as such in reality.   [438]

The transition in the exchange is a manifold, divided, externally

22. Value and price are being regarded as universal and equal for everyone. An equal and fixed price is a necessary presupposition of exchange between individuals. Law is passive or at rest in value and price, but it comes into movement in exchange. In economics Hegel usually followed, first Sir James Steuart, and later Adam Smith. Here his intention is to move from abstract to concrete, from equality or sameness to a synthesis of differences.

connected series of the single moments of the whole transaction. It may take place in one moment, in a single present instant, by the transfer of the possessions of both parties from one to the other. But if the object is manifold, the transition is likewise manifold, and the desired *quid pro quo* is something manifold, and the opposite *quid pro quo* is not there until it is complete; it is not there at the start or in the continuation, except as only an advance.[23] Therefore exchange is itself something uncertain because of these empirical circumstances, which appear as the gradualness of the execution of the exchange, the postponement of the whole execution to a later date, etc.; the present moment does not appear here. The fact that the *execution* of the transaction is something inner and presupposes sincerity is something entirely formal, for the point about it is that the exchange has not happened. The transaction and transfer has not become a reality, and the uncertainty depends on the manifold aspects [of the transaction], on their dispersal, and on the possibility of abstraction [i.e., withdrawal] from it or of freedom.

(The third moment of this second level (b))

(γ) This irrationality or the antithesis between (i) this empty possibility and freedom and (ii) actuality and what appears, must be superseded, or the inner [intentions] of the intelligent agents who are making the exchange must emerge. This freedom must become equivalent to necessity, so that the transaction is deprived of its empirical contingenc[ies], and the middle term of the transition, i.e., identity, is established as something necessary and firm. The nature and form of the exchange remains, but the exchange is taken up into quantity and universality.

This transformation of exchange is *contract*. In it the absolutely present moment in a pure exchange is formed into a rational middle term which not only admits the empirical phenomena in exchange but, in order to be a totality, demands them as a necessary difference which is undifferentiated in a contract.

Owing to the necessity acquired by the transition in a contract, the empirical aspect, the fact that the two sides of the bargain are fulfilled separately at different times, becomes unimportant—it is something accidental which does no harm to the security of the whole. It is as

[439]

---

23. Two people may make an exchange on the spot. But if the transaction is a complicated one, e.g., involving cargoes of goods, the exchange will take time and the *quid pro quo*, e.g., payment for the goods, will not be there until the whole transaction is at an end, unless some advance is made by agreement a jump ahead of the due date.

good as if the bargain had already been carried out. The right of each singular party to his property is already transferred to the other and the transfer itself is regarded as having happened. The outwardly apparent fact that the transaction has not yet been executed, that the transfer has not yet been empirically carried out in reality, is wholly empirical and accidental; or rather it has been nullified, so that the property has been entirely deprived of the external tie whereby it is not only marked as a possession but is still in the possession of the one who has already transferred it.

[∂] Thus since contract transforms the transfer from a real one into an ideal one, but in such a way that this ideal transfer is the true and necessary one, it follows that in order to be this it must itself have absolute reality. The ideality or universality which the present moment acquires must thus exist, but reality itself transcends the sphere of this formal level. This much results formally, that ideality as such, and also as reality in general, can be nothing other than a spirit which, displaying itself as existing, and wherein the contracting parties are nullified as single individuals, is the universal subsuming them, the absolutely objective essence and the binding middle term of the contract. Owing to the absolute oneness in the contract, freedom and possibility are superseded with respect to the members of the transfer. This oneness is not something inner like fidelity and faith, in which inner being the individual subsumes identity under himself; on the contrary, in face of the absolutely universal, the individual is what is subsumed. Thus his caprice and idiosyncrasy are excluded because in the contract he invokes this absolute universality. But though the whole force of universality likewise enters the contract, this still happens only formally. The determinate provisions linked by that form and subsumed under it are and remain determinate provisions; they [are] only empirically infinitely posited as this or that or the other, yet they subsist. They are treated as the singular aspect of the individuals or of the things about which the contract is made. And for this reason true reality cannot fall within this level. For the aspect of reality here is an explicitly subsisting finitude which is not to be annihilated in ideality, and it follows that it is impossible for reality here to be a true and absolute one. [440]

c) [*The Level of the Indifference of (a) and (b)*]

The third level is the indifference of the preceding ones; that relation of exchange and the recognition of possession, which therefore is property and hitherto had a bearing on the single individual, here becomes a totality, but always within individuality itself; or the second relation is taken up into universality, the concept of the first.

(α) Relative identity or the relation.

The surplus set into indifference, as something universal and the possibility of [satisfying] all needs, is *money*, just as labor, which leads to a surplus, leads also, when mechanically uniform, to the possibility of universal exchange and the acquisition of all necessities. Just as money is the universal, and the abstraction of these, and mediates them all, so *trade* is this mediation posited as activity, where surplus is exchanged for surplus.

(β) But the intuition of this totality, yet of this totality as singularity, is the individual as the indifference of all specific characteristics, and this is how he displays his individuality as totality.

(i) Formally, in simplicity or intuition, the individual is the indifference of all specific characteristics and as such is in form a *living being* and is recognized as such; just as he was recognized previously only as possessing single things, so now he is recognized as existing independently in the whole. But because the individual as such is purely and simply one with [his] life, not simply related to life, it is impossible to say of life, as it could be said of other things with which he is purely in relation, that he possesses it. This has sense only in so far as the individual is not one such living thing but an absolutely entire system, so that his singularity and life are posited like a thing, as something particular. The recognition of this formal livingness [of the individual] is, like recognition and empirical intuition in general, a formal ideality. Life is the supreme indifference of the single individual, but it is also something purely formal, since it is the empty unity of individual specific characteristics, and therefore no totality and no self-reconstructing whole is posited out of difference. As what is absolutely formal, life is for this very reason absolute subjectivity or the absolute concept, and the individual, considered under this absolute abstraction, is the *person*. The life of the individual is the abstraction, pushed to its extreme, of his intuition, but the person is the pure concept of this intuition, and indeed this concept is the absolute concept itself.

In this recognition of life or in the thinking of the other as absolute concept, the other [person] exists as a free being, as the possibility of being the opposite of himself with respect to some specific characteristic. And in the single individual as such there is nothing which could not be regarded as a specific characteristic. Thus in this freedom there is just as easily posited the possibility of nonrecognition and nonfree-

[441]

dom. All things are likewise, owing to their concept, the possibility of being the opposite of themselves; but they remain in absolute determinacy or are lower levels of necessity; they are not all indifferently identical but absolutely different from one another. But intelligence or human life is the indifference of all specific characteristics.

(ii) This formal, relationless, recognition, [presented] in relation and difference or according to the concept.

At this [level] a living individual confronts a living individual, but their power (*Potenz*) of life is unequal. Thus one is might or power over the other. One is indifference, while the other is [fixed] in difference. So the former is related to the latter as cause; indifferent itself, it is the latter's life and soul or spirit. The greater strength or weakness is nothing but the fact that one of them is caught up in difference, fixed and determined in some way in which the other is not, but is free. The indifference of the one not free is his inner being, his formal aspect, not something that has become explicit and that annihilates [his] difference. Yet this indifference must be there for him; it is [442] his concealed inner life and on this account he intuits it as its opposite, namely, as something external, and the identity is a relative one, not an absolute one or a reconciliation [of internal and external]. This relation in which the indifferent and free has power over the different is the relation of *lordship and bondage* [or master and servant].

This relation is immediately and absolutely established along with the inequality of the power of life. At this point there is no question of any right or any necessary equality. Equality is nothing but an abstraction—it is the formal thought of life, of the first level, and this thought is purely ideal and without reality. In reality, on the other hand, it is the inequality of life which is established, and therefore the relation [of lordship] and bondage. For in reality what we have is shape and individuality and appearance, and consequently difference of power (*Potenz*) and might, or the relative identity where one individual is posited as indifferent and the other as different. Here plurality is the plurality of individuals, for, in the first level, absolute singularity has been posited in the formality of life, posited as the form of the inner life, since life is the form of external [identity or] absence of difference. And where there is a plurality of individuals, there is a relation between them, and this relation is lordship and bondage. Lordship and bondage is immediately the very concept of the plurality relation. There is no need for transition or conclusion here, as if some further ground or reason were still to be exhibited for it.

Lordship and bondage are therefore *natural*, because individuals confront one another in this relation; but the relation of lordship and obedience is also set up whenever individuals as such enter into [a moral] relation in connection with what is most ethical, and it is a question of the formation of the ethical order as framed by the highest individuality of genius and talent. Formally this [moral] relation is the same [as the natural one]; the difference consists in the fact that in ethical lordship and obedience the power or might is at the same time something absolutely universal, whereas here it is only something particular; in ethical lordship individuality is only something external and the form; here it is the essence of the relation and on this account there is here a relation of bondage, since bondage is obedience to the single individual and the particular.

[443]   The master [or overlord] is the indifference of the specific characteristics, but purely as a person or as a formally living being. He is also subject or cause [as opposed to object or instrument]. Indifference [or identity] is subsumed under "being the subject" or under the concept; and the bondsman is related to him as to formal indifference or the person. Because the commander is here *qua* person, it follows that the absolute, the Idea, the identity of the two is not what is posited in the master in the form of indifference and in the servant in the form of difference; on the contrary, the link between the two is particularity in general, and, in practice, need. The master is in possession of a surplus, of what is physically necessary; the servant lacks it, and indeed in such a way that the surplus and the lack of it are not single [accidental] aspects but the indifference of necessary needs.

(iii) This relation of bondage or of person to person, of formal life to formal life, where one is under the form of indifference and the other under that of difference, must be undifferentiated or subsumed under the first level, so that the same relation between persons, the dependence of one on the other, remains, but that the identity is an absolute one yet inner, not explicit, and the relation of difference is only the external form. But the identity must necessarily remain an inner one, because at this whole level it is either only a formal one (legal right) hovering over the particular and opposed to it, or an inner one, i.e., one subsumed under individuality as such, under the intuition of particularity, and so appears as nature, not as an identity subjugating a pair of antitheses or as ethical nature in which that antithetic pair has been likewise superseded, but in such a way that particularity and individuality are what has been subsumed.

This indifference of the lordship and bondage relation, an identity in which personality and the abstraction of life are absolutely one and the same, while this relation is only something *qua* apparent and external, is the [patriarchal] *family*. In it the totality of nature and all the foregoing are united; the entire foregoing particularity is transformed in the family into the universal. The family is the identity:

(α) of external needs

(β) of sex-relationship, the natural difference posited in the individuals themselves, and

(γ) of the relation of parents to children or of natural reason, [444] of reason emergent, but existing as nature.

(α) On account of the absolute and natural oneness of the husband, the wife, and the child, where there is no antithesis of person to person or of subject to object, the surplus is not the property of one of them, since their indifference is not a formal or a legal one. So too all contracts regarding property or service and the like fall away here because these things are grounded in the presupposition of private personality. Instead the surplus, labor, and property are absolutely common to all, inherently and explicitly; and on the death of one of them there is no transfer from him to a stranger; all that happens is that the deceased's participation in the common property ends.

Difference is [i.e., it has here] the superficial [aspect] of lordship. The husband is master and manager, [but] not a property owner as against the other members of the family. As manager he has only the appearance of free disposal [of the family property]. Labor too is divided according to the nature of each member of the family, but its product is common property. Precisely because of this division each member produces a surplus, but not as his own property. The transfer of the surplus is not an exchange, because the whole property is directly, inherently, and explicitly common.

(β) The sex relation between husband and wife is naturally undifferentiated. I have said in (α) that in respect of personality, i.e., as holders of property, they are definitely one. But the sex relation gives a special form to their indifference, for it is something inherently particular. When the particular as such is made into a universal or the concept, it can only become something empirically universal. (In religion things are different.) Particularity becomes persistent, enduring, and fixed. The sex relation is restricted entirely to these two individuals together, and it is established permanently as *marriage*.

Because this relation is grounded on a particular character of individuals—though its peculiarity is settled by nature and not by some capricious abstraction—this relation seems to be a contract. But it would be a negative contract which annuls just that presupposition on [445] which the possibility of contract in general rests, namely, personality or being a subject [possessing rights]. All this is nullified in marriage, because there the person gives himself [or herself] up as an entirety. But what is supposed in a contractual relation to become the property of the other could simply not come into his or her possession. Since the relation is personal, what is supposed to be transferred remains the property of the person, just as, in general, no contract is inherently possible about personal service, because only the product, and not the personality, can be transferred into the possession of the other. The slave can become property as an entire personality, and so can the wife; but this relation is not marriage. There is no contract with the slave either, but there can be a contract with someone else about the slave or the woman, e.g., among many peoples the woman is bought from the parents. But there can be no contract with her, for in so far as she is to give herself freely in marriage, she gives up, along with herself, the possibility of a contract, and so does the man. The terms of their contract would be to have no contract and so the terms would be immediately self-destructive.

But by a positive contract each party [in a marriage] would make himself [or herself] a thing in his own possession, would make his whole personality into a determinate characteristic of himself to which he is absolutely linked at the same time; yet as a free being he must not regard himself as absolutely bound up with any single characteristic of himself, but as the indifferent identity of all of them. We would have to think, as Kant does,[24] of the sexual organs as this characteristic. But tc treat one's self as an absolute *thing* (*Sache*), as absolutely bound up with a specific characteristic, is supremely irrational and utterly disgraceful.

(γ) In the child the family is deprived of its accidental and empirical existence or the singularity of its members, and is secured against the concept whereby the singulars or subjects nullify themselves. The child, contrary to appearance, is the absolute, the rationality of the relationship; he is what is enduring and everlasting, the totality which produces itself once again as such. But because in the family, as the supreme totality of which nature is capable, even absolute identity remains something inner, and is not posited in the absolute form itself, it follows that the reproduction of the totality is an appearance, i.e.,

---

24. *Metaphysik der Sitten*—Rechtslehre §§ 24–27 (*Akad.* VI, 277–80—omitted in Ladd's abridged translation).

the children. In the true totality the form is entirely one with the es- [446]
sence, and so its being is not the form driven into the separation of its
constituent features. But here what is persistent is other than what *is*;
or, reality surrenders its persistence to something else which itself endures over again only in the sense that it becomes, and transmits to
another its being, which it cannot retain itself. The form, or infinity,
is thus the empirical or negative [form] of being other, which cancels
one determinate characteristic only by positing another, and is only
really positive by being always in another. Might and the understanding, the differentiating characters of the parents, stand in an inverse
relation with the youth and force of the child, and these two aspects of
life fly from and follow one another and are external to one another.

2. THE NEGATIVE OR FREEDOM OR TRANSGRESSION

The foregoing has singularity as its principle; it is the Absolute subsumed under the Concept; all the levels express specific characteristics,
and the moments of indifference are formal; universality as opposed
to particularity is undifferentiated only in relation to lower particulars,
and these moments of indifference are themselves particulars once
again. There is thus plainly no [moment that is] absolute; any one
can be cancelled. The indifference which is the absolute totality of
each level is not inherent, but lies beneath the form [of singularity]
which is the subsuming moment.[25] The cancellation of specific characteristics must be absolute in itself, the assumption of all specific characteristics into absolute universality.

This assumption is absolute and positive, but it is also purely negative. Just as, in the foregoing, absolute form expressed itself as the
persistence of antithesis, so it expresses itself here in its opposite, or
in the nullification of antithesis.

But when this nullification is purely negative, it is dialectical, i.e., it
is cognition of ideality and the real supersession of specific character- [447]
istics. [Here] the negative is not fixed, it is not in antithesis [to the
positive], and thus it is in the Absolute. Absolute ethical life rises

25. Thus, for example, all family relations are summed up in, explained by, and
get their meaning from the infant in the cradle. "Contrary to appearances," as
Hegel puts it, the child is the way in which the Concept (of Reason) subsumes
the Absolute (of Life). But as he or she grows up, he or she passes through all
the relations that are subsumed.

above specific determinacy because the Absolute cancels the determinacy, though in such a way that the Absolute unites it with its opposite in a higher unity; thus the opposite is not left by the Absolute to persist in truth but is given a purely negative meaning; but owing to the perfect identity with its opposite, its form or ideality is cancelled by the Absolute, which precisely deprives it of its negative character and makes it absolutely positive or real.

The cancellation of the negative is quite different. It is itself cancellation of cancellation, opposition to opposition, but in such a way that ideality or form likewise persists in it though in a converse sense; i.e., cancellation maintains the ideal determinate being of singularity and so determines it as negative; thus it allows the singularity and oppositeness of determinate being to persist, and does not annul the antithesis but transforms the real form into the ideal one.

In the foregoing every level and every reality of a level is an identity of opposites, absolutely inherently. The identity is subsumed under the form, but the form is something external. The real persists; the form is what is on the surface, and its determinacy is enlivened, made indifferent; the real is indeed something determinate, but it is not determinate for itself; the real is not determined, and its essence is not posited, as determinate. But now the form, as negative, is the essence. The real becomes posited as something ideal; it is determined by pure freedom.

This is the same transformation that occurs when sensation is posited as thinking. The specific characteristic remains the same; red as sensed remains red as thought, but the thought is determined at the same time as something nullified, cancelled, and negative. The freedom of intelligence has raised the specific character of the sensation of red to universality; it has not deprived the sensation of its opposition to other determinate sensations, but has only made the false attempt to do that. It has reflected on the sensation, raised it to infinity, but in such a way that finitude remains definitely persistent. It has transformed the objective reality of time and space into a subjective one. Objective ideality is "being other," i.e., having other [colors] around it; quite simply and in every respect ideality and infinity are posited empirically as something everywhere "other." Subjective ideality cleanses infinity of this multiplicity, gives to it the form of unity, binds the specific character itself together with the infinity which lies objectively outside it and is manifested as "being other," and in this way makes infinity into a unity as the absolute determinacy of the subjective or ideal as opposed to the real. And while the

[448]

determinacy as real, as sensation, had the form, infinity, as it were on the surface outside it, it is now bound up with it.

Similarly in the practical sphere what in and by itself is negative is a determinacy posited by the same moment of negation according to the preceding level of necessity; it is itself something objective, ideal, and universal. The negation of this practical positing is the restoration of the first original particularity of the antithesis. Because the former objectivity is superseded, the practical sphere falls under the control of the inorganic and objective levels. Murder does away with the living thing as an individual or subject, but ethical life does this too. But ethical life does away with subjectivity or with the ideal specific character of the subject, whereas murder does away with his objective existence; it makes him something negative and particular which falls back under the control of the objective world from which he had torn himself free by being something objective himself. Absolute ethical life directly cancels the individual's subjectivity by nullifying it only as an ideal determinacy, as an antithesis, but it lets his subjective essence persist quite unaffected. And he is allowed to persist, and is made real, as subject precisely because his essence is left undisturbed as it is. In ethical life intelligence remains a subjectivity of this kind.

This negative, or pure freedom, leads to the cancelling of the objective in such a way that the negative makes the ideal specific determinacy, which in the sphere of necessity is only external and superficial, into the essence.[26] Thus it negates reality in its specific determinacy, but it fixes this negation.

But against this negation there must be a reaction. Since the cancellation of the specific determinacy is only formal, determinacy [as such] persists. It is posited ideally, but remains in its real specific character. And in it life is only injured, not elevated [to a higher level], and therefore must be restored. But in its actuality an injury of life cannot be restored (restoration by religion does not affect actuality);   [449] but the restoration here does affect actuality, and this reconstruction

26. This sentence is a crux. The text reads: "Dieses Negative oder die reine Freiheit geht also auf die Aufhebung des Objektiven so, daß es die ideelle, in der Notwendigkeit nur äusserliche oberflächliche Bestimmtheit, das Negative zum Wesen macht, also die Realität in ihrer Bestimmtheit negiert, aber diese Negation fixiert." Our rendering takes "das Negative" as a nominative specifying the referent of "es." It can be taken as an accusative (a second object which "Dieses Negative . . . macht zum Wesen"). In that case the translation should be augmented. Our second sentence should read: "It makes itself into the essence; thus it negates reality etc." The sense does not appear to be materially affected.

can only be a formal one, because it affects actuality as such and the fixedness of negation. It is therefore external equality; the negating [subject] makes himself a cause and posits himself as negative indifference, but therefore the proposition must be converted upon him [who was the subject of it] and he must be posited under the same characteristic of the indifference as he posited. What he negated is to be equally really negated in him, and he has to be subsumed just as he subsumes. And this conversion of the relation is absolute, for in what is determinate it is only possible for Reason to assert itself as indifference, and so in a formal mode, by positing the two opposites symmetrically.

There is an absolute link between *crime* [or transgression] and the *justice of revenge*. They are bound together by absolute necessity, for one is the opposite of the other, the one is the opposite subsumption of the other. As negative life, as the concept constituting itself into intuition, transgression subsumes the universal, the objective, and the ideal; conversely, as universal and objective, avenging justice subsumes again the negation which is constituting itself as intuition.

It must be noticed here that what is in question is the real reaction or reversal, and that the ideal, immediate, reversal according to the abstract necessity of the concept is included in general, but in this form of ideality it is only an abstraction and something incomplete. This ideal reversal is *conscience* and it is only something inner, not inner and outer simultaneously; it is something subjective but not objective at the same time. The criminal has directly injured something he regards as external and foreign to himself, but in doing so he has ideally injured and cancelled himself. Inasmuch as the external deed is at the same time an inner one, the transgression committed against a stranger has likewise been committed against himself. But the consciousness of this his own destruction is a subjective and inner one, or a bad conscience. It is to that extent incomplete and must also manifest itself externally as avenging justice. Because it is something inner and incomplete, it presses on to a totality. It betrays itself, reveals [450] itself, and works of itself until it sees the ideal reaction or reversal confronting it and threatening its reality from without and as its enemy. Next it begins to be satisfied because it descries the beginning of its own reality in its enemy. It produces an attack on itself so as to be able to defend itself, and through its resistance to the attack it is at peace by defending against the threatened negation the most universal demand, that of indifference and totality, i.e., life, of which the conscience is one specific characteristic. [But] through victory in this set battle the same pang of conscience returns, and conscience is reconciled only in the danger of death and ceases [only] in that danger. But with the coming of every victory the fear becomes greater, the fear which is an ideal state of annihilation. It presses on the force of life and so brings with it weakness and also the reality of avenging justice. And it engenders this justice [even] when the enemy does not at once appear externally and when the conversion of the subsumption is not present as a reality.

(a)

The first level of this thus determined negation is the formal one in accordance with the subsumption of concept under intuition. Annihilation by itself, apart from being related to something else, presupposes a specific deficiency, but a completely indeterminate and general one, affecting nothing individual but directed rather against the abstraction of culture as such.[27] This is *natural annihilation* or purposeless destruction and havoc. Nature is thus turned against the culture imparted to it by intelligence, as well as against its own production of the organic. And just as the element [the forces of unconscious life], the objective, is subsumed under intuition and life, so the element in return subsumes under itself, and destroys, what is organic and individualized; and this destruction is havoc. Thus culture alternates with destruction in human history. When culture has demolished inorganic nature long enough and has given determinacy in every respect to its formlessness, then the crushed indeterminacy bursts loose, and the barbarism of destruction falls on culture, carries it away, and makes everything level, free, and equal. In its greatest magnificence, havoc occurs in the East, and a Genghiz Khan and a Tamerlane, as the [451] brooms of God, sweep whole regions of the world completely clean. The northern barbarians who continually invaded the south belong to the level of understanding; their miserable enjoyment, which they have developed into [at least] a narrow range of culture has therefore a specific character, and their havoc is not mere havoc for the sake of

27. The context implies that the hostility is directed against culture and all its aspects and products generally. Hegel's specific references show that the "inorganic element" here is the *vital* forces of *human* nature that have not been *organized* by reason. He habitually uses the contrast between organic and inorganic in a contextually relative way, just as Aristotle does with the contrast between form and matter.

havoc. The fanaticism of havoc, being absolutely elemental and assuming the form of nature, cannot be conquered from outside, for difference and specific character succumb before indifference and indefiniteness. But, like negation in general, it has its own negation in itself. The formless drives itself on towards indeterminacy until, because it is not after all absolutely formless, it bursts, just as an expanding bubble of water bursts into unnumerable tiny drops; it departs from its pure unity into its opposite, i.e., the absolute formlessness of absolute multiplicity, and therefore becomes a completely formal form or absolute particularity and therefore the maximum of weakness. This advance from havoc to absolute havoc and hence to the absolute transition into its opposite is *fury* [or *mania*]; since havoc is wholly within the concept, mania must intensify purity, the very opposite of havoc, *ad infinitum*, until that opposite becomes opposed to itself and so has annihilated itself. Standing at the extreme, i.e., at absolute abstraction, mania is the absolute and unmediated urge, the absolute concept in its complete indeterminacy, the restlessness of the absolute concept's infinity. This restlessness is nothing but this [extreme], and in its annihilation of the opposites by one another, it annihilates itself, and so is the real being of absolute subjectivity. The absolute concept, the immediate opposite of itself, is real because what it produces is by no means an identity of subject and object, but pure objectivity or formlessness.

(b)

This havoc, subsumed under the concept, is, as a relation involving difference and specific determinacy, directly turned against the positive relation of difference. The havoc of nature, so far as it is specifi-
[452] cally determined, can only tear possession away [from him who has it]; the presupposition is that havoc is in precisely the same characteristic position as what confronts it, and thus it lets this position persist; the indifferent moment of possession, the aspect of legal right, does not concern it; it only affects the particular situation. But ethical life, owing to its nature as intelligence, is at the same time objective and universal, and so in an identical relation with an "other"; the nullifying of a particular character of the other—and no other nullifying act is relevant here except one directed at an ethical being—is at the same time the nullification of indifference and the positing of it as something negative; the positive aspect of this positing lies in the fact

that the specific thing remains as such and is only posited with a negative specification. Such letting the specific characteristic persist, though
along with the nullifying of the indifference of recognition, is an infringement of the law. As a phenomenon, i.e., as a real nullifying of
recognition, this infringement is also the cutting of the tie between the
specific thing and the individual subject. For recognition recognizes
precisely this tie (in itself purely an ideal one) as a real one; owing to
recognition, it is a matter of indifference whether the subject has absolutely and inseparably united this specific thing with himself or whether its connection with him is only relative and this unification is put
only formally as a possibility. By recognition the relative connection
itself becomes indifferent and its subjectivity also objective. The real
cancellation of recognition cancels that tie too and is *deprivation*, or,
when it purely affects the tied object, *theft*. In this tie between the
object and the subject, which is what property means, the nullification
of the [moment of] indifference or legal right makes no difference to
the specific thing, which remains unaffected; the object stolen remains
what it is, but the subject does not, for here, in the particular case, he
is the indifference of the connection. Now in so far as it is not the abstraction of his tie with the object which is cancelled [as in voluntary
alienation], but he himself who is injured in respect of that tie, something is cancelled in him—and what is cancelled in him is not the dim-
inution of his possessions, for that does not affect him as a subject;
on the contrary it is the destruction of his [being] as indifference by
and in this single act. Now since the indifference of specific characteristics is the *person* and this personality is injured here, the dimunition
of his property is a personal injury, and this is necessarily so throughout this whole level of particularity. For the injury is directly nonper-   [453]
sonal if it is only the abstraction of the subject's tie with the object
that is infringed; but at this level this abstraction is not made as such;
it does not yet have its reality and support in something itself universal [i.e., a legal system], but solely in the particularity of the person.
And therefore every deprivation is personal. The tie here is personal,
as it is elsewhere only when it is a real or empirical one; the possessor
has the object he possesses directly before his eyes, or he holds it, or
has made it secure in some other way in his premises,which is how he
regards the space he occupies along with his possessions. This empirical connection, as a specific type, is here the type prevailing at this
level generally, for at this level there is still no suggestion of any way
whereby the empirical connection itself could be indifferenced and
property protected without it, i.e., a way in which the ideal connection

could be real without being empirical, so that personal integrity would not be infringed by the infringement of the ideal tie of possession *qua* property.

Consequently theft is both personal and a deprivation; and the subsumption of a possession, which is a property, under the desire of someone else (or the negation of indifference, and the assertion of a quantitatively greater particularity against a quantitatively lesser one, of the subsumption of the more different under the lesser) is might, not in general, but against property, or robbery must have its reaction or the converse subsumption. Just as there is subjugation here, i.e., the lesser might is subsumed under the greater, so conversely what is momentarily the greater might must be posited as the lesser. And in accordance with absolute Reason this reversal is just as absolutely necessary as the former subsumption is actually robbery. But robbery exists only where the relation of lordship and bondage does not. But where this relation exists, where an individual is more indifferent, where thus the higher level is there as the other one, then there is naturally no robbery except in so far as robbery is pure and simple havoc and destruction, not in so far as if it were robbery proper. Therefore, because robbery becomes personal, person tries conclusions with person and the one subjugated becomes the bondslave of the other; and this entry to bondage is strictly the appearance of that relation which, in this relation of subsumption, accrues to each of the individuals; they cannot be beside one another without being connected. Robbery is the singular subsumption, not affecting the totality of the personality, and consequently the [individual] who makes this personal injury a matter of his entire personality must get the upper hand, and make the conversion real, because he posits himself as a totality while the other [the robber] posits himself as particularity only, and the reality of this relation is subjection, but the phenomenon of its coming-to-be is *subjugation*.

[454]

In the foregoing relation [havoc] the reversal is absolutely annihilating, because annihilation itself is absolute, and so the reaction, like the treatment of an animal on the rampage, is absolute subjugation or death. But in this relation the reaction cannot be simply the recovery of what was stolen, on account of the personal character of the injury, but instead is only the moment of an establishment of lordship and bondage—the fact that being subsumed is real in the robber only for a moment and only in the determinate respect that corresponds with the determinate character of the personal injury that arose from his act ["an eye for an eye," etc.]. But precisely because the assailant has not put his whole personality into his attack, the relation too cannot end with the totality of the personality in a subjecting relation, but can only exist for a moment. It is only through warfare that there is occasion for bondage, a war between men, a case of mutually self-recognizing personality, or of necessity in respect of life as a whole— but otherwise men are slaves by nature. But except in war, the reaction [to injury] is formally the entirety of this relation, [like] adoption into the family, but materially it is equally single and particular. For the robber is too bad to be a slave, for he has not justified any trust in his own entire personality, since he has remained on the level of particularity.[28]

(c)

The indifference or totality of both these negations affects the indifference of specific determinations, or life, and the whole personality; and the reversal (which is established equivocally and is not one-sided as it would be if the relation were quite definitely and certainly on one side) is likewise the loss of personality through slavery or death. Because the negation can only be one specific determinacy, this determinacy (the whole being out of the question) must be intensified into a whole. But because it is personal, it is immediately the whole, for the specific determinacy belongs to the person who is the indifference of the whole. And a particularity of a person, once denied, is only an abstraction, for in the person it is absolutely taken up into indifference. Denial here is an injury to life. But because this indifference has over against it the abstraction of the injured particularity, through the latter the former is posited ideally too, and what is injured is *honor*. Through honor the singular detail becomes something personal and a whole, and what is seemingly only the denial of a detail is an injury of the whole, and thus there arises the battle of one whole person

[455]

28. Hegel seems to want to distinguish three cases: (a) natural slavery, where the pressure of natural necessity leads a man to accept bondage on condition that his "necessary desires" are satisfied from the surplus of the family to which he is bonded. (b) Subjection of a surrendered enemy, where trust is founded on the fact that each side knows how far the other is prepared to go if injury arises—so the *whole* relation of lordship and bondage can be *materially* realized. (c) Retribution for injury where the *lex talionis* is accepted by the offender. His acceptance of it makes the material realization of the *whole* relation unjust—but also imprudent, for if he is willing to pay the penalty without a death struggle, we can expect him to offend again.

against another whole person. There can be no question of the justice of the occasion for such a battle; when the battle as such starts, justice lies on both [sides], for what is established is the equality of peril, the peril of perfect freedom indeed, because the whole [personality of both] is at issue. The occasion, i.e., the specific point which is posited as taken up into indifference and as personal, is strictly nothing in itself, precisely because it is only a personal matter. Anything can be posited as such in innumerable ways; nothing can be excluded and no limit can be set. Might, or rather might individualized as strength, decides who dominates; and here, where the entire real personality is the subject, the relation of lordship and bondage must enter immediately. Alternatively, if absolute equality, the impossibility of such a relation between differents, is presupposed, and so the impossibility of one being the indifferent and the other the different, then in battle, as absolute difference and reciprocal negation, indifference is to be maintained, and the strife is to be assuaged solely by death, in which subjugation is absolute, and precisely through the absoluteness of the negation the downright opposite of this absoluteness, freedom, is upheld.

But it is a different thing when there is inequality in the negation and one-sidedness in the battle, which in that event is no battle. This inequality, where domination is purely on one side—not swaying from one to the other—and where the centre is set as possibility and therefore the indifferent possibility of either, is *oppression* and, when it proceeds to absolute negation, murder. Oppression and murder are not to be confused with battle and the relation of mastery. Genuine and unrighteous oppression is a personal attack and injury in a manner whereby all battle is simply cancelled. It is impossible for a person attacked to foresee the attack and thereby start a battle. But in itself this impossibility cannot be proved and demonstrated—the Italians advance as a reason for the lawfulness of assassination the immediacy of a declaration of war resulting from the offense—only in that event the impossibility is to be regarded as actually present when no offense is present and the murder is committed not at all on personal grounds but for the sake of robbery. But even if an offense has preceded, so that personality and the whole [individual] is in question, the offense is wholly unlike total negation on the side of reality; honor indeed has been injured, but honor is distinguishable from life. And since life is brought into play in order to restore to honor its reality, which as injured honor is only ideal, the linking of the ideality of honor with its reality is achieved only by raising to full reality the specific aspect injured; and honor consists in this, that when once one specific aspect

[456]

is negated, then life, or the totality of specific aspects, is to be affected too. Thus the man's own life must be brought in question as the means whereby alone that negation of a single detail is made into a whole as it should be. (*margin*: 3 levels: (a) murder, (b) revenge, (c) duel. The centre is battle, swinging to and fro. Duel, personal injury on some singular point).

This totality of negation must be conceived under its three forms:

($\alpha\alpha$) Crude totality, the absolute indifference of negation without relation and ideality, is the transformation of specific determinacy into personality, and the immediate establishing of the reality of the negation or [in other words] *murder* simply. Murder precludes the recognition of this relation, the other's knowing about this relation, and prevents equality of peril from preceding; moreover the injury is materially wholly unequal.[29]

($\beta\beta$) The second level must be the formal indifference in accordance with which domination and its reversal occur according to the law of equality, but in such a way that the equality as form, as consciousness, hovers over the opposition of the individuals, is not a consciousness and recognition of the opposition. Thus the form of equality is missing along with the equality of peril, for peril is nothing but the approach of negation; yet the knowledge of the negation, the indifference, is here not in the peril but is purely material; the relation is subsumed under the concept. The true and real reversal of the subsumption lies in this equality and is *revenge*. What has been killed must itself make the reversal, but as killed [it] is purely something ideal. Out of its life, which is its blood, only its spirit can rise in revenge. *Either* this spirit can so long pursue the murderer until, in whatever way, he sets a reality over against himself and himself creates a body for the spirit of the man he has slain, a body which, being no longer the same external appearance of the man slain, appears as something more generally universal, and the spirit wreaks its revenge in the form of fate. *Or*, however, the real life properly belonging to the spirit has remained; the spirit has preserved its body and the murder has destroyed only one single member or organ of the whole, and so this still living body, i.e., the family, takes on itself the work of revenge. Revenge is the absolute relation against murder and the individual murderer; it is simply the reverse of what the murderer has done; what he has done can in no other way be superseded and made rational. Nothing can be abstracted from it, for it has been established as an actuality which as

[457]

---

29. What the victim suffers is far greater than what the murderer suffered through the initial injury.

such must have its right, i.e., Reason demands that the opposite of the situation created shall be created. The specific character of the relation remains, but within that character the relation is now transformed into the opposite one; what dominates is dominated. The only thing altered is the form.

(γγ) The totality of this relation is what is rational and it makes the middle term emerge. The indifference of the justice which lies in revenge, but as something material and external, enters the individuals as a like consciousness of the emerging negation, and therefore the [458] reality of this emergence is alike too [on both sides]. Consequently an injustice seems to prevail, since the man who made the attack, the first unequal and one-sided domination (and both the opposed dominations must appear and display themselves as following on one another), should be in the wrong, but, owing to consciousness, would simply come into an equality of peril. When revenge is in question, undoubtedly only the man who was the murderer must be dominated in turn in some sure way, and the avengers thus escape from the equality of strength and they wreak revenge either by a superiority of might or by cunning, i.e., by the evasion of strength as such. But here in the totality of the relation, things are different, i.e., it directly excludes singleness in such a way that for revenge the avenger is not a stranger or even only a single individual, nor is the assailant, but the member of a family and so not an abstraction. But since this is the case, murder is not an absolute negation; the spirit has lost only one member of its body, and neither can revenge be an absolute negation. In the totality of revenge the form must be put as absolute consciousness, and so the injured party himself, and no stranger, must be the avenger—and this is only the family. Similarly the injurer is not a single individual; it is not as single individual but as the member of a whole that he has done injury; in the totality [of revenge] he is not posited as an abstraction. In this way the middle term is directly posited at the same time, i.e., negatively as the cancelling of the superiority and lack of consciousness in the one, and equality of peril for both, i.e., *battle*. Given perfect outward equality, the difference for the relation is in the inner life (and therefore the battle is a divine judgment): one side is only defending itself, the other side also attacking. Right is on the side that has been injured, or this side is the indifferent and dominant one. This it is absolutely because absolute equality must be displayed by the reversal and the side dominated was before now the one dominating. But with the magnitude of the still living body the loss of the lost member is diminished, and therefore also the right, and the right or indifference

becomes honor and therefore equal on both sides, because the particularity of the injured party's action is made into the indifference of the
whole, into an affair of the whole. Through honor the bad conscience, [459]
the urge to self-destruction, is cancelled, for honor is the urge to dominate. And the injured party who utterly repudiates the singularity of
the deed (which as this singular event is not his own) is given by hon-
or exactly the same right as, in an isolated case of personal injury, the
injured party has, because he is protecting his life. This equality [of
rights], in the face of which the aspect of legal right and necessary
subsuming [or subjection] vanishes, is *war*.[30] In war the difference of
the relation of subsuming has vanished, and equality is what rules.
Both parties are identical; their difference is what is external and formal in the battle [i.e., they are on different sides], not what is internal,
but something absolutely restless continually swaying to and fro (Mars
flits from side to side), and which [side] will be subsumed [or con-
quered] is entirely doubtful and has to be decided. *Either* a decision is
reached by the complete defeat of one party[31]—and since as a totality
it is itself immortal, this means not that it is extirpated but that it is
subjugated and enslaved. In this case it is a higher principle, not the
trivial question of the original injury that is decisive, but the greater or
lesser strength of the totality which submits in battle to that equality,
and the test of it—an equality which was previously something merely
ideal, and existed only in thought, while the parties lived side by side
without connection. The question as to which of the totalities is truly
more indifferent or stronger is submitted to the decision of battle,
which may thus end with the [establishment of a] relationship of mastery. —*Or* there may be no absolute decision which would affect the
entirety of the total individuals [i.e., families or clans]; on the contrary
they find that they are more or less equal and, at least for the experienced moment, incapable, even in the case of an obvious superiority
of one party, of carrying out to a finish the real constitution of the
relationship. The abstract preponderance of one party would indeed
be there, but not its reality at this moment of battle, since the force of
this preponderance is necessarily devoted, not to the battle, but to
other natural necessities not affecting the battle directly but the inner

30. Legal right requires that an offender should be punished (this is the "necessary subsuming"). But ordeal by battle takes no account of who committed the
offense—this difference (the relation of the parties as injuring and injured) disappears.
31. I.e., one tribal family as subjected to the other when its champions are de-
feated; the warriors may be killed, but the family does not perish.

stability of the totality. Animus ($\theta\nu\mu\sigma$) diminishes, because it is the feeling of the unrealized relation of the indifference of the dominating party. It reverts to the feeling of equality, since the reality of the battle contradicts this fancied superiority of animus. And so a *peace* is made in which—whether one side acquires the position of victor and the other that of being vanquished and surrendering some specific things or whether both give up the struggle with a sense of their complete equality—both parties put themselves into the previous position of difference from one another, difference without connection or relation, and thus with the cessation of their connection all interest ceases too. Hence the rationality of this totality is, in the antitheses, the equality of indifference, while the middle term [between the opposites] is their unity in their complete confusion and uncertainty.

[460]

3. ETHICAL LIFE

The foregoing levels incorporate the totality of particularity in both its aspects, particularity as such and universality as an abstract unity. The former is the family, but it is a totality such that, while in it all the levels of nature are united, intuition is at the same time involved in a relation. The really objective intuition of one individual in another is afflicted with a difference; the intuition [of the father] in the wife, the child, and the servant is not an absolutely perfect equality; equality remains inward, unspoken, still unborn; there is an invincible aspect of involvement in nature in it.[32] In universality, however, freedom from relation, the cancellation of one side of the relation by the other, is what matters most, and the cancellation is only rational as the absolute concept, in so far as it proceeds to this negativity.

But at none [of the previous levels] does absolute nature occur in a spiritual shape; and for this reason it is also not present as ethical life; not even the family, far less still the subordinate levels, least of all the negative, is ethical. Ethical life must be the absolute identity of intelligence, with complete annihilation of the particularity and relative identity which is all that the natural relation is capable of; or the absolute identity of nature must be taken up into the unity of the absolute concept and be present in the form of this unity, a clear and also

---

32. I.e., ethical individuality remains physically "comprehended" in nature, and so conceptual comprehension can only be in the context of physical nature.

absolutely rich being, an imperfect self-objectification and intuition of
the individual in the alien individual, and so the supersession of natural determinacy and formation, complete indifference of self-enjoy-   [461]
ment. Only in this way is the infinite concept strictly one with the
essence of the individual, and he is present in his form as true intelligence. He is truly infinite, for all his specific determinacy is annulled,
and his objectivity is not apprehended by an artificial independent
consciousness, nor yet by an intellectual intuition in which empirical
intuition is superseded. Intellectual intuition is alone realized by and
in ethical life; the eyes of the spirit and the eyes of the body completely coincide. In the course of nature the husband sees flesh of his flesh
in the wife, but in ethical life alone does he see the spirit of his spirit
in and through the ethical order.

Accordingly ethical life is characterized by the fact that the living
individual, as life, is equal with the absolute concept, that his empirical
consciousness is one with the absolute consciousness and the latter is
itself empirical consciousness, i.e., an intuition distinguishable from
itself, but in such a way that this distinction is throughout something
superficial and ideal, and subjective being is null in reality and in this
distinction. This complete equalization is only possible through intelligence or the absolute concept, in accordance with which the living
being is made the opposite of itself, i.e., an object, and this object itself is made absolute life and the absolute identity of the one and the
many, not put like every other empirical intuition under a relation,
made the servant of necessity, and posited as something restricted,
with infinity outside itself.

Thus in ethical life the individual exists in an eternal mode; his
empirical being and doing is something downright universal; for it is
not his individual aspect which acts but the universal absolute spirit
in him. Philosophy's view of the world and necessity, according to
which all things are in God and there is nothing singular, is perfectly
realized in the eyes of the empirical consciousness, since that singularity of action or thought or being has its essence and meaning simply
and solely in the whole. In so far as the ground of the singular is
thought out, it is purely and simply this whole that is thought, and the
individual does not know or imagine anything else. The empirical consciousness which is not ethical consists in inserting into the unity of
universal and particular, where the former is the ground, some other   [462]
singular thing between them as the ground. Here [in ethical life], on
the other hand, absolute identity, which previously was natural and
something inner, has emerged into consciousness.

But the intuition [individualization] of this Idea of ethical life, the form in which it appears in its particular aspect, is the *people*. The identity of this intuition with the Idea must be understood—viz., in the people the connection of a mass of individuals with one another is established generally and formally. A people is not a disconnected mass, nor a mere plurality. Not the *former*: a mass as such does not establish the connection present in ethical life, i.e., the domination of all by a universal which would have reality in their eyes, be one with them, and have dominion and power over them, and, so far as they proposed to be single individuals, would be identical with them in either a friendly or an hostile way; on the contrary, the mass is absolute singularity, and the concept of the mass, since they are one, is their abstraction alien to them and outside them. Also not the *latter*, not a mere plurality, for the universality in which they are one is absolute indifference. In a plurality, however, this absolute indifference is not established; on the contrary, plurality is not the absolute many, or the display of all differences; and it is only through this "allness" that indifference can display itself as real and be a universal indifference.

Since the people is a living indifference, and all natural difference is nullified, the individual intuits himself as himself in every other individual; he reaches supreme subject-objectivity; and this identity of all is just for this reason not an abstract one, not an equality of citizenship, but an absolute one and one that is intuited, displaying itself in empirical consciousness, in the consciousness of the particular. The universal, the spirit, is in each man and for the apprehension of each man, even so far as he is a single individual. At the same time this intuition and oneness is immediate, the intuition is not something other than thought; it is not symbolical. Between the Idea and reality there is no particularity which would first have to be destroyed by thinking, would not be already in and by itself equal to the universal. On the contrary the particular, the individual, is as a particular consciousness [463] plainly equal to the universal, and this universality which has flatly united the particular with itself is the divinity of the people, and this universal, intuited in the ideal form of particularity, is the God of the people. He is an ideal way of intuiting it.

Consciousness is the infinite, the absolute concept, in the form of unity, but in empirical consciousness the concept is posited only as relation: the opposites [united] in the concept *are*, and so are opposed and their unity is as such a hidden one; it appears in both as quantity, i.e., under the form of being possibly parted (in one consciousness) and the actuality of this "being parted" is precisely opposition. But in ethical life this separation is in the eyes of empirical consciousness it-self an ideal determinacy. Such a consciousness recognizes in its oppo-site, i.e., its object, absolutely the same thing that the object is, and it intuits this sameness.

This intuition is absolute because it is purely objective; in it all sin-gular being and feeling is extinguished, and it is intuition because it is within consciousness. Its content is absolute because this content is the eternal, freed from everything subjective. The antitheses [of the eternal], appearance and the empirical, fall so completely within abso-lute intuition itself that they display themselves as only child's play. All connection with need and destruction is superseded, and the sphere of practice which began with the destruction of the object has passed over into its counterpart, into the destruction of what is subjective, so that what is objective is the absolute identity of both.

This totality must be treated according to the moments of its Idea and therefore: first, at rest[33] as the constitution of the state, secondly, its movement, i.e., the government; first, the Idea as intuition, second-ly, the Idea according to relation, but in such a way that now the es-sence, the totality itself, is absolute identity of intuition and concept. And the form under which this identity appears is something super-ficial throughout. The extremes of the relation are simply the totality itself, not abstractions which would exist only through relation.

First Section[34]   [464]

The Constitution of the State

The people as an organic totality is the absolute identity of all the spe-cific characteristics of practical and ethical life. The moments of this totality are, as such, the form of (i) identity or indifference, (ii) differ-ence, and finally (iii) absolute living indifference; and every one of these moments is not an abstraction but a reality.

33. *Desselben* seems to be a misprint for *derselben*.
34. There is no second. But this First Section, though headed *The Constitution of the State*, is divided into two parts corresponding to what is described above as (i) rest and (ii) movement; and the second subsection is headed *Government*. (The problem of whether "Government" is the "Second Section" or whether the proper complement of this section remained unwritten is discussed in the Intro-ductory Essay, pp. 61–63).

146

G. W. F. Hegel

I. *Ethical Life as System, at rest.*

The concept of ethical life has been put into that life's objectivity, into the annulling of singularity. This annihilation of the subjective in the objective, the absolute assumption of the particular into the universal is

(a) Intuition: [Here] the universal [is] not something formal, opposed to consciousness and subjectivity or individual life, but simply one with that life in intuition. In every shape and expression of ethical life the antithesis of positive and negative is annulled by their integration. But the separation of particular and universal would seriously appear as a slavery of the particular, as something in subjection to the ethical law, and further as the *possibility* of a different subjection. In ethical life there would be no *necessity*. The grief would not endure, for it would not be intuited in its objectivity, would not be detached; and the ethical action would be an accident of judgment, for with separation the possibility of another consciousness is established.[35]

(b) As this living and independent spirit, which like a Briareus[36] appears with myriads of eyes, arms, and other limbs, each of which is an absolute individual, this ethical life is something absolutely universal, and in relation to the individual each part of this universality and each thing belonging to it appears as an object, as an aim and end. The object as such or as it enters his consciousness is something ideal for the individual; but "it enters his consciousness" means nothing but "it is posited as individual." But it is different if the individual subsumes [465] absolute ethical life under himself and it appears in him as his individuality. Here, and generally, it is not by any means meant that the will, caprice, specific things posited by the individual have dominated ethical life so that they have come to command it and make it negative as an enemy and fate. On the contrary dominion is wholly and entirely the external form of subjectivity under which ethical life appears, though without its essence being affected thereby. This appearance of ethical life is the *ethical life of the single individual*, or the *virtues*. Because the individual is single, the negative, possibility, specific determinacy, so too the virtues in their determinate character are something negative, possibilities of the universal. Here, then, there is established the difference between morality and natural law; it is not as if they

35. This paragraph is a summary of Hegel's critical reactions to the "reflective philosophy [and religion] of subjectivity"—which were stated in detail in *Faith and Knowledge*. See further the Introductory Essay, 00–00, and *Faith and Knowledge*, pp. 183–87.
36. In Greek mythology a hundred-handed giant.

If Opportunity

Doesn't Knock,
Build A Door,

—Milton Berle

were sundered, the former being excluded from the latter, for on the contrary the subject matter of morality is completely contained in natural law; the virtues appear in the absolute ethical order, but only in their evanescence.

Now ethical life is

(α) as *absolute ethical life*: not the sum but the indifference of all virtues. It does not appear as love for country and people and law, but as absolute life in one's country and for the people. It is the absolute truth, for untruth lies only in the fixation of something specific; but in the eternity of the people all individuality is superseded. It is the absolute process of formation (*Bildung*), for in what is eternal lies the real and empirical destruction of all specific things, and the exchange of all of them. It is absolute unselfishness, for in what is eternal nothing is one's own. Like every one of its moments, it is supreme freedom and beauty, for the real being and configuration of the eternal is its beauty. It is serene and without suffering, for in it all difference and all grief are cancelled. It is the Divine, absolute, real, existent being, and unveiled, yet not in such a way that it would first have to be lifted up into the ideality of divinity and first extracted from appearance and empirical intuition; on the contrary absolute ethical life is absolute intuition immediately.

But the movement of this absolute ethical life (as it is in the absolute concept) runs through all the virtues, but is fixed in none. In its [466] movement ethical life enters difference and cancels it; [its] appearance [is] the transition from subjective to objective and the cancellation of this antithesis.

This activity of production does not look to a product but shatters it directly and makes the emptiness of specific things emerge. The above-mentioned difference in its appearance is specific determinacy and this is posited as something to be negated. But this, which is to be negatived, must itself be a living totality. What is ethical must itself intuit its vitality in its difference, and it must do so here in such a way that the essence of the life standing over against it is posited as alien and to be negatived. It is otherwise in education, where the negation, subjectivity, is only the superficial aspect of the child. A difference of this sort is the *enemy*, and this difference, posited in its [ethical] bearing, exists at the same time as its counterpart, the opposite of the being of its antithesis, i.e., as the nullity of the enemy, and this nullity, commensurate on both sides, is the peril of battle. For ethical life this enemy can only be an enemy of the people and itself only a people. Because single individuality comes on the scene here, it is *for* the people that the single individual abandons himself to the danger of death.

But apart from this negative aspect there also appears the positive aspect of difference, and likewise as ethical life, but as ethical life in the single individual, or as the virtues. Courage is the indifference of the virtues; it is virtue as negativity, or virtue in a determinate form, but in the absoluteness of determinacy. It is thus virtue in itself, but formal virtue, since every other virtue is only *one* virtue. In the sphere of difference, specific determinacy appears as a multiplicity, and therefore there appears in it the whole garland of virtues. In war as the manifestation of the negative, and the multiple and its annihilation, there thus enters the multiplicity of specific relations, and in them of virtues. Those relations appear as what they are, established by empirical necessity, and therefore they quickly vanish again, and with them the existence of the virtues, which, having this speedy chasing of one another, are without any relation to a specific totality (the whole situation of a citizen) and so are just as much vices as virtues.[37]

[467]   The exigency of war brings about supreme austerity and so supreme poverty and the appearance first of avarice and then of enjoyment, which is just debauchery, because it can have no thought for tomorrow or the whole of life and livelihood. Frugality and generosity become avarice and supreme hardheartedness against self and others (when supreme misery demands this restriction)—and then prodigality; for property is thrown to the winds since it cannot remain secure, and its disbursement is wholly disproportionate to the use and need of self and others. Likewise the reality which has not been completely taken up into indifference is the immoral aspect of the specific situation, but what *is* present is existence in its negativity or the highest degree of annihilation.

It is the same with labor as it was with the ethical aspect of the virtues. The exigency of war demands supreme bodily exertions and a complete formal universal unity of the spirit in mechanical labor as well as supreme subjection to an entirely external obedience. *Just as* the virtues are without outer and inner hypocrisy—for in the case of the former its appearance and externality would be created by the caprice of the subject, who, however, would have had something different in his own mind and intention; this, however, cannot happen here because the ethical is the essence, the inner mind of the subject; neither can the inner hypocrisy occur, because it knows its ethical substance and through this consciousness maintains its subjectivity and is morality; (*margin*: in the former case there is an outward show of

37. Courage is a virtue in war, where the other virtues are shown up as vices.

of it, the fact that duty illuminates itself before the eyes of the individual himself)—*so too,* labor is without an aim, without need, and without a bearing on practical feeling, without subjectivity; neither having done one's duty, in the latter an inner one, the consciousness has it a bearing on possession and acquisition, but with itself its aim and its product cease too.

This war is not one of families against families but of peoples against peoples, and therefore hatred itself is undifferentiated, free from all personalities. Death proceeds from and afflicts something universal and is devoid of the wrath which is sometimes created and annulled again. Firearms are the invention of a death that is universal, indifferent, and nonpersonal; and the moving force is national honor, [468] not the injury of a single individual. But the injury which occasions the war comes entirely home to every individual owing to the identity of the [national] honor [in everyone].

(β) *Relative ethical life.* This bears on relations and is not freely organized and moved in them but, while allowing the specific determinacy in them to subsist, brings it into equality with its opposite, i.e., into a superficial and partial determinacy which is only conceptual. Thus this form of ethical life fashions legal right and is *honesty.* Where it acts or is real, it clings to the right that his own shall accrue to everyone and, at that, not in accordance with written laws; on the contrary it takes the whole of the case [into account] and pronounces according to equity if the legal right has not been decided, and otherwise it must keep to legal right. But in equity it mitigates the objectivity of legal right according to pressing needs, whether it be a matter of empirical necessitous circumstances, or of an ignorance that is called pardonable, or of a subjective trust. The totality of relative ethical life is the empirical existence of the single individual, and the maintenance of that existence is left to devolve upon himself and others.

Honesty cares for the family in accordance with the class to which the family belongs, and so for fellow citizens; it relieves the necessities of single individuals and is enraged about a bad action. The universal and absolute aspect of ethical life and the manner in which this aspect should have been present in its reality, and in which reality should have been subjugated, is for honesty a *thought.* Honesty's highest flight is to have many sorts of thoughts about this, but at the same time its rationality is that it sees how the empirical situation would be changed, and this situation lies too near its heart for it to let anything happen to it. Thus its rationality is to perceive that absolute ethical life must remain a thought.

In connection with the negative and with sacrifice, honesty offers from its acquisitions (a) to the people, for universal ends according to a universal principle, in taxes according to an equality of justice, and (b) in particular cases, for the poor and the suffering. But it may not sacrifice either [a just man's] entire possessions or his life, since indi-

[469] viduality is a fixture in it, and so person and life are not only something infinite but something absolute. Thus it cannot be courageous, neither may it go through the whole series of virtues or organize itself purely momentarily as a virtue. For purely momentary virtue is itself without aim and without connection with a totality other than the one it has in itself. The empirical totality of existence sets determinate limits to unselfishness and sacrifice and must stay under the domination of the understanding.

(γ) *Trust* lies in the identity of the first (α) and the difference of the second (β), so that that identity of absolute ethical life is a veiled intuition, not at the same time taken up into the concept and developed outwardly, and therefore this identity in the form of its intellectuality lies outside it. For intuition's solidity and compactness, which lacks the knowledge and form of the understanding and so also the active use of it, precisely the same intuition, when developed, is a might against which that solidity is different but also mistrustful, because singular individuality, in which that might comes in question, may seem to destroy the whole and cannot illumine for it the identity of absolute intuition and form as a singular middle term. It is not by understanding—for from that quarter it fears, as is only fair, to be betrayed—that it [is] to be set in movement but by the entirety of trust and necessity, by an external impulse and so one affecting the whole.

Just as trust's ethical intuition is elemental, so is its labor. This labor does not issue from the understanding, nor is it differently parcelled out in the way [characteristic] of honesty, but is entire and solid. It does not proceed to the destruction and death of the object but lets utility act and produce naturally.

So too, without knowledge of the legal right, trust's property is preserved for it, and any dispute is composed by passion and discussion. This trust is after all capable of courage because it relies on something eternal.

In the real absolute totality of ethical life these three forms of it [i.e., the three social classes] must also be real. Each must be organized

[470] independently, be an individual and assume a shape [of its own]; for a confusion of them is the formlessness of the naturally ethical and the absence of wisdom. Of course since each is organized, it is for that

very reason a totality and carries in itself the other levels of its form, but conformably to themselves and unorganized, as they have already been exhibited in each case according to their concepts.

Individualization, vital life, is impossible without specification or dispersal. Each principle and level must unquestionably reach its own concept, because each is real and must strive after its own self-satisfaction and independence. In its concept or in its own indifference it has completely taken into itself its relative identity with the other's concept and has thus formed itself; to this self-formation everything which is at one level must press on; for infinity is strictly one with reality, although within infinity there is the difference of levels.

The fact that physical nature in its own way expresses the levels in their pure shape and makes each of them independently alive appears more readily acceptable only because, according to the principle of the multiplicity of nature, each single thing should be something incomplete, while in ethical life each must be something absolutely complete; and each makes for itself a plain claim to absolute real totality, because the singularity of each one is the absolute totality, or the pure concept, and so the negation of all specific determinacies. But this absolute concept and negation is precisely the highest abstraction and immediately the negative. The positive is the unity of this form with the essence, and this is the expansion of ethical life into a system of levels (and of nature), and the level of ethical life, self-organized, can only be organized in individuals as its material. The individual as such is not the true but only the formal absolute: the truth is the system of ethical life.

Therefore this system cannot be thought as if it exists in purity in the individual, i.e., as developed, completely distributing itself in its levels; for its essence is ethereal, elemental, pure, having subordinated unities to itself and dissolved them out of their inflexibility into absolute malleability. The singularity of the individual is not the first thing, [471] but the life of ethical nature, divinity, and for the essence of divinity the singularized individual is too poor, i.e., too poor to comprise divinity's nature in its entire reality. As formal indifference it can display all features momentarily, but as formal indifference it is the negative, time, and destroys them again. But the ethical [reality] must apprehend itself as nature, as the persistence of all its levels, and each of them in its living shape; it must be one with necessity and persist as relative identity, but this necessity has no reality except in so far as each level has reality, i.e., is a totality.

The levels of ethical life as it displays itself in this reality within the perfect totality are the *classes*, and the principle of each one of them is the specific form of ethical life as expounded above. Thus there is a class of absolute and free ethical life, a class of honesty, and a class of unfree or natural ethical life.

According to the true concept of a class, the concept is not a universality which lies outside it and is an *ens rationis*; on the contrary universality is real in the class. The class knows itself in its equality and constitutes itself as a universal against a universal, and the relation between the different classes is [not] a relation between single individuals. On the contrary [by] belonging to a class the single individual is something universal and so a true individual, and a person. Consequently the class of slaves, for example, is not a class, for it is only formally a universal. The slave is related as a single individual to his master.

(a) The *absolute class* [i.e., the military nobility] has absolute and pure ethical life as its principle, and in the above exposition of that life it has itself been set forth, for its real being and its Idea are simply one, because the Idea is absolute ethical life.

But in the real being of absolute ethical life we have only to consider how this class behaves in respect to the persistence of difference and how its practical being can be differentiated in it. In the Idea itself, as was explained above, the life of practice is purely and simply negative, and [contained] in its reality are the relations and the virtues [472] connected with them which are self-motivated and committed to empirical contingency. But, for this class as the reality of ethical life, the need and use of things is an absolute necessity which dogs it, yet one which is not allowed to dog it in its above-described form, in its separatedness; for the work of this class may only be universal, while work to supply a need would be singular. The satisfaction of a need is certainly itself just something particular, but here nothing is to occur in the shape of the satisfaction of a need or the particular character of something purely practical; for this satisfaction is as such pure destruction of the object, absolute negation, not a confusion of the ideal with the object or the prolongation of the consequences of this confusion, not a partial putting of intelligence into the object, nothing practical, not a development of something lifeless, the result of which would yet be destruction. Instead the work [of this class] can be nothing but the waging of war or training for this work; for its immediate activity in the people is not work but something organic in itself and absolute.

The labor of this class can have no relation to its needs, but its needs cannot be satisfied without labor, and consequently it is necessary for this labor to be done by the other classes and for things to be transmitted to it which have been prepared and manufactured for it. All that is left to it is direct consumption of them in enjoying them. But this relation of this class to the other two is a relation in existing reality that has to be taken up into the indifference [of the ethical totality] in the [only] way possible. The way here is equality. And since the essence of the relation is the utility which the other classes have for the first one, so that they provide it with its necessities and it makes the goods and gains of the others its own, it must in turn, in accordance with equality, be useful to the others. But this it is [first] in the highest way and then, too, in their way.

In its content the tie of mutual utility is partly one of difference on both sides, whereby the first class is the absolute power over the others, and partly one of equality, whereby it is negative and so immanent for them in the way they are immanent for it.

The former utility is that the first class is the absolute and real ethical shape and so, for the other classes, the model of the self-moving and self-existent Absolute, the supreme real intuition which ethical nature demands. These classes, owing to their nature, do not get beyond this intuition. They are not in [the sphere of] the infinite concept whereby this intuition would only be posited for their consciousness as something external, [but] strictly [i.e., in their conceptual knowledge] it would be their own absolute moving spirit overcoming all their differences and determinacies. Their ethical nature's achievement of this intuition, this utility, is provided to them by the first class. Since this, displayed in the shape of something objective, is their absolute inner essence, it remains for them something hidden, not united with their individuality and consciousness.

[473]

The latter utility, according with the mode of the other classes, lies in the negative [i.e., in labor], and on the part of the first class labor is established likewise, but it is the absolutely indifferent labor of government and courage. In its bearing for the other classes, or to them, this labor is the security of their property and possessions, and the absolute security is that they are excused from courage, or at least the second class is.

(b) The *class of honesty* [the bourgeoisie] lies in work for needs, in possessions, gain, and property. Since the unity involved in these relations is something purely ideal, an *ens rationis*, on account of the

fixity of difference, it acquires reality only in the people. It is the abstract empty might in general, without wisdom[38] its content is settled by the contingency of real things and by the caprice involved in them, in gain, contracts, etc. The universal and legal element in these relations becomes a real physical control against the particularity which intends to be negative towards it. This immersion in possession and particularity ceases here to be slavery to absolute indifference; it is, as far as possible undifferentiated, or formal indifference, [i.e., what it is] to be a person, is reflected in the people, and the possessor does not lapse, owing to his difference, with his whole being and so does not lapse into personal dependence; on the contrary, his negative indifference is posited as something real, and he is thus a burgher, a bourgeois, and is recognized as something universal. In the first class all the particular character in individuality is nullified, and thus it is related as a universal to the second class, which in this way is itself
[474] determined similarly, but, owing to the fixity of its possession, it [is] only something formally universal, an absolute singular.

Since the labor [of this class] is likewise universal, the result is that, for the sake of the satisfaction of physical need a [system of] universal dependence is set up because labor here affects the totality of need, not materially but only conceptually. The value and price of labor and its product is determined by the universal system of all needs, and the capricious element in the value, grounded as it is on the particular needs of others, as well as the uncertainty whether a surplus is necessary for others, is completely cancelled. —The universality of labor or the indifference of all labor is posited as a middle term with which all labor is compared and into which each single piece of labor can be directly converted; this middle term, posited as something real, is *money*. So too the active universal exchange, the activity which adjusts particular need to particular surplus, is the *commercial* class, the highest point of universality in the exchange of gain. What it produces is to take over the surplus available in particular activities and thereby make it into a universal, and what it exchanges is likewise money or the universal.

Where barter or, in general, the transfer of property to another is ideal—partly owing to the universally known possession of the one, a universal recognition hindering the transfer (because property and its certainty rests in part on the transfer), partly because the two sides of the simultaneity of the barter become empirically separate—that

38. A reminiscence of Plato's *Republic*, where it is only the Guardians who are wise.

ideality is posited in reality (by the fact that the whole might of the state hangs on it) as if that had actually happened which was to happen, and the empirical appearance of the exchange did not matter. Just as the empirical appearance of possession or nonpossession does not matter either, and what is important is whether the inward absolute tie between the individual and the thing is close or distant, [i.e.,] whether the thing is his property or not. Both together constitute *justice* in connection with property in things.

Personal injury was infinite at the natural stage; it was a matter of honor and the whole person; in the system of reality it becomes this specific abstraction of injury; for since the indifference of the individual is here absolute indifference, i.e., the people (which, however, cannot be injured [by civil wrong]), nothing is left but precisely the specific and particular character of the injury. In a citizen as such the universal is as little injured, and is so little to be revenged or in jeopardy, that nothing remains but to liberate the particular by superseding it, i.e., the injurer is subjected to the very same treatment. Revenge is transformed in this way into punishment, for revenge is indeterminate and belongs to honor and the whole [family]. Here it is undertaken by the people, since in the place of the particular injured party there enters the abstract but real universality, not his living universality, the universality of the individual. [475]

But, for honesty, the living totality is the family, or a natural totality, and a situation of property and livelihood which is secured, so far as possible, for the empirical totality of its life as a whole and for the education of the children.

This class is incapable either of a virtue or of courage because a virtue is a free individuality. Honesty lies in the universality of its class without individuality and, in the particularity of its relations, without freedom.

The greatest height which this class can attain by its productive activity is (a) its contribution to the needs of the first class and (b) aid to the needy. Both are a partial negation of its principle, because (a) is labor for a universal according to the concept, while (b) is devoted to something particular according to an empirical necessitous case. The former universal sacrifice is without vitality, while the latter more living sort of sacrifice is without universality.

So too the inner relation of the family is determined according to the concept. Whoever out of necessity binds himself to the head of the house does so, despite all the personal aspects of the bond of service, only as an absolute person by way of a contract and for a definite term. For since each member of the household is an absolute person, he should be able to attain a living totality and become a paterfamilias. [476] This is precisely the relation when the bond is less personal and only for specific services and labor.

(c) The class of crude ethical life is that of the *peasantry*. The shape that the levels [of ethical life] have for it is that it is certainly involved with physical needs; it falls likewise into the system of universal dependence, though in a more patriarchal way, and its labor and gain forms a greater and more comprehensive totality.

The character of its labor is also not wholly intellectual, nor is it directly concerned with the preparation of something to meet a need; on the contrary it is more of a means, affecting the soil or an animal, something living. The peasant's labor masters the [organic] potency of the living thing and so determines it, though the thing produces itself by itself.

The ethical life of this class is trust in the absolute class, in accord with the totality of the first class, which must have every relation and every influence. The crude ethical life of this third class can only consist in trust, or, when placed under compulsion, it is open to the parcelling out of its activity.[39] On account of its totality it is also capable of courage and in this labor and in the danger of death can be associated with the first class.

II. Government

In the preceding level the system of ethical life was set forth as it is at rest: the organic independently, as well as the inorganic absorbing itself in itself and forming, in its reality, a system. But this [present] level treats of how the organic is different from the inorganic; it knows the difference between universal and particular, and how the absolutely universal transcends this difference and everlastingly cancels and produces it; in other words, the Absolute is subsumed under the absolute concept, or we have the *absolute movement* or process of ethical life. This movement, spread throughout the unfolding of all levels and really first creating and producing this unfolding, must be displayed in this level. And since the essence of this level is the difference between [477] universal and particular, but also the supersession of this difference,

39. The reference seems to be to the possibility of serfdom. Where the peasantry is reduced to legal serfdom, it is "parcelled out" to particular "lords." Thus it would cease to have the character of a true class and, being under compulsion, would cease to trust the nobility who lead it in war and speak for it in politics.

and since this organic movement must have reality (and the reality of the universal consists in its being a mass of individuals), this antithesis is to be so interpreted—since the universal is real or in the hands of individuals—that these are truly in the universal and undifferentiated, and in the separation [of universal and particular] adopt such a movement that through it the particular is subsumed under the universal and becomes purely and simply equal to it.

So far as might is concerned, the universal in its reality is superior to the particular, for, no matter at what level, the government is formal, it is the absolutely universal; the might of the whole depends on it. But the government must also be the positively and absolutely universal, and hence it is the absolute level [i.e., the first class], and the question is always about the difference that the government is the true power against everything particular, whereas individuals necessarily dwell in universal and ethical life.

This formal characterization of the concept of a *constitution*, the reality of the universal in so far as it is in contrast to something particular and so enters as power [*Potenz*] and cause, must also be recognized as a totality in the separation of powers. And this system—determined according to the necessity in which they are separated, and as the power of the regime is framed at the same time in this separation for each of these determinate features—is the true constitution. A truly ethical totality must have proceeded to this separation, and the concept of the government must display itself as the wisdom of the constitution, so that the form and consciousness is as real as the Absolute is in the form of identity and nature. The totality exists only as the unity of essence and form: neither can be missing. Crudity, with respect to the constitution in which nothing is distinct and the whole as such is directly moved against every single determinacy, is formlessness and the destruction of freedom; for freedom exists in the form, and there in the fact that the single part, being a subordinate system in the whole organism, is independently self-active in its own specific character.

This government is therefore directly divided into absolute government and government through the single powers.

A. *The Absolute Government* [478]
seems immediately to be the first class because that class is the absolute power for the others, the reality of absolute ethical life, the real intuited spirit of the others, while they are in the [sphere of the] particular. But the first class is itself one class in contrast to the others,

and there must be something higher than itself and its difference from the others.

As absolute universal reality this class is, of course, the absolute government; but organic nature proceeds to the annihilation and absorption of the inorganic and the latter maintains itself by its own resources, by the inner spirit which posits organic nature and its reflection as an inorganic nature. This latter stands in the concept as something absolutely universal, and the annihilation and the empowering of it by organic nature necessarily affects its particular character. Inherently it is the particular, though assumed into the concept and infinity, and this is what its persistence means.

Similarly the absolute class is the ethical organic nature in contrast to the inorganic nature [of the relative classes] and it consumes the latter in its particularity, so that [the relative classes] must provide the absolute one with the necessaries of life and work, while the first class is individualized in intuition by this contrast, and therefore, as a class, the first class has in its consciousness the difference of the second class and the crudity of the third, and so it separates itself from them and maintains a sense of its lofty individuality or the pride which, as an inner consciousness of nobility, abjures the consciousness of the non-noble and, what is precisely the same as that consciousness, namely, the action of the non-noble.

This spiritual individualization, like the former physical one, sets up a relation of organic to inorganic nature, and the unconscious limitation of this movement and of the annihilation of inorganic nature must be posited in ethical life as known, must emerge as the newborn and appearing middle term; it must not remain left to itself or fail to retain the form of nature; on the contrary it must be known precisely as the limit of the particularity which is to be annihilated. But such knowledge is the *law*.

The movement of the first class against the other two classes is assumed into the concept by reason of the fact that both of them have [479] reality, both are limited, and the empirical freedom of the one is cancelled like that of the others. This absolute maintenance of all the classes must be the supreme government and, in accordance with its concept, this maintenance can strictly accrue to no class, because it is the indifference of all. Thus it must consist of those who have, as it were, sacrificed their real being in one class and who live purely and simply in the ideal, i.e., the Elders and the Priests, two groups who are strictly one.

In age the self-constitution of individuality vanishes. Age has lost from life the aspect of shape and reality, and at the threshold of the death which will carry the individual away entirely into the universal, it is already half dead. Owing to the loss of the real side of individuality, of its particular concerns, age alone is capable of being above everything in indifference, outside its class, which is the shape and particularity of its individuality, and of maintaining the whole in and through all its parts.

The maintenance of the whole can be linked solely to what is supremely indifferent, to God and nature, to the Priests and the Elders, for every other form of reality lies in difference. But the indifference which nature produces in the Elders, and God produces in his Priests who are dedicated to him alone, appears to be an indifference lying outside ethical life, and ethical life seems to have to take flight out of its own sphere, to nature and the unconscious. But this must be because here the question is about reality, and reality belongs to nature and necessity. What belongs to ethical life is the knowledge of nature and the linkage (a) of that level of nature which formally and explicitly expresses the specific character of an ethical level with (b) that ethical level.

Nature is here related [to ethical life] like a tool. It mediates between the specific Idea of ethical life and its outward appearance. As a tool it must be formally adequate to that Idea, without indeed having any independent ethical content of its own, but corresponding with the Idea according to its formal level and specific character. Or its content is nothing but precisely possibility, the negative of ethical specific character. This latter, posited ideally, requires a tool, or alternatively its subjective reality, its immediate, inherently undifferenti- [480] ated body, taken up into its unity, appears, considered by itself, as its tool; and for the Idea, posited ideally, opposed to reality, this its body appears to reality as something accidental, something that finds itself, fits in, and conforms.

In nature the soul frames its body directly and one can neither be supposed, nor conceived, without the other. There is an original unity, unconscious, without separation. But in ethical life the separation of soul from body is the primitive thing, and their identity is a totality or a reconstructed identity. Thus for the ideal the body is to be sought as something present, formal, inherently negative and to be bound up with the ideal; and herein consists the essence of the construction of the government, namely, that (a) for the specific character of the soul or the specific ethical character whose reality is to be known, that shall be found which lies outside difference, in the sense that what is found is a specific ethical character; but that (b) at the same time this tool shall not be something universal, adequate for many other things, but precisely and only for this specific function. For, for one thing, the tool would otherwise be restricted against its own nature, and, for another thing, it would be, for that on account of which it is restricting, power in general, predominance, and not one with it in essence and spirit. It must have its entire shape in common with that, [be] one with it in respect of particularity, or, so to speak, have the same interest as it has except that the antithesis of ruler and ruled is the external form of the indifferent in contrast to the different, of the universal in contrast to the particular.

Thus age is the body of absolute indifference against all the classes. It lacks the individuality which is the form of every single person; and although the priesthood exists as the indifference not abandoned to nature but extorted from it and destructive by self-activity of what is individual, it must be noticed (a) that the Elders of the first class have led a divine [i.e., consecrated] life by belonging to it; (b) that the Elder of the first class must be a priest himself and, in the transition from an adult into a higher age, live as a priest and so must produce [481] for himself an absolute and true age; (c) that the true priest needs the outward age as his body, that his consummation cannot be put, against nature, into an earlier age, but must await the highest one.

The preservation ([the] absolute relation) of the whole is consigned simply to this supreme government; it is absolute rest in the endless movement of the whole and in connection with that movement. The wisdom of this government affects the life of all the parts, and this life is the life of the whole and is only through the whole. But the life of the whole is not an abstraction from the life force but absolute identity in difference, the absolute Idea. But this identity in difference is in its absolute and supreme outward articulation nothing but the relation of the classes constructed in the first level [i.e., within the absolute class itself]. It is the Absolute as something universal, without any of the specific determinacy which occurs at the particular levels.

This indifferent Idea of the supreme government does not affect any form of the particularity and determinacy which is manifest in the ramification of the whole into its subordinate systems. The government does not have to repeat this Idea in these, for otherwise it would be a formal power over them; on the contrary once this difference of the classes is established, it proceeds to maintain it. Thus to this extent it is negative in its activity, for the maintenance of a living thing is negative. It is government and so opposed to the particular; the absolute positive soul of the living [social whole] lies in the entirety of the people itself. By being government, government is in the sphere of appearance and opposition. Thus as such it can only be negative.[40]

But this absolute negation of everything that could conflict with the absolute relation of the absolute Idea and that had jumbled the distinction of the classes, must have a supreme oversight of the way in which any power is determined. No ordering whatever of any such power is exempt from its control, neither in so far as such a power establishes itself, nor in so far as it proposes to uphold itself when it [is] restricted by the movement of a higher power, either in general, in such a way as still to remain in existence, or as to be wholly superseded for a time.

Anything that could have an influence on disturbing the relation [between the classes] or the free movement of a higher power is in an absolute sense organic and within the competence of the supreme government. But the government's negative business in the field of appearance is not to be so conceived as if it behaved simply in a supervisory capacity and negatively in prohibitions by veto. On the contrary its negative activity is its essence, but it is the activity of a government, and its relation to the particular, or its appearance, is a positive activity, precisely in so far as it emerges in opposition to the particular. Thus it is legislative, establishing order where a relation is developed which intended to organize itself independently, or where some hitherto insignificant feature gradually develops itself in its previous unrestrictedness and begins to get strong. Above all it has to decide in every case where different rights of the systems [i.e., the class structures] come into collision and the present situation makes it impossible to maintain them in their positive stability.

In all systems, theoretical or actual, we come across the formal idea that an absolute government is an organic central authority, and, in particular, one which preserves the constitution. But

[482]

40. If a living thing is to be preserved, it is necessary continually to negate or destroy what threatens it. Even its food has to be "negated" in order to be absorbed. A glance at Hegel's later *Philosophy of Nature* will show that he always continued to think of the most primitive aspects of growth and self-maintenance as a continual breaking down of determinate forms previously built up. The living body literally consumes its own substance in order to maintain its organic unity. There is thus a struggle for existence among the "organs"; and each must have *its own* self-asserting, self-defending form. This is the analogy which Hegel here applies to his theory of social structure.

(α) such an idea, like Fichte's ephorate,[41] is entirely formal and
empty in its negative activity,

(β) and then there has to be ascribed to it every possible
oversight in the government of every single case, and consequently this oversight involves a crude confusion of
universal and individual. It is supposed to dominate everything, giving commands and operating as predominant,
and yet at the same time [that it dominates] to be nothing
nevertheless;

(γ) the absolute government is only not formal because it presupposes the difference of the classes and so is truly the
supreme government. Without this presupposition the whole
might of reality falls into a clump (no matter how the
clump might otherwise ramify internally) and this barbarian
clump would have at its apex its equally barbarian power
undivided and without wisdom. In the clump there cannot
be any true and objective difference, and what was to hover
over its internal differences is a pure nothing. For the abso-
[483] lute government, in order to be the absolute Idea, posits
absolutely the endless movement of the absolute concept.
In the latter there must be differences and, because they are
in the concept, universal and infinite, they must therefore
be systems. And in this way alone is an absolute government and absolute living identity possible, but born into
appearance and reality.

The external form of this government's absolute might is that it
belongs to no class, despite the fact that it originated in the first one.
From this one it must proceed, for in reality the crude living identity,
without wisdom and undifferentiated, is the third thing, the third class,
while the second is the one in which difference is fixed, and although
it has unity as formal universality united with itself, it still has this
unity floating over it. But the first class is clear, mirror-bright identity,
the spirit of the other classes, though since it is fixed in antithesis [to
the others], it is the infinite side, while the others are the finite one.
But the infinite is nearer to the Absolute than the finite is, and so, if
the expression be allowed, rising from below, the Absolute mounts up

41. Fichte, *Science of Right*, Part II, Book II, § 2 (Kroeger, pp. 259–78; compare
also Hegel's *Philosophy of Right*, § 273 (Knox, p. 177).

and swings forth directly out of the infinity which is its formal and negative side.

This government is absolute power for all the classes because it is above them. Its might whereby it is a power is not something external whereby it would be something particular against another particular, would have an army, or whatever else, to execute its commands. On the contrary it is entirely withdrawn from opposition; there is nothing against which it could set itself as something particular and thereby make itself into something particular. On the contrary it is absolutely and solely universality against the particular; and as this Absolute, this Ideal, this Universal, in contrast with which everything else is a particular; it is God's appearance. Its words are his sayings, and it cannot appear or be under any other form. It is the direct Priesthood of the All Highest, in whose sanctuary it takes counsel with him and receives his revelations; everything human and all other sanction ceases here.

It is neither the declaration that such an authority is to be inviolable nor the whole people's choice of its representatives that gives this gov-   [484] ernment its sanctity; on the contrary such a sanction rather detracts from it.

Choice and declaration is an act proceeding from freedom and the will and so can just as easily be upset again. Force belongs to the empirical and conscious will and insight, and every such single act of will and judgment occurs in time, is empirical and accidental, and may, and must, be able to be retracted. A people is not bound by its word, its act, or its will, for all of these proceed from its consciousness and from the circumstances. The absolute government, on the other hand, is divine, is not made, has its sanction in itself, and is simply the universal. But any and every making of it would issue from freedom and the will.

B. *Universal Government*
Absolute government is the restful substance of universal movement, but universal government is this movement's cause; or it is the universal in so far as the universal is opposed to the particular in the form of something particular; yet in its essence the universal is still the universal and, on account of its form, it is the determinant of the particular.

Now since universal government is related to movement, while movement occurs in the sphere of individuality, shape, and relation, the content and object of this government is a universal situation. For what abides absolutely is the essence of absolute government; all that can accrue to universal government is a formal universal, a universal accident, a determinate situation of the people for this period of time. For this situation must itself not be an abstraction, something belonging in its reality entirely to the particular and not being any modification or particularization of the universal, as, for example, the fact that every man lives, has clothes, etc. Such characteristics are only abstractions as universal and are needs of the single individual. But universal government is directed on what there is in those needs which qua universal is a power and subsumes the whole under itself and makes it a power. Universal government provides for the need which is universal, and provides for it in a universal way.

[485] The movement of the whole is a persistent separation of the universal from the particular and a subsumption of the latter under the former. But this particular is the persisting separation, and on this account there is stamped on it the form of the Absolute or its moments as mutually external to one another. And the movement is determined in ways that are similarly manifold.

The particular against which the universal moves at the level of inwardly concealed identity and outwardly revealed difference determines the movement as one proceeding to nullity; for what is flatly set down as particular and cannot bring identity to birth, and so is not absolute concept or intelligence, can only become one with the universal through nullification.

But the particular itself, as absolute concept and as organic totality, i.e., a people, is a particular; and consequently both particulars fail to recognize one another when they posit themselves as ideally negated —the aspect of negation in the absolute concept—and not as ideally persistent. The people that finds itself unrecognized must gain this recognition by war or colonies.

But self-constituting individuality is not itself at this second level a level which takes its inorganic aspect, the absolute concept confronting it, up into itself and makes it really and absolutely one with itself. War produces only a recognition, an ideal positing of equality, a true living being.

Since government is a subsumption of the particular under the universal, in this concept the moments of the universal opposed to the particular may be distinguished into two, like the subsumption itself; so this subsumption is again a double one, i.e., the real one and the ideal one—the former being the one in which it is formal universality under which the particular is posited, the latter being the true one in which the particular is posited as one with the universal. The moments in question are those which have been conceived as the different powers in the state: (i) the positing of the universal as the legislature, (ii) its ideal subsumption of the particular as the judiciary, or justice in general, and (iii) real subsumption as the executive. (Kant has conceived the real subsumption or the conclusion of the syllogism as the judicial power, but the ideal subsumption, or the minor premise as real subsuming, as the executive power.)[42]

Every real or living movement is an identity of these three moments, and in every act of government all three are united. They are abstractions to which no reality of their own can be given or which cannot be constituted or organized as authorities. Legislation, giving judgment, and executive action are something completely formal, empty, and devoid of content. A content makes them real, but by this linking of form and content each of them would immediately become an identity of universal and particular, or, as movement, a subsumption of the particular under the universal, and so a movement which has united all three moments in itself.   [486]

These abstractions may of course acquire reality; each of them may be independently linked with individuals who limit themselves to them. But in that case their true reality lies in the one which unites the three; or, since the conclusion [of the syllogism], the executive, is this unification, the executive is properly alw : the government; and whether the others are not pure abstractions, ..npty activities, depends on the executive, and this is absolutely the government; and after the above-mentioned distinctions [between legislature, judiciary, and executive have been made] and the ineffective authorities set up, the first problem comes back again, the problem of knowing the executive, not as such, but as government.

Therefore the movement of the people is government, because movement *as such* is something formal, since in it it is not absolutely determinate which of the terms standing in relation in the movement is power and which is the particular, and the fact that they are related in the movement seems accidental, whereas in the movement *of the people* universal and particular are plainly bound together; the absolutely universal as such is plainly determined and therefore the particular is too.

Organic movement must be recognized, so far as intuition subsumes the concept and the concept intuition. But because what is self-moving

42. *Rechtslehre*, § 45. (*Akad.*, VI, 313; Ladd, pp. 77–78).

is essentially organic, this distinction is formal throughout. The intuition which subsumes the concept is itself absolute concept, and the concept which subsumes intuition is itself absolute intuition. The appearance of this form of this antithesis is outside the organic itself; the antithesis lies in reflection on the movement. For the organic itself the antithesis is set up in such a way that, in so far as it is the concept which appears as subsuming, the organism is posited as an individual, as an independent single entity contrasted with other individual peoples as single entities; in so far as it is intuition which is subsuming, the organism is really and truly subsumed; it is the universal, the determinant of the particular, which is inherently nullified. In so far as the people, the totality, is directed against its own inner particular character, what is proper to the totality is this particular, because here the universal is posited as what is implicit.

[487]

This separation, as was said, is a formal one. The movement itself is nothing but an alternation of these two subsumptions. From the subsumption under the concept, where the opposites are single individuals, indifference arises and ideally intuits the single individual, which is thus posited outside the organism as what is proper to indifference, but itself still in the form of particularity, until indifference intuits the single individual as also really itself, or absolute identity is reconstructed.

Subsumption under the concept would be the abstraction of the mutual relation [of the people] to foreign peoples as individuals; but the organic process is directly an ideal cancellation of this difference, or the specific determinacy is directly the one belonging to the people, a difference in the people itself, and the living movement cancels it absolutely. There can thus be no absolute basis for the division of government into internal and external affairs; neither is an organic system comprehended within the universal system and subordinate, but at the same time independent and organic. But the moments of the absolute intuition, since they are known as organic, must themselves be systems in which those forms of inner and outer are subordinate. Those moments, being systems, must have difference wholly from outside, in reflection; but implicitly they must have absolute identity in themselves in such a way that it has hovered over them, not as such, but only as a form.

The *first* system of movement in the totality is thus this—that absolute identity is wholly concealed in it as feeling.

The *second* is the separation of universal from particular and thus is something duplex in its movement: *either* the particular remains

what it is and the universal is therefore only formal, or the universal [488]
is absolute and the particular is completely absorbed in it. The first is
justice and war, the second is education, culture, conquest, and colonization.

a) [The first system of Government: System of need]

The system of need has been conceived formally above as a system
of universal physical dependence on one another. For the totality of
his need no one is independent. His labor, or whatever capacity he
has for satisfying his need, does not secure its satisfaction for him.
Whether the surplus that he possesses gives him a totality of satisfaction depends on an alien power (*Macht*) over which he has no control. The value of that surplus, i.e., what expresses the bearing of the
surplus on his need, is independent of him and alterable.

This value itself depends on the whole of the needs and the whole
of the surplus, and this whole is a scarcely knowable, invisible, and
incalculable power,[43] because this power is, with respect to its quantity, a sum of infinitely many single contributions and, with respect to
quality, it is compounded out of infinitely many qualities. This reciprocal action of the single contribution on the whole, which is composed of such contributions, and of the whole in turn, as something
ideal, on the single contribution, determines value and so is a perpet-
ual wave, surging up and down, in which the contributor, determined
by the whole as possessing a high value, amasses his assets and hence
there comes to be in the whole a surplus included in the entirety of
need. As a result of this circumstance, the indifference of the whole,
regarded as a mass of the other qualities, appears as a ratio between
them, and this ratio has altered. These other qualities are necessarily
connected with that surplus, and this which previously had a higher
value is now depreciated. Every single kind of surplus is rendered indifferent in the whole, and through its reception into the whole it is
measured to fit the whole of the general need; its place and worth is
appointed for it. For this reason it is just as little the single contributor
who determines the value of either his surplus or his need, or who can
maintain it independently of its relation to everything else, as there [489]
is anything permanent and secure in the value.

Thus in this system what rules appears as the unconscious and
blind entirety of needs and the modes of their satisfaction. But the

43. *Eine wenig erkennbare, unsichtbare, unberechenbare Macht.* Is there here
an echo of Adam Smith? (See further the remarks in the Introductory Essay, pp.
74 and 95 note 87).

universal must be able to master this unconscious and blind fate and become a government.

This whole does not lie beyond the possibility of cognition, in the great ratios treated *en masse*. Because the value, the universal, must be reckoned up quite atomistically, the possibility of knowledge in respect of the different kinds [of surplus] thus compounded is a matter of degree. But from the value of the kind itself it is possible to know how the surplus stands in relation to need; and this relation, or the value, has its significance from two aspects: (a) whether the production of such a surplus is the possibility of [meeting] the totality of needs, whether a man can subsist on it, and (b) the aspect of universality, i.e., whether this value of one sort of need is not disproportionate to the totality itself, for which the need exists.

Both must be determined by intuition, in terms of the whole of what a man necessarily wants, and this is to be ascertained, partly from primitive natural conditions, according to the different climates, and partly from cultural conditions, by taking the average of what in a [given] people is regarded as necessary for existence. Natural influences bring it about automatically that sometimes the proper equilibrium is maintained with insignificant oscillation, while at other times, if it is disturbed more seriously by external conditions, it is restored by greater oscillations. But precisely in this last case the government must work against the nature which produces this sort of overbalancing sway through empirical accidents whose effect is sometimes more rapid—e.g., poor harvests—sometimes slower—e.g., the development of the same work in other districts and the [resulting] cheapness [of the product] which cancels elsewhere the symmetrical relation of the surplus to the whole; and since nature has cancelled the peaceful mean [of the stable price system], the government must uphold that mean and the equilibrium. For the lowering of the value of one sort of sur- [490] plus and the impracticability of that surplus's meeting the entirety of need [i.e., the impossibility of making a living by producing that commodity] destroys the existence and confidence of part of the people, since that part has tied its existence to the practicability of this, with trust in the universal.[44]

44. Earlier [p. 489] Hegel said that the universal must be able to master "this unconscious and blind fate and become a government." So "trust in the universal" could mean confidence in the stability of an existing economic system which has not yet "become a government" (i.e., an economic plan or policy actively developed and pursued by government). But when once trust is shaken, distrust is exhibited toward the government which has allowed some economic crisis to de-

The government is the real authoritative whole which, indifferent to the parts [of the people], is not anything abstract and thus is indeed indifferent to the singular type of surplus to which one part links its reality, but is not indifferent to the existence of that part itself. When one sort of surplus is no longer adequate to supply the totality of needs [of those who produce it], the abstraction of equilibrium is sure to restore this proportion, and so the result will be that (a) only so many people will busy themselves with that sort as can live off it and their value will rise and that (b) if there are too few of them for those to whom this surplus is a need, their value will fall.[45] But [on the one hand] reality and the government have a concern about a [price] value that is too low because it puts in jeopardy some part [of the people] whose physical existence has been made dependent on the whole [economy] and is now [threatened] with complete ruin by it; and, on the other hand, the government is concerned about values [i.e., prices] being too high, which disturbs everyone in the totality of his enjoyment and customary life. These concerns are ignored by the abstraction of equilibrium, an abstraction which in the equilibrium's oscillation remains outside it as the passive indifference of reflective observation, while the government remains outside [the oscillation] as the real authoritative indifference and the determinant of difference.

But these empirical oscillations and formal nonnecessary differences, to which the government is authoritatively indifferent, are accidental, not the necessary differential urge which proceeds to the destruction of the equilibrium.

The organic principle of this level is singleness, feeling, and need, and this is empirically endless. In so far as it is independent and is to remain what it is, it sets no limits to itself, and since its nature is singleness, it is empirically endless. True, enjoyment does seem to be fixedly determinate and restricted; but its endlessness is its ideality,

---

stroy the livelihood of a significant number of the people. It is the task of government to maintain the reliability of the "universal system of needs." This system, whether "governed" or not, seems to be the "universal" here.

45. There may be something wrong with the text here, because Hegel appears to be contradicting the "law of supply and demand" on which he is plainly relying. It is when there are too many goods, services, or producers in the market to meet the existing demand that the *supplier's* "value" falls. Of course the purchaser's "value" (his purchasing power) *falls* in a situation of scarcity. What Hegel seems to have *meant* is "only so many . . . as can live off it, and if there are too few of them for those to whom this surplus is a need, their value will rise. But if there are too many of them, their value will fall."

and in this respect it *is* endless. As enjoyment itself it idealizes itself
[491] into the purest and clearest enjoying. Civilized enjoyment volitilizes
the crudity of need and therefore must seek or arrange what is nob-
lest, and the more different its impulses, the greater the labor they
necessitate. For both the difference of the impulses and also their indifference and concentration, these two aspects which the reality of
nature separates, should be united. The neutrality which the natural
product has by being a totality in itself should [be] cancelled and
merely its difference should remain to be enjoyed.

Moreover this ideality of enjoyment displays itself also as "being
other," as foreignness in the external connection of the product [i.e.,
it comes from "abroad"], and it is linked with scarcity; and this foreign sort of satisfaction, as well as the most domestic sort, the one
already made most peculiarly our own by its manner of preparation,
makes charges on the whole earth.

Empirically endless, the ideality of enjoyment finally displays itself
in objectified restricted enjoyment, in possession, and in this respect,
consequently, all limitation ceases.

Over against this infinity is the particularity of enjoyment and possession, and since possible possession—the objective element in the
level of enjoyment—and labor have their limits, are determinate in
quantity, it follows that with the accumulation of possession at one
place, possession must diminish at another.

This inequality of wealth is absolutely necessary. Every natural inequality can express itself as inequality of wealth if what is natural
turns to this aspect. The urge to increase wealth is nothing but the
necessity for carrying to infinity the specific individual thing which
possession is. But the business that is more universal and more ideal
is that which as such secures a greater gain for itself.

This necessary inequality divides itself again within the business
class (*Erwerbsstand*) into many particular types of business (*Stände
des Erwerbs*), and it divides these into estates (*Stände*) of different
wealth and enjoyment. But owing to its quantitative character, which
is a matter of degree and is incapable of any definition except in degree, this inequality produces a relation of master [and servant]. The
individual who is tremendously wealthy becomes a might; he cancels
the form of thoroughgoing physical dependence, the form of dependence on a universal, not on a particular.

Next, great wealth, which is similarly bound up with the deepest
[492] poverty (for in the separation [between rich and poor] labor on both
sides is universal and objective), produces on the one side in ideal uni-

versality, on the other side in real universality, mechanically. This purely quantitative element, the inorganic aspect of labor, which is parcelled out even in its concept, is the unmitigated extreme of barbarism. The original character of the business class, namely, its being capable of an organic absolute intuition and respect for something divine, even though posited outside it, disappears, and the bestiality of contempt for all higher things enters. The mass of wealth, the pure universal, the absence of wisdom, is the heart of the matter (*das Ansich*). The absolute bond of the people, namely ethical principle, has vanished, and the people is dissolved.

The government has to work as hard as possible against this inequality and the destruction of private and public life wrought by it. It can do this directly in an external way by making high gain more difficult, and if it sacrifices one part of this class to mechanical and factory labor and abandons it to barbarism, it must keep the whole [people] without question in the life possible for it. But this happens most necessarily, or rather immediately, through the inner constitution of the class.

The relation of physical dependence is absolute particularization and dependence on something abstract, an *ens rationis*. The constitution creates a living dependence and a relation of individuals, a different and an inwardly active connection which is not one of physical dependence. To say that this class is constituted inwardly means that within its restrictedness it is a living universal. What is its universal, its law and its right, is living at the same time in the individuals, realized in them through their will and their own activity. This organic existence of this class makes every single individual, so far as there is life in him, one with the others; but the class cannot subsist in absolute unity. Thus it makes some of the individuals dependent, but ethical on the score of their trust, respect, etc., and this ethical life cancels mere mass, quantity, and the elemental, and creates a living relation. The wealthy man is directly compelled to modify his relation of mastery, and even [others'] distrust for it, by permitting a more general participation in it.[46] The external inequality is diminished externally, just as the infinite does not give itself up to determinacy but exists as living activity, and thus the urge to amass wealth indefinitely is itself eradicated. [493]

This constitution belongs rather to the nature of the class itself and

46. In a marginal note Hegel refers to the "Athenian law for defrayment of festival expenses by the richest men of the quarter"—i.e., the law affecting "liturgies."

its organic essence, not to the government; to the latter it is the external restrictions [that belong]. But this is its particular activity, i.e., provision for the subsistence of the single classes within this sphere by opposing the endless oscillations in the value of things. But the government, as the universal, itself has universal needs: (i) in general, for the first class which, exempt from property and business, [lives] in continual and absolute and universal need, (ii) for the formally universal class, i.e., for that which is the organ of government in the other classes and labors purely in the universal field, (iii) for the need of the community, of the entire people as a universal, e.g. for its [public] dwellings, etc., its temples, streets, and so forth.

The government must earn [enough for] these needs, but its work can only consist in taking directly into its possession without work the ripe fruits [of industry] or in itself working and acquiring. The latter—since it is against the nature of the universal to rest in the particular, and here the government is something formally universal—can only be a possessing and a leasing of this possession, with the result that acquiring and working affect the government not directly but in the form of utility, a result, something universal. But the former is the appropriation of the ripe fruits, and so these ripe fruits are work completed and so in the form of something universal, as money or as the most universal needs. These are themselves a possession of individuals and the cancellation of this possession must have the form of formal universality or justice.

But the system of taxes falls directly into the contradiction that while it should [be] absolutely just for each to contribute in proportion to the magnitude of his possessions, these possessions are not landed or immovable but, in industry, something living, infinite, and incalculable. Looked on abstractly, the calculation or estimation of the capital involved according to the income obtained is possible, but the income is something entirely particular, not something objective, knowable, and ascertainable, like landed property. So in this way private possessions cannot be taxed in accordance with justice because, by being private, they do not themselves have the form of something objective.

[494]

But the objective, i.e., landed property, can be interpreted according to the value of its possible productivity (even though here, too, particularity always has a part to play); but because at the same time possession in the form of particularity is present as skilfulness, not everything is comprised under that value; and if the products of landed property are prodigiously assessed, the value of the product is not set in equilibrium, for the mass always remains the same, being that on which the value depends, and if production diminished, the state's revenues would diminish to the same extent; production would have to be taxed all the more in a progressive rise and its receipts would behave in the opposite way. Thus skilfulness has to be taxed at the same time, not according to its receipts, which are something particular and one's own, but according to what it expends; for the thing it buys makes the passage through the form of universality out of its particularity, or it becomes a commodity. And on account of the same circumstance, namely that the mass either remains the same, in which case the value of the article is not altered and this working class is impoverished, or, what follows in that event, less is produced, with the result that the revenue is less, and the same is the case on whatever branch [of industry] the tax falls; thus [the tax] must extend to the maximum possible particularity [of commodities]. Although for this reason it likewise results that less is needed, this is precisely the [best] external means for restricting gain, and in the taxes the government has a means of influencing this restriction or extension of single parts [of the whole economy].

b) *The second system of Government: System of justice*　　　[495]
In the first system the opposition of universal and particular is formal. Value, the universal, and needs and possessions, the particular do not determine the essence of the matter but are outside it. The essence remains its connection with a need. But in this system of the separation [of universal and particular] it is ideal determinacy which is the essence. The thing which is tied to need is, qua property, so determined that, even as this particular possession, it is essentially something universal; its connection with need—and the need is something entirely single—is something recognized. The thing is mine, and as mine has not been nullified. But the relative identity, in which I stand with it, or the ideality of nullification (i.e., posession), this objectivity is posited as a subjective one, existing in men's minds. For this reason, as this identity, it [i.e., the property] is intuition, not a single intuition of this single thing, but absolute intuition. That connection [with need] has objective reality. The self is universal, established, and has being; that tie is determined as a universal one.

The middle term, the reality of this connection is the government. The fact that a tie of possession is not something ideal but is also real is the fact that all selves establish this connection, that the empirical self of the tie exists as the whole mass of selves. This mass, according to the abstraction of its quantity, is the public authority, and this public authority as thinking and conscious ([*sich*] *bewusst*) is the government here as the *administration of justice*.

As this administration, government is the entirety of all rights, but with complete indifference toward the interest of the connection of the thing with the need of this specific individual. For the government this individual is a completely indifferent universal person. All that comes in question in pure justice is simply the universal, the abstract aspect of the manner of possession and gain. But justice must itself be a living thing and have regard to the person.

Right in the form of consciousness is law, which is here related to singular cases; but this form is arbitrary, although it is necessary for right to be present, in the form of consciousness, as law.

[496]   Right concerns singular cases and is the abstraction of universality, for the singular case is to subsist in it. This singular case is either the living being of the individual or a relative identity of his [i.e., some piece of his property] or the life of the individual himself regarded as something singular or as relative identity.

So too the negation of singular individuality (a negation produced by a single individual and not by the absolutely universal) is a negation of [his right of] possession purely as such, or the negation of a single living aspect of the individual, or the negation of the entirety of the living individual. The second negation is a violent deed, the third is death.

Absolute government could in this matter leave the second class and the third (which through the first lies under civil law) to themselves and leave them alone in the vain endeavor to assume into the infinite the absolutely settled finitude of possession. This endeavor is displayed as the [attempted] completeness of the civil laws, as an absolute consciousness about judicial procedure, such that the rule would be self-sufficient in its form as rule and the judge would be purely an organ, the absolute abstraction of the singular case under discussion, without any life and intuition of the whole.

This false infinite must be set aside by the organic character of the constitution, a character which, as organic, assumes the universal absolutely into the particular.

The organic principle is freedom, the fact that the ruler is himself the ruled; but since here the government, as universal, remains opposed to the collision [of rules] involved in the single individual, this identity [of ruler and ruled] must in the first place be so established that the equality of birth [typical of] the same [noble] class, the constitution [appropriate] for a narrower circle of [noble] families, is expanded into a whole [of all classes] as dwelling together under the same citizenship, and this dwelling together as citizens constitutes the living unity. Secondly, in the actuality of single legal judgments the abstraction of the law must not be the absolute thing; on the contrary the whole affair must be a settlement according to equity, i.e., one that takes account of the whole situation of the parties as individuals, a settlement productive of satisfaction and reached with the conviction and assent of the parties.

This principle of freedom in its mechanical constitution is comprehended as the organization of law courts and is an analysis of the dispute and the decision thereon.

In the administration of the civil law it is only determinacy as such [497] that is absolutely negated in the dispute, and the living employment, work, what is personal, may become what is determinate.

But in criminal law it is not anything determinate which is negated, but individuality, the indifference of the whole, life and personality. Negation in civil law is purely ideal, but in criminal law real, for the negation that effects a totality is real for that reason. [In a case of civil wrong] I am in possession of someone else's property, not by robbery or theft, but because I claim it as mine and justly so. In this way I recognize the other man's competence to possess property; but force and theft deny this recognition. They are compulsive, affecting the whole; they cancel freedom and the reality of being universal and recognized. If crime did not give the lie to this recognition, it could equally well surrender to another, to the universal, what it accomplishes.

Justice in civil matters therefore simply affects something determinate; but penal justice must also cancel, apart from the determinate thing, both the negation of universality and also the universality put in place of the other—opposition is opposed by opposition.

This cancellation is *punishment*, and it is determined precisely by the determinate way in which universality has been cancelled.

1. Civil punishment. 2. Penal punishment. 3. War. Here universality and singular individuality are one, and the essence is this totality.

In 1 the essence is universality, in 2 singular individuality, in 3 identity: the people becomes the criminal who is in 2 and sacrifices the possessions of 1; it sides with the negative in 1 and 2; for the first class, 3 is appropriate.

c) [The] *third system of Government: [System of Discipline]*

In this system the universal is the Absolute, and purely as such the determining factor. In the first [system] the universal is the crude, purely quantitative, and wisdomless universal, in the second the universality of the concept, formal universality, recognition. Thus for the absolutely universal, difference exists too; this difference superseded the universal in the universal's movement, but it is a superficial and formal difference, and the essence of the differents is absolute universality. Similarly in the first [system] the essence of the different is feeling, need, and enjoyment, in the second the essence of the different is to be a singular [person], something formally absolute. The universal, the cause, is determined by its essence like the particular.

[498]

I. Education; II. Training (*Bildung*) and Discipline (*Zucht*); the first consists formally of talents, inventions, science. What is real is the whole, the absolutely universal, the inherently self-moving character of the people, the absolute bond, the true and absolute reality of science. Inventions affect only something singular, just as the single sciences do, and where these are absolute in the shape of philosophy, they yet are wholly ideal. Training in the truth, with the destruction of all appearance, is the self-developing and deliberating and conscious people; the other side is the police as disciplining singular cases. The great discipline consists of the universal *mores*, the [social] order, training for war, and the testing of the reliability of the single individual in war.

III. Procreation of children; the way that a people becomes objective to itself as this people; the fact that the government, the people, produces another people. Colonization.

[C. *Free government*]⁴⁷

47. A and B are "Absolute Government" and "Universal Government," the latter having been divided into a, b, c. (This heading was added by Lasson.)

Possible forms of a free government: I. Democracy. II. Aristocracy. III. Monarchy.

Each is capable of becoming unfree: I. Ochlocracy. II. Oligarchy. III. Despotism. The external and mechanical element is the same. The difference is caused by the relation of ruler to ruled, i.e., whether the essence is the same and the form of opposition is only superficial.

Monarchy is the exhibition of the absolute reality of ethical life in one individual, aristocracy in several individuals. The latter is distinguished from the absolute constitution by hereditariness, still more by

landed estate, and, because it has the form of the absolute constitution and not its essence, it is the worst constitution. —Democracy
exhibits this absolute reality in everyone; consequently it involves
confusion with possession, and there is no separation of the absolute
class. For the absolute constitution the form of aristocracy or monarchy is equally good. That constitution is democracy too in the [or-
ganization of the] classes.

In monarchy a religion must stand alongside the monarch. He is the [499]
identity of the whole, but in an empirical shape; and the more empirical he is, the more barbaric the people is, and the more the monarchy
has authority, and the more independently it constitutes itself. The
more the people becomes one with itself, with nature and ethical life,
all the more does it take the Divine into itself and suffer loss [lose
<faith>?] in this religion that resists it; and then by reconciliation
with the world and itself it passes through the lack of imagination that
typifies irreligion and the understanding.

This is the case also in aristocracy, but on account of its patriarchal,
or pap for the children[48] character, there is little imagination or religion.

In democracy absolute religion does exist, but unstably, or rather
it is a religion of nature; ethical life is bound up with nature, and the
link with objective nature makes democracy easy of access for the intellect. For the positing of nature as something objective—Epicurean
philosophy—the religion must be purely ethical, and so must th
imagination of the absolute religion, and art, too, which has produce
a Jupiter, an Apollo, a Venus—not Homeric art, where Jupiter and
Juno are air and Neptune is water [so that it is natural, not ethical].
This separation must be complete, the ethical movement of God absolute, not crime and weakness [as in the Homeric gods] but absolute
crime—death [as in the Crucifixion].

48. Lasson misread *Brey tornBergriff* here.

Appendix

THE SUPPOSED CONCLUSION OF THE *System of Ethical Life* AND THE CON-
TINUATION OF THE LECTURE MANUSCRIPTS UPON WHICH IT WAS BASED (*as
reported by Rosenkranz in his Life of Hegel, pp. 132–41*).[1]

132]   Hegel made the conclusion[2] of his philosophy of spirit at the end of
the system of philosophy itself initially by seeking to make out the
necessity of philosophy in [the life of] a people as the *ideal complement of war*. The *absolute labor* is simply death, in that it suspends
the determinate singularity; for this reason *military valor* brings into
[the life of] the State the *absolute sacrifice*. But since for those who
do not die fighting, there remains the *humiliation of not being dead*,
and of still having the selfish enjoyment of their own singularity,
[133] there remains only *speculation* as the *absolute cognition of truth*, as
the form in which the simple consciousness of the infinite is possible
without the determinacy of the individual, independent, life. "The
absolute consciousness of the individuals of the people, the living spirit of the same, must be pure, absolute, consciousness, absolute spirit
both in respect of form and in respect of content; and the *spirit of
the people* becomes spirit of the *natural and ethical universe*. Only
then is the spirit absolute in its absolute self-equality, in the aether of
its simple Idea [so that] the end of philosophy returns again to its beginning."[3]

1. The further additions quoted from the manuscript itself by R. Haym (*Hegel
und seine Zeit*, Berlin 1857) have been inserted in their proper place.
2. Rosenkranz is certainly wrong about this. See note 3 below.
3. The fragment which Rosenkranz has here summarized and from which he
quotes the end, was certainly not part of the *System of Ethical Life*. The continuity between our manuscript of the *System of Ethical Life* and Hegel's "oral
communication of his philosophy" is evident enough. On the other hand Rosenkranz would not have been tempted to see in his fragment the missing conclusion of Hegel's supposed "Frankfurt" system if it formed part of a lecture course
for which he had a continuous manuscript. (He treats the lecture manuscripts
that are recognizable as such as "didactic modifications" of the "Frankfurt" system.) What he quotes here, must therefore have been a loose fragment even
when he had it. It is unmistakably (to us, as to him) the conclusion of a "system,"
and Hegel's reference to "the natural and ethical *universe*" virtually guarantees
that it is not later than 1804. It *could* conceivably be earlier than the *System of
Ethical Life*. But in all probability it was the end either of the "First Philosophy

But this ending did not satisfy Hegel when he came later on in Jena to the oral communication of his philosophy. He worked out the concept of the distinction of constitutions further and identified the free estate in Monarchy as the Nobility, which stands over against Majesty [i.e., against the Monarchy] in a tacit *battle* that has the *form of obedience*. But more especially he followed out the concept of the religious *cult* as that in which a people comes to its highest self-enjoyment; and he did this in a fashion notable for its simplicity and intelligibility. He claimed that in *Religion* the reality of the objective world itself, and subjectivity and particularity along with it, are posited *as superseded*. Where it [i.e., subjectivity and particularity] is still held on to as *negative freedom* in this highest region of universal rationality, even just as virtuosity (as he remarked in criticism of Schleiermacher's *Discourses on Religion*, which were epoch-making at the time) then there is no serious intent to let the *spirit appear in spiritual shape*. On the contrary it is the essence of religion that the spirit is not ashamed of any of its individuals [meaning that the religious community does not need virtuosos of religious experience]; it does not refuse to appear to anyone, and everyone has power over it, power to conjure it up. The supersession of subjectivity is not the sheer nullification of it, but just the nullification of its empirical individuality, and by this means it is a purification for the absolute enjoyment of its [i.e., the spirit's] absolute essence. For in religion the ideal shape of the spirit is real, while its real side is ideal; and in it the spirit appears for the individual. Hence it has for him, *imprimis*, the shape of an objective [power] which lives and moves in the people as its Spirit, and is alive in all of them. In Science the spirit appears in an objective [134] shape, the shape of being, but it is still the spirit that is also subjective. In respect of its *subject matter speculative knowledge (das Wissen) has no particular advantage over Religion*. Religion's essence drives the spirit back together, out of the extension of empirical existence, into the supreme point of intensity, and sets it forth objectively for intuition and for thought, so that spirit has enjoyment of itself and of its own intuition, and in this enjoyment it is at the same time real, i.e., it recognizes itself in the individual, and the individual recognizes himself in it. As the totality of empirical existence setting itself forth *objectively*, the *essence* of God has a history for the spirit. His living

---

of Spirit" of 1803/4 or of its immediate predecessor the *philosophiae universae delineatio* of summer 1803. (See further the Introduction to the "First Philosophy of Spirit," pp. 200–01).

being is events and actions. The most living God of a people is its *national God*, in whom its spirit appears transfigured, and not just its spirit but also its empirical existence, the untruth and uncertainty of its life, appears as a sum of singular traits. In religion the spirit is not in the ideality of philosophic science, but is in connection with reality; so it necessarily has a limited shape, which when fixated for its own sake, makes up the positive side of every religion. The *religious tradition* thus expresses two things at once: on one side the *speculative Idea* of the spirit, and on the other the limitation derived from the *empirical* existence of the people—not the limitation of the Idea in the way that *art* must employ such limitation in general. And since religion, qua religion, must exclude philosophic science and art, therefore it is an *activity* which complements art and science; it is the cult which raises subjectivity and freedom to their highest enjoyment, because it *offers up* a part of its singularity to the great spirit in divine service and by this sacrifice makes the rest of its property free. Through the reality of the nullification of singularity in the offering the subject saves itself from the onesidedness of the deception (*Betrug*) that its exaltation is only a matter of thought. This action, the irony toward the mortal and profitable activity of men, is reconciliation, the basic Idea of religion. In so far as singularity wants to maintain itself against rational universality, it comes to be in *sin*, it comes to *transgression*. Here the spirit is reconciled only as *fate in punishment*. Reconciliation is exalted above punishment and appears therefore as justified necessity.[4] For since reconciliation in general is directed only to the spirit and cannot supersede the [causal] chain of determinate existence, *nothing in fate is changed by it.* Only the essence of the actual battle (*Energie des Kampfes*) against fate—as the potentiality of setting at risk the whole range of empirical existence—is also the potentiality of reconciliation with fate, since the spirit has torn itself free from fate through the ethical character of the battle.

[135]

Religion must, as Hegel expressed it in the style of nature-philosophy that was then fashionable, come on the scene of world history in the following three forms (in accord with the three universal dimensions of Reason and within the bounds of *climatic* modification according to its empirical difference):

1) in the form of Identity, in the original reconciliation between spirit and its real being in individuality;

4. *Gerechte Notwendigkeit*—i.e., reconciliation involves both justice (like punishment) and necessity (like fate).

2) in the form where the spirit begins from the infinite difference
of its identity and reconstructs from this difference a *relative*
identity and reconciles itself;

3) this identity, subsumed under the original absolute one,
will posit the being-at-one of Reason in its spiritual shape
with Reason in its real being or in individuality as original,
and will posit at the same time its infinite antithesis, and
its reconstruction.

In the first dimension, as original reconciliation, religion is *nature
religion*. For the imagination of its pantheism nature is in and for itself
a spirit and is holy. Its God has not retreated from any element. A
curse may have lain on the heads of single individuals, but no universal aspect of nature is abandoned by God. The spirit may be wroth
against such peoples at isolated moments, but they are certain of their
reconciliation. The daily round of life is a converse with the Gods,
a reciprocal giving and receiving from them, and every outward motion is full of significance as a word of fate. The *shapes of the Gods*
cannot be resolved into actual things, or historical explanations, or
thoughts. The *eternity of the ideals of a beautiful mythology* rests neither on its perfect artistic beauty, nor on the truth of the Ideas that
they express, nor on the actuality ʰat belongs to them, but precisely [136]
on the identity of all of these fa ᵣₛ and their *indivisibility*.

In a second period this beautiful world of the Gods must pass away,
along with the spirit that enlivens it. It can abide only as a memory.
The unity of the spirit with its reality must be rent. The ideal principle
must constitute itself in the form of universality, while the real principle sets itself up firmly as singularity, and nature is left lying between them as a *desecrated corpse*. The spirit must abandon its dwelling in living nature and raise itself up as a potency against it. Ethical
grief (*Schmerz*) must be infinite. The time of this grief came when
the Romans smashed the living individuality of the peoples, putting
their spirits to flight and destroying their ethical life, before extending
the universality of their lordship over the dismembered singular parts.
At the time of this dismembering, for which there was no reconciliation, and of this universality that had no life, in this *boredom of the
world* when peace was lord over all of the civilized earth, the original
identity had to rise out of its rent condition, it had to lift its eternal
force above its grief and come again to its own intuition. Otherwise the
human race must have perished inwardly. And the first theatre for
the *appearance* of ethereal Reason reawakened in the world that had

ceased to be Nature, had to be the very people which in the whole course of their existence has been the *most rejected* of the peoples, because in it the *grief* was bound to be deepest, and its utterance must have had a truth intelligible to the whole world.

In this way Christ became the founder of a religion, because he uttered the suffering of his whole world from the inmost depth; he raised the force of the divinity of the spirit above it, the absolute certainty of reconciliation, which he bore in himself; and by his *confidence* he awoke the confidence *of others*. He uttered the suffering of his time, which had become untrue to nature, in his absolute *contempt* for a nature become *worldly* and his absolute confidence of reconciliation, *in his certainty that he is one with God.*—The contempt that he [137] expressed towards the world was necessarily bound to be avenged upon him as his fate by his death; and this death had to vindicate the contempt of the world and make it the fixed point [*scilicet* of the new religion]. These two necessary elements had to become the pivot of the new religion: the expulsion of the Gods from nature, hence contempt for the world; and the fact that in this infinite division a man still bore within himself the confidence of being one with the Absolute. In this man the world was again reconciled with the spirit. Since the whole of nature had ceased to be divine, only the nature of this man could be divine and nature could become *hallowed* again only from him as focus. But because man, being certain that he was not himself divine, could look upon divinity *only* in this man and had to make the coming of individuality to oneness with the absolute spirit hang upon his *personality*, his finite existence (*sein Dasein*) became the starting point of this religion itself. The more striking tendency of this religion was bound at first to be contempt for the world and of the universal which existed as *State*; and the symbol of this contempt was the *cross*, which, being the gallows of the world, was the most shameful and dishonorable thing. [*According to Haym, Hegel's actual words were*: "In the context of our ethical customs this new religion would have had to make the gallows, which is now what the cross was then, into its battle-standard."][5] A more distinctive or unambiguous [literally "necessary"] signal of absolute division from the world and of total war against it to wipe it out could not be established.

The other side of the infinite grief of this absolute division was its reconciliation in the faith that *God has appeared in human form* and has thus reconciled human nature with himself in this singular shape as the representative of the species. This single human shape expressed in its history the whole history of the empirical existence of the human race; it had to do this in order to be the *national God of the race*. But at the same time it expressed this history only so far as it was the history of God. In other words the principle is infinite grief, the absolute rending of nature. Reconciliation has neither meaning nor truth without this grief. In order for this level [*Potenz*] of religion to exist *it must eternally produce this grief so as to be able to reconcile it eternally*. The empirical condition of the world in which the religion originated was bound to be superseded through the struggle of this reconciling religion, so that the world was really happier and more [138] reconciled, and the religion must in this way surpass itself. So it must bear within itself the principle by which the infinite suffering is aroused in order to reconcile it infinitely. It has this principle, the fate of the world, necessarily in the history of its God who has died the death of a transgressor. The death of a transgressor could itself be just a single death. The view of death as a universal necessity can arouse no infinite religious grief, but he who died on the cross is simultaneously the God of this religion and as such his history expresses the infinite suffering of nature deprived of its gods. The divine was bruised in the *everyday routine of life, the divine was dead.* The thought that God himself had died on earth, that alone expresses the feeling of this infinite grief; just as the thought that he is *resurrected* from the grave expresses its reconciliation. By his life and death God is humbled, by his resurrection man has become divine. This religion cannot let the infinite grief and the eternal reconciliation depend on the accidental empirical existence of the single [believers]. It must constitute itself as a cult through which the grief is aroused and the reconciliation shared. Nature religion must leave it to *chance* how far the original reconciliation is alive in a single [worshipper]. But the religion that proceeds to the reconstruction of the indifferent harmony must produce that infinite difference by doing violence to nature so as to make it possible for its reconciliation to be a reconstructed one.

This then is what has happened with perfect *wisdom* in the Christian religion. Man is led up to the grief of the divine death and of the mortality of all life by an infinite sum of *instituted situations*, and then awakened from this death, and hallowed in oneness with the God-Man again (in whom the race is reconciled) by the eating of his body and the drinking of his blood, the most inward type of union. The history of God is the history of the whole race and every single human being goes through the whole history of the race. All nature is

[139] hallowed again, beginning from the reconsecrated man; it is a temple of the newly awakened life. *The new consecration is extended to everything.* The lordly authority of the monarch is consecrated by religion; his sceptre contains a piece of the Holy Cross. Every land has been provided with special messengers of God and is marked by their traces. Everyone of them can boast its own sacred history of reconciliation and has *individualized* the new consecration. To every single act and everything in the highest and lowest activities the consecration is given anew that they had lost; —the old curse that lay on all things is dissolved; the whole of nature is received into the state of grace and its grief reconciled.

Through this reconstructed religion the other side, the ideality of the spirit in the *form of thought*, is added to the only form of spiritual ideality that can exist in nature religion, namely, *art*, and the folk religion must contain the highest Ideas of speculation expressed not just as a mythology but in the *form of Ideas*. It reveres the Absolute in the form of *Trinity*. God as the *paternal principle* being *absolute thought*; then his reality, the Father in his creation, *the eternal Son*, who, as the divine reality has two sides, the one being that of his genuine divinity, according to which the Son of God is God, the other the side of his singularity as world; finally the eternal identity of the objective world with the eternal thought, the *Holy Spirit*. Since religion proceeds from the infinite grief, the reconciliation of this grief has this connection objectively at the same time in the reconciled God as love; and the divinity in which this love finds its own felicity must come to be the *Mother of God* herself.

In *Catholicism* this religion has come to be a *beautiful* one. *Protestantism* has superseded the poetry of consecration, the individualization of holiness, and has poured the color of universality over a *patriotically* hallowed nature, transposing the *patria* of religion and the appearing of God into the distance once more—far from the peo-

[140] ple's own fatherland. It has changed the infinite grief, the sense of life, the confidence and peace of reconciliation into an infinite *yearning*. It has imprinted on religion the whole character of *northern* subjectivity. Since it has in general transformed the whole cycle of grief and reconciliation into yearning, and yearning into thinking and knowing about reconciliation, and since the violence and [external] necessity with which the grief was aroused thus falls away in it, its character as infinite grief and reconciliation became the prey of chance, and this form of religion could pass over into empirical reconciliation with the actuality of existence (*Dasein*) and an unmediated and

untroubled immersion in the common round of empirical activities (*Existenz*) and necessities of everyday. The religious exaltation and hallowing of empirical existence, the *Sabbath of the world*, has disappeared and life has become a common unhallowed workaday matter.

Though Hegel at that time considered Protestantism to be just as much a finite form of Christianity as Catholicism (a fact which emerges clearly enough from the above report), still he did not, like many of this contemporaries, on that account go over to Catholicism. He believed rather that through the *mediation of philosophy* a *third* form of religion would emerge out of Christianity. He said in this connection: "Since that beauty and holiness [of Catholic Christendom] has gone under [in nationalism], it can neither *come back again*, nor can we *mourn* for it. We can only recognize the *necessity of its passing* and surmise the higher thing for which it has to prepare the way and which must take its place. —From what we have already said, in other words, it is evident that the reconstruction occurs within the sphere of the antithesis from which the grief came, and the whole form of religion up to this point belongs primarily in the *Potenz* of the *relative antithesis*, for Nature is hallowed, but not by a spirit of its own; it is reconciled, but it remains for itself a secular thing as it was before. Consecration comes to it from something external. The entire spiritual sphere has not risen up into the spiritual region from its own ground and soil." [*Haym continues here*: "This idealistic sphere forms an adventurous realm without rules; it has tumbled together at random from the histories and the imagination of all peoples and climates, without significance or truth for nature, which is placed in subjection to it, and equally without allowing that the spirit of the individuals of a people can maintain their right within it; it is without personalized (*eigentümliche*) imagination, as it is without personalized consecration."][6] "The infinite grief is permanent in the hallowing, and the reconciliation itself is a sighing for Heaven. —Once the alien conse- [141] cration has been withdrawn from Protestantism, the spirit can venture to hallow itself as spirit in its own shape, and reestablish the original reconciliation with itself in a *new religion*, in which the infinite grief and the whole burden of its antithesis is taken up. But it will be resolved purely and without trouble, when there is a free *people* and Reason has found once more its reality as an ethical spirit, a spirit which is bold enough *to assume its pure shape on its own soil and in its own majesty*. Every single [person] is a blind link in the chain of

6. *Hegel und seine Zeit*, (1962), p. 165.

absolute necessity on which the world develops. Every single [person] can extend his dominion over a greater length of this chain only if he recognizes the direction in which the great necessity will go and learns from this cognition to utter the magic word which conjures up its shape. This cognition, which can both embrace in itself the whole energy of the suffering and the antithesis which has ruled in the world and all the forms of its development (*Ausbildung*) for a couple of thousand years and can raise itself above it all, this cognition only philosophy can give." [*Haym*: Through philosophy "Reason gets its vitality (*Lebendigkeit*) and nature gets its spirit back again."][7]

7. *Loc. cit.*

Hegel's First Philosophy of Spirit

(being Part III of the "System of
Speculative Philosophy" of 1803/4)
translated with an Introduction
by H. S. Harris

For the Summer term of 1803 Hegel announced his first "encyclopaedic" course: *philosophiae universae delineatio* or an "outline of *universal* philosophy." In the language of the Identity Philosophy *Universum*
was the technical term for the Absolute as a *totality*. Thus we have in
the language of the announcement a flicker of evidence to confirm that
the system of 1803 is structurally similar to that of 1801.[1] Hegel was
lecturing (or at least offering to lecture) on "Naturrecht" regularly
every term, and I have suggested in my "Interpretation" that the so-
called "System of Ethical Life" was distilled out of his regular lectures
on "natural law" in a form which he thought would be suitable for
direct incorporation into the system of "universal philosophy" as he
then conceived it.

But in order to complete the "universal philosophy" Hegel had for
the first time to write a systematic sketch of his own philosophy of
Nature. The "Introduction to Philosophy," which he gave during his
first term, began with an outline of the Idea of Philosophy, in which
the reality of the Idea was divided into two moments: body and spirit.
Nature, and *imprimis* the solar system, was declared to be the real
body of the Idea; *Sittlichkeit*, and ultimately the life of a free people,
was likewise its real *spirit*. Between these two stable realities the immortal process of the earth and the mortal process of human life and
consciousness made the bridge for the transition from nature to spirit.[2]
So the philosophy of Nature must "come down from heaven to earth"
and reach its culmination in the theory of the living organism that is
rational, whereas the philosophy of spirit must "rise up" from the first
dawn of cognitive awareness to the systematic exposition of the "intuition of the *Volk*."

Hegel's first two attempts at a philosophy of Nature fit directly into
this pattern.[3] So does the *System of Ethical Life* on the other side of
the central turning point. But the *System of Ethical Life* does not quite
touch the center point properly. It begins—as a *practical* philosophy
naturally would—with the development of need, labor, and enjoyment
out of the primitive unity of feeling. In short it begins with *desire*
(*Begierde*). But the parallel between "natural" and "transcendental"
philosophy in the *Difference* essay requires, (and the introductory lecture of 1801 confirms) that the first phase of the "resurrection" must
be theoretical. Not *die Begierde* but *das Vorstellen* is the first *Potenz*
of the philosophy of Spirit.[4]

In the *Difference* essay itself Hegel speaks of the "self-constitution of intelligence as a point" (i.e., the individuated human mind) as a turning point which is external to both alike, but at the same time as the "center where Science establishes itself."[5] He experienced the difficulty that arises from this ambivalence in his efforts at theory construction. Each of the two sciences of the "real Idea" tends toward this center; but the philosophy of nature "tends" toward its culmination in man as the embodiment of theoretical Reason, whereas the philosophy of spirit seeks its point of origin in the free spontaneity of practical reason. Thus Reason (considered as a "totality" and for itself) is half inside and half outside of each of the two "philosophical sciences." When the science of the Idea is expounded as one single whole, it is the higher science that is most seriously affected by the proper completion of the "totality." For now its point of origin, which in the practical science as an independent whole was defined from the point of view of the final goal, or *realized* totality, is itself the totality of rational nature concentrated into a point and known as a point. Nature is the reality of the Idea as simple substance or being; Spirit is the reality of the Idea as thinking substance, or *conscious-being*. Thus the initial *totality* that we arrive at as we pass over from nature to spirit in the continuous exposition is that of being-conscious, it is the moment of absolute contraction of Nature into the living self where *Bewusst-sein* or *consciousness* comes to birth.

The fact that the "concept" of spirit is *consciousness* is not mentioned in the *System of Ethical Life*. But one might think that it is so clearly implicit there that it can be made explicit by simple addition. I assume that this is what Hegel himself believed when he began to compose the *System of Ethical Life* for an "outline of universal philosophy" which still had a gaping hole at its center. If that hypothesis is correct, then we must add that Hegel became dissatisfied with his exposition very soon, when he tried to fill the hole in this simple additive way. We can see from the philosophy of Spirit of 1803/4 that having once laid it down that "Bewusstsein" is the "concept" of spirit, he was unwilling to abandon the standpoint of "consciousness" at all. In the philosophy of Nature the great stages of the Idea's expression are *spatially* distinct. First there is the "system of the Sun," and then (within it) there is the earthly system. Within that again, but distinguished from it by mortality, there is the system of the living organism. Life reaches its point of *absolute contraction* in the *consciousness* of the cognitive organism. But the expansion of that "point of contraction" ought now to take place *continuously from within*. The need for a spatial stage upon which the drama can be observed is what typifies Nature as opposed to Spirit. There ought to be no need to look at Spirit from the outside, to observe it as we observe the "natural history" of an organic species. Spirit, as conscious-being, must evolve for itself—or from within—continuously, passing from the small, temporal auditorium of mortal organic awareness, to the greater one of the *Volk* and its history, in a continuous unbroken flow (and from there to the eternal history of the divine life in which the "logic" of the Idea would receive its experimental confirmation). The process does indeed involve an observer, for the identity of the conscious self with the world that it is conscious of can only become evident initially to a third (observing) consciousness. But it is a process that takes place within consciousness, and the function of the philosopher is not just to observe it, but to participate practically in bringing it to consciousness.[6]

In the *System of Ethical Life*, however, natural consciousness, and even *Sittlichkeit* itself, the ethical consciousness of the free people, is viewed from a speculative point of view which is sometimes inside the evolution of consciousness itself and sometimes outside it. Sometimes we *move with it* as it unfolds for itself, and sometimes we observe it from an eternal standpoint which reduces the motion and sequence of forms to the flickering of shadows in the firelight.

For the Identity Philosophy a flickering show is, indeed, what all the motion and sequence of empirical consciousness amounts to. But if I understand Hegel's position rightly, he held that it ought to be possible to exhibit the ideal evolution of spirit itself without any flicker. The speculative philosopher is (as the name implies) an *observer*. But when he is observing the development of spirit itself, there is no need for a continual alternation of the historical-genetic and the conceptual-analytic standpoint (such as we find in the *System of Ethical Life* at least until we arrive at the level of *Sittlichkeit* itself). The evolution of spirit is itself a steady movement toward logical or absolute cognition. Its phases only need to be identified in the flickering light of ordinary experience and the connecting thread pointed out as they are arranged. Conscious-being *is* in itself a rational process of evolution, since it is the realization of Reason for itself rather than outside of itself.

At any rate what distinguishes the philosophy of Spirit of 1803/4 is the evident determination to bring out the "infinity" (of natural being) which is focussed in the "simplicity" of immediate awareness, without abandoning the standpoint of consciousness itself. The most important, and the most difficult, step toward understanding the text as a whole is the comprehension of Hegel's theory of consciousness. That this is indeed difficult is evident enough from Hegel's own struggles to state it. He wrote it out four or five times in different ways. But once we are over this initial hurdle, the development and sequence of the argument is much easier to follow than the logical thread of the *System of Ethical Life*; and since the content of Hegel's views has not changed much, the later manuscript will be found very helpful for the understanding of the earlier one.

The best way to approach Hegel's own struggles is from the end. When he gives up the attempt to say what consciousness *is* and begins to tell us what it *does*, he finally touches upon some traditional problems in a way that is illuminating. There is a traditional dispute, with a long history, about whether colors, sounds, and other "secondary qualities" exist really "in the thing" (realism) or only "in the mind" (idealism). Hegel's discussion of this problem shows us how different the standpoint of "consciousness" is from either of these traditional positions. "The thing" and "the mind" are just the antithetic "sides" of the *a priori* synthesis of consciousness. To look for the "ground" of color, etc. in either of these sides is to lose sight of the real problem about color, which is the problem of relating particular colors, (and color-perceptions) with the universal "color." "Color" *exists* in three "potencies." First, there is "sensation." A sensation is a determinate event "in the thing" (the objective world of bodies). This is the justification of "realism." Secondly, colors exist as *imagined concepts*. Hegel does not refer to Hume's problem about the "missing shade of blue," but it is plain that he would hold that we *can* imagine it. And what we *imagine* exists "in the mind." This is the justification of subjective idealism. But what is interesting is the power of memory to classify the imagined shades by *names*. Thus "blue" embraces many shades—and the color vocabularies of different communities vary considerably in the way in which they divide up the array of discriminable color sensations.[7]

If we think about *this* problem, instead of the traditional one, we can begin to see the power, and the attraction, of Hegel's doctrine. Determinate sensations are bodily states of an organism interacting with an environment. The *consciousness* of them that the organism *is said* to *have* is the expression of a power to discriminate and organize sensations which the organism does not have, *could not* have, in isolation from other conscious organisms. Consciousness is free and spontaneous, for my sensations are uniquely mine, and only I can express the consciousness of them. But as a medium of expression consciousness cannot be private to me. Anything that I can express, even to myself, is in principle *universal*, or communicable to other conscious beings. Consciousness is essentially a universal *medium*, and only a *community* of beings capable of becoming conscious can produce any actual conscious beings. What distinguishes human from animal existence is man's communal capacity to rise into this "aether" and to shape its absolute plasticity into definite patterns of communication.

If we take this theory of language (the first *Potenz* of consciousness) back with us to the beginning of the manuscript, I think that most of Hegel's struggles to present the bare concept, the aether of the spirit itself,[8] will become comprehensible. He is trying to find the most abstractly general description of the unformed element or medium, which takes on different shapes and patterns in every human language and in every other aspect of communal life and experience. Inevitably, in order to avoid the limited perspective that is directly implied in any *one* formulation (a limitation that is bound to give rise to pseudoproblems like the one about "secondary qualities" in our own philosophical tradition), he is driven to offer several alternative formulations side by side. But he cannot decide how to order them or array them in relation to one another.[9]

The formula that is basic to all of his drafts, because it is the one that is structurally necessary for the "indifference point" between Nature and Spirit in the Identity theory, is that "consciousness is the concept of the union of the simple with infinity." Thes re the two "sides" (mind and thing-world) which we have alrea met in our quick look at the controversy between realists and idealists. But now the sides are so abstractly characterized that mind and world can each take either role. Already, in dealing with the dialectic of intuition and concept in the *System of Ethical Life*, we saw that we must sometimes view "Nature" as the realization of "the concept" (i.e., as the instantiation of the range of real possibility). This is no harder really than thinking of it as a Parmenidean equilibrium of simple being.[10] Common sense avoids that extreme but likes to insist, with Bishop Butler, that "everything is what it is, and not another thing." What Hegel is asking us to see is that "everything is what it is" in the context of an evolving system of interpretation (apart from which we cannot speak of *things* at all). This system of conscious interpretation enters into the constitution of "things." The mistake of the realists is their commitment to "nominalism." Nothing that can be *named* is absolutely singular, because conceptualizing consciousness is the medium of existence for nameable "singular" things.

On the other side the status of "the mind" is absolutely ambivalent in the same way. In its theoretical activity it appears to be the "place of forms" as Aristotle called it; its whole activity is a generation of universal entities (as was instanced in the case of "blue"). At the same time we are *always* conscious of ourselves as uniquely *singular*, once we become conscious of ourselves at all. When we begin to *act*, this singular self-consciousness becomes unavoidable; and in the action of the uniquely singular being the ontological ambivalence becomes fully explicit; for here the agent consciousness stands forth as the singularized *concept* imposing itself upon the stuff of the world.

All this ambivalence receives both its explanation and its justification from the fact that Hegel is trying to get away from the normal opposition of self and world and to find a neutral position from which this opposition itself can be comprehended. "Consciousness," as he defines it, *is* this neutral position. We ordinarily think of "consciousness" as a peculiarly subjective thing—perhaps I should even say *the* peculiarly subjective thing. Each of us has his own and it is uniquely private to him. That is why it is essential, for the correct understanding of Hegel's doctrine to pay particular attention to the universal, shared aspect of consciousness, its essentially communal basis and origin.

Because every conscious mind appears to itself to be indubitably singular and unique, the communal aspects of experience naturally appear to us to be the necessary structures of the individual mind itself (as a mental entity). This is to say these structures make up the "concept" of the mind itself. Thus when Kant recognized that our "objective world" is a product of conscious interpretation, he simply assumed, as did everyone else schooled by Descartes and Locke, that he was discovering the fixed structures of the human mind as a singular thing. It becomes quite evident that he was not doing any such thing, that he was identifying rather the commonly posited structures of the *conscious world* of the great scientific revolution, as soon as we examine his theory of the mind from the standpoint of an earlier scientific culture like that of the Greeks.

The conscious world of the Greeks is as full of spiritual agencies as Kant's world of scientific understanding is devoid of them. The scientific thinkers of the Greek world formulated their theory of the rational totality of experience in terms of the "divine life"; and it is not at all hard to see why they did so. Since the singularity of every rational consciousness is an indubitable certainty for it, there is an inescapable tendency to formulate our awareness of the universal, communal, basis of consciousness in terms of one *great* consciousness that is as singular as the individual minds that depend on it. Kant felt this pull just as the Greek thinkers did. He responded by banishing all of this imaginative *religious* consciousness to the noumenal realm of faith. But it is just as "necessary" as the structures of the phenomenal realm. If the "necessities" of consciousness conflict, we can properly speak of "dialectical illusion"; but it is a mistake to suppose that we can certainly identify where the *illusion* is. That certainty is *itself* a dialectical illusion. Hegel's object, in seeking to establish the standpoint of "consciousness" as a *neutral* one vis à vis the great conceptual dichotomies of self and world, singular and universal, is to avoid precisely *this* pitfall.

All of the rational *certainties* from which dialectical illusions (and hence conflicts) arise have their origin in the indubitability of our own existence as singular consciousnesses. Greek mythmaking is the projection of this certainty at the intuitive (or imaginative) level. Kant's noumenal world is the projection of it at the conceptual level (the level of "Understanding"). But according to Hegel, "the highest existence of consciousness is when for the individual his opposite itself has its being as absolute consciousness, that is, as *unity* of what is conscious, with what it is conscious of, the singularity of the individual is *eine aufgehobene*."[11]

Once we have comprehended the basic perspective and the ultimate goal, the sequence of the argument should be fairly easy to follow. We have already dealt briefly with the evolution of imagination into language, via memory. The practical correlate of this is the transformation of the physical world by human labor. We should notice at once that the essential relation between consciousness and nature (especially the natural sensory existence of the living organism) is one of *domination*.[12] Imagination, memory, and conceptualization (which begins with *naming*) involve the *domination* of natural sensation, its subjection to the higher purposes of conscious existence. Once we recognize this, we can begin to see why the transition from natural existence to properly social (or *rationally* conscious) existence must necessarily involve a "struggle for recognition."[13]

The development of language and labor begins in the context of a kinship-organization—the family. This is the *natural* level of conscious existence, where the spirit is in *bondage* (*gebunden*).[14] When we do reach political existence, we shall find Hegel claiming that the

Greeks were right in holding that prepolitical man is "barbarian," i.e., he cannot talk properly.[15] Apparently he means that the speech of a small tribe must express the untransformed natural environment, not the physical subjection of nature in practical consciousness. Since the active subjugation of nature is essential to the development of consciousness, tribal societies that have accommodated to a natural environment are bound to have all their values wrong. Language must express the viewpoint, not just of man the maker, but of man the self-maker, the creator of institutions and values, the educator.

This same transvaluation of values explains the contrast between the *natural* labor which Hegel analyses[16] under the *Potenz* of "the tool" here and the slave labor that is his concern in the *Phenomenology*. In our manuscript he is thinking of the free labor of Greek artisans. This *is* the *real* subjugation process through which the foundations of human culture are laid. But again, when he came to analyse labor in modern society, Hegel found that the natural value of labor as self-expression is inverted.[17] No doubt this was what caused him to focus his attention in the *Phenomenology* upon the servile labor that results from surrender in the life-and-death struggle.

The family is treated here, just as it was in the *System of Ethical Life*, as the "totality" of natural consciousness. It is the natural community that makes free consciousness possible, through the process of self-recognition in the other, which distinguishes human sexual relations from the natural drive of the brutes. Once more we may note that Hegel was obliged in the *Phenomenology* to focus attention on a "struggle for recognition" between the sexes in order to account for the transformation of natural ethical existence into the conscience-governed freedom of his own rational world. But there is no hint of that inevitable rift in the domestic lute as yet.

What we *do* find here, but not in the *Phenomenology*, is the keystone for the theory of domestic education as the natural relation of "independent and dependent" consciousness.[18] The child passes from an unconscious to a conscious state of being by recognizing his real self in the conscious world of his parents. The relation of dependence is mutual, for the parents know that their achieved consciousness, their self-possession or independence, can only be preserved by transmitting it to the child. The parents know that they are mortal, and their education of the child is a conscious preparation for the day when they will step aside, and he will take their place. "In this way the totality of consciousness is in the family the totality as an evolution into being for self."[19] Self-possession involves conscious family responsibility. Without that there would never be an independent consciousness prepared to embark upon the struggle.

Because the text is fragmentary, we cannot say for certain how Hegel intended us to regard the transition from consciousness in the bonds of nature to the free consciousness of the *Volk*. It seems best to follow the structural analogy of the *System of Ethical Life* and to take "the Negative" as a moment of transition from the lower level to the higher one. But since Hegel was evidently writing under pressure and giving only the barest summary of his views even about the higher level of communal consciousness, the articulation of the system becomes very sketchy even in the fragments that we do have.[20]

The import of the text itself is fortunately quite clear. The independent consciousness that emerges from the family with a full awareness of its responsibility must be prepared to lay down its life for the sake of its independence. There are of course—as Hegel has already noticed in his treatment of "lordship and bondage" in the *System of Ethical Life*[21]—naturally submissive or dependent individuals. But for the maintenance of a free community a military élite is essential. So the self-sacrificing independent consciousness of the fighting man must be developed within the natural community before a truly free social consciousness will be possible. This is the consciousness of the biblical "strong man that keepeth his goods."

Hegel obviously delights to lay out the structure of the ethics of "honor," because it shows forth "consciousness" both in its *integrity* (honor allows no distinction between subject and object, the tiniest trifle in the "outer world" can become a "point of honor") and in its dialectical character (in order to prove that he is strong enough to keep his goods, the independent consciousness must sacrifice all goods, even life itself). The dialectic of independence thus leads to the real conquest of nature. The free consciousness must regard *all* natural goods (even its own self-preservation) with *contempt*.[22] In this way singularity is consciously "superseded." The noble consciousness contradicts itself in its own self-assertion, since it accepts death willingly. In the *natural* course of ethical life the conscious recognition of mortality is the great educational force, for it is the acceptance of death as inevitable that makes education the ultimate concern of the family. But the willing *acceptance* of death for the sake of whatever "whole" the natural course of ethical life has generated makes a new kind of whole, and a new kind of ethical life based on free decision, possible.

This great transition, from the natural bondage of self-preservation to the freedom of self-sacrifice for the *polis*, is what Hegel was principally interested in. It has to be conceived as a struggle for recognition, it has to be based on an ideal of *personal* honor, *personal* integrity, because simple self-sacrifice is evidently not enough. The warriors of warlike tribes can exhibit a natural bravery that wreaks *havoc* in the lives of their more civilized neighbors. But unless they have arrived at *understanding* of the civilization that they conquer (so as to have *lordship* over it as their conscious aim), their bravery is not the virtue of courage.[23] It will have educational significance, if any, only for their opponents. *Independent* existence is an essential presupposition of *self*-consciousness, and *self*-consciousness is the transformed medium of *free* ethical life.

Very soon Hegel will become conscious of the educational significance of *defeat* in the struggle. We can see this already in the "Philosophy of Spirit" of 1805/6, where *tyranny* is treated as an essential moment in the establishment of the rule of law.[24] In the *Phenomenology* defeat assumes focal significance. But in the first philosophy of Spirit, as in the *System of Ethical Life*, the resurgence of the vanquished goes unnoticed. The long history of class struggle *within* the *polis* is simply ignored. It is as if Athens had no history between Theseus and Themistocles. We pass directly from the mutual recognition of tribal chieftains or feudal barons to the legal equality of the Napoleonic Code.

It would seem that during the period of his commitment to the Identity theory Hegel saw very little that was of speculative interest in the great stretches of human history that lay between periods of ideological revolution. Speculative philosophy was for him the final flowering of a revolutionary period, the birth of the new age in consciousness;[25] and since on the side of *theory* it was always the same speculative vision that was reborn,[26] the capacity to leap from peak to peak over vast tracts of historical time was a mark of speculative insight. Speculation itself comes to birth when it is *needed*; and the need arises when the unity of social consciousness has broken down, when the aether of human communication is riven by the separate existence of great categoreal worlds within which independent consciousness is possible.[27] Speculation itself must recollect and harmonize all of the "imperfect" philosophies that express this independent consciousness.[28] But Hegel does not yet see any need for it to recollect the development of the consciousness of the age as a whole. It must rather "collect" the consciousness of the new age by organizing it into the new speculative synthesis. This is what Hegel appears to be doing in the final pages of his first philosophy of Spirit. The great leap from Theseus to Napoleon is taken as intuitively obvious. We could not be doing speculative philosophy, as we know that we are, if we were not at a point of history that can be recognized as a new beginning.

There can be little doubt that in his Platonic "collecting" of the aspects of true or free social consciousness Hegel intended to display the necessity of the class structure which he takes as basic in the *System of Ethical Life*. For the same structure reappears in the "Philosophy of Spirit" of 1805/6.[29] We can even surmise with some confidence that he meant to do this by repeating the cycle of finite consciousness (or consciousness in natural bonds), since the pattern of repetition is clear enough in what remains to us of the manuscript.

The first level of communal consciousness, Language, is the great medium of spiritual unity. We have already considered the difference between tribal speech and the language of a free *Volk*, and no more needs to be said about that here. We should notice, however, that free language is the medium within which all social differences are to be articulated and that after this articulation has taken place, it will be the medium of cultural reunification through the artistic and religious experience of the community. We can see fairly clearly from the original lecture announcement that this final synthesis is no longer regarded by Hegel as a separate part of the system of speculative philosophy.

When Hegel began the *practical* articulation of social consciousness, with labor and possession, however, a problem declared itself, which puts the wisdom, and even the feasibility, of his direct leap from tribal origins to modern times in doubt. Even the *System of Ethical Life*, with its evident echoes of the *Republic*, was a design for modern living. But the first philosophy of Spirit is conceived more straightforwardly in the terms of the great "contract theories" that it seeks to replace. The Hellenic inspiration is clear enough; it becomes quite clamant in the first pages on the *Volk*. But the attempt to develop communal consciousness in the world of machine manufacture and international trade forces Hegel to spell out the enormous difference between the ancient *polis* and the modern state. In a passage which anticipates Marx,[30] he shows quite clearly why the consciousness of a modern laborer must differ *toto coelo* from that of a classical artisan. The economic process in which he is only a vanishing element, replaceable on the instant, is inexorably forcing him back into the bondage of natural need, without even the reasonable hope of natural enjoyments.

The modern social order is one where dependence on nature has been replaced by dependence on the understanding. The economic structure is like the solar system; it is a dead body which moves mechanically. But unlike the solar system it does not move reliably. Consciousness, which is parcelled out in it, can only suffer the fate of Job under its domination.

Hegel's analysis breaks off as he is moving from labor to possession, from the worker to his employer. It is clear enough that he had no thought of going in a Marxist direction. He would have dismissed the idea of a classless society as a Utopian dream, and the goal of scientific communism he would have attacked (as he attacked the socialism of Fichte)[31] as an extreme form of tyranny—the tyranny of abstract understanding. As soon as we put the theory of the natural classes in the *System of Ethical Life* into the context of the "consciousness" theory of the first philosophy of Spirit, we can see why he always thought of civil society in terms of self-regulating "corporations." These communal systems are the necessary foundation of individual self-awareness. If he were alive now, he would be a keen analyst of pressure groups and lobbies, and especially of the relations between trade unions, employers' unions, corporate interests, and the central government. The economic machine is to be caged and fenced in, like our not very domesticated stock. We can expect to change it to the same limited degree (and in the same indirect and very gradual ways) as we do our stock.

It is obvious enough in the last pages of our manuscript that Hegel is compressing and summarizing his material. No university course could end where our manuscript does; he must either have written more than we now have or else used older material for the completion of his lecture program at the end of the term. Minimally, he had to run through the forms of social consciousness required by the class structure of the *System of Ethical Life*, moving from the bourgeoisie to the military aristocracy and from that to the "absolute consciousness" of the intellectuals—artists, priests, and philosophers.

If we accept the hypothesis that the fragment which Rosenkranz took to be the "lost" conclusion of the *System of Ethical Life* is actually the conclusion of the "outline of universal philosophy" of Summer 1803, then we have good evidence that Hegel had already brought one such survey of the "forms of consciousness" to an extremely rapid and condensed conclusion. This is the most natural hypothesis, because that fragment seems so plainly to be the closing of a survey based on the earlier quadripartite plan (Logic—Real Body—Real Spirit —Absolute Idea). In that case Hegel did have a usable survey available which he could easily adapt to his newer triadic model. So perhaps he simply used it and never did finish our manuscript.

On the other hand we can quite plausibly argue that the Rosenkranz conclusion does not seem to come from a survey in which the "resumption of the whole into one" was accorded an independent treatment. Perhaps the use of the "parallel universes" terminology is simply an accidental employment of the familiar language of the Identity theory at the end of the new tripartite scheme. Hegel continued to use a *parallel* division of philosophy ("Speculative" and "Real" philosophy, with the former divided into Logic/Metaphysics and the latter into philosophy of nature/philosophy of spirit) until 1806, in spite of the absorption of the fourth part of his original scheme into the third. So perhaps the Rosenkranz fragment is in fact the conclusion that Hegel wrote for our present manuscript. It is certainly *summary* enough, and the emphasis on *death* as the "negative absolute" is perfectly appropriate. But no *decisive* argument is possible from the internal evidence, precisely because this emphasis is one of the major links between the *System of Ethical Life* and the first philosophy of Spirit. Hence the Rosenkranz fragment has much the same import as an indication of how Hegel conceived the culmination of the philosophy of Spirit whether he wrote it in 1803 or in 1804.

Instead of speculating idly about what we do not have, or cannot be certain about, we must appreciate the significance and the varied relevance of what we do have and what we can be sure of. At first sight our present manuscript appears very difficult in itself. But all of its difficulties really boil down to the initial one. Once the basic conception of "consciousness" is grasped, this manuscript has two great values. First it helps us to understand the more complete *System of Ethical Life* which preceded it. That is the reason why it is published here alongside that first statement of Hegel's social philosophy; and the main object of my commentary upon it here has been to maximize this usefulness. But secondly it anticipates Hegel's more ambitious attempt to systematize the forms of "consciousness" in the *Phenomenology*. I have tried to illustrate that aspect too, but I have not been able to offer more than the most general pointers. All of the Jena "systems" must be viewed *together* for the proper appreciation of what any one of them contributes to that end. The two documents translated in this volume (with their appendixes) are perhaps the most important and the most obviously relevant ones. I believe that any thoughtful student who studies them together will find, first, that they are each of them more intelligible than they are when considered independently, and secondly, that they help more in the understanding of Hegel's first great published work, when taken together, than they do taken separately.

NOTES

1. The use of the term *universum* is attested for 1801 (and explained) in the fragmentary lecture manuscripts recently discovered (see *N.K.A.* V). In 1802 Hegel used it to formulate his published critique of Schleiermacher (*Faith and Knowledge*, pp. 150–52). The fragment which Rosenkranz wrongly believed to be the conclusion of the *System of Ethical Life* (see note 3, pp. 178–79) is almost certainly not earlier than 1803, and the way the term is used there suggests quite strongly that it is the conclusion of this "outline of universal philosophy." In that case the hypothesis of structural continuity between 1801 and 1803 must be regarded as securely confirmed. Hegel's conception of the "System" developed considerably in the interim (as the newest manuscript finds reveal, and the essay on *Natural Law* confirms). But the fourfold articulation of the Absolute as a "Substance" is maintained.

2. Compare the "system outline" given by Rosenkranz and cited in full on p. 6. The fragments upon which his summary was based will be published in *N.K.A.* V. The scheme differs from that given in *Difference* (pp. 166–72) because of the insertion of Logic at the beginning as the fundamental science of the Idea. Hegel's own comments upon this addition were

quoted by Rosenkranz and are translated in Appendix, p. 262.

3. It is fully confirmed in the system of 1804/5 (which is continuous until it breaks off altogether at the beginning of the theory of the organism). The system of 1803/4 is fragmentary, and no part of the theory of the solar system has survived. But the "transition to the earthly system," which we do have refers back to it in a summary fashion that is quite unambiguous (*N.K.A.* VI, 4, lines 2–7).

4. I could see this implication clearly in the *Difference* essay before the lecture manuscript was discovered (see *Difference*, pp. 59–60). Of course my conjectural reconstruction there does not agree perfectly with the lecture manuscript, but I do not think that the *Difference* essay itself agrees perfectly (at p. 168) with the lecture manuscript either. I assume that in the months after Schelling's "breakthrough" Schelling and Hegel continually discussed and reformulated the plan for the systematic exposition of "the Idea."

5. See *Difference*, pp. 169–70.

6. We can see the method of the *Phenomenology* coming to birth in Hegel's explicit discussion of this problem on pp. 212–14.

7. See especially pp. 224–25.

8. There is nothing particularly metaphorical about Hegel's description of consciousness as "aether." *His* concep-

tion of the aether (for which, see p. 205, n. 3) is better exemplified by consciousness than by anything in nature. It is not at all surprising, to my mind, that although he no longer made any use of his concept of the aether in his mature *Philosophy of Nature*, he always continued to employ it in the *Philosophy of Spirit*. Of course, as K. L. Michelet pointed out long ago, Hegel's conception of the aether has little or nothing in common with any physical theory of the aether. That is why I have chosen to maintain the initial diphthong—which reminds us that we are speaking of one of the Greek elements.

Even Hegel's continual appeals to the four elements of this mortal world are not poetic or metaphorical. For instance, when he says that "consciousness steps forth from the earth" (pp. 207–08 n.), he certainly means us to remember the myths of Deucalion and Pyrrha and of Cadmus, (as opposed to the story of the making of Adam). But he is interested in the *scientific* sense of the Greek myths. The natural existence of man is that of a living organism generated and sustained within the immortal organic process of the earth (compare pp. 214–16). I have generally chosen to ignore Hegel's philosophical theory of the natural background of spirit. But this is not because I consider it unnecessary or unimportant. Rather it is because the historical interpretation of it is generally quite simple and because a proper revision of it in terms of our own scientific world view is not at all simple. Such a reconstruction is, in my view, highly desirable. But it is also, for the most part, beyond my competence.

9. The dialectic of "sense certainty" in the *Phenomenology* was his eventual solution to this problem. But the complex of drafts in which he originally confronted the problem casts as much light on this "solution" as the solution does upon them—see especially pp. 218–20.

10. This is what the solar system exemplifies once its proper periodicity (the so-called "Great Year") is known. Hegel is obviously pointing an analogy with this reconciled unity of rest and motion in nature in the cancelled passage in note 7 on p. 207.

11. See p. 207, note 8 (the emphasis is mine). The passage comes from the first draft and was subsequently cancelled (see pp. 204, 212–13 for revised versions that were allowed to stand). As both of the revised versions show, Hegel was here interested in the "individuation" of the *Volk* in its God-consciousness. But "absolute consciousness" as defined here is *not* properly the consciousness of God as a great *individual*. Singularity is *aufgehoben* in it; that is to say, it is more like Fichte's impersonal concept of God as the "moral world order," except that the gulf between the phenomenal and noumenal worlds is overcome in the Hegelian version. In other words it is the absolute consciousness of the human historical experience as a community of conscious world interpretation. Religious consciousness is in the mode of imaginative *presentation*. Speculative philosophy gives it the conceptual form of "absolute consciousness." Compare the fragmentary "conclusion" quoted by Rosenkranz and translated on p. 178 above.

12. Compare pp. 217 and 221–22. Collingwood's theory of consciousness as the domination of sensation is a direct development of this Hegelian position—see his *Principles of Art*, Book II, and *New Leviathan*, pp. 18–66.

13. Compare pp. 227–28.

14. See p. 216.

15. See p. 245.

16. See p. 229–31.

17. See pp. 245–49. Compare the *System of Ethical Life*, pp. 117–18.

18. I believe that it *is*, in fact, present in the *Phenomenology* as the bare concept which Hegel states before proceeding to develop the experience of the struggle: see *Phenomenology*, trans. Miller, sections 178–84. But Hegel does not make this explicit. The whole pattern is not made explicit here either, since Hegel develops the totality in terms of mutual self-sacrifice. But if we read the discussion here (pp. 233–35) in the context of the theory of the family and of education in the *System of Ethical Life* (pp. 109–11), the whole relation emerges quite clearly.

19. p. 234–35.

20. See note 45 to p. 235.

21. See p. 125.

22. Compare here the passage quoted by Rosenkranz and translated in Appendix 2 at p. 261.

23. Compare the *System of Ethical Life*, pp. 133–34.

24. *N.K.A.* VIII, 255–60.

25. See the passages from lectures cited by Rosenkranz (Appendix 2, pp. 255–56, 260, 263–64.

26. See, for instance, *Difference*, pp. 87, 88, 114; and the passage from the "Logic and Metaphysics" lecture of 1801 cited in *Faith and Knowledge*, pp. 10–11.

27. The "need of philosophy" is discussed at length in *Difference*, pp. 89–94. Hegel was still concerned to explain it in the lectures of 1803 (see the fragments in *N.K.A.* V).

28. See *Faith and Knowledge*, pp. 56–66, 189–91.

29. See *N.K.A.* VIII, 266–77.

30. This has been brought out very well by Avineri, *Hegel's Theory of the Modern State*, pp. 92–95.

31. See *Difference*, pp. 144–49.

Hegel's First Philosophy
of Spirit

An Interpretation

(Jena 1803/4)

The first part of [the system of speculative] philosophy[1] constructed[2] the Spirit as Idea; and it arrived at the absolute self-identity, at absolute substance which in coming to be through the activity against the passivity within the infinite antithesis absolutely *is* just as it absolutely *comes to be*. [In the second part] this Idea fell absolutely apart in the philosophy of Nature; absolute Being, the Aether,[3] sundered itself from its Becoming or Infinity, and the union of the two was the inner aspect, the buried [essence] which lifted itself out in the organism and exists in

[268,
Fragment
16]

1. The three "parts" of the system are: I: Logic and Metaphysics, II: Philosophy of Nature, and III: Philosophy of Spirit. Nothing survives from the "first part of the present system."

2. "Construction" is Schelling's technical name for the method by which each *Potenz* of the Absolute Identity is developed from an original "identity" to a "totality." Construction replaces the method of "transcendental deduction" in the Critical Philosophy and its many epigones. From Hegel's formal definition of it in the *Logic* of 1804 (*N.K.A.* VII, 113) it is evident that the method is thought of as analogous to the procedure of "construction" in Euclidean geometry. Thus the terminology was adopted as a conscious homage to Spinoza's "geometric method." But the procedure itself, at least as conceived by Hegel, owes more to Plato and Socrates than to Spinoza. It is the process by which a formal definition is shown to involve what it excludes, or by which a division is generated, of which the universal concept thus "constructed" is the relating ground. The clearest illustration of the procedure meant is the *System of Ethical Life* itself. But the conceptual thread of that work is difficult to follow precisely because the procedure is there exemplified without being explained.

3. In the fragments of 1803/4 no discussion of the "aether" survives. In 1804/5, however, Hegel describes it thus: ". . . the absolute ground and essence of all things, is the aether or absolute matter, that which is absolutely elastic and despises every form, but which is likewise absolutely plastic, giving itself and expressing every form. . . . The aether is not the living God; for it is only the Idea of God; but the living God is he who [is] self-cognitive from his own Idea and cognizes himself as himself in the other of himself. The aether, however, is absolute spirit which relates itself to itself, [but] does not cognize itself as absolute spirit" (*N.K.A.* VII, 188, lines 4–13). In 1805/6 Hegel restates this theory of the aether, but he makes it clear that his "aether" is not really a physical hypothesis (see Hegel's *Philosophy of Nature*, trans. M. J. Petry, I, pp. 188–89).

the form of singularity, that is, as a numerical unit; [finally] in the philosophy of Spirit it exists by taking itself back into absolute universality, it is really the absolute union [of Being and Infinity, essence and existence] as absolute Becoming.[4]

[A: THE FORMAL CONCEPT OF CONSCIOUSNESS.]

[265, Fragment 15]

[266]

In the spirit the absolutely simple Aether has returned to itself by way of the infinity of the earth; in the earth as such this union of the absolute simplicity of aether and infinity exists; it spreads into the universal fluidity, but its spreading fixates [i.e., fragments] itself as singular things; and the numerical unit of singularity, which is the essential characteristic (*Bestimmtheit*) for the animal becomes itself an ideal factor, a moment. The concept of Spirit, as thus determined, is *Consciousness*, the concept of the union of the simple with infinity;[5] but in the spirit it exists for itself; or as the genuine infinity; the *opposed* [moment] in the [genuine] infinity in consciousness is this *absolute simplicity of both* [singularity and the infinite][6] This concept of Spirit is what is called *Consciousness*; what is opposed to it is itself a simple [being] such that it is implicitly infinite, a *concept*; every moment [of consciousness] is in itself completely the simple *immediate* opposite of

---

4. This first paragraph is written on a separate sheet. Hegel did not make any insertion sign in his continuous manuscript. However the same sheet contains two other passages which were written for insertion at points that are securely identifiable in the revised text a little further on, and only one of these insertions is clearly marked by Hegel himself. It is clear enough that the passage was drafted while Hegel was revising his first version, and the heading itself (which is repeated from his main manuscript) shows exactly where the new text was intended to go. The new beginning makes a short digressive intermission in the continuity of the argument in the first version. But it appears to me to be supplementary to Hegel's review of the philosophy of nature there, rather than alternative to it. So I have, rather hesitantly decided to treat it as an *insertion* (like the other passages on the sheet) and not as a *parallel* text (which Hegel either abandoned or remained undecided about). The reader should note that the considerations that have influenced my decision were bound to be weighed by Düsing and Kimmerle, since Hoffmeister had already treated the text in my way. But they decided, nonetheless, to segregate this passage as a distinct fragment.

5. This passage "and the numerical unit . . . the simple with infinity" is written on the same sheet as the opening paragraph (see note 4) and clearly marked for insertion at this point.

6. I have tried here to translate exactly what Hegel wrote: "das entgegengesetzte in der Unendlichkeit in ihr ist diese absolute Einfachheit beyder selbst."

itself;[7] the singular taken up in universality without conflict; but *consciousness* is likewise itself the immediate simple opposite of itself, [for] on the one hand it opposes itself to the one [being] of which it is conscious, by sundering itself into active and passive; and on the other hand [it is] the opposite of this sundering, the absolute union of the distinction, the union of the distinction both in being and superseded. [267]

[At this point the continuity of the revised version is broken. The continuous first draft, which we have, has been crossed out— including a revision which was partially crossed out. It seems clear that both text and revision were cancelled because Hegel wrote a new version of the whole passage on a separate sheet which has been lost. The final state of the cancelled text is given here in angled brackets.]

<In the animal the immediate experience of supersession (*Aufgehobenwerden*) was indeed restricted and an opposite for it; but this opposite was itself another than itself [i.e., its mate] in such a way that the other-being, was the unity outside it; the animal is in itself the simple universal, but because what was opposed to it was not the universal, this universality [of the rational consciousness] did not exist as such, but is for itself always just a particular [animal]. The existence of this universality is what is identical in both antitheses, it is that wherein the intuiting and the intuited infinity are one.[8] <266>

<269>

7. At this point the first version continues: "and as simple infinity, an infinity brought to rest. Both [simplicity and infinity] are strictly at one without movement, absolute rest in absolute motion, and absolute motion in absolute rest." (The next paragraph of the cancelled first version is printed in the text.)

8. Here Hegel began his revision. But he cancelled the first sentences of his revised text (down to the point where the angled brackets end in our text). The original text (which was, of course, also cancelled) continued as follows: <269> The universality exists as consciousness; but the consciousness of the individual is at the same time the consciousness of singularity, [and] as such it is nothing *qua* universal. It is the unity of the infinite as a single being and as a universal self-identical being; the individual is a single being and is the unity of both [singular and universal] as consciousness. The highest existence of consciousness is when for the individual his opposite itself has its being as absolute consciousness, that is, as unity of what is conscious with what it is conscious of, [and] the singularity of the individual is a suspended one. The infinity of consciousness is the supersession of the opposite in its simplicity; the essence is always this middle, within which the superficial, self-cancelling antithesis of what is conscious with what it is conscious of has its being (*ist*). This middle, i.e., consciousness as absolute, must realize itself. It is not real, insofar as it is consciousness of the individual, for this is rather its ideality, its cancelled characteristic. It steps forth

Consciousness, the concept of spirit, is within itself the opposite of itself in its simple unity. The form of the opposite is determined by the essence of consciousness; the terms of its antithesis are as absolutely simple as it is itself; the one is posited under the form of simple unity, the other under that of simple multiplicity. > The simple essential multiplicity is the thus determined concept, the single [being] immediately taken up into positive universality, the single [being] as self-identical, or its other-being, its nonidentity made identical with itself. What is opposed to it is *unity as absolutely unequal* [or] *as absolutely exclusive,* [i.e.,] *numerical one;* this is indeed self-identical but in its self-identity it is the direct other of itself as absolutely negating [itself], or the absolute singularity.[9]

[269, Fragment 17]

[270]

In as much as the concept of Spirit [is] the absolute union of absolute *singularity* (for the multiplicity as negated) with the absolute mul-

---

from the earth as consciousness of the singular [being]. Its existence in this mode is rather the being of the individual and subsumes it under singularity; only the abstraction of consciousness is posited. Its true existence is [such] that in it the individuality that the individual brings with him from his animal existence cancels itself, and that consciousness is negative in subjecting the animal organization under itself and positive in organizing itself as absolute consciousness within itself; as this pure consciousness it supersedes itself as an opposite along with what is opposed to it. In antithesis to the individual generally, pure consciousness is itself <270> the abstraction, it only exists with the characteristic of singularity.

Because it exists as absolute middle, it exists equally absolutely as something that is in the individuals, and as something opposed to them, etc. (as in text at p. 209, line 15).

9. Here Hegel cancelled his first revision and wrote a new version on the back of sheet 115—the sheet already used for two previous additions to these opening pages of his third section. He did not indicate clearly that this passage was to be inserted here, but, as the reader will see, the sequence of thought is natural at the beginning. The word flow from this insertion on to the back of the present sheet can also be construed naturally (see note 10). The cancelled revision continued to the bottom of the recto of this present sheet (117) as follows:

"The Earth was, in general, the element of the numerical unit; but [it was] only this unit as infinite divisibility, i.e., the unit itself was only [there] as possibility, it existed as individual [for the first time] in the organism; but vegetable as well as animal singularity is only directed to this end, to maintain itself for itself; but according to its essence [its end is] to supersede itself; and its return into itself, its coming to absolute singularity is just the supersession of itself and the coming to be of another singularity [i.e., its offspring]; its maintenance of singularity [is] not in absolute singularity. In consciousness the numerical unit which negates all multiplicity exists for the first time truly and the negated multiplicity [exists likewise] as a simple multiplicity."

tiplicity which is itself positive or implicitly universal, simple multiplicity, the concept must *realize* itself.

The whole consciousness—this unity of singularity, [or] negative
unity, with the posited implicitly universal multiplicity of the determinate concept—must elevate itself to absolute singularity, [and] must
elevate singularity as such to totality; and from this self-shaping of the
individual [consciousness must] pass over likewise into its opposite;
and just as, in the former [the self-shaping of the individual], the absolute concept of consciousness exists as absolute singularity, so in the
latter [i.e., the plurality of individuals] [it must] exist outwardly as determinate concept, i.e., as something essentially multiple within itself;
and must resume itself out of both sides into absolute totality[10] so that
it exists equally as one great individual, [or] as the spirit of a people
which absolutely is in the individuals who are its singular [moments],   [271]
[or] organs; and as opposed to them even in their organic functions
[for] it exists as object of their singular consciousness, as something
external, because although they are absolutely one in it, they likewise
cut themselves off from it and are on their own (*für sich*). It is their
universal unity and absolute middle; and [is that] wherein they are
posited ideally, as superseded, yet their supersession in it is at the same
time [posited] for themselves; in their supersession the living spirit of
the people *is*; their supersession is for themselves; it is implicitly the
consciousness of any one of them, even in so far as it is a single [being];
and hence it appears; it exists at the same time as *something distinct
from them, something intuitable*; as another being of the individuals,
than they are [on their own account]; but in such a way that this other-
being of theirs is [their] absolutely universal self for themselves.

In so far as we are cognizant of the *organization* of the spirit, we do
not regard consciousness as the merely inner aspect of the individuals,
or the way in which the *moments of the* antithesis appear in the *individuals* as such as distinct capacities, inclinations, and passions, etc.
which are related to particular objects as to *determinate concepts.* Instead, because we recognize consciousness generally, according to its
concept, as the absolute union of singularity and the determinate concept, we take cognizance of its organic (*organisierenden*) moments too,   [272]

10. This is the end of the insertion from the back of sheet 115, where half of
the page is left empty. The following clause, "So that . . . spirit of a people" is
written in the margin of sheet 117 verso and forms a bridge joining the inserted
passage to the running revision of the main text. The connection of this marginal
bridge passage with the insertion and with the body of the text eluded Hoffmeister. But it is completely convincing as soon as the sequence is recognized.

in the way that they are on their own account as moments of the absolute consciousness, not as something which is merely, in the form of
the individual, one side of the absolute consciousness; [i.e., not merely]
as if it were passion, drive, inclination, etc. but [the absolute conscious-
ness] as it absolutely is for itself, and as it organizes itself on its own
account, and is thus assuredly in the *individuals*, but directly as their
other side, the one which they set against themselves as individuals;
but consciousness is the essence of both.[11]

[280,
Fragment
19][12]
The first form of the existence of the spirit is consciousness in general, the concept of spirit as it makes itself into the totality, whether as
this concept [i.e., ideally] or as consciousness [i.e., really]; [for consciousness in general is] its purely theoretical existence, [and] here in
its [mere] concept its opposed moments are similarly universal concepts in general; hence they are not internally related (*sich beziehende*)
to one another as absolute opposites [i.e., in real existence] but have a
formal internal connection in the simple element of consciousness; they
are unimpaired (*unangegriffen*) in their being for themselves and are
only reciprocally self-cancelling in their form, still subsisting on their
own account apart from this. But because consciousness takes their

11. In the first version this paragraph read as follows: <271> "Hence, in so far
as we are cognizant of the organization of the spirit, we do not regard consciousness as the merely inner aspect of the individuals, but rather as existing, as what
[really] is in them, their essence, but likewise as set against them in as much as
its infinity is real; consciousness is at one time such that even while it is the
consciousness of individuals, it is their supersession as individuals, and likewise
an external [object] for them; we treat it, therefore, not in the form of possibilities, capacities of the individuals, but as it is for itself outwardly with equal absoluteness, and as having its own necessary organization in this being for itself."
[Between the cancelled draft and the new one Hegel inserted: "*absolute unity.*"
This may be meant as a paragraph heading.]

12. We have now come to the end of sheet 117. It is quite likely that sheet 99
followed next in the first version. Hegel wrote two different later drafts which
contain revised versions of the first lines of sheet 99. One of them (fragment 18)
begins with other material and is continuous with the main body of following
text (fragments 20, 21). Fragment 19, which I have inserted here, is more distant-
ly related to the first lines of sheet 99 but deals with much less extraneous
ground. The probability is, therefore, that it was the latest version. But given the
state of our evidence it has to be treated as a "parallel" discussion, not as part
of the more or less continuous manuscript. I have therefore chosen to place it
here, because the continuum is broken here in any case, rather than make an
artificial break for it (as the editors of the Critical Edition do) or relegate it to a
footnote at the point of closest parallel (which seems inappropriate for what may
well be Hegel's most considered statement of this phase of his argument). Further
justification for not following either of these courses will be found in note 14.

form from them in this way, it determines the antithesis as absolute form subsisting on its own account, absolute introreflection, absolute emptiness of the concept, on one side, and absolute matter on the other. Consciousness exists, first as *memory* and its product *speech*, and by way of the understanding (as the being of the determinate concept) it becomes the simple absolute concept, absolute introreflection, the emptiness of the formal capacity of absolute abstraction; and the connection of the antithesis becomes a superseding of [terms that] implicitly differentiate themselves in mutual opposition; the theoretical process passes over into the *practical* process in which consciousness likewise makes itself into totality [and] thus gains here[13] a real existence opposed to the previous ideal one; for in *labor* it becomes the middle as the *tool*; whereas in the first potency [i.e., memory and speech] it proved its ideal lordship over nature, here it proves its real lordship and thereby constitutes itself as spirit for itself withdrawn from nature and independently self-shaped; it has superseded the antithesis on the external side, so that it falls apart within itself and realizes itself in mutually differentiating moments, each of which is itself a consciousness, in the difference of the sexes, in which it likewise supersedes the singular desire of nature, and makes it an *abiding* inclination, having come to the totality of singularity in the family, and raised up inorganic nature into a family holding, as the singularly enduring outward means for the family (*Mitte derselben*); and from here it passes over to its absolute existence, to *ethical life*. [281]

Both of these [processes], the ideal constitution of consciousness as formal *Reason*, absolute abstraction, absolute emptiness [and] singularity, and its real constitution as the family, the absolute riches <cancelled: absolute fulfillment> of the single being, are themselves just the ideal moments of the existence of the spirit, or the way in which it organizes itself immediately in its *negative* relation to nature. Spirit comes forth as ethical essence, free being for itself and enjoying its own absolute self: in the organization of a *people* the absolute nature of spirit comes into its rights.

13. The words "so hier" come from the middle of a cancelled passage and were, perhaps, left standing by mistake. Hegel originally wrote: ". . . makes itself into totality, <and just as it becomes absolute emptiness, simplicity against absolute multiplicity, in the critical process, so here [*not* cancelled] [it comes] to riches within itself, a totality of being,> it *gains* etc."

14. Hegel wove part of his first draft into the *third* sheet of this revised version. It is possible that some of the first draft was suppressed or destroyed when he completed this version. But it is a bit more likely that the first pages here were written either as a *review* of the doctrine already expounded, or—more radi-

[273,
Fragment
18][14] *The essence of consciousness* is that there is absolute unity of the antithesis immediately in an aetheric identity. It can only be this *in as much as immediately, so far as it is opposed,* both terms *of the antithesis are consciousness itself,* [and are] *in themselves, as terms of the antithesis, immediately the opposite of themselves,* [i.e.,], they are the absolute difference cancelling itself, they are the superseded difference, they are simple. —In this unity of the antithesis, that which is self-conscious is one side, and that of which it is self-conscious is the other side of the antithesis. Both sides are *essentially the same*; both [are] an immediate unity of singularity and universality. But this *being-conscious*, and that of which *it is self-conscious*, only is this unity of consciousness for a third [consciousness] not for the unity itself; for in the antithesis of the conscious being and that of which it is conscious, the one is rather not what the other is; consciousness arises as a self-conscious being from itself as consciousness, [i.e.,] as the actively negating identity which, from its becoming conscious to itself of something other than it is, returns into itself, and supersedes this other, by the expedient of passing on to yet another. *Consciousness* itself, although in its essence it is equally the supersession of both, appears only on one side, the side which is characterized as *active* and hence as cancelling; it posits only itself as consciousness, not that of which it is conscious; and it is therefore only singular, formal, negative, not absolute consciousness;

[274] for that which it is conscious of, it does not posit *as like itself*; this *self-equality it has only* in a *negative way*, in that it supersedes this [object] that it is conscious of as something not like it; but it only is consciousness so far as it *opposes* itself as an *other*; it must therefore let another that is unlike it enter in the place of the other [that is itself] it cancels *every such unequal*; but it arrives in this way only at the empirical external infinity, which the other of itself always has outside it. But this *empirical consciousness* must be absolute consciousness, i.e., it is immediately the other of itself, it must have its other-being, its positive equality with consciousness, in itself. It is absolute consciousness, when

cally—to *take the place of* the earlier draft as a whole (except for its introductory paragraph). If Hegel wrote the new draft with either of these ideas in mind, then his subsequent writing of fragment 19 represents at least a *tentative* decision either to return to his previous draft (if he had been thinking of replacing it) or not to burden it with so much repetition (if review was what he has had in mind). In either case fragment 19 belongs logically with the preceding discussion and forms an alternative transition, or bridge-passage, to the systematic exposition ("Fragments" 20, 21) from which "fragment" 18 has been artificially separated by Düsing and Kimmerle.

this other than itself is its own perfected consciousness,[15] without any being on its own account, without any genuine distinction, only distinct from it through the *empty contentless* form of other-being, so that the form, because it is so devoid of content, is implicitly universal and [only] ideal. —This is the goal, the absolute reality of consciousness, to which we have to elevate its concept. It is the totality which it has as the spirit of a people, spirit which is absolutely the consciousness of all, for they *intuit* it, and as consciousness set themselves against [it], but directly recognize all the same that their opposition, their singularity is superseded in it, i.e., they recognize their consciousness as an absolutely universal one.

Consciousness as its [own] concept has raised itself directly from the animal *organization* [*margin*: This consciousness, having come into being, it must come to be for itself]; we have freed it from that; in as much as we have recognized in principle the suspension of the antithesis as a being, [or] as something subsistent, not implicitly ideal, [but] as it is in nature; [in other words, we have recognized] that everything differentiated, [and] opposed is in virtue of its difference immediately in its opposite implicitly, and therein it is not. Consciousness is the simple-being of infinity, but since it is consciousness, it must be this supersession of the antithesis for itself; it must itself for the first time become real consciousness apart from its concept. Up to this point, in nature, wherein the spirit does not exist as spirit, it is we who have been in *our cognition* the existing spirit of Nature,[16] which does not exist in it as spirit, but as entombed [or] is only in nature as something other than itself. What is in the sphere of spirit, is its own absolute activity; and our cognition, in that it raises itself out of nature, [and] the antitheses that have standing in nature are ideal, having been cancelled, must be recognized as a cognition of the spirit itself. Or [it must be recognized as] spirit's coming to be, i.e., its merely negative relation with Nature. This *negative relation with* nature is [the] negative side of spirit in general, or how it organizes *itself within itself as this negative*: or in other words, how it becomes [the] totality of consciousness of the

[275]

---

15. In Hegel's text the comma comes earlier: "It is absolute consciousness in as much as this other than itself is, etc." But I think the intended sense is the same, and it is clearer when the comma is moved.

16. Again I have been forced to move a comma (following this time, the example of Hoffmeister). What Hegel wrote translates literally as "We have in *our cognition* the existing spirit, of nature been which in it . . ." But the German auxiliary is "we are" not "we have," so Hegel's comma made sense as it came from his pen. The tense shifted from present to past as he wrote.

single [mind]. For consciousness [in] itself, as active, as negative, as cancelling the being of its other-being,[17] is consciousness as one side of it only; it is subjective consciousness, or consciousness as absolute singularity.

Consciousness is the ideality of the universality and infinity of the simple in [the] form of opposition; as universal it is undistinguished unity of both [universality and infinity]. But as infinity [it is] the ideality in which its opposition *is*; and the two [aspects of universality and infinity] are distinct and external to one another in consciousness, they separate themselves; their unity thus appears *as a middle* between them, as the *work* of both, as the third whereby they are related, in which they are one, but [as] that wherein they likewise distinguish themselves; the conscious being distinguishes this middle from himself, just as he distinguishes himself from what is distinguished in conciousness; but with the difference (*Unterschied*) that he also relates both [himself and the object of consciousness] to this middle; absolute universality comes to be the *middle* only in the subject, in the isolating of the antithesis. As this middle it [subjective consciousness] is itself an opposite, or it has therein the form of its existence; for its existence is that wherein it is an opposite. *Hence,* when *we* are cognizant of *the articulation of consciousness* to its totality, we cognize it as it is [for] itself as a moment, [or] in a determinate aspect, and it *is* as determinacy, as one [term] in [a pair of] opposites[18] in as much as it is a middle; and its organization in the reality of its moments [is] an *organization of its forms* as middles. It must be for itself as [an] absolutely universal simple [being] likewise become the opposite of itself, it must go through the antithesis; or [it must] be synthetically opposed [in the] product; and it is only a determinate [subject], posited *as moment* of its totality, insofar as it is as [a term] in the antithesis; or it exists in as much as it is that wherein both terms, the self-conscious being, and that of which he is self-conscious, are posited as one, and also oppose themselves to it; in other words consciousness itself is in this way something afflicted with a determinate character, an existent.

[276]

The being of consciousness in general is, to begin with—when it posits in itself the reflection that was previously ours—that it is the *ideality of nature*; in other words it is at first in [a] negative relation with nature, and in this negative relation it exists as tied to nature itself

---

17. Again I follow Hoffmeister in moving the comma (which Hegel placed after "cancelling"!)

18. The reading of Hegel's erratic shorthand is uncertain here. Quite possibly "e in" is simply "ein," so that the translation should read simply "as an opposite."

within the relation; the mode of its existence is not a particular [or] a singular aspect of nature, but a universal [moment] of nature, an *element* of it; the elements in which [consciousness] exists as middle are just the elements of air and earth, as the indifferent self-identical elements, not the unrest of fire and water; for consciousness only is qua absolutely self-identical,[19] and qua existing middle it is itself posited as a quiescent indifferent middle.

As *concept* of consciousness this *middle* is in that element which is the simple self-identical one among the elements; its external middle [medium][20] is *the air*.

Thus the first three moments of the existence of consciousness are [i] that it exists as [something] ideal, *as something not stable*, but *evanescent* in its appearance, in *the element of air*.[21] Next, [ii] that it sinks [277]

19. Hegel's first impulse was simply to say this, and he finally returned to it. But he was momentarily tempted into an analogy from his philosophy of the organism: "for already in the plant, the absolute unity of these two [i.e., fire and water] is posited, and they have gone into supersession." (The whole passage about the four natural elements is an insertion made after the writing of the final brief paragraph about the air, with which Hegel made his transition back to the revision of his first draft.)

20. Hegel wrote first: "external middle." He then wrote in "medium" below the line but failed to cross out "middle." Both Hoffmeister and Düsing-Kimmerle think that it was only left standing through an oversight. My reasons for thinking otherwise are given in the next note.

21. We have now reached sheet 99, where Hegel begins once more to revise his first draft. The two paragraphs of the first draft (which must enter into consideration for the comparative study of fragments 18 and 19) originally read as follows:

<277> The first form of its existence is that it exists as [something] ideal, as something not stable, but evanescent in its appearance, in the element of air, next, that it sinks down from the air into the earth, and comes forth from this as surpassed (*geworden*) earth. And these three forms of its existence constitute precisely the ideal potency of its existence, since it is itself submerged in externality, in nature, at this stage: it must free its existence from this [natural externality], and consciousness itself must also be the form of its existence, its externality.

That first existence in bonds is its being as speech, as *tool*, and as possession; <278> but the second [existence is] as people.

Fragment 19 preserves less of the content above. But it *begins* with the same phrase (which is altered in fragment 18). Since Hegel preserved both versions, we may tentatively conclude that he never quite decided whether he wanted earth, air, fire, and water in his discussion here or not. The fact that he left both *Medium* and *Mitte* standing in the previous paragraph confirms this hypothesis. The air as external *medium* belongs with fragment 19 (and the sentences inserted down from the air into the earth itself as a singular individuality; [a] changeable external element, and there stabilizes itself, becoming a middle for itself, as it moves out of its concept, the form of its simplicity, to become practical—a middle in which the opposite [aspects] of consciousness are really connected; and [iii] this mode of its existence as earth singularized, *overcome* (*geworden*), or subdued, comes forth as an earth which is posited like a *third element*, a universal earth [risen] out of its natural singularization. But as consciousness is absolutely free on its own account, it tears itself away from this [mode of] its existence in the determinate elements, and its element is just the absolute element of *the Aether.*

That first existence of consciousness as middle in bonds, is its being as *speech* [in the air], as *tool* [in the earth], and as [family] goods. Or as simple union [of the opposites, rather than middle between them, it is] *memory, labor,* and *family. For the standpoint of* [subjective] *con-* [278] *sciousness* which only *looks at the antithesis* of consciousness, these *two* [moments] *of consciousness* itself appear on the *two sides of the antithesis; memory* [in the simple union] *appears on the side of that which is self-conscious; speech* [the middle] *on the other side;* similarly labor and family are on the self-conscious side, tool and family goods on the other. But the truth is that speech, tool, and family goods are not merely the one side of the antithesis that is opposed to [the subject] who posits himself as conscious, they are just as much connected with him; and the middle [is] that in which he separates himself from his true antithesis: *in speech,* from others to whom he speaks; in the tool, from that against which he is active with the tool; through the family goods, from the members of his family. He is qua agent; these middles are not what he acts against—not *against speech, tool* as such, family goods as such—but they are the middles, or as it is called, the means, whereby, *through which,* he is active against something else.

Likewise [the subject] is only active through the other side of the middle, through memory, labor, and *family;* the activity of the individual can be directed against either side and against their single moments [e.g., most obviously, tool, labor, family goods]; and it can posit the

---

about the elements (p. 215 lines 3–8) would have been cancelled, if *Medium* and fragment 19 were finally adopted). On the other hand the air as "external middle" belongs with the revised text of fragment 18 as we have it. For this reason I have ventured to disagree with both German editions and have given it pride of place.

moments themselves as ideal. But not in the way that it can posit single things as ideal, [by] destroying [them], for the moments are absolutely necessary [and] *universal*; and for all that they appear to him as "his," as posited ideally in him, they are none the less absolutely necessary in themselves, and it is the individual who as a single being stands under their lordship, rather than they under his. But in principle, there is here no lordship relation either of or over the individual, for the individual is only a formal side of the antithesis, whereas the essence is the unity of both sides, and this unity is consciousness, which, as such, presents itself as universal on both sides of its universality. Each of these two sides in their opposition is the unity of both, [i.e.,] the unity of that ideal antithesis of the conscious individual and what is opposed to him; the unity both as universal—memory, labor, and family—and also as existing unity or as middle [speech, tool, and family goods]; [both unities] are the absolute universal. The existing unity is the universal as existing, and as existing absolutely: as *enduring*, having universal existence.[22] The sides of the antithesis, on the other hand—the active individual and his passive object—are only enduring as antithesis in general,[23] and this universality of theirs as antithesis is precisely the existing middle; what they are on their own account is the changeable [or] contingent [aspect], that belongs to the *empirical necessity* of nature as such. What [is] essential in them, [or] universal, is this middle. Consciousness as existing certainly exists in the antithesis of active against passive; but what is (*das Seyende*) in this opposition itself, just that is the middle of existing consciousness. Those ideal sides of the antithesis of consciousness are like the ever-changing and perishing fire and water; but consciousness as universal and as middle [is like] air and earth. In coming to be this middle [consciously], consciousness gains existence; it comes to an *enduring absolute* product, while nature on the other hand could not [come] to any *enduring product*; it never arrives at any genuine existence, but always is just the difference, and for this reason, too, it never reaches *the fifth element* [the aether]; in the animal it only gets as far as the sense of voice and hearing, i.e., to the immediately vanishing hint of the [real] process [of consciousness] reduced to simple being (*einfach geworden*) and the wholly formal existence of the inner [conceptual side].

[279]

22. Hegel added "as existing IN ITSELF" (doubly emphasized). But he crossed it out.

23. I.e., no single agent, object, conflict, or product endures, but the concept always has application.

First Level: [Speech]

As spirit, the product of Reason, the first product is the middle as its own concept, [or] as consciousness; and it realizes itself in consciousness, i.e., it is *memory* and *speech*; from this middle the spirit generates the practical antithesis through understanding and *formal* Reason, and supersedes it in labor.[24]

[283] *[a) Intuition].*

Consciousness in its ideal potency, *as concept*, has elevated itself immediately out of *sensation*; sensation, posited as ideal or as superseded is a singularity for which other-being is something else outside it, *not immediately itself* [*margin*: another sensation than that of the sensing [organism], or another sensing of the thing, which is the same]. The ideality of sensation, or its coming to be consciousness, has as its immediate goal that [active] sensation shall become in consciousness something inwardly opposed that has its other-being, and hence precisely the object sensed, in itself, and the sensing [subject] shall become in himself a universal. Sensation as singular is to become infinitely singular. *Singularity as such*, which is implicitly infinite, so that in this singularity it abides wholly in its determinacy, or separated infinity in the immediate existence of its concept, is time and space, and consciousness intuits *in time and space* immediately; in space the singular as a subsistent, and its own other-being outside itself; but as it is equally posited in time, it is as something transient, something implicitly ideal, being no longer, even while it is; not that it just passes away in time, but that it is posited with reflection as being in time. It does not intuit space and time as such, they are universal and empty, higher idealities in themselves, concepts, but it intuits them only as both being and not being qua universal; [being] when it posits them as singular particular-

---

24. The first version began: "A. *Formal Existence* / I. Level of Speech/" [Hegel did not cross these headings out and may have intended to use at least the second one].

"Consciousness is as such something external [for] itself; it does not exist in flame and water, for it is as absolutely quiescent infinity, not the former [fire], and since in its simplicity it still moves itself from within, it is not identical in form with the latter [water]. Its external element can only [be] the one that is in itself simple, the air, and the synthetic one whose essence itself is also this simplicity [i.e., the earth]." (The material here was mostly absorbed in fragment 18. See especially the insertion on p. 215 at lines 3–8).

ized [contents] as filled [time and space]; [not being] because even   [284]
while space and time are the positive universal [side] of consciousness,
it makes them at the same time immediately and formally the opposite
of themselves and particularizes them; that being of consciousness [i.e.,
its positing space and time] is just as much theoretical, passive, as it is
practical; the theoretical side consists in its being in the form of positive
universality, and the practical in its being simultaneously in negative
universality, and particularizing this universality itself. This form of
consciousness is *empirical imagination*; as positive universality, *intuition* is in the continuity of time and space generally; but at the same
time [empirical imagination is] breaking it up, and turning it into determinate singular beings, i.e., making it into filled pieces of time and
space.

b) [Imagination].

But this *singularizing* remains immediately in the *universal element*
of consciousness [i.e.,] in the universal space and the universal time
within consciousness itself. And it abides in such a way that (a) this
space and time of consciousness is immediately just as much an absolutely empty simplicity as it is a full one; those singularities of intuition
have disappeared in it now, and it is their universal possibility. Within
this empty possibility they have been set free from the side of sensation, which they had in them. The side of sensation was their singularity, [i.e.,] an external contextual dependence on other [singular things]
according to their [causal] necessity. But now they belong only to the
universality of consciousness. But [b] this empty time and space of
consciousness particularizes itself just as absolutely once more, and re-
calls every [intuited] bit within itself. With respect to its content this   [285]
particularization is just those primary sensible representations, but the
universal [form] *that is particularized* is the *universal element* of consciousness itself, its empty infinity as time and space; the recalling
within itself of intuitions had previously or in another place. The determinacy of the sensation, the *this* of time and space,[25] is abolished *in
it*, and their succession and coordination appears as a free one, it is
quite contingent (*gleichgültig*) for the universal element; [it is] an active reproducing, since it is this universal element that is particularized.
    This *formal being* of consciousness has no genuine *reality*, it is *some-*

25. Reading "das *dieses* der Zeit und des Raumes, getilgt," instead of Hegel's
"das *dieses*, der Zeit und des Raumes getilgt."

thing subjective, it does not exist externally; it only is as the form of
the abstract, pure, *concept* of infinity, as space and time, the concept of
infinity as it immediately is as consciousness; and consciousness as this
empirical imagination is a waking or sleeping dream, *empty* and *without truth*, [occurring in human experience] either as permanent de-
rangement, or as a transient state of sickness, when consciousness falls
back into the animal organism, and only is as its concept.

This *dumb consciousness* is its *formal being* in its own univeral element of infinity, and only the formal specification of this universal ele-
[286]   ment; it must gain an existence, become external,[26] or [in other words]
posit what is then distinguished in the formal way in intuition as something external, [the point] at which the two opposites, the intuiting and
the intuited, are separated, and consciousness is as an existing middle.
This existence of consciousness will be just as inadequate and formal, as
consciousness itself is in its universal aspect [i.e., existence will match
concept]. It can express nothing in itself, [except] that what is intuited
should quite generally be posited as something other than it is, but that
consciousness is still not truly for itself therein, but only as something
that is still connected with the antithesis to a subjectivity, something
opposed to the being of the subject, just as it is to what is opposed to
the subject; and precisely for this reason the opposed [object] remains
what it is, it still has *its being on its own account*, and its other-being
is only posited as something that ought to be; consciousness, as its own
concept falling apart into space and time, is, so to speak, just too weak
to suspend the antithesis of subject and object completely; and in its
externalization [it is too weak] to represent the actual union [of its concept and its existence] as more than an ought. Consciousness as this
existing middle of its concept is thus just a *sign* in general, in which
something intuited, wrenched out of its context, is posited as connected
to another, but [only] ideally, because it still subsists in truth in its context; the significance is its ideality as external to it, and [the sign] is

---

26. The first version continued: "[it must] be on its own account, outside of
the individual. This externality is, in the first place, something wholly universal
[and] <286> indifferent; and precisely for this reason consciousness is not yet in
it for itself, since this externality is not at the same time a negatively infinite,
[or] self-cancelling one. This positively universal externality does indeed, qua
universality of consciousness, supersede the intuited [single sense-impression] as
what it is, and posits it as a universal, as something other than it is; but it remains what it is, it still has its being on its own account, and its other-being is
not immediately [and] as such in it. This externality is *signifying* in general, in
which, etc., [at line 4 from bottom].

itself a being that subsists,[27] *a thing*; [it is] infinite in this respect, that   [287]
it means something other than it is, it is posited as something other
than it is on its own account; [it is] contingent for that of which it is
the sign; [and] no longer having being by itself on its own account.
And the supersededness of the subject is no more posited in the sign
than the supersededness of the intuited [object]; the meaning of the
sign is only in relation to the subject; what the subject thinks by means
of the sign depends on his caprice, and is only comprehensible through
the subject; the sign does not have its absolute meaning within itself,
i.e., the subject is not superseded in it.

c) [Memory].

This *dumb signification* must absolutely cancel the indifference of the
subsistence of the ideal terms;[28] the *meaning* must be on its own account, in opposition to that which it means and that for which it has
meaning; and the sign as *something actual* [must] thus directly vanish.
The idea of this existence of consciousness is *memory*, and its existence
itself is *speech*.

Memory, *the Mnemosyne of the ancients*, is according to its true
meaning, not the fact that intuition, or what have you, is the product
of memory itself in the universal element, and has been recalled from
it, while the element gets specified in a formal way that does not affect
the content at all, but the fact that memory makes *what we have called
sense intuition* into a *memory-thing*, a thought content: it suspends the
form of space and time in which they [the sense-impressions] have
their other outside of them, in time [that is] likewise ideal, and posits
them implicitly as other than themselves. In this [product] consciousness gains for the first time a reality, because the connection to the outside gets nullified in that which is only ideally in space and time (i.e.,   [288]
has its other-being outside it): and it gets posited ideally on its own
account, in that it becomes a *name*; in the *name* its empirical being as
a concrete internally manifold living entity is cancelled, it is made into
a strictly *ideal*, internally simple, [factor]. The first act, by which Adam
established his lordship over the animals, is this, that he gave them a
name, i.e., he nullified them as beings on their own account, and made

27. Only the sign satisfies this condition. Hence the emendation proposed by
Düsing and Kimmerle—*dieses (das Zeichen)* for *diese (die Idealität)*—is probably
correct though not unavoidably necessary.

28. Hegel added here in his first draft: "it is theoretical, it must become practical."

them into ideal [entities]. This sign was previously, qua [natural] sign, a *name* which is still something else than *a name* on its own account; it was a thing, and what is signified has its sign outside it, it was not posited as something superseded, so that the sign does not have its meaning in itself, but only in the subject, one must still know specifically what the subject means by it; but the name is in itself, it *persists*, without either the thing or the subject. In the name the *self*-subsisting reality of the sign is nullified.

The name exists as *speech*. Speech is the existing concept of consciousness, so that it does not fixate itself, but immediately ceases to be, when it is. It exists in the element of air, as an externality, (i.e., manifestation] of the formless free fluidity [of the aether]; it is as absolutely external to itself as [that fluility] is which has universally communicative existence.[29] The empty voice of the animal gets an infinite, internally determined meaning [*or*: a meaning that is internally determined in an infinite way]. The pure sounding of the voice, the vowel, distinguishes itself, because the organ of voice indicates its articulation as an organ [of conscious spirit] in its distinctions; this pure [289] sounding gets interrupted by the mute [consonants], the authentic restrictions of mere sounding, and the principal means by which every tone has a meaning on its own account. For the distinctions of mere tone in a song are not determinate distinctions on their own, but are determined in the first place through the preceding and following tone. Speech as articulated sounding is the voice of consciousness, because every tone within it has meaning, i.e., because there exists in it a name, the ideality of an existing thing; [in other words] the immediate nonexistence of the thing.

Infinite as it is in its simplicity, speech thus interrupts itself as infinity of consciousness within itself, it organizes and articulates itself; and it becomes a manifold of names. But it recovers itself out of the absolute manifold likewise. The name as such is just the name of the single thing; speech is the *relating* of names, or once again it is the *ideality of*

29. Perhaps I am wrong in seeing an intentional reference to the aether here. But it makes little difference to what is asserted about language. The text *can* be read: "for it [speech] is absolutely external to itself, when it is; it has the absolutely communicative existence." This seems to be the *only* clear sense of the first draft. In that first draft Hegel added: "[it is] the first simple existence of rationality, [or] simple, pure, Reason; for the element of air leaves it free on its own account. (*margin*: "vowels and consonants") (This last clause, with its marginal comment, is more fully explicated in the revised text. The first clause was simply eliminated because, if my reading is right, Hegel elected to refer *back* to the aether rather than *forward* to Reason.)

the multiplicity of names, and it *expresses* likewise this *relation*, the achieved universal (*das gewordene Allgemeine*); in other words it becomes *understanding*. In the universal element of speech names [are] only formally ideal in themselves, they express the concrete determinate [thing]; but the unity of the element in which they are, posits them equally as these determinate [things], i.e., as different from one another, [it posits] their relation, or themselves as absolute particulars, which means that in their determinacy they are likewise self-suspending. "Blue," [for instance,] is to begin with ripped out of the continuity of its [special] being, cut away from the variously specified [field] in which it is; but it is still always this determinate [color]. In memory, however, it is both for itself [i.e., independent] and at the same time also alongside others, and related to others though the *negative unity* [290] *of memory*; it is posited as this relatedness, as implicitly a universal, something other than it is, according to the determinacy of its content; it is *color*, and a concept of the understanding, a determinate concept. It is the universal of distinct colors; but not as if it were something extracted from them, for it is rather an abstraction, that is, their determinacy is immediately a cancelled [aspect] in their being. "Blue" is for the spirit at this level as "color."

Determinacy:[30] The singularity of sensation has thus developed through these stages to the determinate concept. For empirical intuition it was posited generally as a being in space and time, and in a wholly formal way as a superseded being, so that it remained (in this supersession) completely self-dependent (*für sich*), and only the *requirement* that it should become superseded was expressed in its formal supersession. In the name the positing of empirical intuition as ideal is realized, but the name is itself still a single ideality; the negative unity of consciousness must relate it to others, [just] as they are at rest beside and outside of one another in their universal element; and in this relating it must cancel the singularity of their content, and fix them as related to concepts of the understanding. Since we are considering consciousness as such, as unity of what appears as active and what appears as passive within it, the consideration of consciousness as it appears in

---

30. This paragraph was added in the margin. Hegel did not mark a new paragraph in the manuscript but he inserted the word: "Determinacy" between the lines. I have elected to treat this as a topic heading and have therefore made a paragraph break. (The first draft proceeds at once to the controversy about "secondary qualities": "It is here, especially, that what is called 'realism' parts company with what is called 'idealism'—though they are divided about consciousness as a whole—to wit, about whether the somewhat that is 'color', etc." (See p. 224 at line 2 from bottom).

the antithesis (i.e., subjective and objective) has no meaning for us. We
consider the moments of self-organizing consciousness neither on the
side of the subject (in the form of capacities, inclinations, passions,
drives, etc.) nor on the other side of the antithesis, (as a determinacy
of things), but absolutely as it is on its own account, as the unity and
middle of both [subject and object]; there is within it the motion of an
[291]   agent against a patient; but as the *motion* itself it is the unit in which
the antithesis is just implicitly a superseded one, all of its moments are
in the agent as capacities [and] inclinations, just as they are determinacies of the other [side, i.e., the thing]; but the essence is the middle;
and the middle of consciousness, in its being as a moment of the organization of its own totality, belongs to both sides; in other words they
are both [related] to the same [middle], but determined according to
their antithesis; in empirical intuition one [side] is empirically intuitive,
the other empirically intuited, the name giver and that to which the
name gets given, thus the comprehender and the comprehended. It is
superfluous to point this out; but it is quite false [i.e., mistaken] to
treat these moments of consciousness as coming to be put together in
empirical intuition (just as it is [false, i.e., mistaken] in memory and in
conception). [The synthesis is not put together] from the two sides of
the antithesis in such a way that each of the sides contributes a part to
the one whole; and [it is a mistake] to ask what the active [contribu-
tion] of each part is in this putting together. This is the standpoint of
ordinary consciousness, for which consciousness is always just a side
of the antithesis; [from this standpoint] the individual when defined as
active (*in der Bestimmtheit als thätiges*) is pictured as the essence, but
in such a way that this consciousness, as thus defined, is a contingent
one which the individual may either have or not have; for he has
power over its moments and free choice about it. [On this view] consciousness is a property, but on the contrary consciousness is the essence [and] spirit [is] the absolute substance, which has activity within
itself upon one side of the antithesis of its infinity, but activity that is
absolutely ideal and has only a cancelled being.

Thus[31] what are called "realism" and "idealism" are developed entirely at the standpoint of the antithesis, and [part company] on the
question whether the somewhat that is "color" is grounded in the ob-
[292]   ject or in the *subject*, in the active or in the passive side of *conscious-*

31. We now return to the first draft. Again, Hegel did not mark a new paragraph here—but it seems best to assume that he intended one. (The reader should
note, however, that the discussion of "determinacy" continues.)

ness. [The dispute is framed] in such a way that these two sides subsist absolutely in and for themselves and are not rather [present] in consciousness itself only as superseded. Realism leaves to the subject only the formal activity of *comparing the similarity in being;* idealism, which treats the ideal side of the antithesis as the absolutely real, that which is on its own account as absolute substance, leaves nothing at all to the object. There is honestly nothing to be said about such an irrational conflict. *Color* is in its three potencies: in sensation as the determinacy of *blue* (for example), and then in formal ideality [of imagination] as concept, and as name [in memory] as related *to others,* which it is opposed to and which it is at the same time like (in this respect that they are colors); and at this level [memory] it is simply, universally, as color. That [dogmatic] realism and idealism sunders this essential totality of the three levels of determinacy. Realism holds that *determinacy is on its own account,* and relatedness likewise, is so far as it is simultaneously opposed; or the universality of color [is on its own account] in so far as it is submerged in the difference of the colors. It leaves to consciousness, to the subject, only one side of the third potency, the drawing out of the relatedness that already is in the difference, the isolation or abstraction of the universal. Idealism vindicates the claim of the subject at the two higher levels of determinacy and indeed at the first level as well—the determinacy of blue [sensation]. The dispute bears properly upon the potency of the middle, which is in conflict with itself, for this is the level where the determinacies as such and their relatedness are posited together both in unity and as distinct. It emerges from the previous discussion, that *determinacy,* as being on [293] its own account, belongs to nature as the way in which color comes to its totality; at the same time determinacy only *is* in connection with its suspendedness or with the spirit. It *is* as singular sensation. Spirit *as sensing is itself animal,* submerged in nature; in the progress upwards to the relating and distinguishing of colors, and to their coming forth as color, as concept, the nature of color itself becomes spirit; it is just as much as determinate color, as it is not as determinate color. As for the subject himself, in the very crude terms in which realism and idealism set up their disputed question, [viz.,] whether outside the subject the determinate, distinct colors (self-related in their distinction) are something, quite regardless of the existence of the subject, it must be stated therefore, that the subject as such *is* only *a unique singularity,* that is, something such that the totality of determinacies (including the determinate colors) is outside him. But in so far as he is not absolute singularity, but consciousness, they are in him; and likewise in so far as the determinacy of the color "blue" is not a singularity, [the subject or consciousness] is equally the totality of color, apart from which there is no color. But it is a completely ridiculous idealism which takes the subject, the active side of the antithesis, as a term of the antithesis, and as a subsisting (*seyend*) determinacy, yet wants to free it from determinacy, from [any] externality affecting it; for so far as it is freed from determinacy, it ceases to be subject, this one term of the antithesis; and it is nothing but the union of both terms, the spirit, consciousness. This is the Absolute that we are discussing. But properly speaking we ought not to talk about either a subject, or an object, of this kind,

[294] but about the spirit; and in that perspective, we have seen how qua totality it comes to be nature, and how it comes to be spirit. Subject as such, it only is as sensation, that is, as singularity whose immediate other-being is outside it;[32] and the articulation of consciousness is how it comes itself to consciousness, [or] how the inner concept of consciousness posits itself as consciousness proper.

Sensation becomes concept of consciousness when it elevates itself to memory and speech; but it reaches only the concept, that is, only formal consciousness. The singularity of sensation is certainly posited [in memory] as ideal; but these idealities are themselves a mass of idealities, they are not as absolute unity. This multitude must become mutually differentiated, it must raise itself to connection; and their connection, the concept, must be what is posited.

Speech that elevates itself to understanding, once again goes into itself by doing so, it supersedes the *singular* spoken name—the concept itself, like everything else, falls within speech, and [it is] absolutely communicative.[33] The suspended name, the name as posited not according to its singular being, but only according to its relation, i.e., as universal or the concept, must be *absolutely* reflected into itself. Language must fade away in consciousness just as it does in the outer [air]; the concept of the understanding is just the unity of consciousness re-

[295] turning out of the name, self-relating to singularity itself and therefore a *determinate* concept, not the absolute unity of consciousness; it must be in the mode of something absolutely returned [i.e., pure essence],

32. Hegel added in the first draft: "But this is what is self-cancelled in speech, in the being of consciousness." (In his revision he inserted the next paragraph to replace this comment.)

33. Compare note 29. In the first draft Hegel added here: "But as determinate concept it ceases to be an existing [entity] opposed to the conscious being; it makes no difference to the concept whether it is spoken or not." (The long insertion below took care of this point in the second draft.)

not, that is to say, [like] the relation of colors, for example, but absolutely undetermined, the abolished determinacy of relation, pure relating, the absolute *emptiness* of the infinite, the formal aspect of rationality, the simple, absolute abstraction of unity: reflection as point.[34] As this absolute abstraction, consciousness has become absolute in its negative connection; it abolishes all determinacy, [and] is purely self-identical. But because this absolute being is strictly only negative, he is in himself empty, and immediately the contrary of what he wanted to bring to pass within himself; the totality of being confronts this absolutely empty unit; what he negates is the unit of formal rationality, just as much as his absolute negation [of it] is; the consciousness that posited singularity previously within itself as an ideal [factor], as a superseded being, has posited the formal, mere ideality, on its own account, having cut it off from singularity, which last gains an absolute reality. In freeing itself from singularity, that [rational] unit has rather posited the antithesis as absolute, without [its terms] being mutually determined, and the terms of the antithesis subsist as absolutely real against one another. Consciousness has come to be as the unit of individuality.

The unit of individuality previously came to be *for us* [i.e., in the philosophy of Nature] in the Earth the element of singularity, and everything that pertained to it had the *character of this singularity*; but this point of reflection, the absolute being-returned-into-self, was only *our* concept, it is not realized in the Earth as such, it does not exist [296] in it; instead it is only posited as a requirement, namely, as infinite divisibility, i.e., only as the infinite possibility of its being. It exists for the first time in consciousness as its absolutely negative side; it exists first, when consciousness makes itself into this point.

This absolutely simple point of consciousness is its own absolute being; but as a negative, or in other words it is the absolute being of the individual as such, as a singular being. It is the freedom *of his privacy* [obstinacy, *Eigensinn*]; the single being can make himself into

---

34. The long insertion that follows here in the text replaces the following in the first draft: "This is how it [reflection] made itself into the consciousness of the individual in the first place. The consciousness [spoken of] thus far was only the *Idea* of it. As consciousness of the individual, consciousness exists as absolute singularity and absolute universality simultaneously. Just as what precedes always realizes itself in what follows, so the existing Idea of consciousness as language is itself only existent as consciousness of individuals; and as previously the coming-to-be of the individual <296> was a reciprocal exchange between his universality and his infinity itself as a universal, so it is now an exchange between his universality and him as absolutely opposed multiple infinity qua singular [being]. Consciousness qua consciousness of the single being, etc." (See p. 228 at line 13.)

this point, he can abstract from everything absolutely, he can give everything up; he cannot be made dependent on anything, or held to anything; every determinacy by which he should be gripped he can cut away from himself, and in death he can realize his absolute independence and freedom [for] himself as absolutely negative consciousness. But death has the contradiction of *life* within it; just as the point of absolute reflection, the simple empty singularity, instead of superseding singularity in truth, is itself only absolute singularity which is confronted by the totality of determinacies, as something that is just as absolutely on its own account, sundered [from the negative unit] by an absolutely empty gulf with no bridges (*beziehungslose*). So that the antithesis, together with its relation, its ideality, has the opposite form to the one that went before. Consciousness, qua consciousness of the single [being], is set against other single [beings], and it must now posit singularity as something superseded; or it [must be] practical consciousness, consciousness as existing thing against [other] existing things.

[297]   *Second Level: The Tool*

With this absolute opposition consciousness as language has gone out of the middle. There is no middle, in which the terms of the antithesis are connected and by which they are cut off from one another; the middle term [is] invisible, it [is] the entombed spirit[35] of the absolute opposition. This universal indifferent spirit must prove itself as infinite spirit, by cancelling the singularities, and bringing itself to birth as the existing middle.

The consciousness that organized itself in language into the totality of the ideal, began from the concept of infinity, and its organization was carried out in the determinacy of the first level [i.e.,] *in the element of indifferent* universality, so that the opposites in their union subsisted indifferently as universal and particular within one another in the concept, without their implicit contradiction of one another as such being
[298]   posited; or in other words, their opposition in being was abstracted from, it was [treated] as something external to them, not posited in

35. The first version began: "As language consciousness had become consciousness being for itself as singular; as absolute reflection it has gone out of the middle and [is the] invisible middle, the entombed, etc." (The next paragraph was added entirely in the revised draft.)

them. This first level passes of its own accord over into its opposite, into the absolute opposition in being, and that indifferent element of universality in which the opposites are at rest in one another disappears; the opposites, as they emerge from the preceding level, are absolutely opposed, *without relation*. The former *theoretical unity* became the absolute contrary of itself as it was realized; it came to be absolute singularity and opposition; and the relation now posited becomes a *practical* one; absolute singularity must fulfill itself, it must cancel the absolute opposition; but as it thus elevates itself practically, by its own effort, to absolute totality, it again comes to be the contrary of itself. For this practical level, along with the [previous] theoretical one, are only *the two ideal levels*; each posits consciousness only in the abstraction of one form of the antithesis—the theoretical level posits it in the abstraction of indifferent simple universality, the practical level that we are now discussing in that of the absolutely *differentiated*, absolutely opposed relation.

The absolute unit of reflection is itself only a negative one through negation, i.e., through its relation with an opposite to which it is essentially linked; in its absolute reflection it has freed itself from the relation to another, but the absolute reflection itself only is as this relation to another; consciousness, *as absolute reflection*, has *only* changed *the form* of the opposition and relation; it is related to an absolute opposite, *a dead thing*, and it is the contradiction of a relation to something absolutely unrelated; the relation must be realized, and the absolutely singular consciousness is directed against itself as if it were its own nullification[36] as this absolute singularity; and consciousness is as practical relation.   [299]

[a) Desire]

ANIMAL *desire* is a beast-consciousness in which the nullification restricts itself, and the terms of the antithesis are only posited as *going to be cancelled*; desire is an *ought-to-be* nullified; the desired [object], like the actual state of cancellation itself and its *ideality*, a restriction

---

36. This is the only clause that survived from the first version of this paragraph, which read: "For the singularity of conscience, the single [object] is an *absolute opposite* where we have left it, a *dead thing*; and the single consciousness is directed against itself as if it were its own nullification. This *practical* relationship is the opposite of the previous one in which consciousness was determined as universal, while here [it is determined] as a single being absolutely opposed [to the universal]."

of the state of cancellation, are pulled apart from one another in time, but the actual coming-to-pass of the cancellation, the stilling of desire, is an immediate state of cancellation without any ideality, without consciousness; human desire must be [only] ideally cancelled [even] *in the suspending itself*, and the object must abide even when it has been cancelled, and the middle as the abiding supersession of both, must exist as opposed to both; the practical connection is a connection of consciousness, i.e., the simplicity of nullification must even in its simplicity go apart from itself, it must be inwardly restricted and opposed [to itself]. The simplicity of nullification must be the universal unity, the superseded state of both antitheses, and at the same time the middle in which they are one, and in which, as their one, they separate themselves from their superseded state. That is to say, the one side of the antithesis, the side that appears as active, the unit of individuality, must *work on* the other side, the one that appears as passive. In labor

[300] desire wrenches the *object* to be nullified entirely out of its context, specifies it, and posits it as connected with a desiring [being]; in so far as desire as such *is*, both [terms of the antithesis] subsist in this connection, they are at rest; being only ideally cancelled, desire (as moving toward nullification) must:[37] [i] cancel both the object and itself; but [ii] in the cancellation [desire must] itself be consciousness, an ideality of the cancelling. Thus the individual, as *laboring*, is active, and the object gets superseded, while both still subsist. Desire does not come to its satisfaction in its nullification, and the object continues to subsist even as it is nullified. *Labor* is this practical consciousness as [the] connection, [the] universal union of both [terms]; it must likewise be as middle, in which they are connected as opposed, and whereon they abide as separately subsisting; hence labor as such has its abiding existence; [it is] itself a thing. The *tool* is the existing rational middle, the existing universality, of the practical process; it appears on the side of the active against the passive; it is itself passive on the side of the

---

37. This colon replaces a semicolon in Hegel's text. The first version read: ". . . they are at rest; it [desire] is not a cancelling; but it is essentially this [in animal life or as a natural drive], and [in desire] as labor, the individual is active, and the object gets superseded, while both still subsist. Labor as the unifying middle, the middle subsisting in both terms as things, is itself a thing that abides [i.e., the tool], active through desire and passive against it, and active against the object. The tool is the existing rational middle of the practical process, that which endures in traditions, whereas both the subject and object of desire subsist only as individuals and pass away." (Here the "Third Level" begins in the unbroken first draft.)

laborer, and active against what is worked on. It is that wherein laboring has its permanence, that which alone remains over from the laboring and the product of work, that wherein their contingency is eternal-
ized [immortalized]; it is propagated in traditions, whereas both the
subject and the object of desire subsist only as individuals, and pass
away.[38]

[Third Level: Possession and the Family][39]

[Sexual desire, in its natural simplicity?] is a restricted nullification
through need, or something absolutely external. The freedom of consciousness supersedes this need, and restricts the nullification in enjoyment, through consciousness itself; it makes the two sexes into consciousness for one another, into beings on their own account, beings
that subsist; and [they subsist] in such a way that in the being-for-self
of the other, each is him/herself; so that each is conscious of their own
singularity-for-self in the *consciousness* of the other, that is, in his/her
singularity, or being for self; and the connection of the sexes comes to
be one, in which in the being of the consciousness of either party, each
is him/herself one with the other, or [there is] an ideal [union?] . . . .

<But as desire passes over into enjoyment, the individual super-
sedes his antithesis and his activity, as well as his inorganic nature, and
becomes [a] shaped totality which reflects itself into itself as realized
Idea, and which realizes itself in the sundering of the sexes. Desire restricts itself here necessarily, too; the woman comes to be a being on
her own account for the man. She ceases to be [simply] an object of his
desire; desire becomes something ideal, and a [conscious] intuiting, it
comes to be inclination.> Desire thus frees itself from its connection
with enjoyment,[40] it comes to be an immediate union of both in the

[301,
Fragment
21]

[302]
<301>

[302]

---

38. In the first version (see previous note) this is the end of the section. But
Hegel added here an insertion sign and the note "see separate sheet." Unfortunately we do not have this sheet. What we *do* have is the first version (which
shows us how much of the text was replaced) and a half sheet which contains
part of the revised version. It is fragmentary at both ends, so it probably comes
from inside the lost (folded) sheet. It is likely, in any case, that part of the lost
material was a *continuation* of the present discussion of "the tool."

39. The *heading* comes from the cancelled first draft. The *text* is *first* the surviving fragment of the revised version, *then* the cancelled passage from the continuous first draft. The cancelled passage is given—as always—in < >. Thus
where the angled brackets end, we return to Hegel's revised text.

40. The first version continued thus: "and has made itself something abiding

absolute being for self of both, i.e., it becomes *Love*; and the enjoyment is in this intuiting of oneself in the being of the other consciousness. The connection itself becomes in the same [way] the being of both, and something that abides as much as they do [separately], that is, it becomes marriage.

Just as in marriage each [partner] is mutually in the consciousness of the other, so each is mutually consciousness in the other, as his/her *whole* singularity; and the spouses give themselves a wholly communal existence, in which they are one not in the linkage with any one singularity (a particular purpose), but as individuals, according to the totality in which they belong to nature. This bond, as involving the totality of someone's consciousness, is just for this reason sacred, and is wholly removed from the concept of a *contract*, which some have wanted to view marriage as. In this living union of both, for which the consciousness of each has been exchanged, so that it is [both] as his/hers and [as] the consciousness of the other, consciousness is likewise necessarily the middle term, at which the two divide and in which they are one; it is their existing unity. *This middle, wherein* they recognize themselves as one [and] their antithesis is cancelled, and in which they are, just for this reason, once more opposed, is on its own account. The side of it in which they recognize themselves as one, and as superseded, is necessarily a consciousness, for it is only as conscious-

[303]

---

and enduring, as love; it does not die away in enjoyment, but becomes an abiding linkage and comes through Reason to marriage; a sacred bond, wherein the spouses give themselves a wholly communal existence, they are one not in connection with some one singularity, but as whole individuals, according to the totality in which they belong to nature; [a bond] that is just for this reason sacred, and is wholly removed from the concept of a contract. Through the child there comes into being. not, as in nature, an endurance of the being of the middle only for a moment, only a moment of self-cognition in a third, but an essential (*an sich*) enduring of it. And in marriage, for the first time, a middle is posited in the way in which it exists in the individuals themselves or in the way that their opposite is the whole of themselves; speech is likewise only real in individuals, but they are not in it simply as individuals, but only universally as consciousness, and the universal of speech is for the individuals a formal [unity]. The middle here [in marriage] embraces them wholly and completely in itself. Even as it is this spirit of several, and hence is sacred, <303> so also there stands opposed to this sacred middle a dead one (or just because it is the absolute union of both, so too it is opposed to them). The individuals are, first of all, themselves this death coming to pass; which belongs to their nature as single individuals; but in this coming-to-be-dead of theirs, they equally intuit their coming-to-life; the child is not, as in the [breeding] relationships of animals the existing genus, but the parents recognize themselves in it as genus, etc." (See p. 233 at line 4.)

ness that they are one; it is the child in which they recognize themselves as one, as being in one consciousness, and precisely therein
as superseded, and they intuit in the child their own coming supersession. They recognize themselves in it as genus, [i.e.,] themselves
as other than they themselves are, namely, as achieved (*geworden*[
unity. But this achieved unity is itself a consciousness in which the
coming supersession of the parent is intuited, i.e., it is a consciousness in which the consciousness of the parents comes to be; in other
word the parents must *educate* it. As they educate it, they posit
their achieved consciousness in it, and they generate their death,[41] as
they bring their achievement to living consciousness, [for] their reflection into self, the emptiness of absolute singularity, realizes [itself],
and qua achieved consciousness becomes inorganic nature, to the totality of which man as [i.e., in the person of the] child raises himself.
Thus far *absolute opposition, the other of consciousness, was for consciousness a pure other*; here consciousness itself has become another:
for the parents, the child, for the child, the parents;[42] and the education [304]
of the child consists in this: that the consciousness that is posited for
him as other than that which he is himself, shall become his own; or his
inorganic nature, which he consumes inwardly, is an achieved consciousness; the process of individuality is a shaping, and what the
evolving shape consumes inwardly, is achieved individuality. Just as
previously in the practical self-shaping of consciousness, consciousness
appeared as a real being opposed to nature, so here it appears as an
evolution-into-being *for itself*. At the theoretical level consciousness
came to be for itself as its concept, which it had achieved [as simple
being] in the animal; in the theoretical process it came to be for *us* as
an absolutely single [mind] in the formal [element of] rationality; at
the practical level this absolute singularity came to be for itself; *for us*
[it earlier came to be] something that has its consciousness in another;
here it comes to be that for itself. Consciousness becomes something
that another consciousness posits within itself. In his education the
unconscious unity of the child is superseded, it articulates itself inwardly, it becomes cultured *consciousness*; the consciousness of the

41. The first version continued: "with consciousness which, as it previously
was an absolute being, here realizes its reflection into self, the emptiness of absolute singularity, as perishing in sexual enjoyment, and qua achieved, etc." (See
line 13.)

42. The first version continued: "The essence of the relation belongs to nature,
the process of individuality as a natural one is a shaping, and what the evolving
shape consumes inwardly is achieved individuality. In his education the unconscious unity, etc." (See line 2 from bottom.)

parents is its matter, at the cost of which it is formed; they are for the child an unknown, obscure presentiment of himself; they cancel his simple state of self-containment; what they give him they shed themselves; they die in him; for what they give him is their own consciousness. Consciousness is here the coming-to-be of another consciousness in him, and the parents intuit in his evolution their own passing into supersession. The world does not come to this [new] consciousness as a process (*ein werdendes*) as it did previously in the absolute form of *something external*, for it has been penetrated thoroughly by the form of consciousness; [the child's] inorganic nature is the *knowledge of his parents*, the world is already prepared [on his behalf]; and it is the form of *ideality* which comes to the child.[43] Since the world comes to the evolving consciousness as this ideal world, the problem for consciousness is to find the meaning, the reality, of this ideal, to find out how the ideal exists; it must realize this ideality. Hence the previous relationship of consciousness [to the world] is reversed; previously, for active consciousness as one side of the antithesis the EXTERNAL [world] was [there] as the other side, the single [system of things] inwardly determined in a manifold way, but not ideal. Here consciousness is the singular [term], and the other side of its antithesis is the ideal [term], a world as it is in consciousness. Thus the antithesis is superseded for the active consciousness, which has been in antithesis till now; for the other side, which was thus far posited as nonconscious, is itself a consciousness, and so here [the process] is the other way to realize the ideal world. This is how consciousness generates itself for itself as identity of inner and outer. For the child the contradiction between [his] real world, and the ideal world of his parents is present, but for him as evolving consciousness, this contradiction is cancelled, in that his consciousness posits the real side for him ideally (as nonconscious), and realizes the conscious side (the ideal one of his parents). The activity of consciousness as an agent is this absolutely opposed activity; it unites both [sides of the antithesis], and it is in the first place a consciousness that has achieved itself. Thus both the external [world] and the inwardness, the ideality [of the individual], are equally superseded; both are present for it as something external.

In this way the *totality of consciousness* is in the family the totality

[305]

[306]

43. The first version continued: "Culture is the finding of what the existence of the world was for one's parents; it is the reversal of the previous relationship in which the external [world] was idealized in active consciousness; here [the process] is the other way, to realize the ideal world, etc." (See line 25.)

as an evolution into being *for self*; the individual intuits himself in the other; the other is the same whole of consciousness, and it has its consciousness in the other, in the generated [consciousness of the child?] . . . .[44]

[B. TRANSITION TO REAL EXISTENCE: THE NEGATIVE][45]

[There is a lacuna in the text here. One or more sheets are missing. Since the cancelled draft on the next sheet that we have does not overlap very much with the revised version (which begins with a marginal insertion continued from the previous page, now lost) I give both versions in the text. The cancelled version is given first in angled brackets.]

<Every form between absolute singulars is a neutral one, for it makes no difference [formally] whether one makes another a gift, or one robs him and puts him to the sword; and there is no boundary between the least and the greatest outrage. <307, Fragment 22>

44. The sheet is full and breaks off in midsentence. The sheet that follows next does not connect directly with this one even in the first version. Thus at least one sheet is missing. See further the following note.

45. This heading has no textual status whatever. But it is clear that Hegel was approaching his major turning point at the end of fragment 21. The heading of fragment 20, "A. Formal Existence," points to a complementary "Real Existence" somewhere further on. I am assuming that this complement is "Ethical Life" or "The *Volk*." It is probable, however, that Hegel did *not* divide up the levels of the "real existence" of consciousness by the insertion of headings, since he did not mark off the transition to "the people"—which is certainly the *third* level (or "totality" of the development)—in any way. It is transparently clear I think that Hegel was becoming pressed for time. Either his writing time or his lecturing time—and almost certainly both—was running short. For this reason he could not develop the "real" stages of consciousness as fully as he would like, and he did not, therefore, set up a skeleton for which there was no flesh. The "struggle for recognition" *must* however be the second level—the moment of "opposition" or "antithesis"—since he makes his transition directly from it to the "totality." I assume that "the Family" is the "totality" of the first level—the level of "Nature" in the *System of Ethical Life*—and that the "struggle for recognition" is the transition in "consciousness" from the "natural" (i.e., patriarchal) society to a properly political one. On this hypothesis the lacuna in our text need not be, and probably is not, a large one. It may be that we have lost only a single sheet. But then again we may have lost several and my hypothesis about the form of the argument may be quite mistaken. It seems to me, however, that in both versions, Hegel was not so much *developing* his doctrine here as *summarizing* it in order to make a rapid transition.

The single individual is a whole and everything distinguishable in him is posited in this wholeness; [the singular whole] is without the emergence of the universal; the relation of single individuals to one another is a relation between them as wholes, for the emerging universal would be precisely the bringing to an end of their singularity. Since they cannot articulate themselves in their relation, every single negation of property is a negation of the totality [of the one injured], and at the same time this negation must occur.> The single individual is <as such only a rational being (*Wesen*)>, in as much as every single aspect of his possession etc., (see line 21 below).

[307,
Fragment
22>

. . . it is absolutely necessary that the totality which consciousness has reached in the family recognizes itself as the totality it is in another such totality of consciousness; in this cognition each [family head] is for the other immediately an absolute singular. Each posits himself in the consciousness of the other, cancels the singularity of the other, or each [posits] the other in his consciousness as an absolute singularity of consciousness. This is reciprocal *recognition* in general, and we are to see: how this recognition merely as such, as the positing of one's own consciousness as a singular totality of consciousness in another singular totality of consciousness, can exist. The single [family head] is one consciousness, only in as much as every singular aspect of his possessions, and of his being, appears bound up with his whole es-

[308]

sence, it is taken up into his indifference; [in other words,] in so far as he *posits* every moment *as himself*, for this ideal being of the world is what consciousness is. The injuring of any one of his single aspects is therefore infinite, it is an absolute offense, and offense against his integrity, an offense to his honor; and the collision about any single point is a struggle for the whole;[46] the thing, the determinate [prop-

46. Here Hegel wrote a new version of several pages of his text in the margins. When he cancelled the first version after the revision, he forgot to cross out the original draft on the back of the first sheet. This first version (with the actual cancellation shown in brackets) reads: ". . . the whole. <And that collision both must and ought to occur, since it can only be known whether the singular consciousness is, as such, a rational indifference, in as much as he posits every single detail of his possessions and his being in the collision, [and] connects himself with it as a whole [i.e., he is rationally *indifferent* to the distinction between the integrity of his inner and that of his outer personality]; this can only be demonstrated in that he posits [i.e., stakes] his whole existence upon his maintenance [as an external whole] and purely and simply does not divide himself; and the proof> ends only with his death. The appearance of the single [consciousness] against the other, is a manifold holding, his [family] goods, the

erty], does not come into consideration as to its value, or as a thing at all; it is, rather, wholly nullified, wholly ideal; the point is just this, that it is connected with me, that I am one consciousness [and it] has lost its antithetic status as against me. The two [consciousnesses] that mutually recognize one another as this totality of single aspects, and want to know that they are recognized, come forth against each other as this totality; and the meaning which they give one another in their opposition is: [α] that each appears in the consciousness of the other as someone who excludes him from the whole *extension* of his singular aspects; (β) that he is an actual totality in this exclusive agency of his. Neither can prove this to the other through words, assurances, threats, or promises; for language is only the ideal existence of consciousness, but here there are actual [consciousnesses], i.e., they are absolutely opposed absolute beings for themselves in opposition; and their relation

---

external middle; this, by its very nature qua external, is a universal [i.e., it can be anybody's], and the unrelated singular [consciousnesses] are mutually within it. But it is someone's goods; the connection of several with it is negative, exclusive. Whether the exclusive connection of the one [owner] with it is a rational one, whether he is in truth a totality, upon this *recognition* <309> depends the relation of the single [consciousness]; each can only get recognition from the others, so far as his manifold appearance is indifferent in him, [i.e.,] he proves himself as infinite in every single detail of his possession, and avenges every injury to the point of death. And this injury must occur, for consciousness must advance to this recognition, the single [agents] must injure one another, in order to recognize whether they are rational; for consciousness is essentially of this sort, that the totality of the single [consciousness] is opposed to him, and in this othering-process is yet the same as he, that the totality of the one is in another consciousness, and is the consciousness of the other, and even this absolute subsistence that it has for itself, is in this other consciousness. In other words it gets recognition from the other. But this, that my totality as the totality of a single [consciousness] is precisely this totality subsisting (*seyende*), on its own account, in the other consciousness, whether it is recognized and respected, this I cannot know except through the appearance of the actions of the other against my totality; and likewise the other must equally appear to me as a totality, as I do to him. If they behave negatively, if they leave one another alone <then neither has appeared to the other as totality, nor has the being of the one as a totality in the consciousness of the other <310> appeared; there has been neither presentation nor recognition. Speech, declarations, promising are not this recognition, for speech is only an ideal middle; it vanishes as soon as it appears, it is not an abiding, real recognition. But the recognition can only be a real one; for each single [consciousness] posits himself as totality in the consciousness of the other, in such a way that he puts his whole apparent totality, his life, at stake for the maintenance of any single detail, [*this clause was incorporated in the revision* (p. 239 line 12)], he affirms himself in a possession, asserts the negative, exclusive

[309] is strictly a practical one, it is itself actual, the middle of their recognition must itself be actual. *Hence they must injure one another.* The fact that each posits himself as exclusive totality in the singularity of his existence must become actual; the offense is necessary, [since] the other can only make his exclusion of another actual because I disturb him in his apparent phenomenal being; only then can he present himself as consciousness, [show] that this [is] his being, his singularity indifferently, that this external [thing] is within himself; in particular each must be disturbed in his possession, for in possession there lies the contradiction that something external, a thing, a universal [moment] of the earth, should be under the control of *a single* [man], which is contrary to the nature of the thing as an outward universal, for it is the universal as against the immediate *singularity* of consciousness. —Through the necessary injury, which should lead to recognition, both are to posit

---

meaning [of himself] as a totality. The two of them keep this meaning only with their death, since they are the negative totality as much for themselves as with respect to the other; I can only recognize [myself] as this singular totality in the consciousness of the other, so far as I posit myself in his consciousness as of such a kind that in my exclusiveness [I] am a totality of excluding [*this clause was incorporated* (p. 239 line 15)]. I risk my life on it and go to the death; and likewise the other can only appear to me as rational totality in so far as he posits himself for me in the same way, and I must prove myself to be so to him, and must equally have the proof from him.

Hence this absolute recognition immediately contains an absolute contradiction within it; <311> it is only by infinitely sublating itself. [My] singularity as totality shall (*soll*) come to recognition, it shall be for me as in the consciousness of another; every relation of the other to my singularity is itself singular, and such relations must occur on account of the necessity for recognition; I prove myself to be totality in this singularity, I make the connection [of my possessions to me] immediately infinite, and in respect of the other I go out to posit myself in him [in two ways]:

α) as suspending him as totality, [i.e., I go] for his death, since

(αα) he must recognize me, [he must recognize] that I respect life as little in myself as I do in him, [I regard it] as something connected only with singularity;

(ββ) I must for my own part recognize whether he is a rational essence, one that goes to death in its defense and its attack; [and]

β) superseding myself likewise as totality, since αα) I must prove myself to him as totality. If one or the other stops short of death, he only proves to the other that he will accept the loss of his possessions, <312> that he will risk a wound but not life itself; then for the other he is immediately not a totality, he is not absolutely for himself, he becomes the slave of the other].

[Hegel neglected to cancel the following passage at the foot of the page:]

This *recognition* therefore, aims to prove to the other that one is a totality of singularity, it aims at the intuition of oneself in him and likewise of him in one-

themselves in the relationship of opposition to one another as negatively absolute singularity [and] totality. In that each effectively excludes
the other, [and] cancels the possession taken from him in the offense,
he equally offends the other, he denies something in the other, which
the latter posited as his; each must affirm what the other denies, as being in *his* totality and not something external; and must suspend it in
the other; and as each affirms his totality as a single [consciousness]
in this single [point of offense] strictly, it becomes apparent *that each*   [310]
negates the totality of the other; the mutual recognition of the singular totality of either one becomes a negative relation of the totality,
because this one is negated as it enters into relation; each [must] posit
himself as totality in the consciousness of the other, in such a way that
he puts his whole apparent totality, his life, at stake for the maintenance of any single detail, and each likewise must go for the death of
the other. I can only recognize [myself] as this singular totality in the
consciousness of the other, so far as I posit myself in his consciousness
as of such a kind that in my exclusiveness [I] am a totality of excluding, [i.e., so far as] I go for his death; when I go for his death, I expose
myself to death, I risk my own life; I perpetrate the contradiction of
wanting to affirm the singularity of my being and my property; and
this affirmation passes over into its contrary, that I offer up everything
I possess, and the very possibility of all possession and enjoyment, my
life itself; in that I posit myself as totality of singularity, I suspend myself as totality of singularity; I want to be recognized in this [outward]
extension of my existence, in my being and my possessions, but I transform this will in affirming it, because I cancel this existence and get
recognition only as rational. as totality in truth, since when I go for the

---

self; but in the realization of this aim, the totality of singularity cancels itself.
[The recognized victor—Hegel's pronoun refers to the totality] maintains his
property as a whole, and posits the injury of nonrecognition of his exclusiveness
as infinite. He presents himself as defending every single detail with his whole
[power]. But he can only present himself as the whole, in as much as he cancels
his being in the details, in as much as he <surrenders> [the verb is over the page
and is cancelled—therefore we know that this whole passage was only left standing through an oversight] his possessions to destruction in defending them <and
life [too], as the simple appearance which comprehends all sides of the totality
of singularity within itself; he can therefore only be a totality of singularity, in
virtue of sacrificing himself as totality of singularity, and the other consciousness
likewise, by which he wants to be recognized.

This recognition is absolutely necessary, its purely negative side is > that the
singular totality etc. (See p. 240 line 11 from bottom.)

[311]   death of the other, I myself wager my own life, too, and cancel this
extension of my existence, the very totality of my singularity.

This recognition of the *singularity* of the totality *thus brings* the
nothing of death [in its train]. Each must have from the other cognizance of whether he is an absolute consciousness: a) each must put
himself into such an opposed connection with the other as will bring
this to light, he must injure him; and each can only know of the other
whether he is [a] totality in as much as he drives him to the point of
death, and each proves himself as totality for himself likewise only in
that he goes to the point of death with himself. If in his own case he
stops short of death, he only proves to the other that he will accept the
loss of a part or the whole of his possessions, that he will risk a wound
but not life itself; then for the other he is immediately not a totality,
he is not absolutely for himself, he becomes the slave of the other. If
he stops short of death in the other's case, and suspends the conflict
before putting him to death, then neither has he proved himself as totality nor has he come to cognizance of the other as such.

[312]   This recognition of the singular [consciousness] is thus [an] absolute
internal contradiction; the recognition is just the being of consciousness as a totality in another consciousness, but as far as it is actually
achieved, it cancels the other consciousness, and thereby the recognition is suspended too; it is not realized, but rather ceases to be, just
when it is. Yet consciousness only is the gaining of recognition from
another at the same time as it only is as absolute numerical unity, and
that is what it must be recognized as; but that is to say it must go for
the other's death, and for its own; and it only *is* in the actuality of
death.

This cognition of ours, then, that the recognized totality is only consciousness, so far as it cancels itself, is a cognition of this consciousness
itself; it makes this reflection of self into self all by itself, that the singular totality in that it wants to be, to maintain itself as such, sacrifices
itself absolutely, it cancels itself; and thus it does the contrary of what
it aims at; it can only be itself as a superseded state; it cannot maintain
itself as a [simple state of] being, but only as one that is posited as
superseded; and it posits itself herewith as a superseded state and can
only gain recognition in the status, [as] this immediate self-identical
one; it is a self-cancelling [consciousness] and it is a recognized [con-
sciousness], one which is in the other consciousness as it is in itself,
thus it is absolutely universal consciousness. This being of the supersededness of the single totality is the totality as absolutely universal,

[313]   or as absolute *spirit*; it is the spirit, as absolutely real consciousness;

the singular consciousness intuits itself as an ideal, superseded, consciousness, and it [is] no longer singular; for it is itself rather this supersession of itself, and it is only recognized, it is only universal, as this superseded state; the totality as a singularity is posited in itself as a merely possible state, not as being for itself; in its subsistence it is just such as to be ever ready for death, it has made renunciation of itself—it is certainly as singular totality, as family and in possession and enjoyment, but in such a way that this relation is itself an ideal one, and proves itself in its self-sacrifice. The being of consciousness which qua singular totality is as one that has made renunciation of itself intuits itself in another consciousness even in its renunciation, it is immediately itself for itself as another consciousness, or it is *in other* consciousness just as this other consciousness of itself, i.e., as the consciousness of itself as superseded; in this way it is recognized; in every other consciousness it is what it immediately is for itself, [and] in that it is [for itself] a cancelled consciousness in another, its singularity is thereby absolutely saved; I am absolute totality in that the consciousness of the other as a totality of singularity is in me only as cancelled; but likewise my own totality *of singularity* is *one* that is cancelled in others;[47] singularity is absolute singularity, it is INFINITY, the immediate contrary of itself, the essence of spirit, which is to have infinity within itself in an infinite way, so that the antithesis immediately cancels itself. These three forms of being, cancelling, and being as super-   [314]
seded being are posited absolutely as one. The singular totality *is*, for the other singular totalities are posited only as superseded; it posits itself thus in the cancelled consciousness of the others,[48] it gains recognition; in these consciousnesses its own totality is cancelled likewise, and so far as it realizes itself in the recognizing, it is superseded; and *in the recognition* it is *for itself* as a *superseded being*; it is cognizant of itself as superseded, for it, too, only is QUA RECOGNIZED, as unrecognized, as not another consciousness than it is itself, it is not at all; its getting recognized is its existence, and it is in this existence only as a superseded [consciousness]. This *absolute consciousness* is thus a state of supersession of the consciousnesses [that share it] as singular; a superseded being which is at the same time the eternal movement of the one coming to itself in another, and coming to be other within it-

47. The first version continued: "and I am not singularity. These three forms of being, cancelling, and being as superseded being etc." (See line 23.)

48. The first version continued: "it must gain reality, recognition, and there are the single totalities, the consciousness of the others; in these consciousnesses, etc.," (at index 48).

self; it is universal, subsisting consciousness; it is not [the] mere form of the singulars without *substance*, but the singulars are no more; it is *absolute substance*, it is *the spirit of a people*, for which consciousness qua singular is itself only [the] form that of itself immediately becomes another, the side of spirit's motion, the absolute *ethical life*; the single [agent] as member of a people is an ethical essence, whose essence is the living substance of the universal ethical life; he is this essence as singular, as an ideal form; the form of a being, only qua cancelled; the [315] [real] being of ethical life in its living manifoldness is the *customs* of the people. [*Margin*: No composition, no [social] contract, no tacit or stated original contract; [to the effect that] the single [person] gives up part of his freedom, [he surrenders] the whole of it rather, his singular freedom is only his stubbornness, his death].

[C. REAL EXISTENCE: THE PEOPLE][49]

The absolute spirit of a people is the absolutely universal element, the aether which has absorbed all the single consciousnesses within itself, *the absolute, simple*, living, *unique substance*; it must likewise be *the active substance*; and it must oppose itself as consciousness and be the appearing middle of the opposites, that in which they are one and equally that within which they are opposed;[50] that against which they are active, and their nullifying one whose activity against them is their own activity, just as their activity against it is the activity of the spirit; the spirit of the people must eternally come to be the WORK, that is to say, it only is as an eternal coming-to-be spirit. It is achieved as the work when activity is posited in it, which is forthwith against it; and the activity against it is directly the cancelling of itself. This becoming other than itself consists in its connecting *itself as passive* with *itself as active*; as active people it is generally conscious of itself, and passes over into the product or to the self-identical; and since this common

49. There is no heading in the manuscript. Hegel merely began a new paragraph. But he has just made clear that "the people" *is* the real existence of consciousness. And here, as we shall see, he does repeat the moments of "formal existence."

50. The first version continued: "their dead one that nullifies them, outside of which they are as self-connecting; the spirit of the people must eternally come to be the work, or as an eternal coming-to-be spirit. As absolute consciousness it is only so far as it becomes another, and in this other-becoming is immediately itself. This becoming other than itself etc." [See line 4 from bottom].

work of all is their work as conscious beings in principle, they come [316]
to be themselves outside of themselves in it, but this outward [being]
is their deed, it is only what they have made it, it is themselves as active but superseded; and in this outwardness of themselves, in their
being as superseded, as middle, they intuit themselves as one people;[51]
and this their work is their own spirit itself because it is theirs. They
beget it, but they reverence it as something that is on its own account;
and it is for itself, since the activity through which they beget it is the
cancelling of themselves, [and] this cancelling of themselves at which
they aim, is the univeral spirit in being for itself.

Its life is *expiration and inspiration; its going apart from one another*
[is when] *it comes forth as active against itself as passive; it becomes
one, a unity of active and passive,* [as] *the work, but in this work* the
passive and active [opposition] is itself *superseded*; it is the absolutely
universal, it is only work because there is the antithesis of active and
passive, but because the active as such is opposed to [i.e., is in balance
with] the passive, active and passive cease to be an antithesis, and
there is only the absolutely universal. The antithesis [is] just the absolute vanishing of itself. It must have truth, that the single [agents each]
posit their singular totality as an ideal one, not a common deceit of
them all against the whole. The ethical work of the people is the being-
alive of the universal spirit; as spirit it is their ideal union, as work it is
their middle, the cycle of [men] cutting themselves off from the work
as a dead [thing], and positing themselves as singular agents, but positing it as universal work, and so immediately just cancelling themselves in it again, and being themselves only a superseded activity, a
cancelled singularity.

The absolute coming into being of this Idea of the spirit out of its [317]
inorganic nature *as the ethical spirit* is the necessity of its action in the
totality of its work.[52] As absolute ethical spirit it is essentially as the
infinite negative, the superseding of nature, in which it *has only become an other,* the *positing of nature as itself,* and then the absolute
enjoyment of itself, in as much as it has taken nature back into itself.

The first [moment] is *its negative work, its* being directed against
the *appearance of that which is other than it is itself, in other words* its

---

51. The first version continued: "Reason in general exists only in their work;
it comes to be only in their product, and it intuits itself immediately as another
and as itself. The ethical work of the people, etc." (See line 21.)
52. This sentence arrived at its final shape only after some travail. In the first
version Hegel wrote: "The *absolute organization* <of ethical life> of the ethical
spirit is the necessity of its work; it realizes itself in the totality of its work."

inorganic *nature. The* inorganic nature of the ethical spirit, however, is not that which we call "nature" generally—it is not Nature as *other-being* of spirit; i.e., [it is not "nature"] as a moment that subsists in the totality of moments; in consciousness generally this "nature" has been posited as a superseded [moment], in language, by memory, and by the tool;[53] and this status of being posited as suspended, the status of nature as spirit in its negativity is the absolute totality of consciousness as *singularity,* that is, it is the family, taken in its reality as possessor of the family goods. This totality is the *negative positedness of*

[318]   *nature* and [it is] the *spirit itself,* but *differing* [from itself], relating itself to an opposite, and [having as] its totality the realizing of this different [being], [i.e.,] consciousness.[54] But it is this totality that must be freed from its differentiation [literally "different connection"], its existence in nature, and must become an absolutely positive, absolutely universal spirit; and the family as such, the *reality of singularity,* is the *inorganic nature of the spirit* which must posit [itself] as superseded [moment] and elevated [itself] to the level of the universal. We deal first with how it subsists as marked with the character of universality.[55]

[a) The Speech of a People][56]

The preceding levels are in principle ideal, they exist for the first time in a people; *speech only is as the speech of a people,* and *understanding and Reason* likewise. Only as the work of a people is *speech* the ideal *existence of the spirit,* in which it expresses what it is in its essence and its being; speech is a universal [mode of expression], recognized in itself, and resounding in the same way in the consciousness of all; every speaking consciousness comes immediately to be another consciousness in it.[57] In respect of *its content too,* speech comes to be true

53. In other words nature exists for human ethical consciousness as a mass of theoretical concepts and real utilities, or obstacles, not as the living *body* of the divine life (which is its status as a *subsisting* moment of absolute spirit as Hegel envisaged it in 1804).

54. In the first version Hegel wrote here "spirit."

55. In the first version this sentence read: "It [the universal] lets it [the totality of the family] subsist, but marks it with the character of universality."

56. The manuscript has just: "I." But the next section begins: "B. *Die Arbeit und der Besitz* . . ." (the subdivision of that begins with "I.") So it is best to follow Hoffmeister and supply "A. Die *Sprache* eines Volks" here.

57. Because each of us understands what others say, and we speak understandably to them.

speech for the first time in a people, for now it expresses what each one means; barbarians do not know how to say what they mean; they only half say it, or they say the direct opposite of what they want to say; for [ethical nature, which is] what memory, the process of coming to speech, first makes ideal, is only present in a people. Only in a people is it already posited as *superseded, present* as *ideal,* universal *consciousness.* Speech is, of its essence, nature present for itself; posited as ideal; and it is, as it were, mere form, it is a mere speaking, an externality; it is not a producing, but the mere form for making external what has already been produced, in the way it must be said; [the] formal [aspect] of pure activity, the immediate coming of inward being to its contrary, its coming to be outward. The formation of the world to readiness for speaking[58] is present implicitly. As the coming-to-be of understanding and Reason [in the singular consciousness] it falls within education; [speech] is present for the evolving consciousness *as* [an] *ideal world,*[59] or as its inorganic nature, and hence the evolving consciousness does not have to wrench itself free from nature [as such], but rather it must *find the reality for the ideality of its own nature*; it must seek out the meaning for speech that is in being; being also is [there] for it; it remains, so to speak, just the formal activity of relating these [terms] which are already [there] to one another.   [319]

In this way, then, speech is reconstructed in a people, in that although it is the ideal nullification of the external, it is itself *an outward* [being] that must be nullified, superseded, in order to become meaningful language, i.e., to become what it implicitly is according to its concept; thus language is in the people, as a dead other than itself, and becomes totality when it is cancelled as another, and comes to fruition in its concept.

b) Labor *and* Possession

likewise come to be immediately something other in the [life of] the

---

58. Hegel wrote: "Die Bildung der Welt zur Sprechen" (as if he was in two minds between "zur Sprache" and "zum Sprechen"). But the way he continues shows that he has had in mind the fact that *language* is there in the world as a potential that is available to be realized by the consciousness that learns to speak. So I have retained Hegel's *substantive* here (agreeing with Hoffmeister against Düsing and Kimmerle), although we must understand *Sprache* as the referent for *sie* in the following sentence.

59. For the child in the family this just means the achieved consciousness of his parents. But they were just the channel for the *achieved cultural world* of the *Volk.*

people than they are in their concept; labor is, on its own account, concerned with the need *of the singular being as such*, just as possession
strictly pertains to the one single [holder]; labor (and possession too)
becomes here a universal [factor] even in its very singularity.

I. The *labor* that is concerned with the need of a single [agent] becomes
in [public life] α) the labor of a single [agent], but β) even [though it]
is only motivated by his need it is a universal.

α) There is *now* present the requirement of *laboring* as such; [labor-
ing] demands to be *recognized*, it assumes the form of universality; it
is a *universal mode*, a rule of all labor, something that subsists on its
own account, that appears as an external [structure], as inorganic nature, and something that must be *learned*; but this universal [structure]
is for labor the true essence; and natural awkwardness must be conquered in the learning of the universal [skill]; labor is not an *instinct*,
but a [form of] rationality that makes itself universal in the people, and
is therefore opposed to the singularity of the individual, which must be
conquered; and laboring is precisely for this reason present not *as an
instinct* but in the mode of the spirit, because it *has become something
other than the subjective activity of the single agent*; it is a universal
routine, and it becomes the skill of the single [artisan] through this
process of learning; through its process of othering itself it returns to
itself.

[320]

<β> The reverse way: of extraction from the universal.[60]

   The recognition of labor and skill <passes> through the cycle in
the universal [element], the cycle which it has in the single [conscious-
ness] through [the process of] learning. Against the universal skill *the
single agent* posits *himself as a particular*, he separates himself from
[the universal level of skill] and makes himself more skilful than the
others [in the craft], he discovers more useful tools; but whatever is
truly universal in his particular skill is the *discovery* of something universal, *and the others learn it*; they cancel its particularity, and it becomes directly a universal good.

   The tool as such holds off his material nullification *from man*; but

[321]

---

60. The subhead <β> (along with the main verb of the sentence) is restored
from the cancelled opening of this paragraph, which read: "<B. The tool becomes
the *machine*, because in his nullification of nature man posits his own Reason as
a superseded moment, he holds it away from himself. In general> the recognition
of labor and skill <passes> etc." (The new heading comes from a marginal addition at this point.)

there remains a *formal nullification in its use; it is still* his *activity that* is directed on a dead [material], and indeed his activity is essentially the putting [of the object] to death, ripping it out of its living context, and setting it up as something to be nullified as whatever it was before; in the MACHINE man supersedes just this formal activity of his own, and lets it do all the work for him. But this deceit that he practices against nature, and through which he abides stably within its singularity, takes its revenge upon him; what he gains from nature, the more he subdues it, the lower he sinks himself. When he lets nature be worked over by a variety of machines, he does not cancel the necessity for his own laboring but only postpones it, and makes it more distant from nature; and his living labor is not directed on nature as alive, but this negative vitality evaporates from it, and the laboring that remains to man becomes itself *more machinelike*; man *diminishes* labor only for the whole, not for the single [laborer]; for him it is increased rather; for the more machinelike labor becomes, the less it is worth, and the more one must work in that mode.

γ) In other words *his labor, qua laboring* of a single [laborer] *for his own needs,* is *at the same time* a universal and ideal [factor of public life]; he satisfies his needs by it certainly, but not with the determinate thing that he worked on; in order *that that may satisfy his needs,* it must rather become something other than it is; man no longer works up what he uses himself, or he uses no longer what he has worked up himself; that becomes only the possibility of his satisfaction instead of the actual satisfaction of his needs; his labor becomes a *formally abstract universal,* a singular [factor]; he limits himself to labor for one of his needs, and exchanges it for whatever is necessary for his other needs. His labor is for *need* [in general], it is for the abstraction of a need as universally suffered, not for his need; and the satisfaction of the totality of his needs is a *labor of everyone.* Between the range of needs of the single [agent], and his activity on their account, there enters the labor of the whole people, and the labor of any one is in respect of *its contents, a universal labor for the needs of all,* so as to be *appropriate for the satisfaction of all of his needs*; in other words it has a *value*; his labor, and his possessions, are not [just] what they are for him, but what they are for everyone; the satisfaction of needs is a universal dependence of everyone upon one another; for everyone all security and certainty that his labor as a single [agent] is directly adequate to his *needs* disappears; as a singular complex of needs he becomes a universal. Through the division of labor the skill of anyone

[322]

for the labor to be done is immediately greater; all the relations of nature to the singular circumstances of man come more fully under his command, *comfort* increases. This universality, into which private [323] need, and labor, and its aptitude to satisfy need are all elevated, is a formal one; the consciousness of it is not an absoluteness in which these connections are nullified; it is directed toward the cancelling of this privacy, the freeing of the laboring [agent] from his dependence on nature; need and labor are elevated into the form of consciousness; they are simplified, but their simplicity is formally universal abstract simplicity, it is the lying-apart of the concrete [order of nature], which in this external separateness becomes an empirical infinite of singularities;[61] and while man subjects nature to himself in this formal, and false, way, the individual only increases his dependence on it: α) the *division of labor* increases *the mass* of manufactured [objects]; eighteen men work in an English pin factory (Smith, p. 8).[62] Each has a specific part of the work to do and only that. A single man would perhaps not make 20, could not even make one; those eighteen jobs divided among ten men produce 4000 per day. But from the work of these ten in a group of eighteen there would [come] 48000. But in the same ratio that the number produced rises, the value of the labor falls; β) the labor becomes that much deader, it becomes machine work, the skill of the single laborer is infinitely limited, and the consciousness of the factory laborer is impoverished to the last extreme of dullness; [324] γ) and the *coherence of the singular kind* of labor with the whole infinite mass of needs is quite unsurveyable, and a [matter of] *blind dependence*, so that some far-off operation often suddenly cuts off the labor of a whole class of men who were satisfying their needs by it, and makes it superfluous and useless; just as δ) the assimilation of nature becomes greater comfort through the insertion of the intermediate links, so too these stages of the assimilation are infinitely divisible,

61. The passage from "This universality . . . infinite of singularities" was added in the revised draft.

62. This is Hegel's first absolutely certain reference to the *Wealth of Nations* (but compare my query in note 43 to the *System of Ethical Life*). He refers to the Basel edition of the *English* text, 1791. He owned this edition at the time of his death, but it is not known when he acquired it. We know that he was using it here because of the page reference and because, although the figures reported from Smith's text are muddled, they are not muddled in Garve's way (see the note in *N.K.A.* VI, 384–85). Smith records that the ten-man factory could produce about twelve pounds of pins (4000+ pins per pound) per man in a day. Hegel read him as asserting that the whole group produced "about a pound of pins in a day."

and the multitude of conveniences makes them just as absolutely inconvenient once again.

This manifold laboring at needs as things must likewise realize their concept, their abstraction; their universal concept must become a thing like them, but one which, qua universal, represents all needs; *money* is this materially existing concept, the form of unity, or of the possibility of all things needed.

Need and labor, elevated into this universality, then form on their own account a monstrous system of community and mutual interdependence in a great people; a life of the dead body, that moves itself within itself, one which ebbs and flows in its motion blindly, like the elements, and which requires continual strict dominance and taming like a wild beast.

γ. This activity of laboring and need, as the movement of the living dead, has likewise its resting side in *possession*. Like labor, possession becomes within the whole of a people a universal factor in its privacy; [325] it remains the possession of this private [person], but only in so far as it is posited as his by the universal consciousness, or in so far as in the universal consciousness everyone else likewise possesses what is his; that is to say, possession becomes *property*. Its exclusiveness becomes such that all [owners] communally exclude every other likewise, and in the determinate possession [of any one] all equally have their possessions; or that the possession of the private [person] is the possession of all [i.e., it instantiates the *right* of property]. In possession there is the contradiction that a *thing* is universal as a thing, and yet it is to be the possession of just one single [agent]; this contradiction is cancelled by consciousness in that the thing is implicitly posited as the contrary of itself; qua recognized, it is the private possession, yet at the same time it is universal because in this private possession all [owners] have their goods; the security of my possession is the security of everyone's possessions; in *my* property all hold their property, my possession has acquired the form of consciousness, it is determined [as] my possession, but as *property* it is not related to me alone, but universally.

As at the preceding level labor and need have been absolutely parcelled out, so *property* is *parcelled out* at this level; the parcelling out is the positing of the concrete in the universal, the distinctions that it has within itself, as identity of opposites,[63] fall apart, and come to be

63. Or possibly "as opposed to the identity [of the abstract universal]" (Hegel's shorthand will permit either expansion).

[326]

on their own account as abstractions. The *totality of singularity*, which was whole throughout the extension of its existing in whatever it gained the mastery of in each singular case, only is as a superseded state within the whole people, and the private [being] of need and possession falls back into the nature of its privacy; consciousness as totality of the singular [life] was the union of itself and its externality, its possession; in that the two terms [now] fall outside one another, the private [person] ceases to have that [sense of] honor which staked its whole essence on every single detail. In this parcelling out what is related to the totality as an organization, or as self-constituting, what now gets called his *person*, falls directly apart from that which appears to him externally as real thing (*als Sache*), whereas for the sense of honor the distinction is not present; it posits itself as a whole in every relation [and] every possession.

[The rest of the manuscript is lost. The page is full but not the last line, so this is presumably the end of a paragraph. Hegel is just beginning to develop his theory of private right, contract, and distributive justice. Presumably the values of *absolute* spirit —the cultural worlds of Art, Religion, and Philosophy would follow when his account of political life—only just begun here— was complete. The fragment of *ist nur die Form* (printed in Appendix 1) *may belong* to that part of the present "system."]

Appendix 1

[This fragment belongs—by the objective criterion of the hand-writing—to the same period as the "system" of which the third part is here translated. It would fit in neatly enough in the final stages of that system. But the only external evidence that it was part of the system is the fact that it is now bound up in the same volume of posthumous papers. This probably reflects nothing more than the judgment of some earlier student who was not even as well placed to form an objective opinion as modern students are. We are bound, therefore, to ask ourselves whether there are *other contexts* into which the fragment would fit equally well; and it must be conceded that there are. It may, for instance belong to the *philosophiae universae delineatio* of Summer 1803 (see the introduction, pp. 189–90). The *philosophiae systema universum* of Summer 1804 is a less probable alternative, both because of the handwriting, and because it is more probable that that lecture course was not actually delivered.]

. . . . is just the form, the semblance of the absolute independence of [330] the absolute present, and what matters is what the stuff is to which it [the form?] gives this semblance; [what matters is] whether the stuff is absolute in itself.[1] But this stuff we know:

α) the universal as an inward [essence] must remain essentially inward, without [outward] effect [or: expression in work], it is *Love*;

---

1. "Stuff" is a strange word for the Divine Being or the absolute substance. But it becomes much less strange if we apply it to the *history* of man's experience of God. This fragment seems to be part of such a history. Rosenkranz reports that Hegel presented the immanent dialectic of the Absolute, in one course at Jena, as the "development of the career (*Lebenslauf*) of God" (*Hegels Leben*, p. 192). His date for the lecture on the transition from Nature to Spirit, in which Hegel developed this theme (1806), can scarcely be right, since we have the complete text of Hegel's *Realphilosophie* for this period, and such an introduction would not fit into it very well. It would certainly have fitted better into either of the Summer systems mentioned in the headnote. (On *Stoff* see M. J. Petry, *Hegel's Philosophy of Subjective Spirit*, I, cxli–cxlii.)

and when it is shaped, it is Love toward what *is* therefore as *a woman* [the Virgin].

β) The activity itself, the living causal action [or: working], these heavenly beautiful and energetic characters, both masculine and feminine individualities, can only be a *romantic realm of adventure*, with singular deeds and confusion of detail.

γ) But the shapes in which these living singular [agents] *intuit* themselves as absolute consciousness, the founders of religions, are essentially actual existing [agents] in history, not absolutely free shapes [like the gods and heroes of myth]; the heroes of these religions, however, are of the kind who represent the absolute grief in suffering and martyrdom of the most lurid type; and instead of a beautiful self-fulfilling appearance, theirs is in the highest degree unfulfilled and ugly.

δ) Finally there is the relation of that first consciousness, the private one, to the Absolute Consciousness, which would be a living relation, [i.e.,] that a people, as consciousness in the form of singularity brought forth a universal work, in which they intuited their absolute consciousness as shape and themselves likewise as suspended therein, as it is their work, or they are alive in it. But this absolute consciousness, since it only exists as concept, has no presence (*Gegenwart*) in the singular consciousness as such, it does not become a self-fulfilling, here-and-now vital, work; and it is an absolute beyond, in the face of which the individual consciousness can only nullify itself, not live and move in Him. The *stirring* of individuality before this absolute self-enjoyment is therefore no Èpic but a *Comedy*, a divine comedy, however, in which the action of man immediately annihilates itself, only his nullity has absolute certainty, his consciousness is only a dream of a consciousness; his character is eternally a wholly powerless past, over which the man who attends on this stage show can only dissolve in tears.[2]

[331]

The art which gives presence to that love, those romantic deeds, this historic shaping, and this nullification of consciousness cannot through its form remove the essential [quality] of such content, the fact that it has no presence, but has only absolute yearning. The content in which the absolute consciousness appears must free itself from its yearning, from its singularity that has a beyond in the past and the future, and

2. It would seem that Hegel's serious study of Dante did not extend beyond the *Inferno*. Compare *Natural Law* (trans. Knox and Acton), pp. 105–06; and *Faith and Knowledge*, p. 146.

wrest the world-spirit forth in the form of universality; the mere concept of absolute self-enjoyment must [be] elevated out of the reality in
which it has submerged itself as concept, and as it [gives] itself *the
form* of concept, it reconstructs the reality of its existence and becomes
absolute universality. After [. . . .]

[The sheet is full. Thus we can be certain that
it was part of a continuing manuscript.]

Appendix 2

[The following reports and fragments can be plausibly referred
to the years 1801–spring 1805 on internal grounds. A few of
the manuscripts here referred to have now been discovered—see
the notes. *Objective* dating of the rest of this material is not
possible. The dates given by Rosenkranz himself cannot be relied
on. The pagination indicated is that of *Hegels Leben*, Berlin,
1844. These reports were also reprinted in Hoffmeister's
Dokumente [Stuttgart, 1936].

[179] . . . Nor did he lack *favorite metaphors*, such as the one that occurs
so often, where the *transparency* of cognition appears as *the aether of
the spirit*.[1] And there were *favorite concepts* for him, too, which he
developed with characteristic energy and with that transcendent pa-
thos which took mighty hold even on what was striving against his
thought. Here especially belongs the portrayal (oft-repeated, with fas-
cination) of *Greek mythology* and of the *ethical spirit of a people*,
whose work costs its individual members such a bitter effort, but which
[180] is for itself a serene play in its deep seriousness because of the freedom
of its activity. [Hegel] was then inexhaustible in creating new images,
pregnant expressions, ever more precise definitions of concepts.

He spoke once of *genius*, of the *inventive* spirit, with direct reference to fine art, but also in a more general sense:[2] "*Mnemosyne* or the
absolute Muse, Art, undertakes to set forth the aspects and shapes of

---

1. Hegel's references to the aether in its spiritual aspect are not simply metaphorical before 1805/6 (and perhaps not *after* that date either!). Rosenkranz is
here referring to a manuscript of 1803, which has just been recovered.

2. The fragmentary manuscript from which the following quotation was taken
has now been found. From the handwriting it appears to belong to 1803 (see
N.K.A. VIII, 355–56). The reader should note that the fragment "*ist nur die
Form* . . ." would fit neatly into the context of a direct continuation of the discussion from which this quotation was taken. (The analogy with the elements
here makes a link with Hegel's "Philosophy of Spirit" in 1803/4; and what he
says about the duty of the artist at a point of revolutionary transition illumines
the relation between his first philosophy of Spirit and the *System of Ethical Life*.)

the spirit visibly and audibly for intuition. This Muse is itself the universal speaking consciousness of the people. The art work of mythology is propagated in the living tradition. Even as the races (*Geschlechter*) advance in the liberation of their consciousness, so it advances and purifies itself and ripens. This work of art is as much a universal possession as it is the work of everyone. Every generation hands it on to the one that follows beautified, or [in other words] it has labored further on the liberation of absolute consciousness. Those who are called *geniuses* have acquired a certain type of special skill, by which they make the universal shapes of the people into their work just as others do other things [of universal value]. What they produce is not their discovery, but a discovery by the people *as a whole*. It is the *finding* that the people has found its essence. What belongs to the artist as *this man here* is his formal activity, his particular skill in this mode of exposition, and it is precisely to this that he has been educated in the universal skill. He is like a man who finds himself among a gang of laborers building an arch of stone, for which the scaffolding is invisibly present as Idea. Everyone puts a stone in place, the artist too. It happens by chance that he is the last, and when he puts his stone in place, the arch can carry its own weight. He sees that because he has put this stone in place the whole work makes an arch, he says so and he counts as its discoverer. Or when laborers are digging for a spring, the one who happens to take out the last clod has the same work to do as the rest—and for him the spring gushes forth. —With a *political revolution* it is the same. We can think of the people as buried under the earth over which there is a lake. Each believes he works just for himself and for the maintenance of the whole when he takes a bit of stone away from above and makes use of it for his own purposes and for the general underworld edifice. The tension of the air, the universal element, begins to change. It makes men thirsty for water. They are [181] uncomfortable, but they do not know what they lack, and in order to do something for it they dig ever higher with the intent of improving their subterranean condition. The skin of earth becomes transparent. One of them looks at it and cries: "Water." He wrenches the last clod out of the way, and the lake rushes in and *drinks them up* even as it *gives them drink*. —So too, the work of art is the work of all. There is one who completes it and brings it to the light of day, because he is the last to work on it and he is the darling of Mnemosyne— If in our time the living world certainly is not molding the work of art within itself, the artist must transpose his imagination into a world that is dead and gone; he must *dream* a world for himself, but then the character of the dreaming state, of not being alive, of being dead and gone, is ineradicably stamped on it."

The lectures printed after Hegel's death give an adequate impression of some of these pedagogical or propaedeutic expositions—e.g., his general remarks about the singular agent's illusion of setting himself against the universal necessity, his taking his relation to it as something accidental and not seeing the action of necessity repeated in that relation; or about the resolution of the opposition between the slumbering, instinctive consciousness and the awakened critical consciousness, through the movement of the world itself, with the objectivity of which genuine philosophy cannot find itself in contradiction; or about the independence of philosophy, which no more needs another science for its founding than it needs an alien instrument for it, and so on. It is superfluous, therefore, to quote anything from them here, even though many discussions of this kind appear worthy of quotation because of the completeness of their exposition.

Nonetheless we cannot refrain from mentioning in particular one of these introductions to a lecture course on the *whole* system [of speculative Philosophy], because it contains a very decided *polemic* against the degenerations of the *nature philosophy of Schelling* which began at the time to inundate the literature of philosophy.[3] It contains, in addition, important declarations about [philosophical] *terminology* generally—to wit, that as far as possible it should be wholly brought back to the *mother tongue*.[4] Hegel speaks first of how we make the study of philosophy more difficult, partly because we make demands on it [182] that ought not to be made, and partly because we terrify ourselves with pictures of the demands that philosophy makes on us and which are too hard for us to meet. The truth should present itself to us in religion, of course, but for our culture faith is altogether a thing of the past; Reason, with its demand that we should not believe, but know what the truth is, has grown strong, that we should not merely have intuitive consciousness of the truth, but should comprehend it. The truth of his individuality, which the path of his existence traces precisely for him, the single individual is well aware of, but the consciousness of the universal life he expects from philosophy. Here his hope seems to be disappointed when instead of the fullness of life there ap-

3. No such polemic is likely to have occurred before Schelling left Jena in 1803. Winter 1803/4, Winter 1804/5, and Summer 1805 are all *likely* times for this course because of the coincidence pointed out in the next note.

4. We know from his letter to J. H. Voss of May 1805 (excerpted in Kaufmann, *Hegel*, pp. 315–16) that Hegel was much concerned about this at that date.

pear concepts, and in contrast to the riches contained in the world of immediate experience the poorest abstractions are offered. But the concept is itself the *mediator between itself and life*, in that it teaches us how to find life in it and the concept in life. But, of course, only science itself can convince us of this.

"There is, indeed, a *dark halfway-house* between feeling and *scientific knowledge*, a speculative feeling or the Idea, which cannot free itself from imagination and feeling and yet is no longer just imagination and feeling. I mean *mysticism*, or rather the *Oriental* attempt to present the Idea, just as much as *Jacob Boehme's*. The oriental spirit is exalted above mere beauty or limited shape. It is the infinite, the shapeless which it struggles to grasp in its fanciful images, but it is always driven beyond the image by the infinite, it continually cancels its image once more and seeks itself in a new one, which it likewise allows to disappear again. It is therefore just a *splendid rhetoric* which ever confesses the *impotence of the means* (namely, the *images*) to present the essence:—the modern mysticism [i.e., Boehme] is of a *darker cast* and a more sorrowful kind. It steps into the depths of the essence with common *sensuous ideas* (*Vorstellungen*) and fights to make itself master of it and bring it before its consciousness. But the essence will not let itself be grasped in the form of a common sensuous idea. Any representation of this kind that it is grasped in is *inadequate*. It is only made to fit the essence by *violence*, and must equally violently be torn [away from it?]; it presents only the battle of an inward [essence], that is fermenting within itself, and cannot advance into the clear light of day, feels its incapacity with sorrow, and rolls about in fits and convulsions that can come to no proper issue.

[183]

The *clear* element is the universal, the concept, which [is] as deep as it is extensive in its revelation that leaves nothing veiled.

For the *fixation* of concepts there is a means at hand which achieves its end, on the one side, but can also become more dangerous than the evil of being without concepts even, namely, *philosophical terminology*, the vocabulary established for this purpose from foreign languages, [specifically] Latin and Greek. I do not know, for example, what there is to the idea that the expression '*quantitativer Unterschied*' is more definite than '*Grossenunterschied*.' Properly speaking, it belongs to the highest cultural development of the people *to say everything in their own language*. The concepts that we mark with foreign words seem to us to be themselves something *foreign* and not to belong to us immediately as our very own. The elements of things appear to us not to be the *present* concepts with which we are environed and have to deal with all the time and in which the most ordinary man expresses himself. *Being, Not-Being, One, Many, Quality, Size* and so on, are pure essences of this kind with which we *keep house* all the time in ordinary life. Such forms as these appear to us to be not worthy enough, as it were, for the grasping of those high *other-worldly* things, the Idea, the Absolute in them; and something foreign is more apt for it, since the Absolute, the *supersensible world* itself, is foreign to the common round of daily life in which we employ those concepts. But that which is *in itself* must just not have this foreignness *for us*, and we must *not give it this foreign look by using a foreign terminology*, but must count ourselves really convinced that the spirit itself is alive *everywhere* and that it expresses its forms in our own spontaneous natural language. They come up in the speech of everyday, *mingled and wrapped in crude concrete* [particulars], for example, in 'the tree is green.' 'Tree' and 'green' are what controls our representation. We do not in ordinary life reflect on the 'is,' we do not set this *pure being* [184] in relief, make it our object, as philosophy does. But this being is here present and expressed. It is, of course, necessary to have recourse to foreign terminology if we cannot find the determinate characteristics of the concept before us in our own language. It is not customary for us to do violence to language and to mold *new forms out of old words*. Our thought is still not properly at home in our language, it does not dominate the language, as it should, and we cherish in this regard, a blind reverence for what is brought from abroad.

But this foreign terminology, which is used partly in a futile and partly in a perverse way, becomes a great evil because it reduces concepts which are implicitly *movement* to something *stable* and *fixated*, so that the spirit and life of the thing itself disappears and philosophy degenerates into an empty *formalism*, which is very easily supplied for social chat; yet to those who do not understand the terminology it seems very difficult and deep. That is precisely what is *seductive* in a terminology of this kind, that it is in fact very easy to master it. It is all the easier to speak in it, because if I have no sense of personal shame, I can permit myself to utter every possible nonsense and triviality when I am talking to people in a language that they do not understand.

In the study of philosophy you must not, therefore, take this kind of terminology for the essence, you should have no reverence for it. Ten or twenty years ago it seemed very hard to work one's way into the Kantian terminology and use expressions such as 'synthetic judgments *a priori*,' 'synthetic unity of apperception,' 'transcendent,' 'transcendental,' etc. But such a tidal wave of words rushes over us and is gone as rapidly as it comes. The majority get on top of the language, and the secret comes to the light of day *that very ordinary thoughts lurk behind the bogeyman masks of such expressions.* I remark on this principally because of the present aspects of philosophy and especially because of the philosophy of nature, which has made mischief with the terminology of *Schelling. Schelling* has certainly uttered good sense and philosophical thoughts in these forms, but he has done so precisely because he *showed himself to be free in fact* from this terminology, [185] since in almost every successive presentation of his philosophy he has used a *new* one. Yet so far as there is public discussion of this philosophy now, it is really only the *superficial aspect* of his thought that is concealed beneath it. I cannot lead you into the depths of this philosophy, as we see it in so many writings, for [in them] it has no depth; and I tell you this, so that *you will not let yourselves be imposed on,* as if behind these abstruse, weighty words there must be a sense hidden. —All that can be of interest here is to observe the astonishment that it creates in the ignorant mass [of the literate public]. But in fact one can learn this current formalism in half an hour. Instead of saying that something is 'long' for example, one says that it 'tends to length and this length is *magnetism*'; or instead of saying it is 'broad,' that it 'tends to be breadth, and that this is electricity'; instead of 'thick, bodily' 'it tends to the third dimension'; instead of 'pointed,' 'it is the pole of contraction'; instead of 'the fish is long,' 'it stands under the *schema* of magnetism' and so on and so forth."[5]

"I give you prior notice that in the philosophical *system which I am going to lecture on* you will find none of this deluge of formalism. And though I speak now as I have done, about this terminology and the current epidemic use of it, I know well enough that *Schelling's Ideas* must be very clearly distingiushed from the use *that his school makes of them,* and I honor *Schelling's* genuine service to philosophy just as much as I despise this formalism; and since I am well acquainted with *Schelling's* philosophy, I know that its genuine Idea, as it has again awakened in our time, is independent of this formalism."

In such introductions as this, therefore, Hegel was fighting not against Schelling himself, towards whom, indeed, he maintained his

5. This passage should be compared with what Marx and Engels said about the tradition of German idealism generally in the *German Ideology* (for example, *Basic Writings*, ed., Feuer, p. 261). It should be noted that, like Hegel, they themselves took the *project* of a *philosophy of nature* very seriously; and it seems safe to assume that, when they were writing the *German Ideology,* they had already read Rosenkranz's biography of Hegel.

original friendship with unbreakable firmness, but rather against the devastation of thought which his school had begun to wreak. Hegel also attacked *romanticism*, which was seeking to establish itself in philosophy at that time. He protests in the most explicit way against

[186] the idea that by its very nature philosophy existed only for the few *elect*, that it required a special genius and a peculiar organization [of the mind]. "We must note briefly that philosophy as the *science of Reason* is by its very nature meant for *everyone* because of its *universal mode of being*. Not everyone achieves it, but that is not to the point, any more than it is to the point that *not every man gets to be a prince*. The *disturbing* thing about some men being set over others only lies in this, that it might be assumed that they were distinct by nature and were *essentially of another kind*."[6]

With incorruptible sobriety he analyzed the religious *enthusiasm* which was forever promising *revelations of the eternal and the holy*, but never achieved the definiteness of cognition. He rejected the appeal of these insipid enthusiasts to *Plato*, from Plato's own work, since Plato ascribes prophecy not to self-possessed men, but to those who are asleep, when the power of consciousness is fettered; or to the sick and the possessed, the enthusiast who does not know what he is doing, so that the meaning of the words he throws out in divinely inspired madness must first be interpreted by the self-possessed man, according to his Reason; and the Demiurge, too, mindful of the injunction of the Father to make the tribe of mortal men in the best way possible, laid up the power of prophecy in the *liver*, so that *our bad side might in some way be in contact with the truth* [Timaeus 71d-e].

Hegel compared this overheated essential being, who wants to replace the good sense he lacks by vehement assurances about the deeper significance of his words, with the feebleness of modern drama, in which similarly the "outstretched, waving arms, the raging face, the eyes staring fixedly up to heaven, the sucking lips and chewing jaws must give the *meagre words* their first real impact."

Because he presented philosophy in the element of free universality according to logical method, as the inner organization of Reason, because he demanded of the philosophy student [or: philosophizing mind] that by abstraction from all given determinacy he [it] makes himself [itself] into a self-conscious void that stands directly opposed to the whole fullness of the universe; and because he also treated *phil-*

6. This, too, is part of a polemic against the aristocratic conception of philosophy fostered by Schelling (who himself used the analogy of princely birth).

osophy of Nature logically, he soon had in Jena the prejudice arising
against him from the side of the romantics that he did not appreciate [187]
the *poetry of nature*. Since he went beyond Schelling in this respect,
that he did not just coordinate the Spirit with Nature, but rather posited it as the *absolute universal*, he did, indeed, get to the point of
speaking not merely of the *liberation* of the spirit from its bondage to
nature, but even of contempt for nature. But this *ethical* aspect of nature is quite a different thing from its scientific aspect. Hegel said: "In
fact, the single spirit can hold fast to itself, as force of character, and
assert its individuality, let nature be what she will. His negative attitude toward nature, where nature is already something other than
spirit, despises nature's power, and in this contempt he keeps her at a
distance and himself free from her. And actually the single spirit is
only as great and as free as his contempt of nature is great."[7]
Experiencing already even then the prejudice against him, as if he
meant this contempt in a theoretical, not just in a practical sense, Hegel
declared himself by alluding to a passage in Goethe's *Faust*: "Nature
is a whole for the living intuition, or if one wants to call it that, the
poetic intuition. The manifold [phenomena] of nature pass before him
as a series of living [shapes], and he recognizes in bush, in air, and in
water his brothers. For this poetic intuition of nature it is, to be sure,
an absolute living whole. But this vitality is in its [phenomenal] shaping an individuality. The living things are inwardly identical, but they
have an absolute externality of being as against one another. Each one
is on its own account, and their motion against one another is absolutely contingent. In this instantiated (*vereinzelte*) vitality everyone
plays its part with equal right against the others, and, because the infinity of its singularity is its *destruction*, its singularity is not in itself
justified. The intuition of it is a *sensible grief*. The *ethical* individualities step outside of nature. For them it is only a side issue, an instrument. Where it is more than that, where ethical beings (*Wesen*) strive
to keep themselves low enough, so to speak, to enjoy it, —in *idyllic
poetry*—they themselves then fall into that debasing sensibility and
into a limited range of life whose impoverishment can only be interesting in a formal way, as a presentation."[8]
Hegel took considerable care about all the misunderstandings which [188]
are bound to arise from the speculative mode of presentation because

7. This comes from the manuscript of 1803. It seems likely that Rosenkranz is
answering complaints made against the (probably later) manuscript (which we do
not have) with quotations from the earlier one (which we have now recovered).
8. This also comes from the manuscript of 1803.

of the way in which it conflicts with the point of view of common sense, which calls itself the "reasonable" view, of course. *Nature,* for example, is *the negative* moment in *the totality of the spirit,* the moment that is opposed both to the simple Idea and to Spirit that is for itself. Nature is the other-being of the Idea, which gets superseded in the spirit and by the spirit through its freedom as that which thinks the Idea in its ideality as spirit's own self. Now this negativity has been represented both by the *Gnostics* and by *Schelling* as a *going-forth* of the Idea from itself or as a *falling* of the Idea away from itself. But Hegel points out that one *can* only bring what is correct in these verbal pictures to the light of present awareness if one *already knows* in general what is right in them; but that it is misguided to want to possess the truth of the matter in these forms already, since they only express it as a *happening,* an *indifference of connection* [i.e., a contingent relation which need not exist], whereas the concept posits [its] negation essentially—only as a *moment,* but as absolutely *necessary.*

In this way Hegel sought as far as possible to overcome the original [*primitive*] difficulty of his system, striving to make it a more perfect systematic circle by simplifying everything, to make it more comprehensible by examples and by references to the nearest present. Least changed was the basic pattern of the *Logic* and *Metaphysics.* We can, however, see the greatest efforts in his introductions to justify the undertaking [of philosophical logic] in general. It is quite remarkable, thinks Hegel, that modern philosophy *despises* logic and yet all the same logic is *required* by it generally; while, of course, those who still pay homage to the *old forms* of logic are *just as discontented,* yet neither party has generated any new logic. "Fichte's *Science of Knowledge* like the *Transcendental Idealism* of Schelling are both of them nothing else but attempts to expound Logic or speculative philosophy purely on its own account. *Fichte,* admittedly, took the great, but *one-sided* standpoint of consciousness, of the Ego, of the subject, as his starting-point, and this has made a free and complete detailed treatment [of Logic] impossible for him. *Schelling* starts from there too, certainly, but he suspends this [subjective] standpoint in the sequel. [189]   But as far as speculative philosophy itself is concerned, it appears that the very *consciousness was not present* in these essays, that precisely this and nothing else was at issue. In his later views of philosophy *Schelling* sets up the speculative Idea quite generally, *without development* in itself [as Logic], and passes on straight away to the shape that it has qua Philosophy of Nature."[9]

9. This passage does not occur in the newly discovered fragments. Neverthe-

In one of the introductions to what he called speculative philosophy
in the stricter sense, he referred directly to the time when philosophy
in general appears, to wit, that it comes forth in the *epochs of transition*, in which the old ethical form of the peoples is wholly overcome
by a new one. To be sure, this happens more rapidly with smaller peoples than it does with great ones, and especially with the colossal peoples of the modern period. Here Hegel became absorbed for a minute
in the portraying of the *great man* (which he himself was so great at)
before making his way back again to philosophy via Alexander the
Great's education at the hands of Aristotle—a route which was for him
a *stereotype*: "These collected (*besonnenen*) natures have nothing to
do but speak the word, and the peoples will hang upon them. The great
spirits than can do this must, in order to be able to do it, be *cleansed*
of all the peculiarities of the preceding shape [of ethical life]. If they
want to bring the work to completion in *its* totality, they must also
have grasped it in *their* whole totality. They take hold of it, perhaps,
only at one end and bring it forward. But since nature wills the whole,
it casts them down from the peak upon which they have placed themselves and puts others in their place; and if these, too, are one-sided,
there is a sequence of singular agents, until the whole work is completed. But if it was the deed of *one man*, then he must have cognized
the whole and thereby cleansed himself of all limitation. The terrors of
the objective world, along with all the fetters of ethical actuality, and
with them, too, all *alien crutches* for standing in this [ethical] world,
and all reliance upon a firm bond within it—all these must have fallen
away from him, i.e., he must have been formed (*gebildet*) in the school
of philosophy. Starting from here he can rouse the still slumbering
shape of a new ethical world to waking, and go forth into battle boldly
against the old forms of the world-spirit, just as Jacob wrestled with
God, secure [in his own mind] that the forms which he can destroy are
a senile shape [of the divine], and the new forms are a new divine revelation. He can regard the whole complex of present human affairs as   [190]
raw material (*einen Stoff*) for his appropriation. From it his great individuality forms (*bildet*) for itself its body. It is a raw material which is

---

less I think it can be securely assigned to 1801 because Fichte and Schelling are
here treated side by side as speculative philosophers (as in the *Difference* essay).
Fichte has not yet been demoted to the rank of a philosopher of subjective reflection (as in *Faith and Knowledge*). Since Rosenkranz goes on immediately to
summarize and quote from the "Logic and Metaphysics" of 1801 as *distinct* from
the "introduction" he has been quoting, I infer that the present passage comes
from the "Introduction to Philosophy" of the same year.

itself alive, and which forms [by its own activity] the organs both inert and vital of this great [new] shape. Thus it was—to cite the supreme example of a man who wove his own individuality into the web of destiny and gave it a new freedom—thus it was that Alexander of Macedon passed out from the school of Aristotle to become the conqueror of the world."

[The quotation continues with an outline of the structure of Hegel's "Logic" as he proposed to expound it in the Winter term of 1801/2. This is omitted here as irrelevant.[10] We pick up the text of Rosenkranz once more, where he passes on to discuss the development of Hegel's "Metaphysics":]

[192]   In his lectures on metaphysics[11] Hegel strove especially to make the transition to the "real philosophy" [the theory of Nature and Spirit] ever clearer. He did this at that period in a wholly speculative theological context. As late as the Summer of 1806[12] in his lecture course on "Real Philosophy" he called the simple Idea *the night of the divine mystery*, from whose undisturbed density, nature and conscious spirit were let go free into their independent subsistence. With the still half-theosophical conception of the Absolute Idea which he had at that period Hegel would have contented much better all those who nowadays do not know how they are supposed to unite the *concept of the Absolute Idea* with that of the *Absolute Spirit* or the finitude of human

10. The passage omitted here is cited—with only one minor omission—in my introduction to *Faith and Knowledge*, pp. 9–11. Rosenkranz quoted the whole passage—accurately, and with only one or two very small cuts—from the manuscript of 1801. The fragments of the manuscript which he removed for his own use have been recovered (see N.K.A. V).

11. Rosenkranz could hardly have spoken of any manuscript that he had as a "Vortrag der Metaphysik" if Hegel wrote it later than 1805, because the division between Logic and Metaphysics disappears altogether from his writings after that year. But what Rosenkranz says here does *not* refer to the manuscript of 1804/5 which we still have (for he believed that the manuscript belonged to 1800). Hence it must refer to an earlier manuscript.

12. What basis Rosenkranz had for this date we can only surmise. He did not know the date of the "Real Philosophy" of 1805/6—which he assigns positively to 1804/5. But he *did* have communications (both written and verbal) from students who took Hegel's courses at Jena. For Summer 1806 G. A. Gabler was a possible source. (Summer 1806 was probably the last term that Hegel lectured at Jena; and for his lectures on *Philosophia naturae et mentis* he mainly used the manuscript of Winter 1805—which we have. Our manuscript contains nothing that deserves the name "introduction"—yet some kind of initial survey Hegel must certainly have delivered.)

self-consciousness with the *absoluteness of the spirit* in his theory. He even called the immanent dialectic of the Absolute the *career of God* (*Lebenslauf Gottes*). The most important thing was that he entirely dissolved the deadness of the concept of God as a fixed point with equally fixed properties. "The intuition of God as himself is the eternal *creation of the Universe*, in which every point as a relative totality for itself has its own special career. This scattering (*Auseinandergehen*) of the real, this getting-posited of the manifold, is the *goodness* of God. But *the singular also cancels itself as singular* and thereby shows its universality. This act is *the cognition of the intuition*, the absolute turning point, *justice* of God, which brings back the negative side as absolute power over the real and thereby inverts it out of its being- [193] for-self in unity with all other things. In so far as God, *qua eternally self-identical self-consciousness*, is not immediately immersed in this double process of the Universe as both *resting and becoming simul- taneously*, so far, that is, as his recreation of the created absolutely keeps the character of *ideality*, he is eternal *wisdom* and *blessedness*. Every relative totality, even the least of them, is blessed in its life- career. Its relativity certainly breaks off this blessed self-sufficiency (*Insichsein*); but even the *judgment seat* to which the single being is brought cannot give an abstract verdict, since the singular being is limited. God, as judge of the world, must *break his own heart*, because he is the absolutely universal totality. He *cannot judge* the single be- ings, he can only *have mercy* on them." Hegel still loved, even yet, as we already saw above, in his first exposition of metaphysics,[13] to pre- sent the creation of the universe as the *utterance* of the absolute *Word*, and the return of the universe into itself as the *understanding* of the Word, so that nature and history become the *medium* between the speaking and the understanding of the Word—a medium which itself vanishes qua other-being.

[The comments on the philosophy of nature and the philosophy of spirit which follow are all based on the manuscript of 1805.]

13. Rosenkranz is not referring to his exposition of the "metaphysics" of the manuscript of 1804, which he took to be Hegel's Frankfurt system to the "Divine Triangle" manuscript which he thought of as earlier still. (See *Hegel's Leben*, pp. 102–3.)

A NOTE ON THE TRANSLATION

The translation has been made from the magnificent critical edition prepared by Klaus Düsing and Heinz Kimmerle (G.W.F. Hegel, *Gesammelte Werke*, Band 6: *Jenaer Systementwürfe* I, Hamburg: F. Meiner, 1975). The first edition of the text was that of Johannes Hoffmeister (*Jenenser Realphilosophie* I, Leipzig: F. Meiner, 1932) and the only other translation known to me is the French version of Guy Planty-Bonjour, which was made from this edition (Hegen, *Première Philosophie de l'esprit*, Paris, P.U.F., 1969). Hoffmeister's treatment of the text was wrongheaded and unsatisfactory in a number of important ways. But I have occasionally followed him (on points that are all carefully recorded in my notes) and I have profited much from the work of Planty-Bonjour (in ways that are generally impossible to record in detail). Sir Malcolm Knox has saved me from a number of errors; and I have also received valuable advice and help on several points from Klaus Düsing, Heinz Kimmerle and Michael Petry.

My text generally renders the final state of Hegel's manuscript. But I have given a translation of all significant cancelled material in the footnotes. Editorial additions are in square brackets throughout, while material cancelled by Hegel himself is always given in angled brackets. The reader should note, however, that the critical apparatus here is far from complete, and it is probably imperfect even within its intended limits. For a truly exact and exhaustive survey of the state of the manuscripts one must always refer to the edition of Düsing and Kimmerle.

I have been trying for several years to decide what distinctions Hegel intends by the spelling distinctions *formal/formell, ideal/ideell, real/reell*. When I made the translation, I had virtually given up the struggle because it seemed that even if the intended distinctions could be identified there was no convenient way of rendering them. Michael Petry persuaded me, rather late in the day, that the distinctions must, in any case, be acknowledged. So I decided that I should, at least, provide a register of the different occurrences; and the process of making the register finally led me to some conclusions about the meaning of the terms, which makes it virtually necessary to distinguish them. I apologize to the interested reader for the trouble that he must take to mark all of these words in accordance with this list. But he will be able to decide as he does so, whether my conclusions are correct; and if he agrees with me, he will certainly agree that the effort is not wasted. (The *First Philosophy of Spirit* is a rather short text, and two of the forms occur only once each; so I have provided a full register for the *System of Ethical Life* for purposes of comparison.)

formal (*speculative* term): theoretically
or inwardly formal, pertaining
to the living form or essence,
as distinct from the *matter*.
(As applied to the ideal realm,
formal means *abstractly intellectual*).

System of Ethical Life (*page,* line):
104,14; 112,4; 116,2,8,32; 120,29;
124,15,24,27; 126,5,14; 127,13;
132,1,10; 133,10; 134,9;139,15;
148,7,31; 151,34,35; 154,8; 159,17,
22,37; 161,30; 164,40; 166,1;
167,1.

First Philosophy of Spirit:
210,16; 211,7,26; 212,26; 217,8,35;
218,5,note 24(line 1); 219,3,38;
220,8,9,11,14; 221,21; 223,3 [*der
Form nach*],23(25); 225,4; 226,19;
227,3,10,13; 233,28; 245,11,20;
247,1,5,25.

formell (empirical term): practically
or outwardly formal, pertaining
to the visible or imposed form,
as distinct from the *content*.
(As applied to the ideal realm
formell refers to *required* formalities—e.g. conventionally
agreed formulas, protocol, etc.).

System of Ethical Life (*page,* line):
102,3(twice); 103,6; 107,16; 111,34;
112,3; 113,7; 114,10; 115,13;
116,13,19,23; 118,25–26; 122,13;
123,15(both),28; 124,14,28; 125,6,
26; 126,26,27,33; 129,16; 131,27;
137,7; 141,12–13; 144,5; 146,6;
151,25; 152,13; 154,17; 157,10,16;
159,24; 160,38; 162,1,10,31; 163,1;
164,2; 165,13,31; 166,15; 167,6;
164,2; 165,13,31; 166,15; 167,6;
169,22; 172,7,16,24,29[abstractly];
173,21–22; 176,8,14.

First Philosophy of Spirit: 225,9.

ideal (speculative term): belonging to
the "ideal series," *practically*
or concretely *ideal*, whatever is
established as a foundation or
a standard by and for *free*

Reason, *logically* necessary, *a
priori*. Thus space and time are
ideal forms (221) and the *work*
of the *Volk* is its *ideal* union
(243). *System of Ethical Life*
(*page,* line):
106,23; 110,6; 120,3; 121,5,17,
19, 27(both); 132,23; 146,22;
158,39.

First Philosophy of Spirit:
211,12,14,25,29; 213,16; 215,
12,30; 218,8; 221,13,25,28;
228,27; 229,12; 231,18; 234,
25,27; 237,39; 243,22; 244,20,
22; 247,19.

ideell (empirical term): *theoretically*
or abstractly *ideal*, belonging to
personal consciousness, or established by social convention,
hence contingent, changeable;
or *deprived* of practical effect.
Thus *names* are *ideel* (221
etc.) and the family committ-
ment is *ideell gesetzt* for those
who commit themselves to the
work of the *Volk* (243).

System of Ethical Life (*page,* line):
105,12,17,19; 106,20; 107,1,8,13,
17,24,27; 110,27,41; 111,9; 113,30,
36; 114,3,22,29,32,38; 116,21,22
(both), 23,24(both); 117,13,17;
118,21; 119,12,28,33; 120,11;
121,25; 123,11(both); 125,27; 130,
11,14,22,41; 131,5,11,17,22,28;
32,17,20,27,34; 133,4; 135,7,41;
136,2; 137,26; 138,39; 139,25;
141,23; 143,19; 144,34,35; 145,2;
153,40; 154,36; 159,26,29,36; 163,
11; 164,27,28,34,40; 165,4,7; 166,
18,25; 170,28,41; 173, 25; 175,18;
176,19.

First Philosophy of Spirit:
206,9; 209,20; 213,5,28; 217,1,2,4,
12,25; 218,9,23; 220,30; 221,29,32;
222,1; 223,3,26; 224,8["just implicitly"=*nur ideel an sich*],32;
225,5,9; 226,20; 227,12; 230,4,19;
231,25; 234,13,14,15,19,21,29,30;

236,25; 237,2,12; 241,1,8; 242,8; 243,20; 245,5,6,8,16,23.

real (speculative term): belonging to the "real series," *theoretically* real, hence unchangeable. Physically *necessary* (in the given context).

System of Ethical Life (page, line): 104,28["more objectively"= realer]; 107,17,26; 108,2,5,30; 111, 3; 112,5,6,10["absolutely real"],11 [realisiert], 20,24,33; 113,5; 119, 28,32; 120,4[realisiert],17,20,21; 121,12; 129,30; 130,14; 131,28; 132,19; 135,4,7,12; 138,10; 139,23, 32; 141,31; 147,11; 150,37,38; 151, 17; 153,18,20; 155,10[reality],21; 157,3,38; 158,38; 165,9; 175,19.

First Philosophy of Spirit: 210, note 11(line 5); 211,11,14,27; 213,22; 225,5; 227,17; 232,33; 233, 24; 234,27,29; 237,40(both); 240,41.

reell (empirical term): practically real, but hence subject to practical control—e.g. needs. Demonstrably *existent* and effective, but transient or changeable. (The genotype is *real*, the phenotype *reell*). *Reell* almost disappears in the *First Philosophy of Spirit* being supplanted by the verb *existiren* and its cognates.

System of Ethical Life (page, line): 106,17,26; 107,5,14; 110,27; 111,33; 112,10["real in his own eyes"], 13,14; 113,35,38; 115,6; 120,1,12; 121,10,13,25; 123,10; 130,7,17,22, 41; 131,1,19; 132,7; 134,21; 136,1, 28,38; 142,2[unrealized], 19; 144,18; 147,15,17; 151,6; 152,7,17, 19; 154,3,12,29; 155,1[reality]; 157,25; 159,3; 164,33,39; 165,5,6,7, 14; 166,10,21; 167,21; 169,1; 171,1; 175,18; 176,14.

First Philosophy of Spirit: 216,5.

All works referred to in Hegel's text or in the introductions and notes are listed here (and identified as fully as possible) *except* classical and medieval authors (e.g., Aristotle, Dante), where the reference can be found in any good modern edition.

Avineri, Shlomo. *Hegel's Theory of the Modern State.* Cambridge: The University Press, 1972.

Collingwood, Robin George. *The Principles of Art.* Oxford: Clarendon Press, 1936.

——. *The New Leviathan.* Oxford: Clarendon Press, 1942.

Eschenmayer, Karl August (1770–1852). *Sätze aus der Naturmetaphysik.* Tübingen: Cotta, 1797.

Fichte, Johann Gottleb (1762–1814). *Grundlage der gesammten Wissenschaftslehre.* Leipzig: Gabler, 1794. Reprinted in *Werke I.*

——. *Science of Knowledge.* Translated by Peter Heath and John Lachs. New York: Appleton-Century-Crofts, 1970.

——. *Grundlage des Naturrechts.* 2 vols. Jena and Leipzig: Gabler, 1796, 1797.

——. *The Science of Rights.* Translated by A. E. Kroeger. London, 1889. Reprinted by Routledge and Kegan Paul, 1970.

——. *Sämmtliche Werke.* Edited by I. H. Fichte. 8 vols. Berlin: Veit, 1845–46.

Haering, Theodor Lorenz. *Hegel: sein Wollen aund sein Werk.* 2 vols. Leipzig Teubner, 1929, 1938. Reprinted Aalen: Scientia Verlag, 1963.

Harris, Henry Silton. *Hegel's Development I: Toward the Sunlight* (1770–1801). Oxford: Clarendon Press, 1972.

Haym, Rudolf (1821–1901). *Hegel und seine Zeit.* Berlin: Gaertner, 1857. Reprinted Hildesheim: G. Olms, 1962.

Hegel, Georg Wilhelm Friedrich (1770-1831). *Briefe von und an Hegel.* Edited by Johannes Hoffmeister and Rolf Flechsig. 4 vols. Hamburg: F. Meiner, 1961.

——. *Differenz des Fichte'schen und Schelling'schen Systems der Philosophie.* Jena: Seidler, 1801. Reprinted in *Gesammelte Werke* IV, 1-92.

——. *Difference between the Systems of Fichte and Schelling.* Translated by H. S. Harris and Walter Cerf. Albany: State University of New York Press, 1977.

——. *Enzyklopädie der philosophischen Wissenschaften.* Edited by L. von Henning, K. L. Michelet and L. Boumann. Werke VII, 1832 ff. Berlin: Duncker and Humbolt, 1840, 1842, 1845. Reprinted as *System der Philosophie* in "Jubilee Edition" edited by H. Glockner. Stuttgart: From-

mann, 1927-30.
———. *Logic*. Translated from the *Encyclopedia of the Philosophical Sciences* by William Wallace. Second edition, Oxford: Clarendon Press, 1892. Reprinted 1974.
———. *Philosophy of Nature*. Translated from the *Encyclopaedia of the Philosophical Sciences* by A. V. Miller. Oxford: Clarendon Press, 1970.
———. *Philosophy of Mind*. Translated from the *Encyclopaedia of Philosophical Sciences* by W. Wallace and A. Miller. Oxford: Clarendon Press, 1971.
———. *Philosophy of Nature*. Edited and translated (from *Encyclopedia of Philosophical Sciences*) with an introduction and explanatory notes by M. J. Petry. 3 vols. London: Allen and Unwin, 1970.
———. *Philosophy of Subjective Spirit*. Edited and translated (from *Encyclopaedia of Philosophical Sciences*) with an introduction and explanatory notes by M. J. Petry. 3 vols. Dordrecht and Boston: D. Reidel, 1978.
———. *Gesammelte Werke*. Edited by the Rheinisch-Westfaelischen Akademie der Wissenschaften. Hamburg: F. Meiner, 1968 ff. [=N.K.A]
———. "Glauben und Wissen", *Kritisches Journal der Philosophie*, Vol. II, no. 1. Tübingen, 1802. reprinted in *Gesammelte Werke* IV, 313–414.
———. *Faith and Knowledg*. Edited and translated by W. Cerf and H. S. Harris. Albany: State University of New York Press, 1977.
———. *Grundlinien der Philosophie des Rechts*. Edited by J. Hoffmeister. Hamburg: F. Meiner, 1955.
———. *Philosophy of Right*. Translated

with notes by T. M. Knox. Oxford: Clarendon Press, 1942.
———. *Jenenser Realphilosophie I*. Edited by Hoffmeister. Leipzig: F. Meiner, 1932.
———. *La Première Philosophie de l'Esprit*. Traduit et presenté par G. Planty-Bonjour. Paris: Presses Universitaires de France, 1969.
———. "Logik, Metaphysik, Naturphilosophie" (1804–5), in *Jenaer Systementwürfe* II (*Gesammelte Werke* VII). Edited by R. -P. Horstmann and J. H. Trede. Hamburg: F. Meiner, 1971.
———. "Naturphilosophie und Philosophie des Geistes" (1805–6), in *Jenaer Systementwürfe* III (*Gesammelte Werke* VIII). Edited by R. -P. Horstmann with the assistance of J. H. Trede. Hamburg: F. Meiner, 1976.
———. *Phänomenologie des Geistes*. Edited by Johannes Hoffmeister. Hamburg: F. Meiner, 1952.
———. *Phenomenology of Spirit*. Translated by A. V. Miller (with Introduction and Analysis by J. N. Findlay). Oxford: Clarendon Press, 1977.
———. *Schriften zur Politik und Rechtsphilosophie*. Edited by G. Lasson. Second edition, Leipzig: F. Meiner, 1923.
———. *Political Writings*. Translated by T. M. Knox with an Introductory Essay by Z. A. Pelczynski. Oxford: Clarendon Press, 1964.
———. "System der Sittlichkeit". Edited by G. Lasson in *Schriften zur Politik und Rechtsphilosophie* (1923). Reprinted separately, Hamburg: F. Meiner, 1967.
———. *Système de la Vie Ethique*. Traduit et presenté par J. Taminiaux. Paris: Payot, 1976.
———. "Das System der spekulativen

Philosophie" in *Jenaer Systement-würfe* I (*Gesammelte Werke* VI). Edited by K. Düsing and H. Kimmerle. Hamburg: F. Meiner, 1975.

———. *System der Wissenschaft: Erster Teil, die Phänomenologie des Geistes.* Bamberg and Würzburg: Goebhardt, 1807.

———. *Theologische Jugendschriften.* Edited by Hermann Nohl. Tübingen: Mohr, 1907. Reprinted 1968.

———. *Early Theological Writings.* Translated by T. M. Knox with an Introduction and fragments translated by Richard Kroner. Chicago: University of Chicago Press, 1948. Reprinted Philadelphia: University of Pennsylvania Press, 1971.

———. "Tübingen Fragment" (1793). Edited by H. Nohl in *Theologische Jugendschriften*, pp. 3–29. Translated in H. S. Harris, *Toward the Sunlight*, pp. 481–507.

———. "Two Fragments on Love" (translated by C. Hamlin and H. S. Harris), *Clio* VIII, 1978/9. [German text in H. Nohl (ed.) *Theologische Jugendschriften*, pp. 374–78; these are the fragments referred to on p. 92, note 48 above.]

———. "Ueber die wissenschaftlichen Behandlungsarten des Naturrechts", *Kritisches Journal der Philosophie* II, 1802–3 (reprinted in *Gesammelte Werke* IV, 417–85).

———. *Natural Law.* Translated by T. M. Knox with an Introduction by H. B. Acton. Philadelphia: University of Pennsylvania Press, 1975.

———. "Die Verfassung Deutschlands" in *Schriften zur Politik und Rechtsphilosophie*. Edited by G. Lasson. Leipzig: F. Meiner, 1923. [Translated in *Hegel's Political Writings*.]

———. *Vorlesungen über die Philosophie der Weltgeschichte.* Edited by J. Hoffmeister and G. Lasson. 4 vols. in 2. Hamburg: F. Meiner, 1955, 1968.

———. *The Philosophy of History,* Translated by J. Sibree. New York: Dover, 1956.

———. *Lectures on the Philosophy of World History: Introduction.* Translated by H. B. Nisbet with an Introduction by D. Forbes. Cambridge: The University Press, 1975.

Hegel in Berichten seiner Zeitgenossen. Edited by G. Nicolin. Hamburg: F. Meiner, 1970. [Gabler's account of Hegel at Jena is report 92.]

Hegel-Studien. Bonn: Bouvier, 1961 ff.

Jacobi, Friedrich Heinrich (1743–1819). *Über die Lehre des Spinoza in Briefen an den Herrn Moses Mendelssohn.* Neue vermehrte Ausgabe. Breslau: Loewe, 1789. Reprinted in *Werke* IV, 1.

———. *Werke.* 6 vols. Leipzig: Fleischer, 1812–25. Reprinted Darmstadt: Wissenschaftliche Buchgesellschaft, 1968.

Kant, Immanuel (1772–1804). *Gesammelte Schriften.* Edited by the Royal Prussian Academy of Sciences. 24 vols. Berlin: Reimer, 1910–1966. [*Akad.*]

———. *Critik der reinen Vernunft.* Riga: Hartknoch, 1781 [=A]; second edition improved throughout, 1787 [=B]; the two editions collated by R. Schmidt, Hamburg: F. Meiner, 1930.

———. *Critik der praktischen Vernunft.* Riga: Hartknoch, 1788. Reprinted in *Akad.* V.

———. *Critik der Urteilskraft.* Berlin and Libau: Lagarde and Friederich, 1790. Second edition, 1793 (reprinted in *Akad.* V).

———. *Critique of Pure Reason*. Translated from R. Schmidt's collation of editions A and B by N. Kemp Smith. London: Macmillan, 1933. [The pagination of both A and B is indicated in the margin.]

———. *Critique of Practical Reason*. Translated by L. W. Beck. Chicago: University of Chicago Press, 1949. (Paper: New York: Library of Liberal Arts, 1956). [The pagination of *Akad*. V is indicated in the margin.]

———. *Critique of Teleological Judgement*. Translated by J. C. Meredith. Oxford: Clarendon Press, 1928. Incorporated in the complete *Critique of Judgement*, translated by J. C. Meredith, Oxford, 1957. [The pagination of *Akad*. V is indicated in the margin.]

———. *Metaphysik der Sitten* (1797). Reprinted in *Akad*. VI, 203–493.

———. *The Metaphysical Elements of Justice*. Translated by John Ladd. Indianapolis: Bobbs-Merrill (Library of Liberal Arts), 1965. [Abridged version of "Doctrine of Right" from *Metaphysik der Sitten*.]

Kimmerle, Heinz. "Dokumente zu Hegels Jenaer Dozententätigkeit (1801–1807)". *Hegel-Studien* IV 1967, 21–100.

———. "Zur Chronologie von Hegels Jenaer Schriften". *Hegel-Studien* IV, 1967, 125–176.

Kritisches Journal der Philosophie. Edited by F. W. J. Schelling and G. W. F. Hegel. 2 vols. Tübingen: Cotta, 1802–1803. [Reprinted *in toto* in Hegel, *Gesammelte Werke* IV, 113–500.]

Marx, Karl and Engels, Friedrich. *Basic Writings on Politics and Philosophy*. Edited by L. S. Feuer. Garden City, N.Y.: Doubleday

Anchor Books, 1959.

Plutarch. *Lives*. The Dryden Plutarch revised by A. H. Clough. 4 vols. London: Dent (Everymans Library), 1910.

Rosenkranz, Karl (1805–1879). *Georg Wilhelm Friedrich Hegels Leben*. Berlin, 1844. Reprinted Darmstadt: Wissenschaftliche Buchgesellschaft, 1963.

Schelling, Friedrich Wilhelm Joseph (1775–1854). "Darstellung meines Systems der Philosophie" in *Zeitschrift für spekulative Physik* II, Heft 2. Jena and Leipzig: Gabler, 1801. Reprinted in *Werke* IV, 105–212.

———. "Einleitung" for the *Entwurf eines Systems der Naturphilosophie*. Jena and Leipzig: Gabler, 1799. Reprinted in *Werke* III, 269–326.

———. "Fernere Darstellungen aus dem System der Philosophie" in *Neue Zeitschrift für spekulative Physik* I, Heft 1, 1802. Reprinted in *Werke* IV, 333–510.

———. *Ideen zu einer Philosophie der Natur*. Leipzig: Breitkopf and Härtel, 1797. Second edition Landshut, 1803, Reprinted in *Werke* II, 1–343.

———. "Ueber das absolute Identitäts-System" in *Kritisches Journal der Philosophie* I, Heft 1. Tübingen, 1802. Reprinted in Hegel, *Gesammelte Werke* IV, 129–73.

———. "Philosophie der Kunst" (1802–3). *Werke* V, 357–736.

———. *Sämtliche Werke*. Edited by K.F.A. Schelling. 14 vols. Stuttgart and Augsburg: Cotta, 1856–61. [The pagination of this edition is preserved in the photoreprinted *Ausgewählte Werke*, 8 vols., Darmstadt: Wissenschaftliche Buchgesellschaft, 1966–1968.]

———. *System des Transcendentalen*

Idealismus. Tübingen: Cotta, 1800. Reprinted in *Werke* III, 329–634.

———. *System of Transcendental Idealism*. Translated by Peter Heath with an Introduction by Michael Vater. Charlottesville: University of Virginia Press, 1978. [The pagination of the *Werke* III is indicated at the top of the page.]

———. *Von der Weltseele*. Hamburg: Perthes, 1798. Reprinted in *Werke* II, 345–583.

Schleiermacher, Friedrich Ernst Daniel (1768–1834). *Ueber die Religion: Reden an die Gebildeten unter ihren Verächtern*. Berlin, 1799. [Abridged translation; *On Religion: Speeches to its Cultured Despisers*, edited by John Oman, New York: Ungar, 1955.]

Smith, Adam (1723–1790). *An Inquiry into the Nature and Causes of the Wealth of Nations* (1776). Basel, 1791.

———. *Untersuchung über die Natur und die Ursachen des Nationalreichtums*. Aus dem Englischen der vierten Ausgabe neu übersetzt von Chr. Garve. Frankfurt and Leipzig, 1796. [Apparently *not* used by Hegel.]

Spinoza, Benedict de (1632–1677). *Opera Omnia*. Edited by H.E.G. Paulus. 2 vols. Jena: Akademische Buchhandlung, 1802–3.

———. *Chief Works*. Translated by R.H.M. Elwes. 2 vols. New York: Dover, 1951.

Tilliette, Xavier. *Schelling: Une Philosophie en Devenir*. 2 vols. Paris: Vrin, 1970.

INDEX

ABRAHAM: exclusiveness of, 56

Absolute: construction of , 8; and
Potenzen, 15–20, 24–25, 56, 90 n.,
151, 153; and nature, 44, 129; formal
in individual, 151; consciousness,
207–8 n., 209, 210, 212–13, 226, 241–
42, 251–53, 255; as supersensible,
258. *See also* God; Idea; Identity;
spirit

abstraction: abstract totality and concrete unity, 121, 168–69; abstract
unity and concrete totality, 142;
ideal abstraction in thought, 121,
124, 149, 227; real abstraction in
practice, 117–18, 247; intelligence as
principle of, 117, 120

ACHILLES: shield of, 37; wrath of, 50,
54

ADAM: 203 n., 221–22

AESCHYLUS: *Oresteia*, 94

aether: spiritual, 151, 179, 181–82, 193,
198, 202–3, 206, 212, 216, 217, 222,
254; physical, 203 n., 216, 217; defined, 205 n.; *Volk*-spirit as, 242

AGAMEMNON: 60

age, old: significance of, 70–71, 158–
60

ALCIBIADES: 60

ALEXANDER (of Macedon): paradigmatic, 83, 263, 264

animal: labor with, 28–29, 108–9; voice
of, 35, 115–16, 217, 222; defined,
108; level of life, 207, 208 n., 213;
in man, 208 n., 225, 229

antithesis (*Gegensatz*): body/spirit, 6,
63, 114–16, 143, 159–60; necessity/
freedom, 8, 18, 122, 123, 185–86;
subject/object, 9, 17, 29, 34, 104,
114–15, 147, 220–21, 223–26, 229–
31, real/ideal, 11, 17–19, 20, 81, 107,
112, 113, 119–20, 123, 132, 234;
finite/infinite, 11, 18–19, 21, 162;
concept/intuition, 12 (*see* concept);
particular/universal, 13, 22, 29, 100,
102, 109–10, 117, 127, 154, 164, 165,
207; God/Nature, 18, 19, 83–84,
181–86; nature/spirit, 19, 213, 243–
44; nature/ethical life, 19, 56, 159,
244; difference/identity, 24–25, 61,
104, 164, 176; possible/actual, 31–
33, 122; person/possession, 42, 126,
155, 236–40, 249–50; joy/grief, 65–
66, 147; organic/inorganic, 68, 70,
108–9, 156–58, 243–44; internal/
external, 72, 101–2, 132, 211; ruler/
ruled, 79, 101n, 160, 174; one/many,
101–102, 143; male/female, 110, 211,
232; simple/infinite, 113–14, 213–14,
225–28, 240–41; singular/universal,
113, 116, 123, 144, 194, 207–8n;
electricity as, 120; of persons, 126–
27, 236–40; positive/negative, 129,
146; dialectical, 129–30; of clans,
142; relative and absolute, 144–47,
185–86; of peoples, 164; unity/
multiplicity, 208–10; form/matter,
210–11; active/passive, 212–13, 229–
31, 234, 243; theory/practice, 218–20;
life/death, 228, 239–40; all/nothing,
260

ARISTIDES: 67

APELLES: 61, 94

aristocracy: tribal, 55–56; critique of, 79, 80, 176–77; sublated in free state, 174–75

ARISTOTLE: form/matter in, 28; *Nicomachean Ethics*, 67; theory of constitutions, 79; and *Potenz* theory, 91; mentioned, 94; mind in, 194; and Alexander, 263–64

art: as divine service, 9, 63–64, 82; in Schelling, 16, 18; flower of feeling, 35, 116; in Absolute Triad, 82, 180; Christian, 84–85, 184, 252–53; epic and comedy, 252–53; genius and revolution, 254–56; modern drama, 260; idyllic poetry, 261

assassination: *see* murder

Athena: identity of Athens, 60, 81; her wisdom, 72

Athens: democracy at, 72, 80, 177; law of liturgies, 76, 171 n.
See also Athena; THESEUS

atomism: physical and spiritual, 84, 177

Aufhebung: of need in enjoyment, 103–4; of object in labor, 105–7; of family-relation in *Bildung*, 111; of possession in property, 121; self-sublation of labor, 117; negation of negation, 130–31, 135; of relation in freedom, 142–43; of difference in identity, 156; of identity in difference, 176; of singularity in *Volk*, 209, 210 n., 212–13, 243, 250; of externality in tool, 211; of opposition in consciousness, 212, 213, 224–25; of image in name, 221; of name in concept, 226; of desire in labor, 230; of desire in love, 231–32; of parents in child, 232–33; of nature in culture, 233–34; of nature in spirit, 243–44; of private in absolute consciousness, 252

AVINERI, Shlomo: 95, 99, 204n

baby: *see* child

barbarism: of North and East, 48–49, 133–34; and civilization, 54, 55; of intellect, 75, 76–77, 171; and bond-age, 93 n, 136; despotic, 162, 177; speech of, 196, 245

BARDILI, C.G. 9

battle: life and death struggle, 46, 47, 50–54, 56 ,132–33, 136; single combat, 51–52, 53; and transition to *Sittlichkeit*, 57, 67; ordeal by, 77–78, 141–142, 147; sublates guilt, 132–33, 138–39, 140–41; for honor, 137–39, 140–41; of obedience, 179; against fate, 180. *See also* war

Begriff: see concept

Bildung: sublation of labor, 28–29, 109–11; human fulfilment, 29–31; foundation of ethical life, 58–61, 67, 147; as historic tradition, 65; and discipline, 78, 176; of world for speech, 245; philosophical, 263–64.
See also discipline; education

BOEHME, Jakob: mysticism of, 257

bondage (*Knechtschaft*): as natural status, 40–42, 125–26, 197; instituted by violence, 46, 50, 53–54, 136, 240; transitional, 56, 198; as contractual status, 69, 155–56; serfdom, 93n, 156; ethical, 146; economic, 154, 170–171; of spirit in nature, 195–96, 213, 215n, 216

"boredom of the world": 84, 181

bourgeoisie: virtue of, 69, 76, 150, 153–54, 155, 171; judicial function, 77, 174; governing function, 80. *See also* class

BRIAREUS: *Volk* as, 66, 146

BRISEIS: 50

BULIS: 60

burial: significance of, 46–47

BUTLER, Joseph: commonsense identity, 193

CADMUS: 203n

cancel(lation): *see Aufhebung*

CAPULETS: 51

Catholicism: universal consecration, 84, 183–185; life and art in, 251–253

causality: in Kant, 12, 14, 91n; in labor, 107; right as, 120, 136; mas-

tery as, 125, 126; of freedom, 130
child: paradigm of 'feeling', 23, 112;
and parents, 29–30, 42, 43–44, 110–
11, 127, 128–29, 233–35; identity of
natural life, 31–32, 42, 57, 59, 112,
232n; rationality of family, 32–33,
43–44, 113, 128–29, 233–35; as person, 40, 42; rearing as goal, 78
Christianity: and Greek religion, 83–
85; evolution of, 182–86, 251–53,
264–65. *See also* grief (infinite)
civil society: in natural ethics, 56, 69;
corporations in, 200
class(es) (*Stände*): H's theory of, 11–
12, 67–71, 75, 76, 79–80, 150–58,
199–200; political Estates, 71, 95;
absolute, 70–71, 152–53, 157–59,
162; governing, 76, 80; universal,
171; struggle of, 198
cognition (*erkennen*): joins real and
ideal series, 18, 91; negative, 129–
31; of economy, 167–68; of spirit,
213, 214; practical, 240; aether of,
254 (*see* aether); of God, 265
COLLINGWOOD, R.G.: theory of
consciousness, 203n
colonization: theory of, 72, 73, 74, 78–
79, 167; means of recognition, 164,
176
color: *Potenzen* of, 45, 130–131, 192,
223, 225–227
combat, single: *see* battle
commerce: as motion of concept, 39,
124; objective recognition in, 58–59;
market as power, 74–75, 167–68;
taxation of, 76, 173; class of, 154,
170
communication: rational, 29, 30;
spoken and written, 34–35;
animal, 35
concept (*Begriff*): and intuition, H's
use, 10, 12, 14–15, 73–74, 81–82,
90n, 100–1, 108 etc.; nature as, 20–
21; movement of, 21–22, 91n, 102;
as truly particular, 22, 100, 194,
206–29; dominance of, 26, 36–37;
rest and motion of 27, 38, 39, 70,
102, 156; in nature, 28–29; formal

and actual, 32–33, 34–35, 91–92, 102–
3, 116–29; as real negative, 47, 48,
49, 56, 58, 132, 134; as intelligence,
59, 109–116, 117, 120, 142–143, 189–
190. *See also* universal
conscience: inward vengeance, 47–48,
132–33; sublated in honor, 141
consciousness (*Bewusstsein*): political
and religious, 70–71, 84–85; theory
of, 92; empirical and absolute, 143,
144–46, 212, 252–53; absolute, 179,
195, 203 n., 207 n., 208–10, 212–13,
255; as concept of spirit, 190,
206–26; evolution of, 191, 193, 233–
34; communal medium, 192–95,
203n., in bonds and free, 195–98;
formal existence in speech, 218–28;
instinctive and critical, 256; philosophical, 260
consecration: *see* sacred
Constitution: ambiguity of heading,
11, 62; object of intuition, 59–61;
as resting concept, 70, 146–57;
forms of, 79, 176–77; evolution of,
174–75
construction: philosophical method, 8,
9, 205n; constructed line, 20, 56–57,
73, 91n; prophetic use, 86–87; spirit
as reconstruction, 103, 159, 245
contempt: for nature, 182, 197, 261
contract: formal reality of spirit, 38–
39, 58, 122–24; sublated in firmly,
42–43, 127–28; bourgeois principle,
69, 155–56; slavery and marriage
not, 43, 128; not political principle,
242
contraction: and expansion, 189–191,
259
courage: absolute virtue, 66–67, 69,
147–48, 178; of peasants, 150; of
nobility, 152, 153; formal virtue,
179; and havoc, 198; philosophic,
179, 263
craftsman(ship): self-expression in
labor, 33–34, 37, 196, 199; recognition of, 92, 113; labor subsumed
under intuition, 107–8; rationality
of, 246, 255

crime: as negative, 45; justice for, 77,
132, 175; negative of formal right,
118–19, 135
Critical Journal: 3, 5, 88, 94
Crucifixion, the: 80, 84, 177; significance of Cross, 182–84
DANTE: 252n
DAVID (King of Israel): 35
death: natural, 35, 44, 116; violent,
45–46, 47–49; in natural justice, 50,
52–53; noble, 66, 67, 149, 178, 197;
of God, 83–85 (see grief, infinite);
negative absolute, 48–49, 56, 58,
179, 201; accepted, 197, 233–34;
voluntary, 228; for honor, 236–38n,
239–40; of Nature, 261
democracy: direct, 72, 80, 177;
representative, 72, 79–80, 163, 177
DESCARTES: 194
desire: Potenz of feeling, 19, 23–25,
189; and need, 23, 30–33; sexual,
29, 110 (see sex); defines its object,
104–6; human, defined, 229–30
DEUCALION: 203 n
dialectic(al): negation of negation, 129–
30; illusions, 195
Difference Essay: 7, 8, 88 n; resumption of whole in, 9, 63–64, 82, 204 n;
"system" in, 89, 90, 202 n; critique
of Fichte, 86, 96, 263 n; Idea in, 93,
95; single intelligence in, 189–90
discipline (Zucht): system of, 78,
166–67, 176; inversion of natural
practice, 145
"Divine Triangle": 265 n.
domestication: of animals, 28, 108–9
domination: see lordship
drive: in natural ethics, 21–22, 31–33,
102–3; "instinctive" labor, 246
DÜSING, Karl: editing, 206n, 210n,
212n, 215–216n, 221n, 245n
duty: in reflective theory, 65, 66; determined by "station", 66; in war,
149. See Sittlichkeit
Earth: animate, 19, 27; life-process,
189, 190, 203n. See also elements
economy: in natural ethics, 11; governmental control of, 72, 74–76,

164, 167–73; as system, 74–76, 154,
156, 167–73, 199–200, 247–49. See
also commerce; need
education (Erziehung): conceptual
labor, 29, 111, and Bildung, 58;
governmental concern, 72–74, 78,
167; and discipline, 78, 176; and
war, 147; conscious relation, 196–
97, 204n; process defined, 233–34,
245. See also Bildung; discipline
Eigensinn: of individual, 227–28; freedom of, 242
elders: see priesthood
electricity: in Schelling, 18, 259;
analogous with exchange, 38, 92,
120
elements: as divine, 177; H's theory,
203 n.; earth as divisible and
atomic, 206, 208 n., 227; as media
of consciousness, 215–16, 217, 218 n,
222. See also aether; Earth
Empire: Roman, 48, 71, 84, 181;
German, 71–72, 80, 86; emperor,
Roman and Christian, 84, 184
Encyclopaedia: 4, 88 n
ENGELS, Friedrich: German Ideology,
259 n
enjoyment: physical, 25–26, 104–5,
109; none in labor, 26, 106;
spiritual, 28, 31, 58, 106–7, 109, 143;
endless dialectic of, 169–70;
Heavenly, 253. See also satisfaction
EPICURUS: religion of, 80, 83–84, 177
equality: civil status, 77; formal concept, 117, 121, 125, 133; of peril,
138, 140–42
equity: see justice
ESCHENMAYER, K.A.: 15, 90
essence (Wesen): inward, 21, 22, 25,
44, 59, 78, 93, 101–3, 107, 126, 132;
floating above, 21, 22, 25, 49, 55, 59,
78, 93, 101–3, 116–17; as light, 102;
consciousness as, 224; ethical substance as, 242
Estates: see class(es)
ETEOCLES: 50, 54
ethics: see Sittlichkeit   N
EURIPIDES: 60

exchange: as motion of concept, 38–39, 120–22; alienation of property, 119–20; contract and barter, 154–55. *See also* commerce

executive: actual government always, 72, 73–74, 165

Faith and Knowledge: 94, 96, 202 n, 252 n, 264 n; intuition of *Volk* in, 60; infinite grief in, 65, 85; critique of Fichte in, 86, 263 n; critical logic in, 88 n

family: totality of natural ethics, 11, 21, 29, 51, 110–11, 235–36, 244; and society, 36; recognition in, 42–43, 57, 142; sublates relations, 42–44, 126–29; as personal identity, 52–53, 139–40; royal, 58; bourgeois concern, 69, 155–56; as natural consciousness, 195–97, 211, 216; union of love, 231–35

fate: Frankfurt concept maintained, 82–83, 180

feeling: first *Potenz* of nature, 22–25, 35; unconscious, 23, 24–25, 34; formal and real concept, 24, 104; totality of, 30, 110, 112; natural and ethical, 103–5; expression of, 114, 115; as inward essence, 166, 169; and science, 257

FICHTE, Johann Gottlieb: 9; his problem, 8; Ego in, 59, 262; criticism of, 65, 66, 77, 86, 95, 200; ephorate in, 71, 162; H's course on, 88; *Science of Knowledge*, 89 n, 91 n, 262; moral world order, 203 n

finite: *see* infinite; antithesis

firearms: ethical significance of, 66, 149

First Philosophy of Spirit: struggle in, 56; economics in, 75, 95; compared with *System of Ethical Life*, 89 n. 190–92; conclusion of, 178–79 n, 200; value of, 201–202; editing problems, 206–24 nn, 226–239 nn, 241–246 nn, 248–250 nn, lacuna in, 235

fixation: of negative, 46, 52, 53, 55, 106, 129–31; conceptual, 114–15,

223–26, 257–59; of legal status, 116, 118, 150; as untruth, 147; of consciousness, 227–28

form: abstract, 24, 32, 36, 38–40, 74, 116–29; speech as, 34, 115, 218–28, 245; legal, 77; of spirit, 39, 40; concrete, 40, 43, 129, 150–51; of virtue, 67, 68, 148; of indifference, 133–34, 137–38, 140–41, 151, 174; practical inversion of, 130–31; in government, 161–62, 164–67, 176; consciousness as, 206–228. *See also* the note on p. 267

formalism: attack on, 258–59

free(dom): and necessity, 8, 18 (*see* antithesis); personal, 40, 124–25; as formal negative, 45, 130, 131; ethical, 46, 67, 240–41; constitution, 79, 174, 176–77; and reconciliation, 83; Idea of, 85; as causal, 130; religious, 179–80; of *Eigensinn*, 227–28, 242; illusory, 256

future: as "beyond", 252–53

GABLER, G.A.: 88 n, 264 n

GARVE, Christian: 95, 248 n

GENGHIZ KHAN: 133

gesture: 34, 114

German Constitution: 3, 72, 80, 93, 95; hopefulness of, 87; dating, 87n

Gnosticism: criticism of, 262

God: and Universe, 16, 18, 19; Judgment of, 47, 48, 53, 54, 57, 77, 140, 265; of *Volk*, 60, 144, 179–80; death of, 65–66, 80, 83–85, 146, 181–83; history of, 81, 179–80, 183–84, 191, 251 n, 265; Greek gods, 83, 252; incarnation of, 147, 151, 163, 177, 182–83, 189; service of, 158–59, 252; Resurrection of, 183, 190; as world mind, 194–95, 203 n; and aether, 205 n, as mystery, 264; intuited in Creation, 265

GOEBHARDT, J.A.: H's publisher, 89n

GOETHE, J.W. von: quoted, 102 n, *Faust*, 261

Good Friday: speculative and historical, 65, 85

government: motion of Idea, 11, 62;
function of nobility, 68–71, 153;
separation of powers in, 70, 164–
67; defined, 70, 156–57; the absolute, 70–72, 157–63, 174; the
universal, 72–79, 163–67; self-
government, 77, 79–80, 174; free,
79, 176–77
"Greek ideal": recalled, 60–61;
adaptation of, 75–76; influence of,
85–86. *See also* Athens; THESEUS
grief: infinite, 65 (*see* God, death of);
finite, sublated in courage, 66, 147;
for death of Nature, 261
guilt: dialectic of, 47–48, 132–33

HAERING, T.L.: *Hegel*, 99, 102 n
hallucination: purely theoretical consciousness, 219
HARRIS, H.S.: *Toward the Sunlight*,
89, 92, 95, 96
havoc: natural and human, 35–36,
116; dialectic of, 48–49, 50–51, 52,
133–34; no recognition in, 49, 134;
negative of ethical life, 55, 136;
educational potential of, 198
HAYM, Rudolf: on H's lectures, 83,
178 n, 182, 185, 186; on H's mss.,
87 n, 89 n
Hegel-Studien: 87–89nn
HELEN (of Troy): 54
hero: tragic, 59, 60–61; religious, 252;
historic, fall of, 263. *See also*
THESEUS
HERODOTUS: 94
HOFFMEISTER, Johannes: edition,
206 n, 213 n, 214 n, 215–216 n,
244 n, 245 n
holy: *see* sacred
HOMER: 58; God in, 80, 83, 177;
honors craftsmanship, 113
honesty: *see* justice
honor: principle of natural justice,
49–50, 52–54, 137–39, 197–98; personal and national, 69, 149, 155;
sublates guilt, 140–41; sublated by
justice, 155; identity of person and
things, 236–40; disappearance of,
250
hope: principle of, 87
HUME, David: missing shade of blue,
192
hypocrisy: inner and outer, 67, 69, 75,
148–49; overcome in religion, 82

Idea (*Idee*): science of, 6, 8–9, 81,
90 n., 189–190; of *Sittlichkeit*, 10,
58, 61, 99–101, 144–145, 159; in
Kant, 14; rest and motion of, 61–
62, 145; triad of, 82; of freedom,
85; as government, 160–61, 162,
163; of reconciliation, 180; totality,
243; theosophical, 264–65. *See also*
Absolute; Identity
idealism: critical, 8; dogmatic, 192,
193–94; reflective, 224–26. *See also*
philosophy
ideality: beginning of, 38, 120;
theoretical and practical, 45, 130–
31; of enjoyment, 106–7, 169–70;
abstract, 116–17, 119–23; consciousness as, 210–11, 213–17; of sensation, 218–19; of intuition, 221–23.
See also the note on p. 267
Identity: Absolute, 8, 31, 82, 111; of
intuition and concept, 10, 61, 99–
101; and *Potenzen*, 15–17, 19–20;
and difference, 24–25 (*see* antithesis), of need and enjoyment,
30–31; of family personality, 32,
126–29; of self and other, 57–58;
of joy and grief, 66; reconstruction
of, 74, 83–85, 99–100; of man and
God, 84, 182–83; of ruler and ruled,
101 n., 174; formal (contract), 123;
of *Volk*, 143, 145
Identity Philosophy: of H and Shel-
ling, 7–8, 12, 14–17, 89, 90–91, 93;
'Universe' in, 16, 189–90; and
Spinoza, 21; as self-formation of
Reason, 32; and Greek ideal, 60–
61; eternal focus, 63–65, 75, 86, 143;
finite mind in, 189–90, 191, 193;
survival of terminology, 201
indifference: point of, 8, 16–17, 18, 93,
193; child as, 25, 31–32, 112; *Wut*

as, 56, 134; *Volk* as, 61, 144–46; family as, 127–29; form of, 133–34, (*see* form); virtue as, 147; old age as, 158–60

individual: as labor unit, 37, 117, 247–48; defined by recognition, 118; organ of *Volk*, 146, 209; shape of infinite, 151; consciousness, 225–28. *See also* person; singularity injury: unavoidable, 235–36, 237 n., 238. *See also* crime; murder; theft

infinity: formal, 11, 36, 38, 116, 119–21, 174; and finite, 18 (*see* antithesis); grief, 65 (*see* God, death of); concrete, 143, 144, 146, 151; of consciousness, 144, 146, 206–17; as becoming, 205–06; divisibility, 206; of space and time, 219–20

intelligence: *see* concept; Reason; thought

intuition: H's use, 10, 12, 13–15, 100–1; of individual agent, 20, 21, 29–36, 102; as truly universal, 22, 100, 143; as feeling, 22–25; animal as, 28–29; of life as task, 37, 117; of *Volk*, 58–61, 62–63, 144–45, 243; intellectual, 59, 143, 147; of self in other, 110, 111

JACOBI, F.H.: *Letters on Spinoza*, 94
JESUS: significance of, 84, 182
JOB: 200
Judaism: infinite grief in, 84, 181–82
judiciary: moment of concept, 72, 73; ideal subsuming power, 165, 166–67
justice: natural, 47, 49–50, 52, 55, 132; of God, 47 (*see* God, judgment of); definition, 67, 68, 149–50; system of, 72, 74, 76–78, 173–75; bourgeois, 67, 69, 75, 152; as equity, 77, 149, 175; of revenge, 80; of battle, 138; living, 174

KANT, Immanuel: influence of, 8, 12, 258–59; *Critique of Judgment*, 13–15, 90 n.; intuitive understanding in, 13–14, 91; Categorical Imperative, 59, 65, 66; Critiques, 88 n., on marriage, 128; separation of powers in, 165; and Greeks compared, 194–95

KIMMERLE, Heinz: date of H's mss., 87 n, 93n; editing, 206 n., 210 n., 212 n., 215–216 n. 221 n., 245 n.

KNOX, T.M.: translations, 89, 92–96

labor (*Arbeit*): *Potenz* of natural ethics, 11, 19, 211, 216, 217, 218; negation of thing and feeling, 23, 106–7, 112–13, 230–31; levels of, 25–29, 107–10, 245–49; middle of feeling, 30–32; mechanical, 27, 33, 34, 37, 75–76, 107–8, 117, 148–49, 171, 199–200, 247; living, 27–31, 150, 156; rational, 33–34, 109–11; division of, 37, 117–18, 154, 199–200, 246–49; of nobility, 68–69, 152–53; conquers need, 104; death as absolute, 179; free and slave, 196

language: *see* speech

LASSON, George: editing of *Ethical Life*, 90 n, 92 n, 177 n; quoted, 100 n

law: above level of feeling, 26, 107; substance of ethical life, 59–60; civil and criminal, 77–78, 174–75; Roman, 84; indifference of virtue, 147; as middle, 158. *See also* right

Lectures on World History: 95

LEIBNIZ, G.W.: influence of, 91 n.

legislative: in absolute government, 71, 161–62; in reflective theory, 72, 73; bicameral, 80; universal power, 165

lex talionis: 47, 50

life: H's concept of, 19; levels of, 27–29, 107–10, 207, 208 n.; comprehension of feeling, 31–32; essence and right of person, 40, 124–25; violence against, 46, 52, 131; in the *Volk*, 66, 147, 152; harmony of, 82–83, 102 n, 146–47; as identity, 143, 243; transition to spirit, 189, 190; mediated by philosophy, 256–58

LOCKE, John: 9, 194

logic: H's courses on, 4, 5, 8–9, 205 n.
262; place in system, 6, 63, 81, 205;
speculative and critical, 8, 9, 88 n.
*Logic, Metaphysics, and Philosophy of
Nature* (1804/5): aether in, 203 n.
lordship (*Herrschaft*): natural, 40–41,
125; ethical, 41, 126; in family, 42,
127; ideal and real, 211, 217, 221–
22. *See also* bondage
love: natural and spiritual, 29, 57–58,
92–93, 110, 231–32; Divine, 251–52

machine: significance of, 37, 117–18,
246–47; society as, 86
Macht: of life, 40–42, 125–26, 129
magnetism: in Schelling, 18, 259; analogous with labor, 38, 120
mania (*Wut*): 49, 53, 56, 134
marriage: union not contract, 43, 127–
28, 232–33
MARX, Karl: anticipated, 75, 95, 199–
200, 204 n; *German Ideology*, 259 n
MARY (Virgin): 96, 184, 252
memory: *Potenz* of consciousness, 211,
216, 217; beginning of speech, 218,
221, 222, 244
metaphysics: in Jena system, 4, 5, 8–9,
88 n., 262, 264–65
MICHELET, K.L.: on aether, 203 n.
middle: tool as, 33, 112–13; money
as, 38, 124; battle as, 52–53, 54, 56,
57, 140–42; natural and ethical, 57;
Jesus as, 84; child as, 111–12;
speech as, 113–14, 218–28; sign as,
114–15, 220–21; contract as, 123;
law as, 158; nature as, 159, 265;
government as, 173; consciousness
as, 214–16, 223–26; labor as, 230–
31; *Werk* as, 243; philosophy as,
257
mien: 34, 35, 114; ideality of child,
115
Mnemosyne: 221, 254, 255
monarchy: despotic, 71, 162; free, 79,
80, 176–77, 179
money: medium of commerce, 38, 39,
154; real universal, 39, 124, 249
MONTAGUES: 51

morality: *see* virtue
murder: paradigm of negation, 45–46,
51, 139; and assassination, 50, 51,
138; and death penalty, 131, 140
Muse: of *Volk*, 254–56
mysticism: Oriental and German, 257
myth: stand point of, 195, 254–55

names: error of nominalism, 193; ideal
realm of, 221–27. *See also* sign
NAPOLEON: *Code*, 198, 199
nation: honor of, 69, 149, 155; law
of nations, 77; basis of reconstruction, 86; religion of, 184, 185. *See
also Volk*
natural law (*Naturrecht*): H's lectures,
4–7, 87–89 nn., 189; and morality,
146–47
Natural Law: 3, 88 n. 202 n., 252 n.
nature: philosophy of, 6–9, 81, 189–
90, 202 n., 256, 259, 261, 263; in
Schelling, 17–19, 90 n.; and ethical
life, 19; ethics of, 20 (*see Sittlichkeit*); as concept, 21, 22, 44, 101,
129; organic and inorganic, 28, 243–
44; and convention, 32–33; tool of
Reason, 32–33, 159; state of, 44;
religion of, 83–85; levels of, 108–9,
151, 261; and spirit, 213–15, 217,
227, 244, 245; definition, 244, 262
necessity (*Notwendigkeit*): Schelling
on, 18; temporal web of, 185–86, 256
need (*Bedürfnis*): and satisfaction, 23–
25; as life potential, 30–33; met by
family, 42, 127; and *Not*, 46; system
of, 73, 74–76, 77, 154, 156, 167–73;
socially generated, 75, 168, 170; of
philosophy, 94 n (*see* philosophy);
defined, 104–5; universalization of,
117–18, 120–21, 247–48; and natural
bondage, 126; sublated in *Volk*-con-
sciousness, 144; of nobility, 152–53;
as government concern, 164; of
public life, 171
negative: labor as, 23 (*see* labor);
natural, 35–36, 44, 129; *Potenz* of,
44–54, 55; ethical discipline as, 44–
46, 146, 147, 151; crime as, 45,

118–19; fixation of, 46 (*see* fixation); havoc as, 47–49; mechanical, 119; dialectical, 129–130; punishment as, 130; thought as, 130–31, 179, 223, 227; consciousness as, 213–15, 227–28; spirit as, 243–50
nobility: theory of, 12, 19; function of, 68, 152–53; and peasants, 70, 77, 94 n., 156, 174; membership, 71; needs of, 74, 76, 153, 158, 172; criticism of, 79, 176–77; as absolute class, 152, 158; and monarch, 179
nominalism: *see* names
Not: extreme of need, 35, 41, 46, 47, 92, 116; ethical function, 44; war as, 148; equity allows for, 149

obedience: not bondage, 41, 126; in natural ethics, 41, 42, 58, 126; disobedient, 95 n. 179; spiritual, 263
object(ivity): of thought, 9; of purpose, 25–26, 146; subject-objectivity, 100 n. 144; living, 108; bodily, 114–15; and equity, 149. *See also* antithesis, body/spirit and subject/object
OEDIPUS: 60
oppression: defined, 138
organism: constitutive ideal, 7, 14, 86, 169; society as, 17, 146, 150–52, 160–62, 176, 243–44; in Schelling, 18, 19, 91 n.; nature as, 19; classes as, 68, 70, 152, 174; family as, 139–140; government as, 156–61, 164–67; spirit as, 209–11, 213, 214, 243–44

particular: *see* antithesis
Passion: *see* God, death of
past: as "beyond", 252–53
peace: significance of, 54, 56, 66–67, 142, 153
peasantry: theory of, 12, 19; distrustfully trustful, 67, 69, 156; without wisdom, 69, 94, 162; brave, 69–70, 156; taxation of, 76, 172–73; judicial process for, 77, 174

PERICLES: 60
person(ality): abstract concept, 36–37, 39–40, 124; *Knecht* as, 41–42, 125, 126; honor of, 49–50, 52–53, 55, 137–39; family as, 52–53, 127, 139–40; legal status, 77, 174; and property, identity of, 135–39, 236–40; burgher as, 154, 250
PETRY, M.J.: on *Stoff*, 251
Phenomenology of Spirit: as textbook, 4, 89 n; religion in, 10; struggle in, 56, 58, 196, 198, 204 n; Schelling on, 90 n; *Antigone* in, 93 n; noble service in, 94 n. 95 n. Terror in, 95 n; Enlightenment in, 95 n; and Jena mss., 201–2; consciousness in, 202 n, 203 n
PHIDIAS: 61
philosophiae universae delineatio (1803): first "Encyclopaedia", 5–6, 189, 190; conclusion of, 178–79 n, 200–1, 202 n. possible fragment of, 251
philosophy: theoretical and practical, 5, 6, 8, 190; of nature, 6 (*see* nature); of Identity, 7–8 (*see* Identity Philosophy); critical, 8, 9, 65, 66; as speculation, 8, 9, 63–64, 81–82, 84–87, 143, 178, 179, 198; need of, 63–65, 94, 198, 204 n. 263–64; Christian, 81–85, 179–86, 189; and art, 82; and revolution, 85–87, 185–86, 256–57; complement of war, 179; language of, 256–59; democratic, 260
Philosophy of Nature: aether in, 203 n. 205 n
Philosophy of Nature and Spirit (1805/6): 264; tyranny in, 198; classes in, 199
Philosophy of Right: 86–87, 88 n, 100 n
plant: labor on, 27–29, 108; defined, 108, 208 n, 215 n; uses of, 109
PLATO: 67; on speech and writing, 35; *Republic* paradigmatic, 62, 68, 70, 79–80, 85, 199; the Cave, 64; influence of *Laws*, 70; peasantry in,

94 n; logical collection in, 199; *Timaeus* on prophecy, 260
PLUTARCH: *Aristides*, 94
polis: foundation of *Sittlichkeit*, 55; and nation, 85–86
POLYNICES: 50, 54
possession(s): analysed, 25–27, 106–7; realized in property, 38, 119–20, 245–47, 249–50; *Knecht* as, 42; ideal tie, 49, 135; of family, 235–40, 244; contradiction in, 238, 249
Potenz(en): H's use of, 12, 15, 92 n.; Schelling's use, 15–20, 24–25, 90–91 n, 103 n; of practice, 23, 28, 103–5, 210–211; natural ethics as, 31; finite/infinite, 36, 116; freedom as, 46, 129–42; family and polis, 56; organization of, 57; in absolute ethical life, 61–62; social classes as, 68, 151–52; separation of powers through, 73, 157, 161, 162, 165–67; of religion, 83–84, 180–81; relative totality, 142, 265; of theory, 192, 210–11
presence: absolute, 251–52
price: empirical value, 38, 121; fluctuation of, 74, 167–169
priesthood: absolute estate, 56; membership, 70–71, 79–80, 158–60
privacy: recognition of, 60, 69, 154, 249–50
property: conceptual place of, 11, 37, 118, 118; more than possession, 26, 249–50; realized in exchange, 121; of family, 42, 127, 216, 217; crime against, 135–36; basic to justice-system, 154–55
prophecy: H as prophet, 86–87; H on prophecy, 260
Protestantism: principle of, 81, 84–85, 94, 96, 184–85; national emphasis, 184
Prussia: machine-state, 86
punishment: retributive, 48, 50, 52, 130, 131, 132–33; and damages, 77–78, 175
PYRRHA: 203 n

realism: and idealism, 192, 224–26

reality: body and spirit, 6, 61, 159–60, 181, 185, 189; finite, 11, 36, 101 n; infinite as totality, 16–17, 61, 101, 150–51, 189; real series, 17–19, 24, 91 n, 120; real pole, 19–20; subsists in formal treatment, 24, 102 n, 104, 116, 117, 123, 130. *See also* nature; *Sittlichkeit*; middle; and the note on p. 267
Reason (*Vernunft*): theoretical and practical, 8–9, 190; *Potenz* in Schelling, 17–18; as human essence, 25, 31, 40; self-enjoyment of, 29–31; man as tool of, 29, 32–33; as slave of passions, 48; as invisible hand, 69, 154; self-actualizing, 87, 101 n. 191; realized in middles, 112–13 (*see* middle); as single intelligence, 117, 121–26, 129; consciousness as form of, 211; *Werk* of *Volk*, 244–45; revolutionary demand, 256
reciprocity: Kantian category, 12, 91 n.; and reconciliation, 46, 82–83; ethical, 46–47, 52, 132–33, 136–37, 139–40
recognition: "dumb", 35, 115; in speech, 35–36, 111; basis of personality, 39–40, 118, 124; differentiated in family, 42–43, 125–29, 231–35; implicit in theft, 49, 52, 135–37; basis of *Sittlichkeit*, 57–58; creates formal universal, 74, 176, 246–249; basic to civil justice, 77, 173, 175, 249–50; battle for, 137–38, 139–41, 195, 196–98, 236–42
reconciliation: religious, 46, 66, 82–85, 93 n., 131, 147, 180, 182; empirical, 184–85
reflection: Kantian, 14; Schelling's use, 17; philosophy of, 65–66; matter as introreflection, 227; consciousness as introreflective, 229, 233, 240
REINHOLD, Karl Leonhard: 9
relation (*Verhältnis*): H's use, 10–12, 22; ethical category, 12, 19, 61; sex as, 29 (*see* sex); parent-child, 29 (*see* child); relative identity, 29–30, 39; lordship and bondage, 40–42, 46, 125–26, 136, 155–56; husband

and wife, 43; and indifference, 61; State and Church, 81; reciprocity, 46–47 (see reciprocity); absolute (intuition/concept), 100–1, 252–253; of classes, 152–163; of soul and body, 159–60

religion: absolute experience, 6, 9, 63–65, 81–85, 179; intuition of Volk as, 60, 71–72, 81; of infinite grief, 65–66 (see God, death of); arm of government, 71–72, 158–60, 163, 177; natural, 80, 81, 177, 181; tradition in, 82, 180; Potenzen of, 83–84, 180–81; rebirth of, 84–85, 185; reconciliation in, 82 (see reconciliation); philosophical, 181, 185, 256

resumption: of whole, religion as, 6, 81, 84–85, 179, 201; as absolute relation, 101–2; of totality in speech, 116

revenge: see vengeance

revolution: French, 86; and art, 255; philosophy and, 263–264

right (Recht): of property, 38–42, 49–50, 77, 173–74; personal, 39–40, 41, 77, 135–36; to life, 40, 46, 50; and wrong, 58; and justice, 67, 149; origin in surplus labor, 120; unknown to peasantry, 150

romanticism: criticized, 260–261

ROSENKRANZ, Karl: on H's lectures, 3, 81, 83, 85, 202–4; on System of Ethical Life, 3, 10; and H's mss., 87–90, 95–96; reports translated, 178–86, 254–66; "conclusion" fragment, 200–1, 202 n, 203 n

Sabbath: of the world, 185

sacred(ness): constitution as, 60, 71, 72, 143, 163; consecration of nature, 83, 84, 182, 183–85, 261; marriage as, 143, 232; of age, 158–60

sacrifice: significance in religion, 82; of God, 84; of personal interest, 147, 158, 179; Idea of religion, 180

satisfaction: goal of feeling, 23–25, 30–31, 103; and enjoyment, 31; in law, 77, 175

SCHELLING, F.W.J.: and H, 4, 7, 87 n, 88 n, 89 n., 90 n., 94, 202 n; Exposition of My System, 15, 91; Potenz theory, 15–20, 90–91; "On the Absolute Identity-System", 15; Philosophy of Art, quoted, 16–17; Further Expositions, 17; real series in, 24; dynamic series, 18, 92, 120; Ideas for a Philosophy of Nature, 90 n, 91 n; On the World Soul, 90 n; "Introduction to Nature Philosophy", 90 n; criticized, 256–62; school of, 259–60; Transcendental Idealism, 262

SCHLEIERMACHER, F.D.E.: Addresses, 81, 94, 179; critique, 202

sensation: content of thought, 45, 130–31; intuition of speech, 218–19; evolution of, 223, 225–26

sex: natural and ethical relation, 29, 32, 43, 110, 127–29, 211, 231–32; identity of family, 32, 42–43, 57; ground of authority, 42–43, 91 n, 93–94 n, 127

SHAKESPEARE: Macbeth, 47, 93; Romeo and Juliet, 51

shape (Gestalt): of Idea as Volk, 142–43, 185; of classes, 151, 153; of government, 160, 163; of God, 163, 181, 252; of world spirit, 186, 264–65; shaping of consciousness, 209, 211; created by art, 254–55

sign: corporeal, 34–35, 92, 114–15; ideality of tool, 115; formal middle, 220; and same, 222. See also speech

sin: consciousness of, 84, 180

singularity: H's use, 10; principle of natural ethics, 44–45, 54, 117, 121–26, 129; formal not true principle, 129, 151; sacrifice of, 147, 158, 179; bourgeois principle, 154; of consciousness, 206–17; in space and time, 218–19, 223

Sitten: as discipline, 78, 176; as fetters, 146, 263

Sittlichkeit: H's concept, 6, 9, 10–11, 99–100; and religion, 6, 9–10, 63–64, 80–81, 93 n; resting and moving, 11, 21, 61–62, 72–74, 147, 156–57,

163–64; and nature, 19, 211, 243–
44; relative or natural, 19, 22–44,
73, 93, 102–29; absolute or free, 51,
54–80, 142–77; transition, 57–58,
129–30; and barbarism, 134, 136; of
individuals, 146–51; of classes,
152–56
slave(s): as person, 41, 125–26; no
contract with, 43, 128; not a class,
53–54, 68, 93, 152. *See also* bondage
SMITH, Adam: *Wealth of Nations*,
74, 75, 95, 248
sociology of knowledge: H's relation
to, 64
SOPHOCLES: 60; *Antigone*, 93
space: in Schelling, 18; reality of
singularity, 218–19, 223; as universal, 219–20
speculation: *see* philosophy
speech: reality of spirit, 34, 35, 113–
16, 222, 244; formal concept of, 34,
92 n.; medium of *Bildung*, 58, 60;
first *Potenz* of consciousness, 193,
213, 216, 217; barbarian, 196; cultured, 199, 244–45; as actual concept,
218–28; origin in voice, 222; native,
importance of, 256–58; formalism of
alien, 258–59
SPERCHIAS: 60
SPINOZA, Benedict: influence of, 8,
17, 21; *Ethics*, 89 n.
spirit: in H's system, 6, 7; and nature,
19, 56; formal reality in contract,
39, 123; actually in *Sittlichkeit*, 63,
146, 242–250; of family, 139–40;
of *Volk*, 144; concept of, 206; birth
of, 240–41; and Idea, problem, 264–
65
"Spirit of Christianity": 96
Stoff: spiritual, 251–52, 263–64
struggle: *see* battle
subject(ive): and object, 9 (*see* antithesis); thought, 10, 149; negated
in labor, 33; expressed in labor, 33;
subject-objectivity, 100 n., 144; as
intelligence, 109–10, 113; as substance, 114; as self-moving, 118; as
life, 124

subjugation: of thief and barbarian,
50, 136
substance: and accident, 12; ethical,
12, 72; subject as, 112, 114; goal
of logic, 205; consciousness as,
242; *Volk*-spirit as, 242
subsumption: H's use, 10, 12, 18–19,
20–22; in Kant, 13; in Schelling,
17–19, 91; as consumption, 26, 107;
as transformation, 26, 107; reciprocity of, 100–1, 111, 136, 165–66; as
domination, 101 n, 126, 164
sun: solar system, 190, 203 n
supersession: *see Aufhebung*
surplus: product of labor, 37–38, 118,
120; universalized as money, 124;
basis of mastery, 126; dialectic of,
167–69
suspension: *see Aufhebung*
system: evolution of H's, 6–10;
four-part, 6, 7, 10, 63–64, 81, 89,
189, 201, 202 n.; triadic, 6, 7, 10,
88–89; four-part, abandoned, 7, 62,
64; circularity of, 178, 262
"System fragment" (1800): 89 n
System of Ethical Life: date, 3, 87 n.
character of ms., 3–10; "conclusion" of, 10, 202 n. structure of,
10–12, 189–90, 197; meets need of
time, 64; hypothetical completion
of, 80; connection with religion
lectures, 83–84, 178; tensions in,
85–87; use in lectures, 89 n; and
Phenomenology, 90 n, 198; method
of, 191, 193; importance of, 201–
2; education in, 204 n
System of Speculative Philosophy:
triadic, 10, 88–89, 205–6

TAMERLANE: 133
taxation: bourgeois institution, 69, 150,
155; economic control by, 75;
method of, 76, 171–72
theft: paradigm of property violation,
49–50, 135–37
THEMISTOCLES: 198
THESEUS: achievement of, 54, 56,
80, 198

THUCYDIDES: influence of, 85

thought: infinite *Potenz*, 36; negates sensation, 45, 130–31; as recognition, 124; medium of bourgeois virtue, 149; memory as origin of, 221

TILLIETTE, Xavier: *Schelling*, 90 n

time: Schelling, 18; ideality of singular being, 218–219, 223; as universal, 219–20

tool: totality of first *Potenz*, 19, 23, 25–26; man as, 29, 32, 112–13; reality of Reason, 33, 35, 113; and machine, 37, 118, 246–47; and child, 58, 115; middle of intelligence and being, 112–13; speech as, 114; nature as, 159–60; *Potenz* of consciousness, 211, 215 n. 216, 217; middle for consciousness, 228–31, 244

totality: balance of subsumptions, 12; in Schelling, 16–17; relative and absolute, 19–20; family as, 42–44, 127–29; constitution as, 59–61, 144–45; of government, 74, 78, 176; reality as, 189; science as, 190; of consciousness, 209

tragedy: justice of, 47; recognition in, 58

Trinity: speculative doctrine, 84, 96, 184

trust: relation of feeling, 39, 122, 123; ambivalent virtue, 67, 69, 94, 150; requires economic stability, 75, 168, 171; in animals, 108

truth: as the whole, 151, 243

"Tübingen fragment": 93, 95

understanding (*Verstand*): in Kant, 13; intuitive, 13–14, 91; of barbarians, 48, 133; of parents, 129; distinguishes honesty from trust, 150; reflective, 195; as achieved universality, 223, 226, 233–34; *Werk* of *Volk*, 244, 245

unity: concrete usage in Schelling, 17; abstract usage in Hegel, 142. *See also* antithesis

universal(ity): H's use, 10, 22, 24, 100–1; analytic, 13; synthetic, 13; male as, 29, 110; empirical, 43, 93, 127; government, 72–79, 163–176; dominance of, 116–24; abstract, 118, 142, 155; concrete, 146, 160, 163; resting and moving, 163–64; of consciousness, 206–17

Universe: and God, 16, 18, 19; of nature and of spirit, 179; creation of, 265; index for dating, 189, 201, 202 n

utility: as real value, 38, 120, 121; of nobility, 153

value: defined, 38, 121; realized in money, 39, 42; in national market, 154; satisfaction universalized, 247–49

vengeance: as natural justice, 47, 52–53, 132; religion of, 80; as ethical reciprocity, 139–40; sublated in justice, 154

village: community of natural ethics, 55

virtue: as resting Idea, 62; H's theory of, 66–70, 75, 94, 146–52; inward and outward, 67; and morality, 146–47, 148–49; and vice, 148

Volk: ethical substance, 12, 61, 62–63; intuition of, 21, 58–61, 63, 81, 101, 144–45, 146, 179, 189; and horde, 48; transition to, 55–56, 241–42; life in, 68–69, 147, 152; as given not made, 71, 163; history of, 82; Jews as, 84; as totality, 101; defined, 144–145; as spirit, 146, 209, 211, 213, 254; as particular, 164; as self-intuition of God, 179; freedom of, 185; speech of, 195–196, 199, 244–45

war: in natural ethics, 51–54, 55–56; in free ethical life, 51, 53–54, 57; ethical significance, 66–67; tribal and national, 66, 149; function of nobility, 68, 152, 175; peasants participate, 69–70; as moment of policy, 74, 77, 164; and justice,

74, 77–78; occasion for bondage,
137, 138, 141; sublation of right,
141; totality of punishment, 175;
training for, 176
wealth: and poverty, dialectic, 75–76,
169, 170–71, 247–49
wisdom: Plato's justice as, 68; none
in natural ethics, 68, 150, 162;
noble virtue, 69; absent in other
classes, 69, 154, 162; function to
govern, 70, 160; comes with age,
71, 160; of Christianity, 183–84;
of God, 265

word: human, totality of speech, 115–
16; divine, utterance and hearing of,
265
work (*Arbeit*): *see* labor
work (*Werk*): of *Volk*, 242–50, 252;
of art, 255
Wurtemburg: H's 1797 pamphlet on,
72

XERXES: 60

yearning: Protestant principle, 85, 184,
185; Christian generally, 252–53